# Glitter Kiss™

Adrianne Ambrose & Monica Gallagher

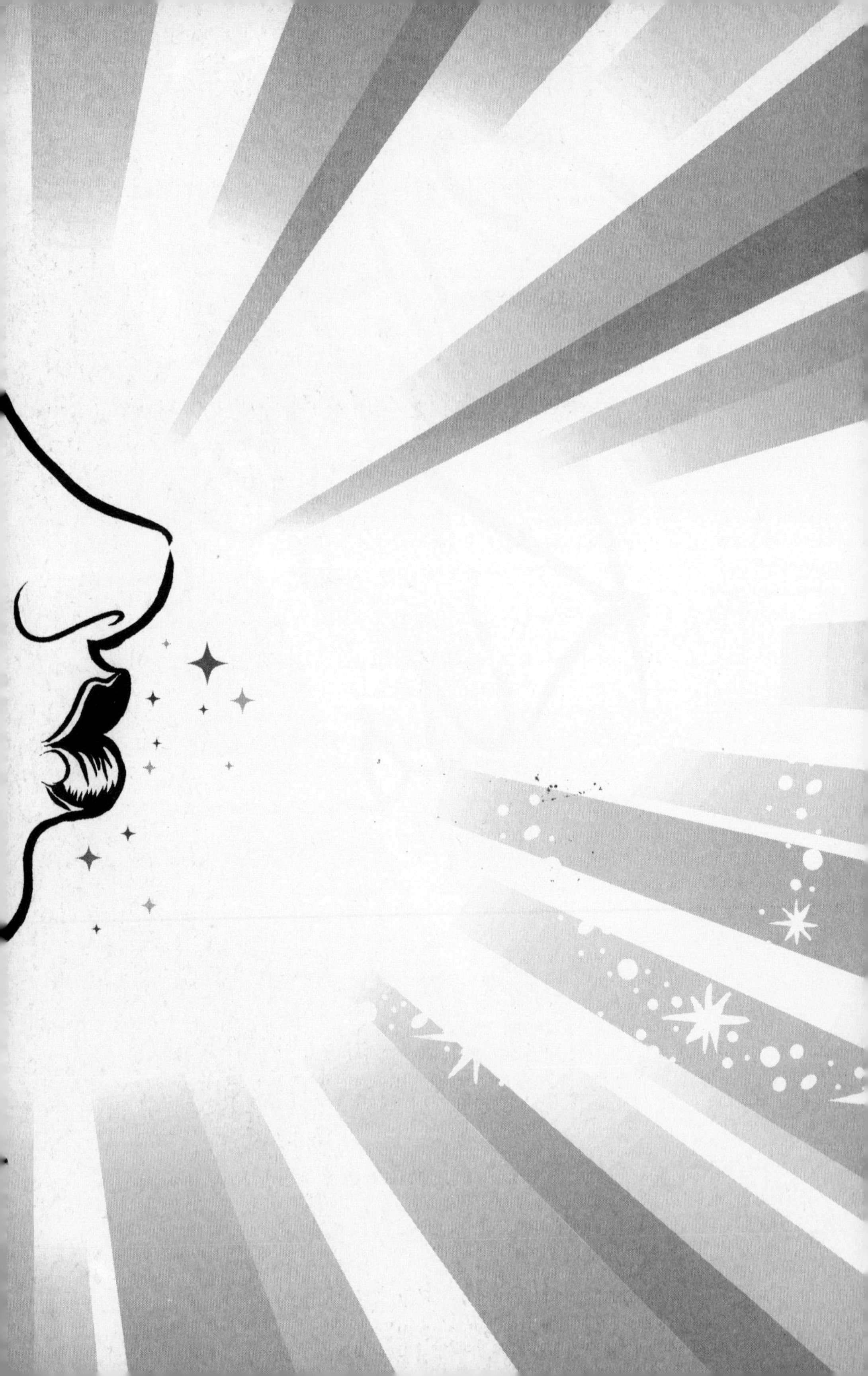

# Glitter Kiss™

written by
## Adrianne Ambrose

illustrated by
## Monica Gallagher

lettered by
### Jared Jones

edited by **Jill Beaton**

designed by **Steven Birch**

## Oni Press, Inc.

publisher **Joe Nozemack**
editor in chief **James Lucas Jones**
art director **Keith Wood**
director of marketing **Tom Shimmin**
director of business development **George Rohac**
editor **Jill Beaton**
editor **Charlie Chu**
digital prepress lead **Troy Look**
administrative assistant **Robin Herrera**

Oni Press, Inc.
1305 SE Martin Luther King Jr. Blvd.
Suite A
Portland, OR 97214

www.onipress.com
facebook.com/onipress
twitter.com/onipress
onipress.tumblr.com
www.eatyourlipstick.com
www.adrianneambrose.com

First Edition: December 2012
978-1-62010-082-0

Printed in U.S.A.

1 2 3 4 5 6 7 8 9 10

Library of Congress Control Number: 2012908713

To J.A.C. for never fearing the glitter kiss. Thank you to Jennifer Corso (for suggesting the Baltics and making silly dares), Mike Glaser (for the usual reasons), and all of the wonderful people at Oni Press.

A very special thanks to Monica Gallagher and Jill Beaton for making this project so much fun. I really couldn't imagine a better team.
-AA


This book is dedicated to my parents for always encouraging my odd behavior, my boyfriend for supporting my hermit lifestyle, and to my loyal friends - the best convention manservants a girl could have.

Thanks to Adrianne Ambrose & Jill Beaton for providing nonstop support, ideas, and for taking an east coast girl out on the town. To Oni Press for making all the magic happen.
-MG

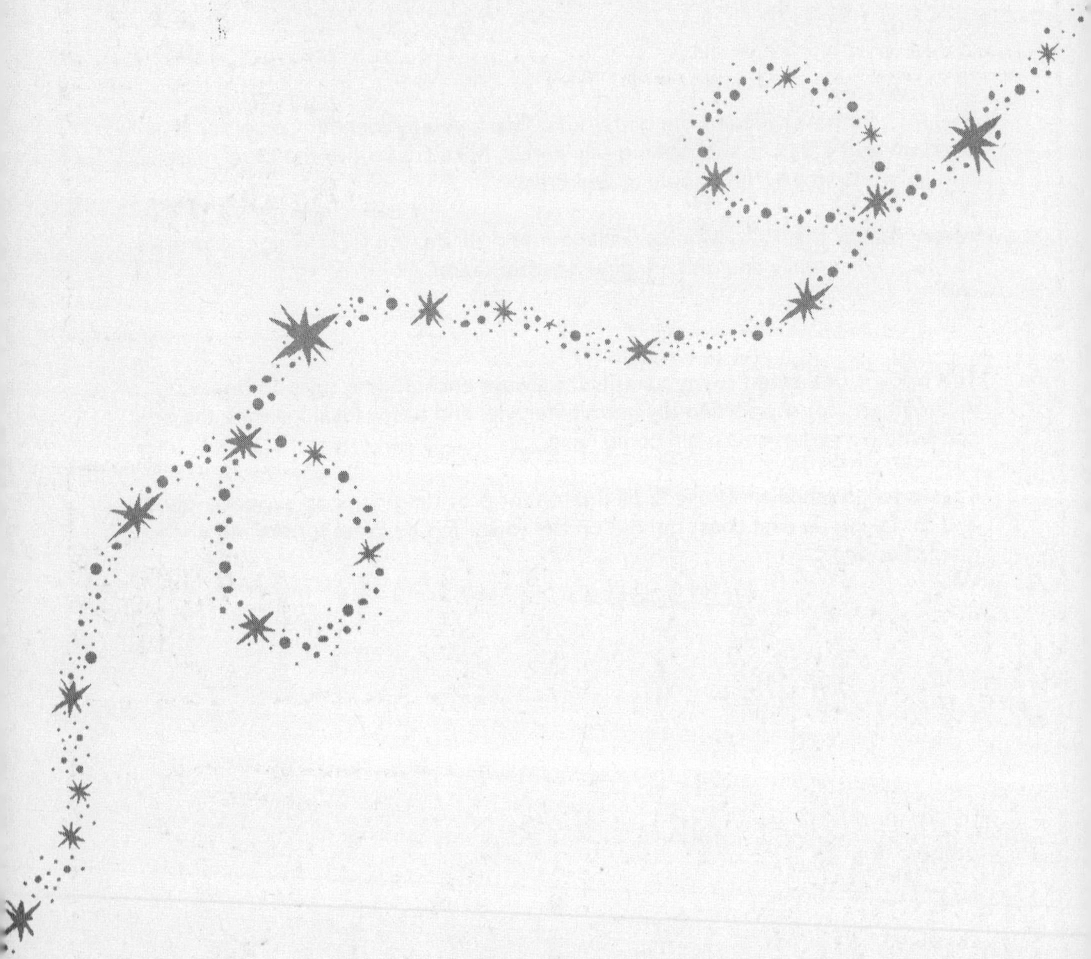

TINKA, IT'S TEN TO EIGHT.

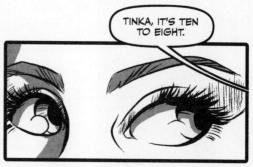

COMING, MOM.

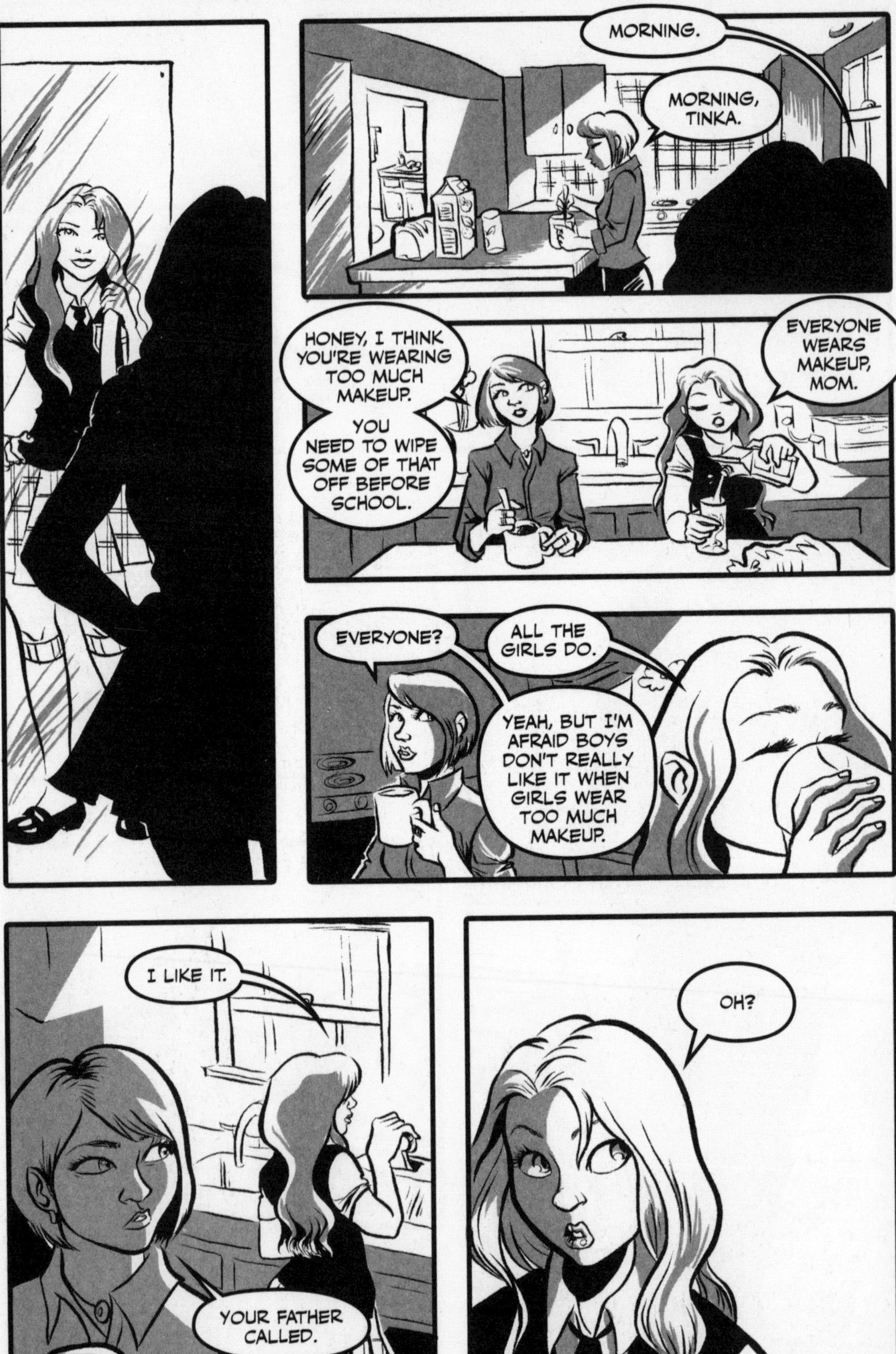
MORNING.
MORNING, TINKA.
HONEY, I THINK YOU'RE WEARING TOO MUCH MAKEUP.
YOU NEED TO WIPE SOME OF THAT OFF BEFORE SCHOOL.
EVERYONE WEARS MAKEUP, MOM.
EVERYONE?
ALL THE GIRLS DO.
YEAH, BUT I'M AFRAID BOYS DON'T REALLY LIKE IT WHEN GIRLS WEAR TOO MUCH MAKEUP.
I LIKE IT.
YOUR FATHER CALLED.
OH?

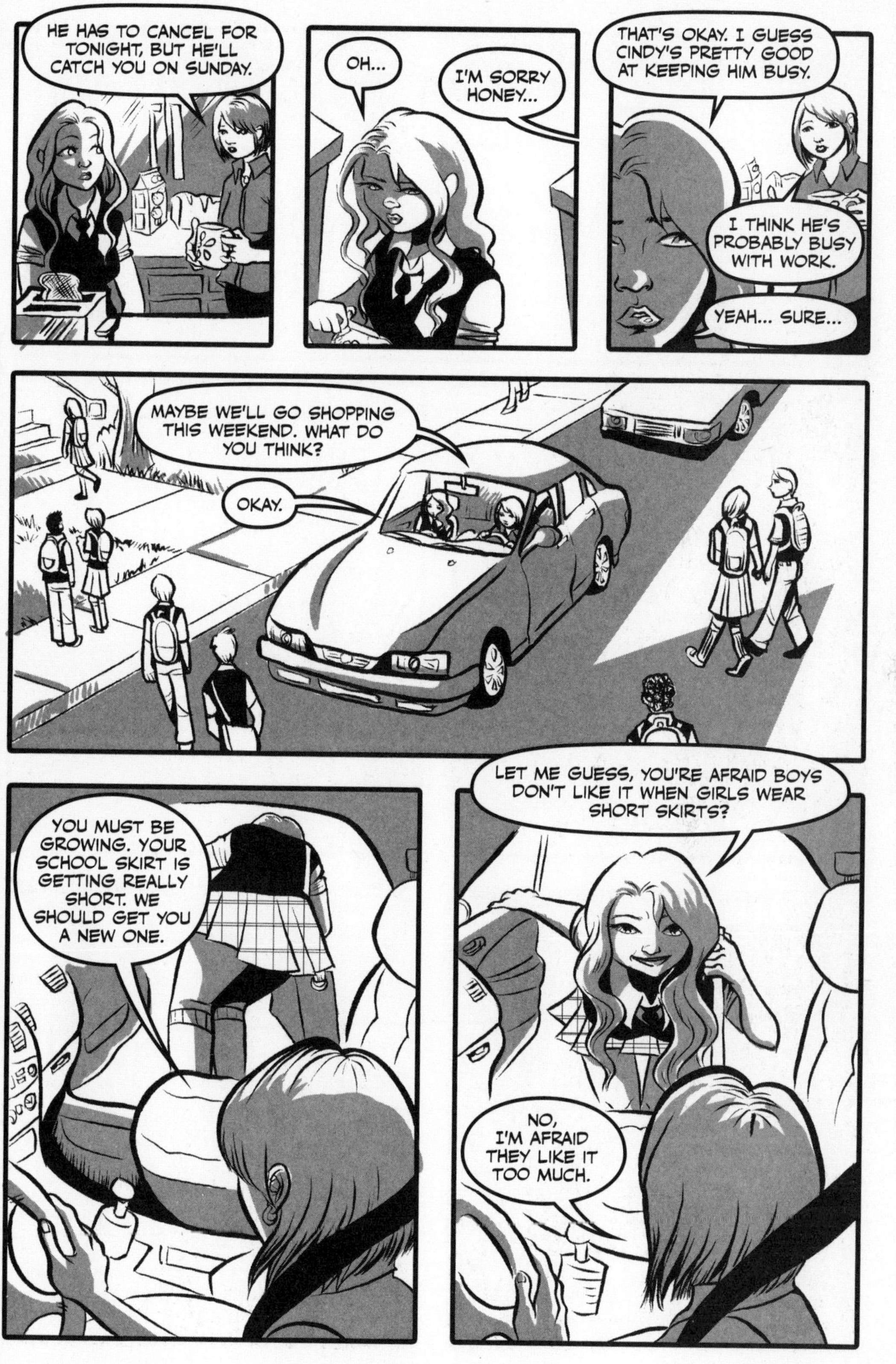
HE HAS TO CANCEL FOR TONIGHT, BUT HE'LL CATCH YOU ON SUNDAY.
OH...
I'M SORRY HONEY...
THAT'S OKAY. I GUESS CINDY'S PRETTY GOOD AT KEEPING HIM BUSY.
I THINK HE'S PROBABLY BUSY WITH WORK.
YEAH... SURE...
MAYBE WE'LL GO SHOPPING THIS WEEKEND. WHAT DO YOU THINK?
OKAY.
YOU MUST BE GROWING. YOUR SCHOOL SKIRT IS GETTING REALLY SHORT. WE SHOULD GET YOU A NEW ONE.
LET ME GUESS, YOU'RE AFRAID BOYS DON'T LIKE IT WHEN GIRLS WEAR SHORT SKIRTS?
NO, I'M AFRAID THEY LIKE IT TOO MUCH.

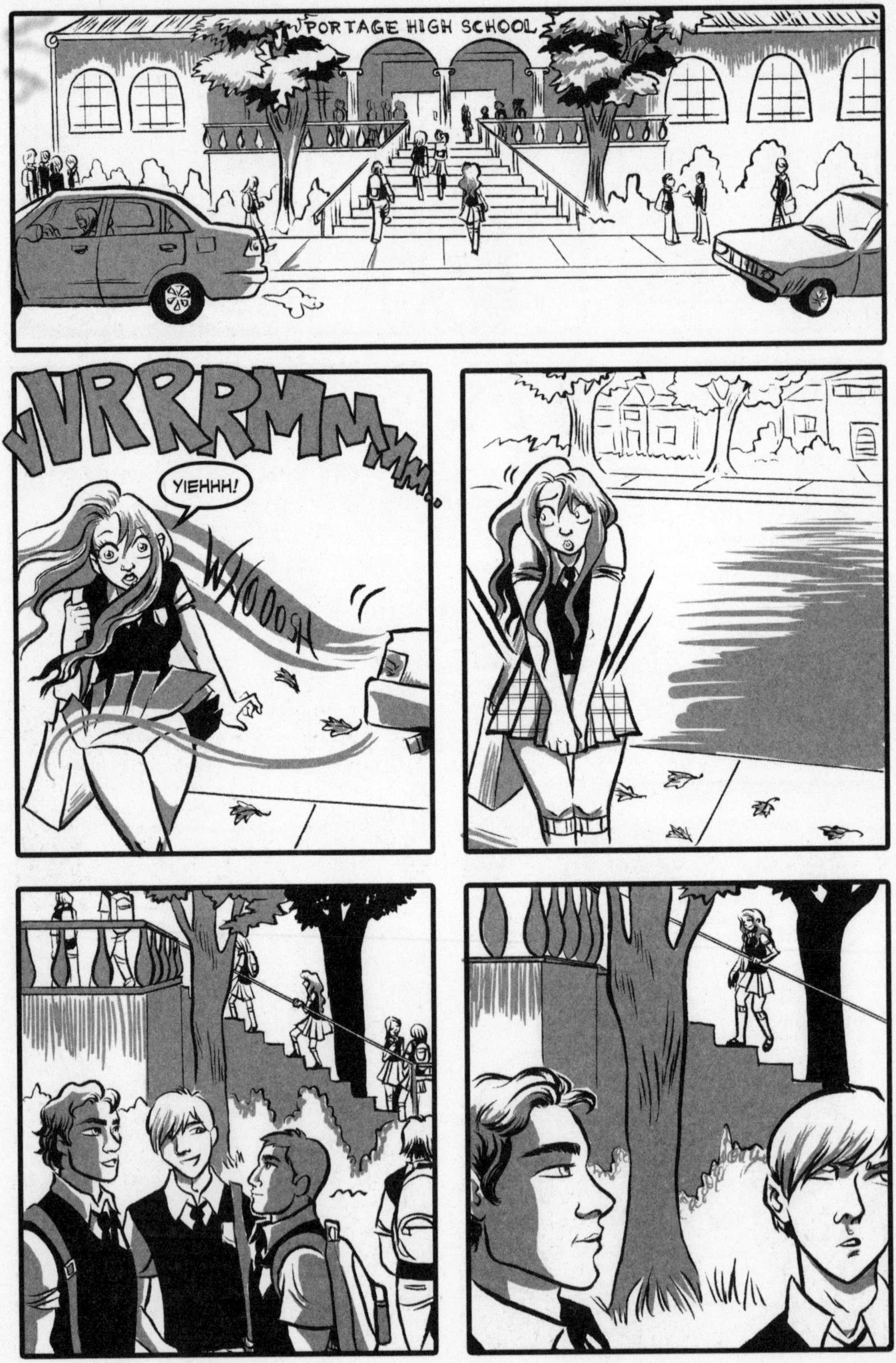
PORTAGE HIGH SCHOOL
VRRRMM...
YIEHHH!
WHOOOM

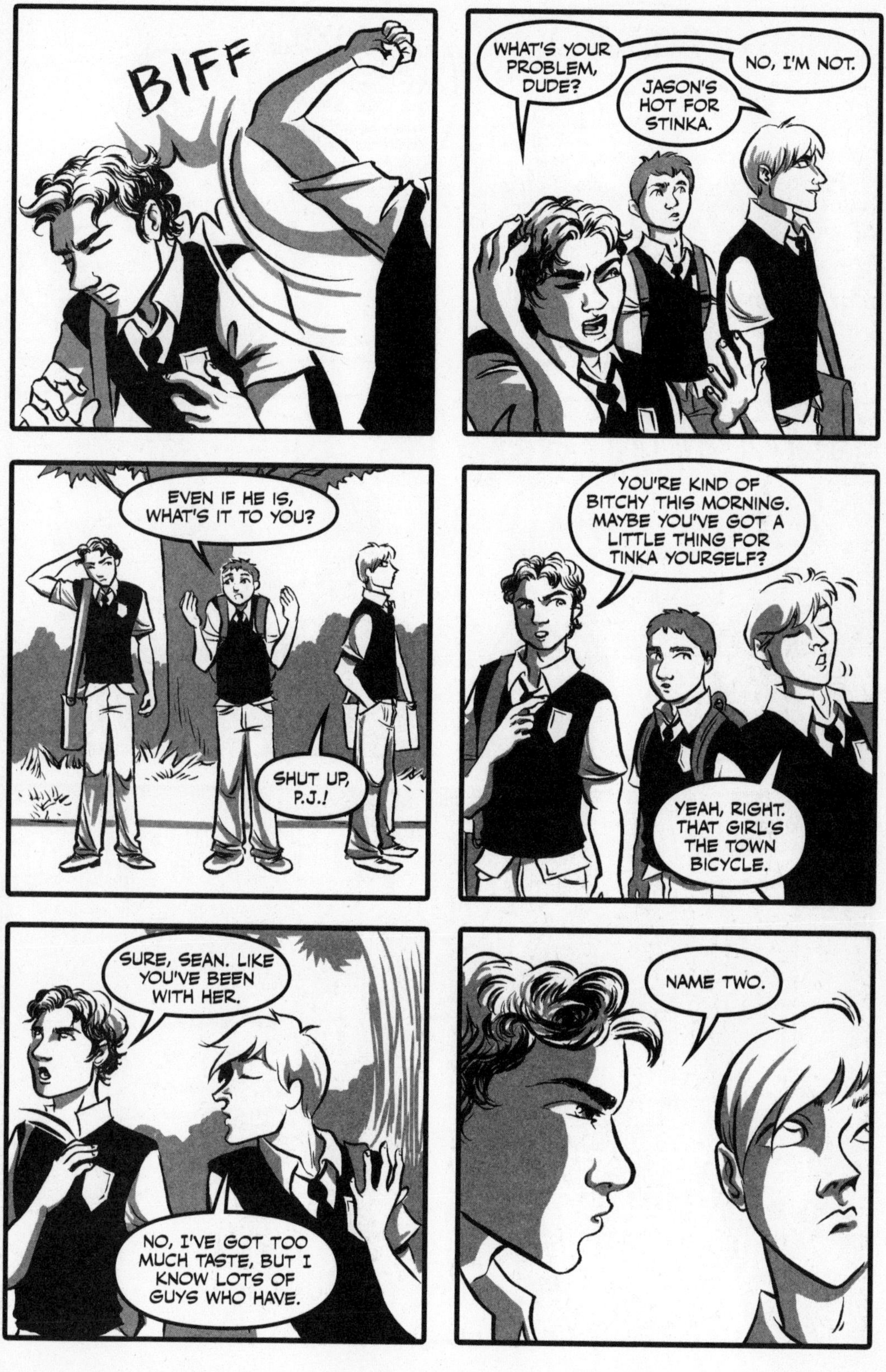
BIFF
WHAT'S YOUR PROBLEM, DUDE?
JASON'S HOT FOR STINKA.
NO, I'M NOT.
EVEN IF HE IS, WHAT'S IT TO YOU?
SHUT UP, P.J.!
YOU'RE KIND OF BITCHY THIS MORNING. MAYBE YOU'VE GOT A LITTLE THING FOR TINKA YOURSELF?
YEAH, RIGHT. THAT GIRL'S THE TOWN BICYCLE.
SURE, SEAN. LIKE YOU'VE BEEN WITH HER.
NO, I'VE GOT TOO MUCH TASTE, BUT I KNOW LOTS OF GUYS WHO HAVE.
NAME TWO.

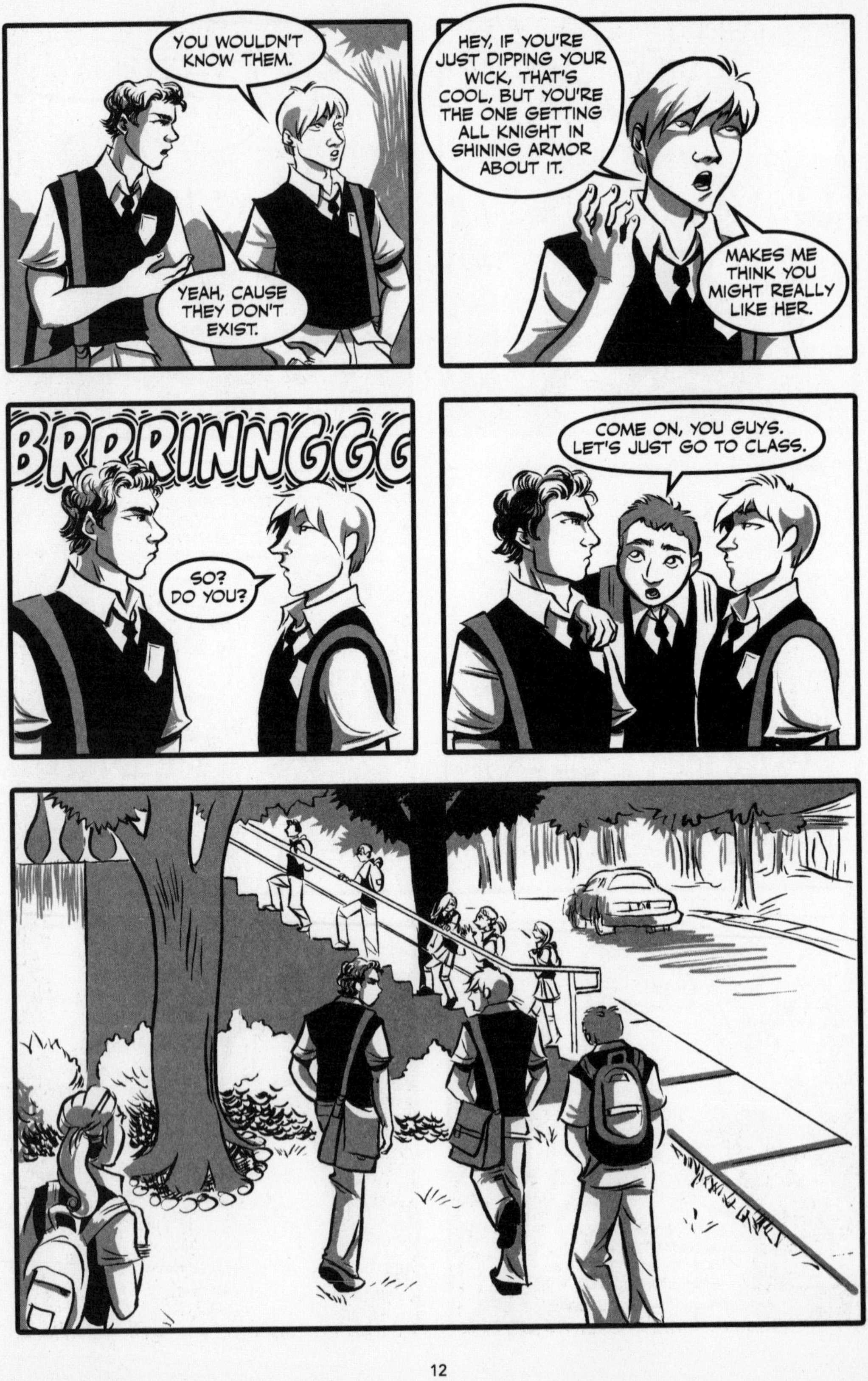
YOU WOULDN'T KNOW THEM.
YEAH, CAUSE THEY DON'T EXIST.
HEY, IF YOU'RE JUST DIPPING YOUR WICK, THAT'S COOL, BUT YOU'RE THE ONE GETTING ALL KNIGHT IN SHINING ARMOR ABOUT IT.
MAKES ME THINK YOU MIGHT REALLY LIKE HER.
BRRRINNGGG
SO? DO YOU?
COME ON, YOU GUYS. LET'S JUST GO TO CLASS.

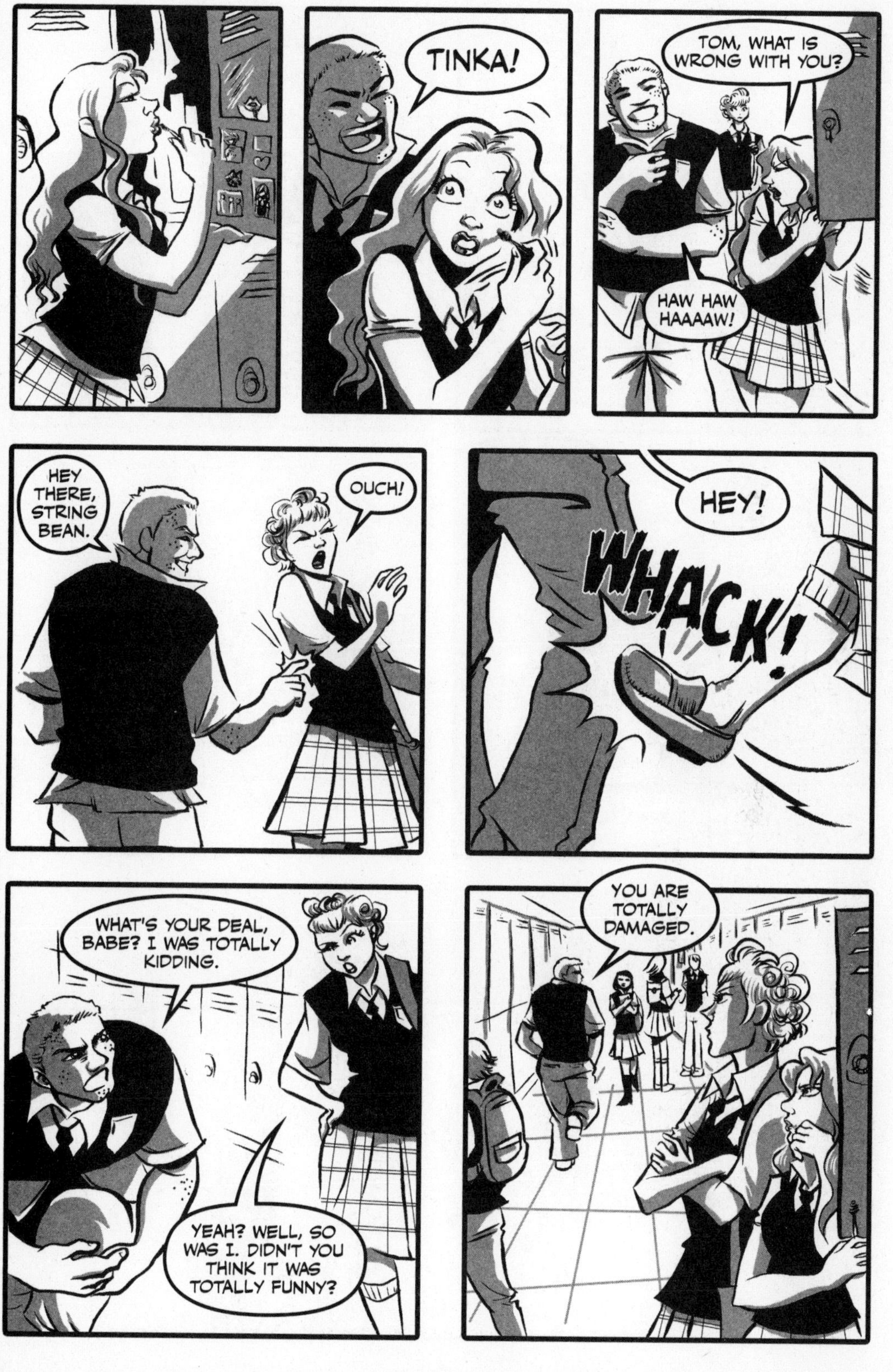
TINKA!
TOM, WHAT IS WRONG WITH YOU?
HAW HAW HAAAAW!
HEY THERE, STRING BEAN.
OUCH!
HEY!
WHACK!
WHAT'S YOUR DEAL, BABE? I WAS TOTALLY KIDDING.
YEAH? WELL, SO WAS I. DIDN'T YOU THINK IT WAS TOTALLY FUNNY?
YOU ARE TOTALLY DAMAGED.

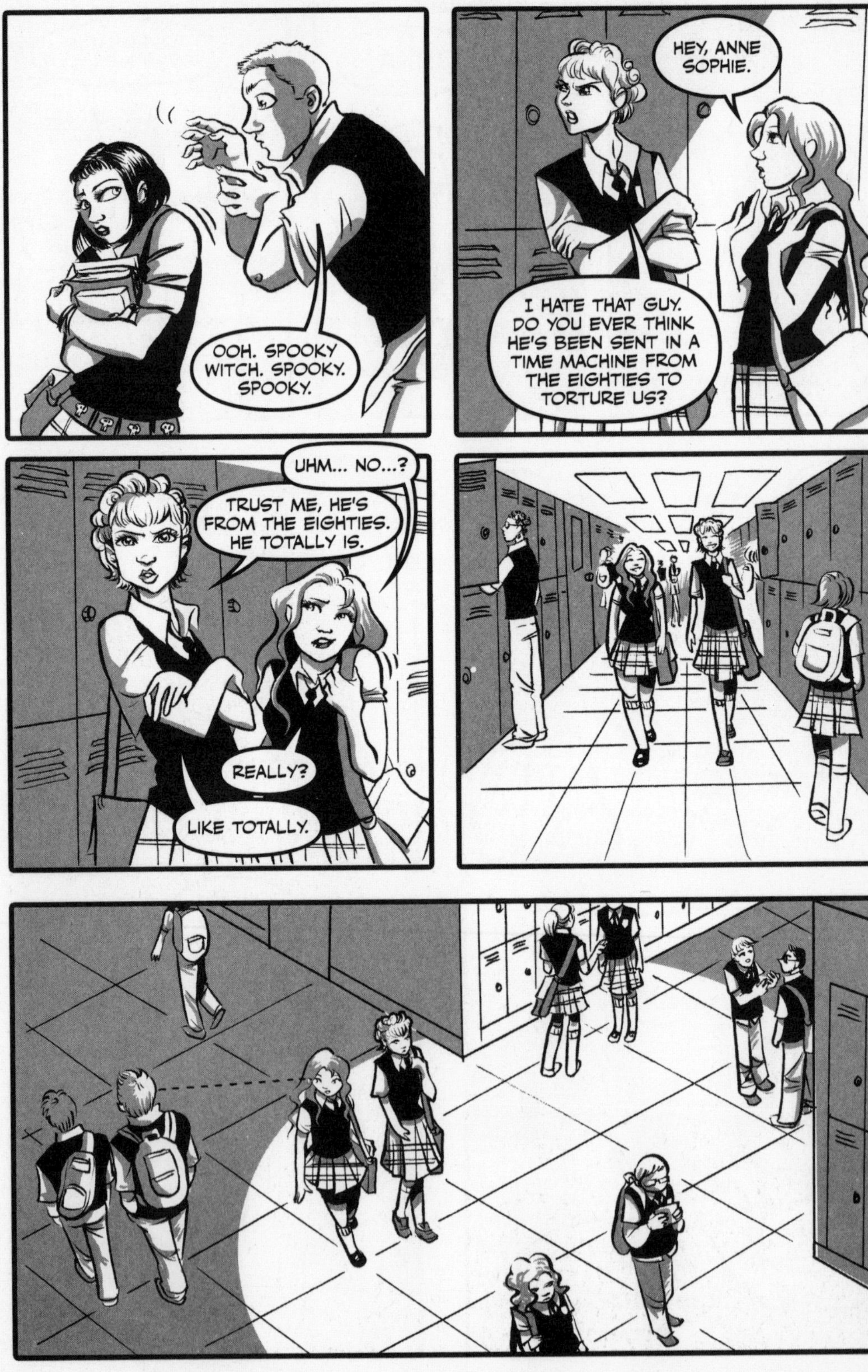
OOH. SPOOKY WITCH. SPOOKY. SPOOKY.
HEY, ANNE SOPHIE.
I HATE THAT GUY. DO YOU EVER THINK HE'S BEEN SENT IN A TIME MACHINE FROM THE EIGHTIES TO TORTURE US?
UHM... NO...?
TRUST ME, HE'S FROM THE EIGHTIES. HE TOTALLY IS.
REALLY?
LIKE TOTALLY.

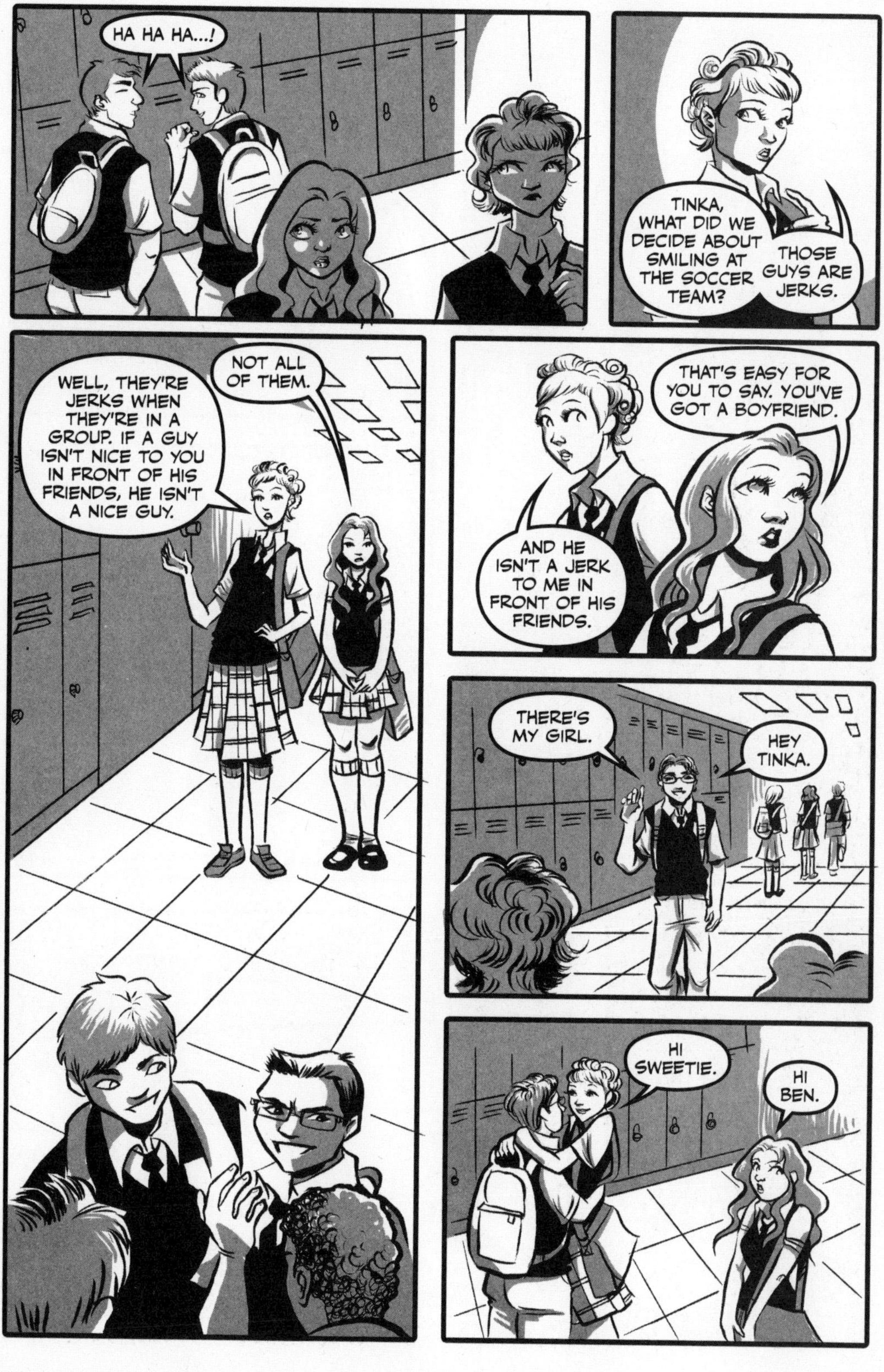
HA HA HA...!
TINKA, WHAT DID WE DECIDE ABOUT SMILING AT THE SOCCER TEAM?
THOSE GUYS ARE JERKS.
NOT ALL OF THEM.
WELL, THEY'RE JERKS WHEN THEY'RE IN A GROUP. IF A GUY ISN'T NICE TO YOU IN FRONT OF HIS FRIENDS, HE ISN'T A NICE GUY.
THAT'S EASY FOR YOU TO SAY. YOU'VE GOT A BOYFRIEND.
AND HE ISN'T A JERK TO ME IN FRONT OF HIS FRIENDS.
THERE'S MY GIRL.
HEY TINKA.
HI SWEETIE.
HI BEN.

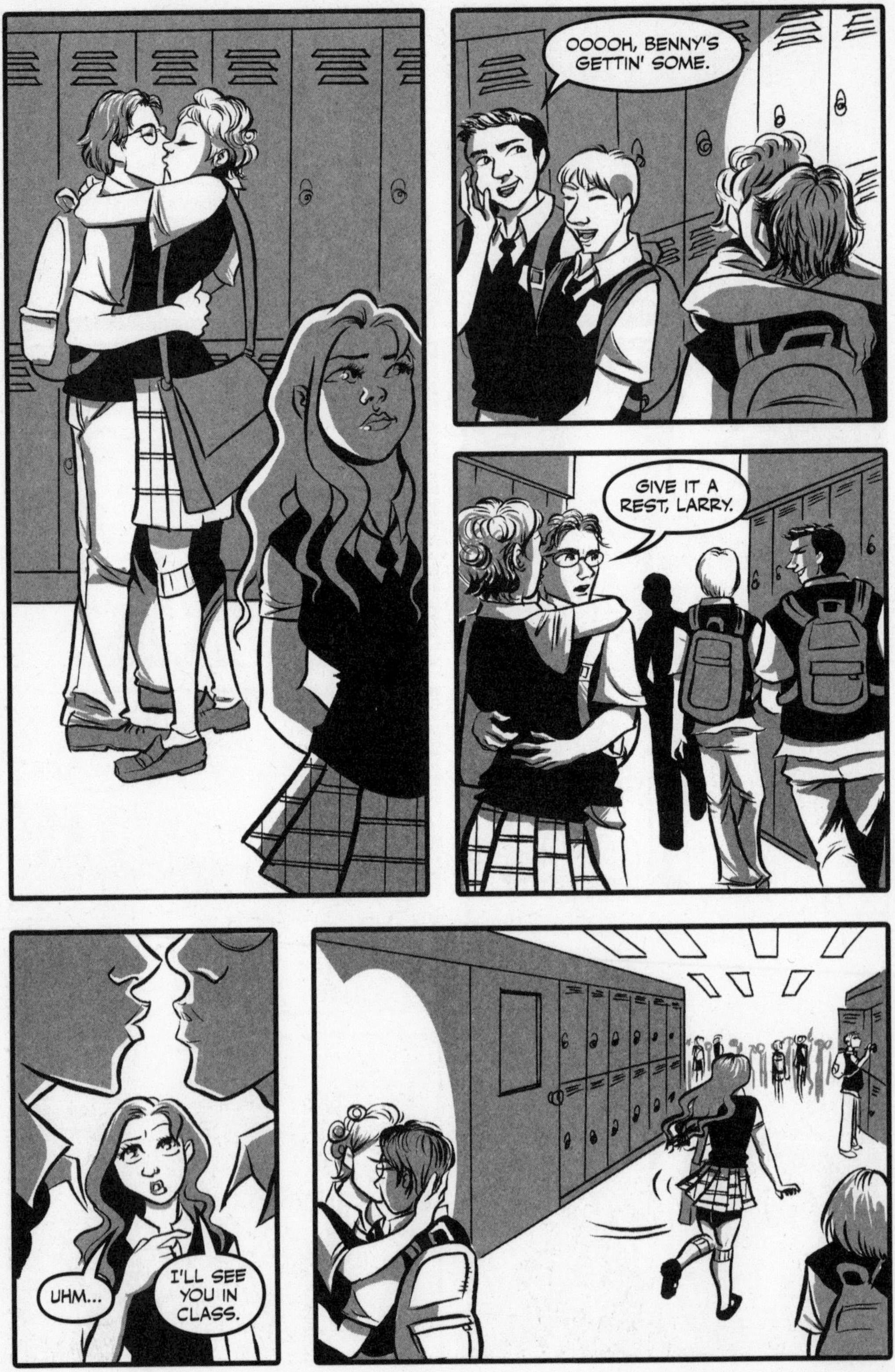
OOOOH, BENNY'S GETTIN' SOME.
GIVE IT A REST, LARRY.
UHM...
I'LL SEE YOU IN CLASS.

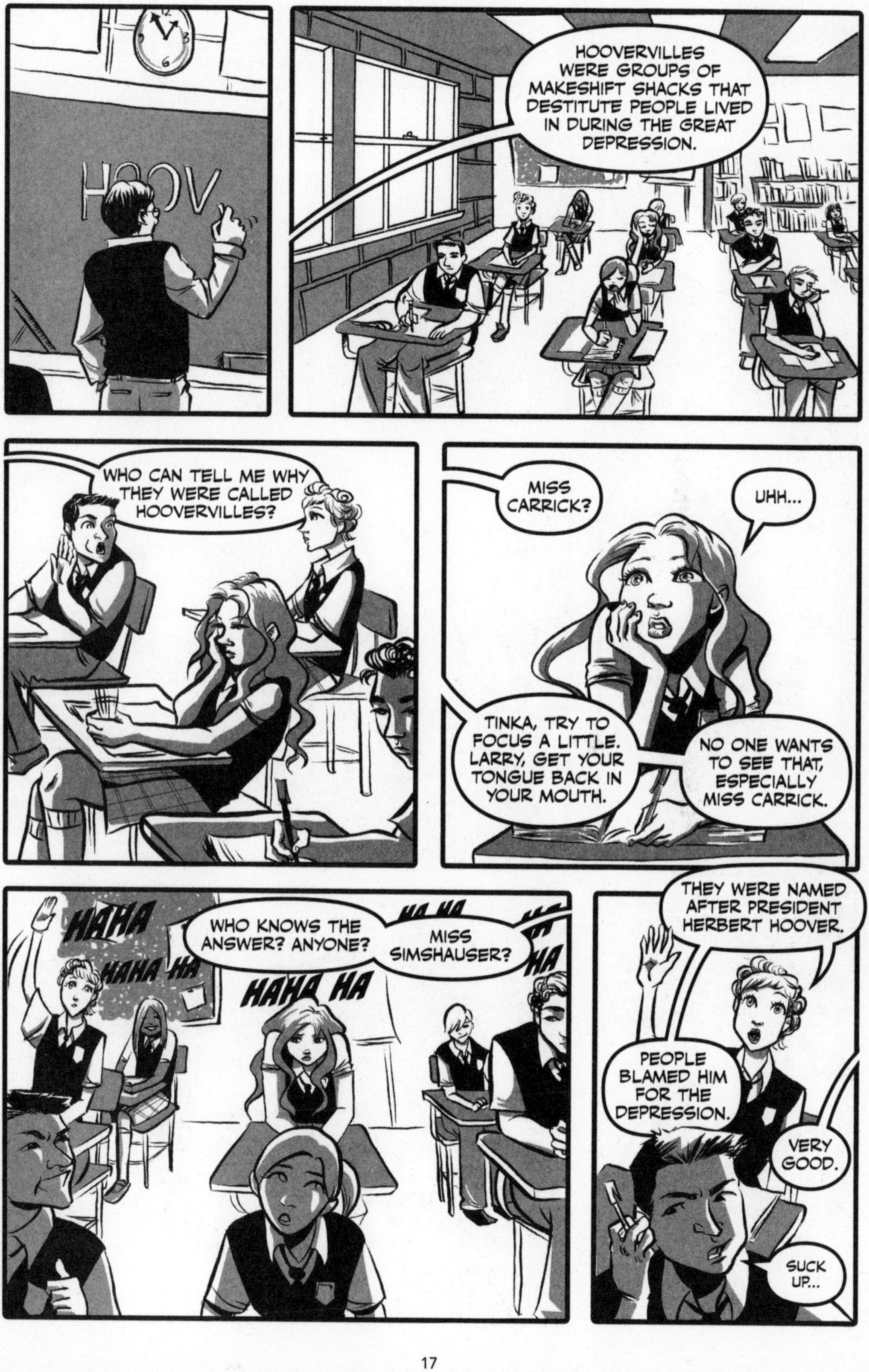
HOOV
HOOVERVILLES WERE GROUPS OF MAKESHIFT SHACKS THAT DESTITUTE PEOPLE LIVED IN DURING THE GREAT DEPRESSION.
WHO CAN TELL ME WHY THEY WERE CALLED HOOVERVILLES?
MISS CARRICK?
UHH...
TINKA, TRY TO FOCUS A LITTLE. LARRY, GET YOUR TONGUE BACK IN YOUR MOUTH.
NO ONE WANTS TO SEE THAT, ESPECIALLY MISS CARRICK.
HAHA
HAHA HA
HAHA HA
WHO KNOWS THE ANSWER? ANYONE?
MISS SIMSHAUSER?
THEY WERE NAMED AFTER PRESIDENT HERBERT HOOVER.
PEOPLE BLAMED HIM FOR THE DEPRESSION.
VERY GOOD.
SUCK UP...

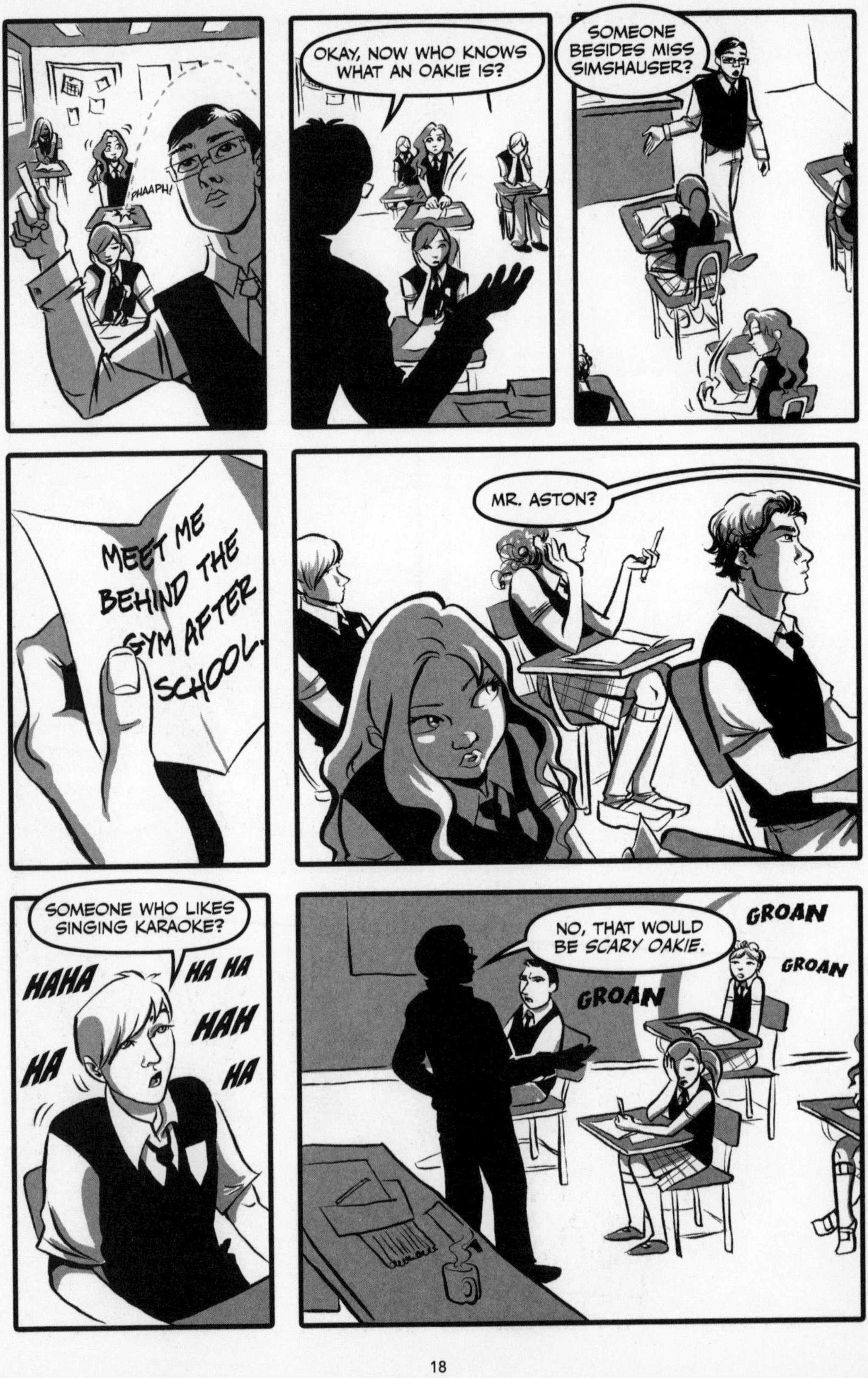
PHAAPH!
OKAY, NOW WHO KNOWS WHAT AN OAKIE IS?
SOMEONE BESIDES MISS SIMSHAUSER?
MEET ME BEHIND THE GYM AFTER SCHOOL.
MR. ASTON?
SOMEONE WHO LIKES SINGING KARAOKE?
HAHA
HA HA
HAH
HA
HA
NO, THAT WOULD BE *SCARY OAKIE*.
GROAN
GROAN
GROAN

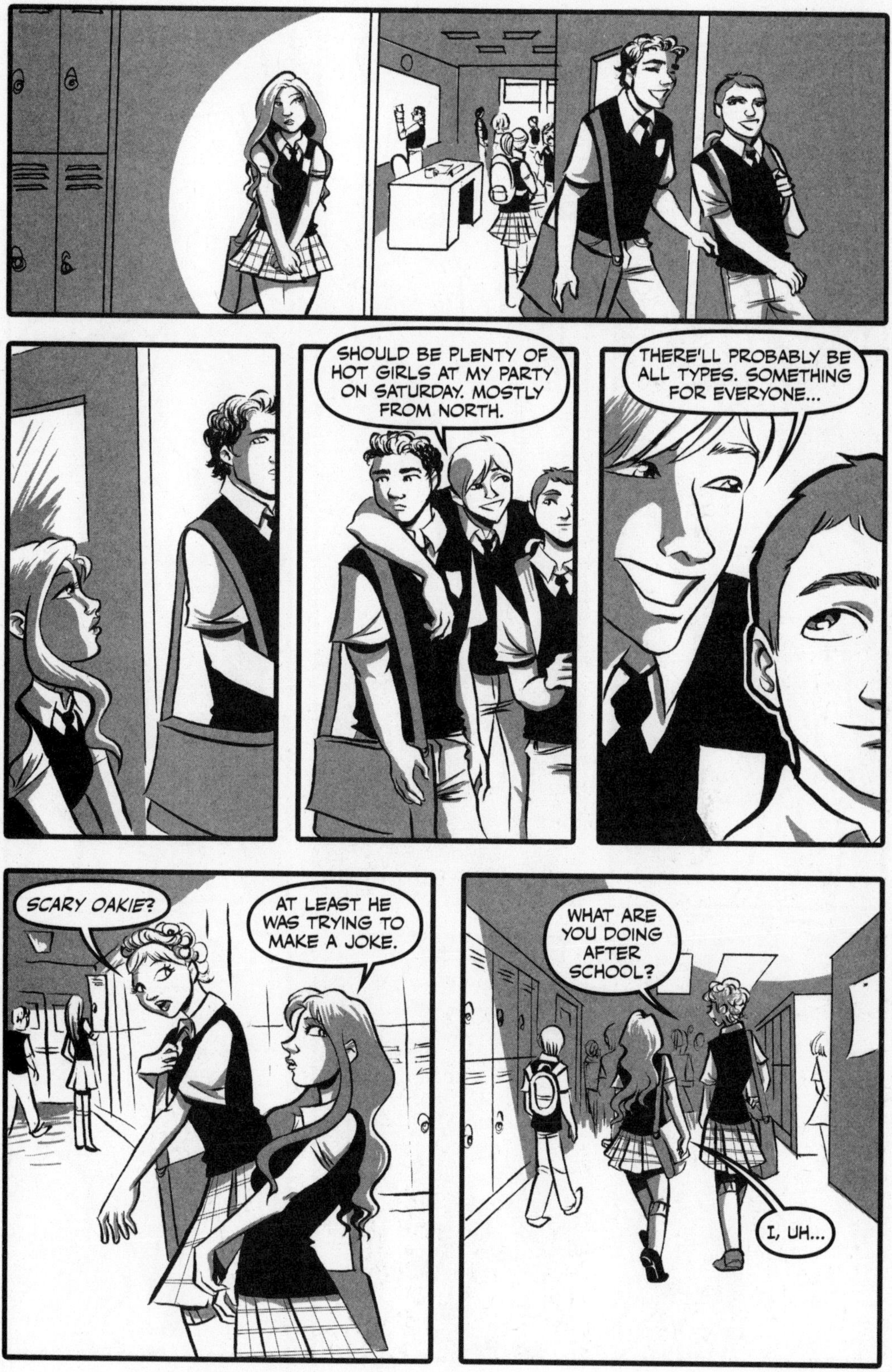
SHOULD BE PLENTY OF HOT GIRLS AT MY PARTY ON SATURDAY. MOSTLY FROM NORTH.
THERE'LL PROBABLY BE ALL TYPES. SOMETHING FOR EVERYONE...
SCARY OAKIE?
AT LEAST HE WAS TRYING TO MAKE A JOKE.
WHAT ARE YOU DOING AFTER SCHOOL?
I, UH...

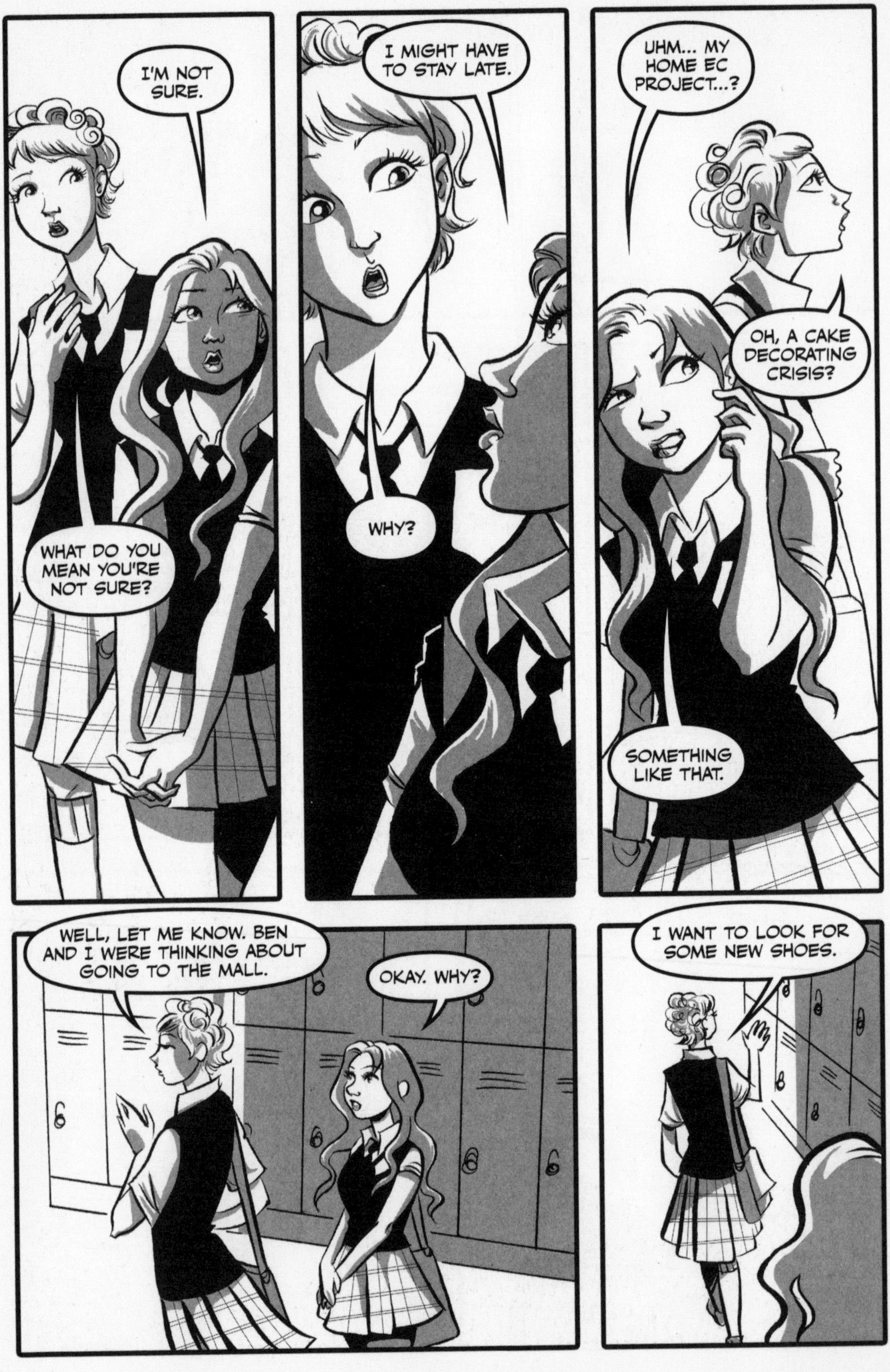
I'M NOT SURE.
WHAT DO YOU MEAN YOU'RE NOT SURE?
I MIGHT HAVE TO STAY LATE.
WHY?
UHM... MY HOME EC PROJECT...?
OH, A CAKE DECORATING CRISIS?
SOMETHING LIKE THAT.
WELL, LET ME KNOW. BEN AND I WERE THINKING ABOUT GOING TO THE MALL.
OKAY. WHY?
I WANT TO LOOK FOR SOME NEW SHOES.

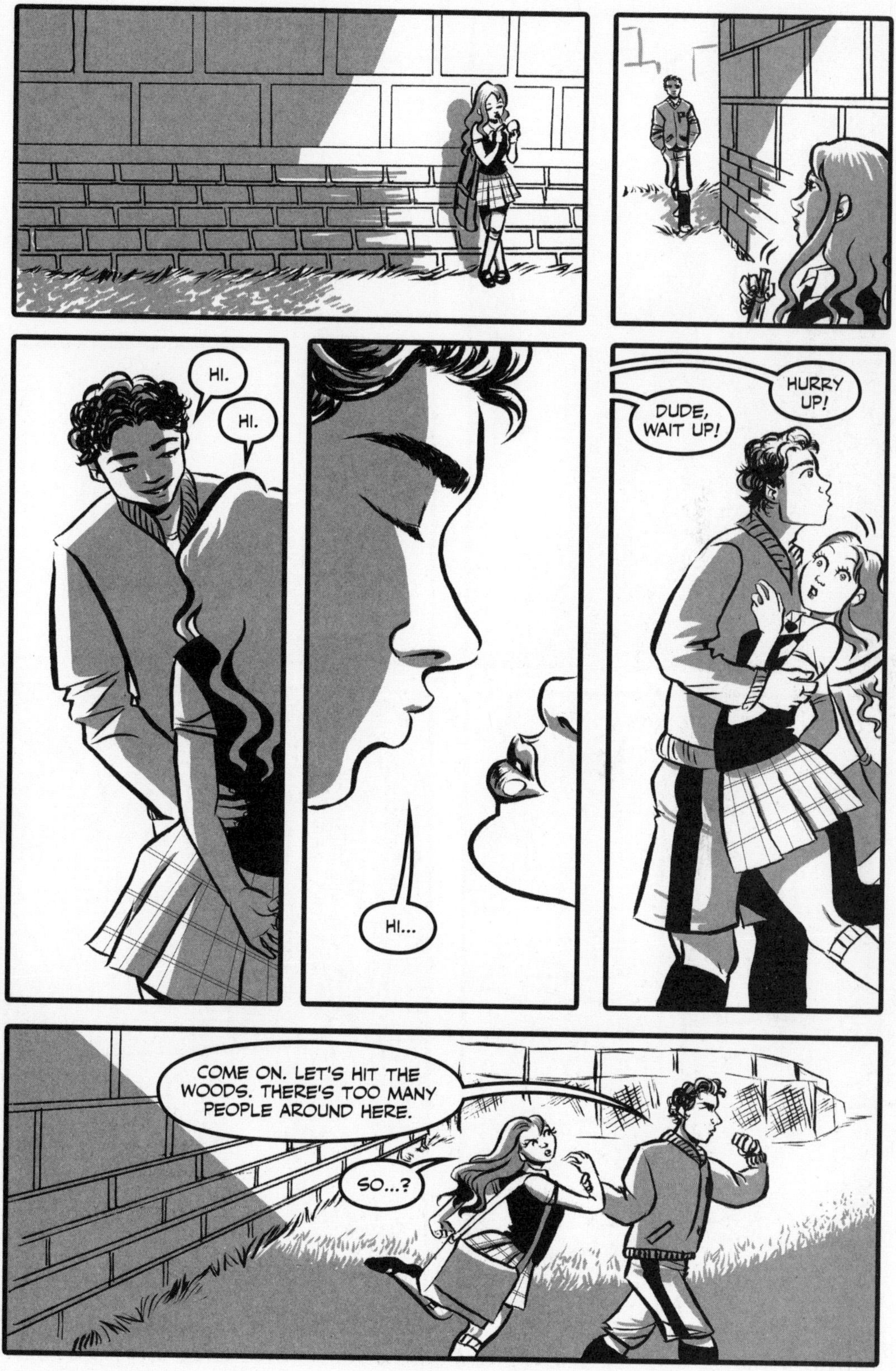
HI.
HI.
HI...
DUDE, WAIT UP!
HURRY UP!
COME ON. LET'S HIT THE WOODS. THERE'S TOO MANY PEOPLE AROUND HERE.
SO...?

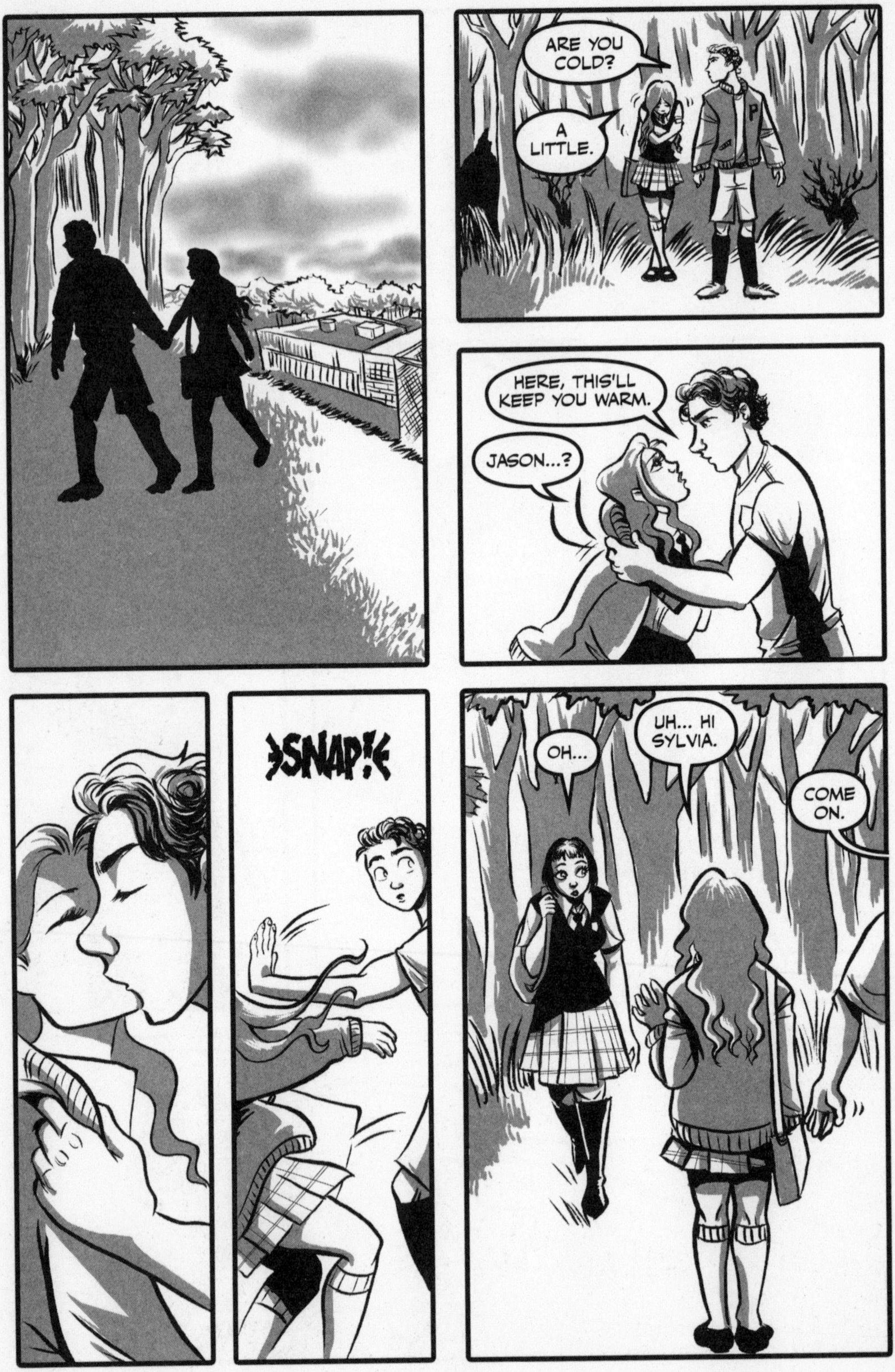
ARE YOU COLD?
A LITTLE.
HERE, THIS'LL KEEP YOU WARM.
JASON...?
SNAP!
OH...
UH... HI SYLVIA.
COME ON.

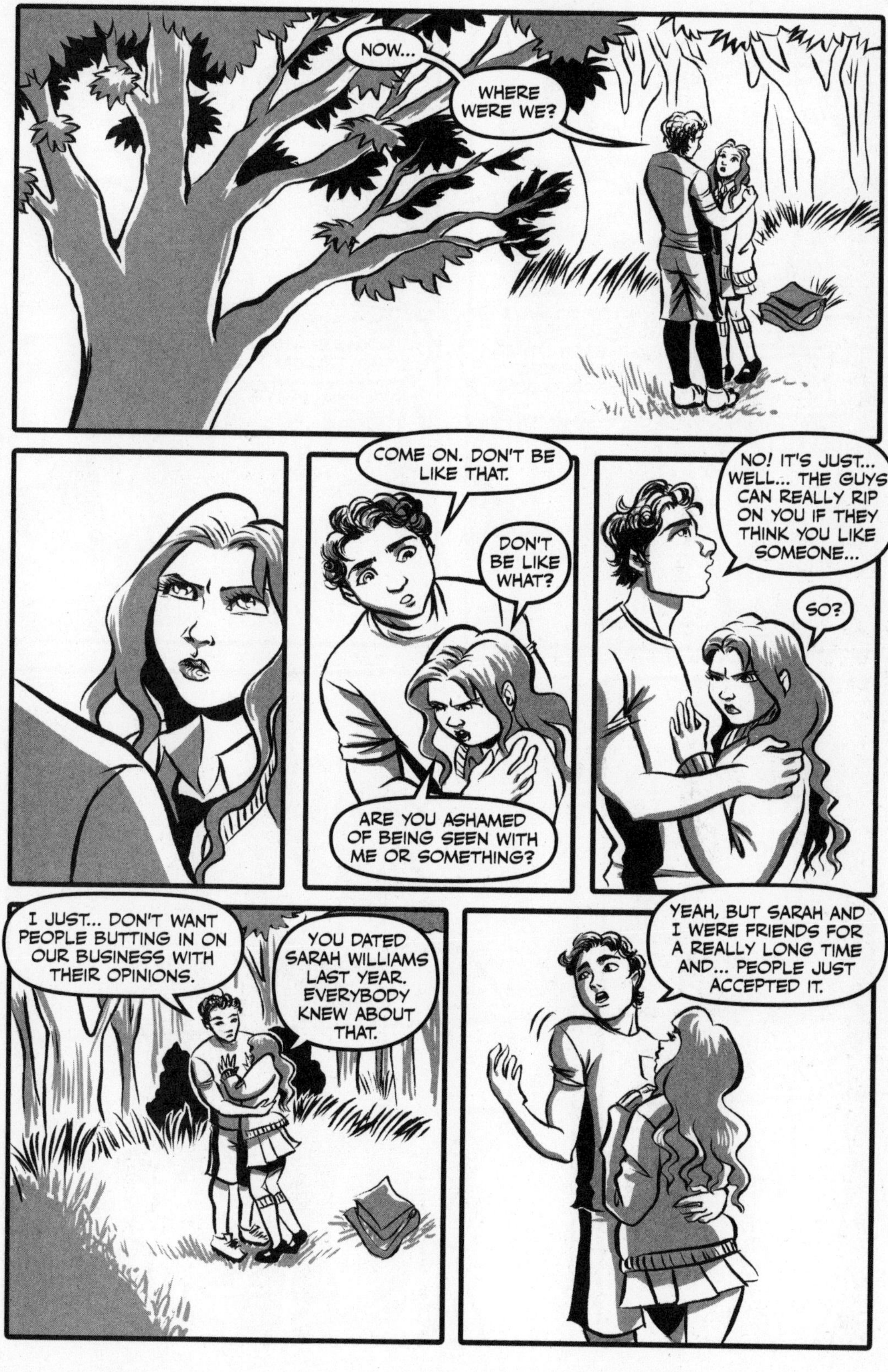
NOW...
WHERE WERE WE?
COME ON. DON'T BE LIKE THAT.
DON'T BE LIKE WHAT?
ARE YOU ASHAMED OF BEING SEEN WITH ME OR SOMETHING?
NO! IT'S JUST... WELL... THE GUYS CAN REALLY RIP ON YOU IF THEY THINK YOU LIKE SOMEONE...
SO?
I JUST... DON'T WANT PEOPLE BUTTING IN ON OUR BUSINESS WITH THEIR OPINIONS.
YOU DATED SARAH WILLIAMS LAST YEAR. EVERYBODY KNEW ABOUT THAT.
YEAH, BUT SARAH AND I WERE FRIENDS FOR A REALLY LONG TIME AND... PEOPLE JUST ACCEPTED IT.

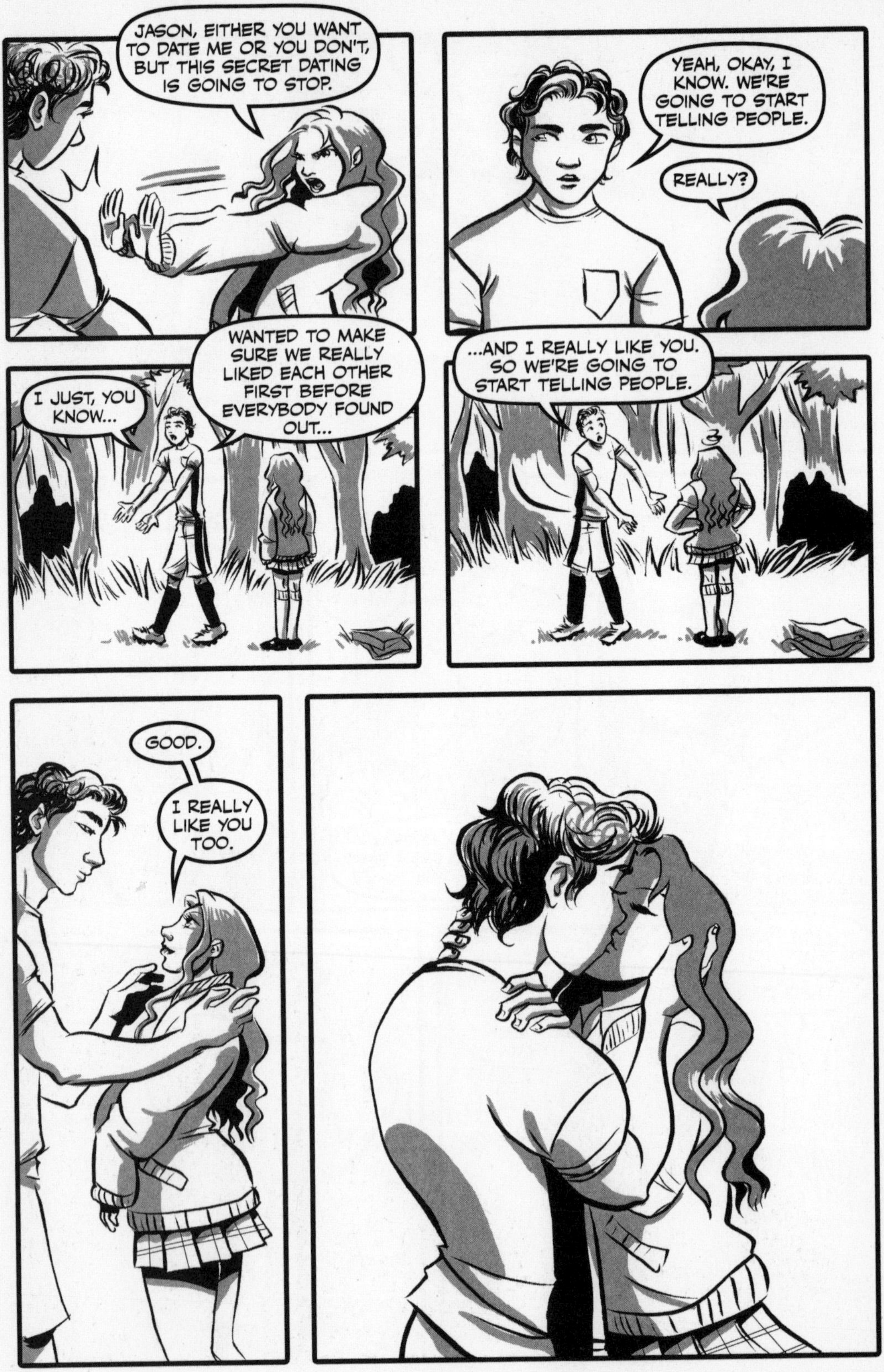
JASON, EITHER YOU WANT TO DATE ME OR YOU DON'T, BUT THIS SECRET DATING IS GOING TO STOP.
YEAH, OKAY, I KNOW. WE'RE GOING TO START TELLING PEOPLE.
REALLY?
I JUST, YOU KNOW...
WANTED TO MAKE SURE WE REALLY LIKED EACH OTHER FIRST BEFORE EVERYBODY FOUND OUT...
...AND I REALLY LIKE YOU. SO WE'RE GOING TO START TELLING PEOPLE.
GOOD.
I REALLY LIKE YOU TOO.

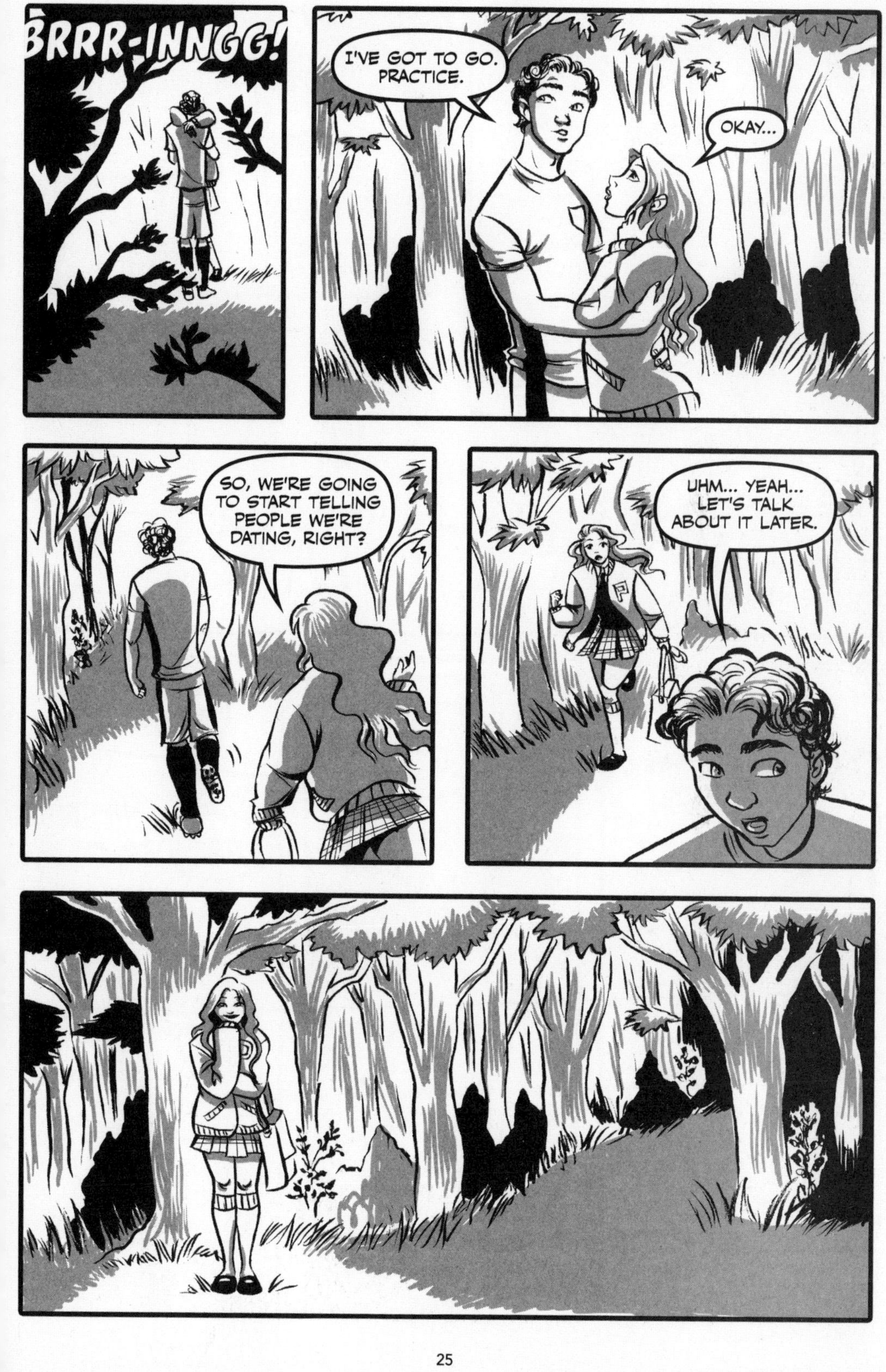
BRRR-INNGG!
I'VE GOT TO GO. PRACTICE.
OKAY...
SO, WE'RE GOING TO START TELLING PEOPLE WE'RE DATING, RIGHT?
UHM... YEAH... LET'S TALK ABOUT IT LATER.

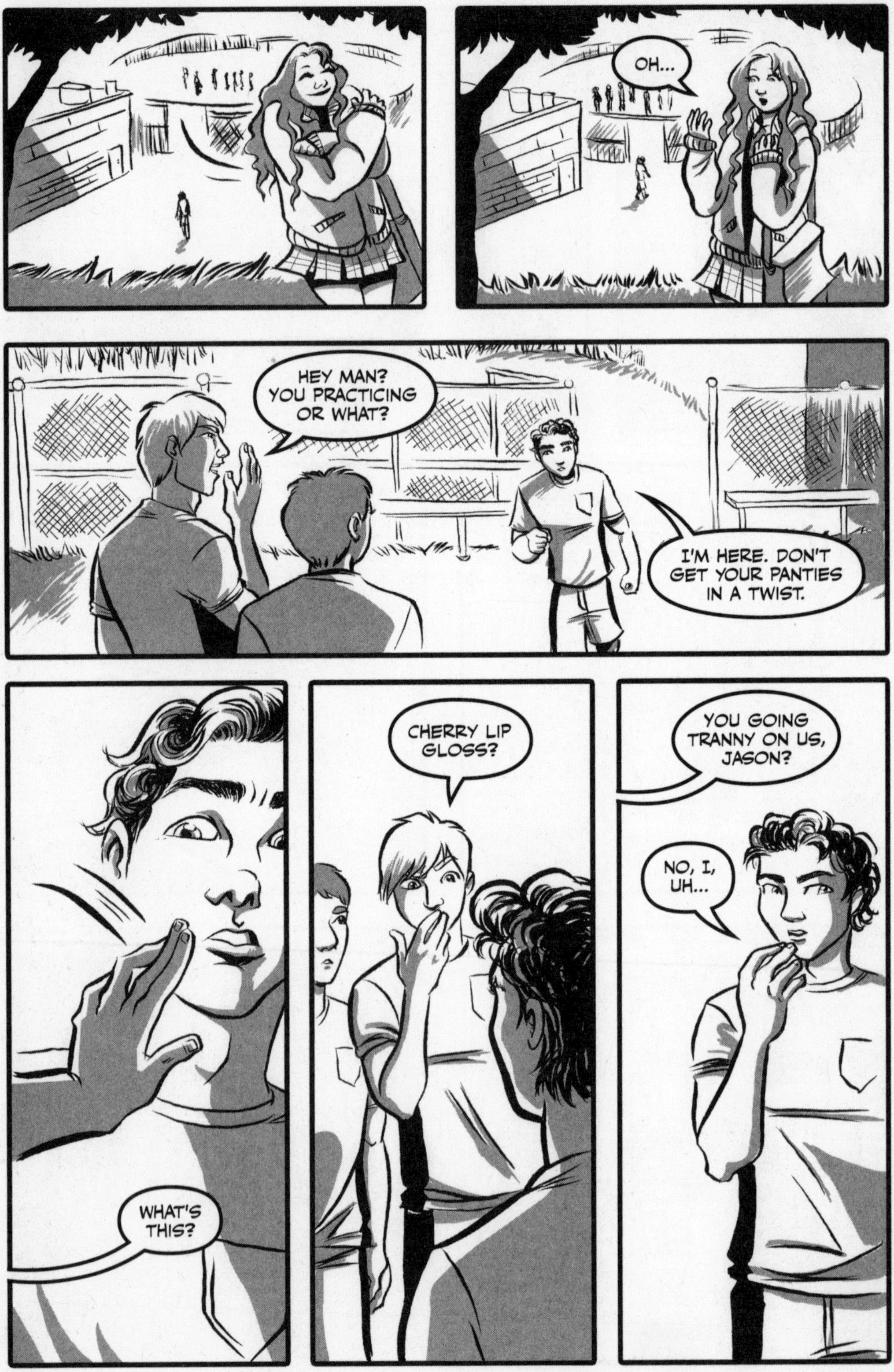
OH...
HEY MAN? YOU PRACTICING OR WHAT?
I'M HERE. DON'T GET YOUR PANTIES IN A TWIST.
WHAT'S THIS?
CHERRY LIP GLOSS?
YOU GOING TRANNY ON US, JASON?
NO, I, UH...

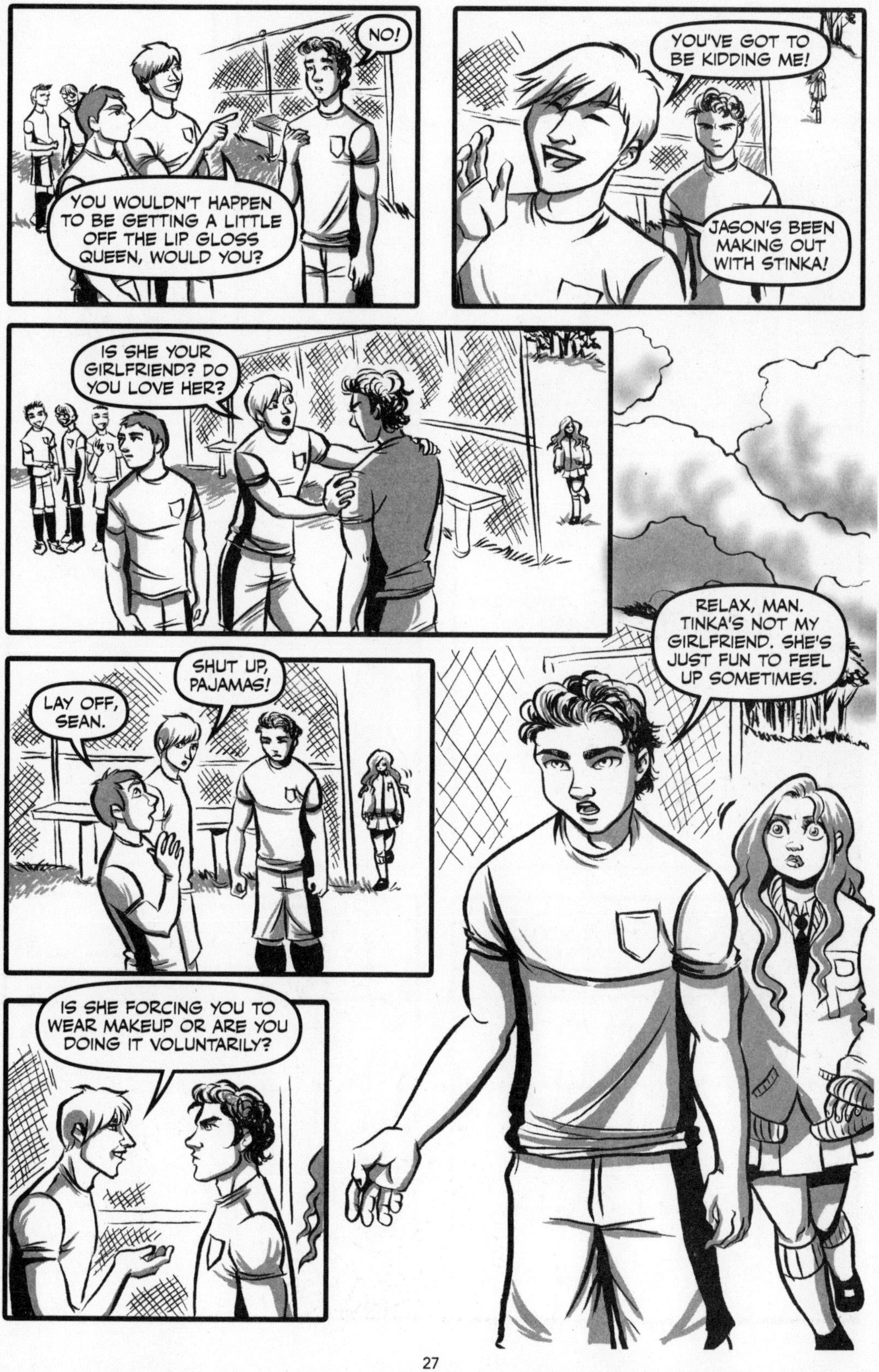
NO!
YOU WOULDN'T HAPPEN TO BE GETTING A LITTLE OFF THE LIP GLOSS QUEEN, WOULD YOU?
YOU'VE GOT TO BE KIDDING ME!
JASON'S BEEN MAKING OUT WITH STINKA!
IS SHE YOUR GIRLFRIEND? DO YOU LOVE HER?
LAY OFF, SEAN.
SHUT UP, PAJAMAS!
IS SHE FORCING YOU TO WEAR MAKEUP OR ARE YOU DOING IT VOLUNTARILY?
RELAX, MAN. TINKA'S NOT MY GIRLFRIEND. SHE'S JUST FUN TO FEEL UP SOMETIMES.

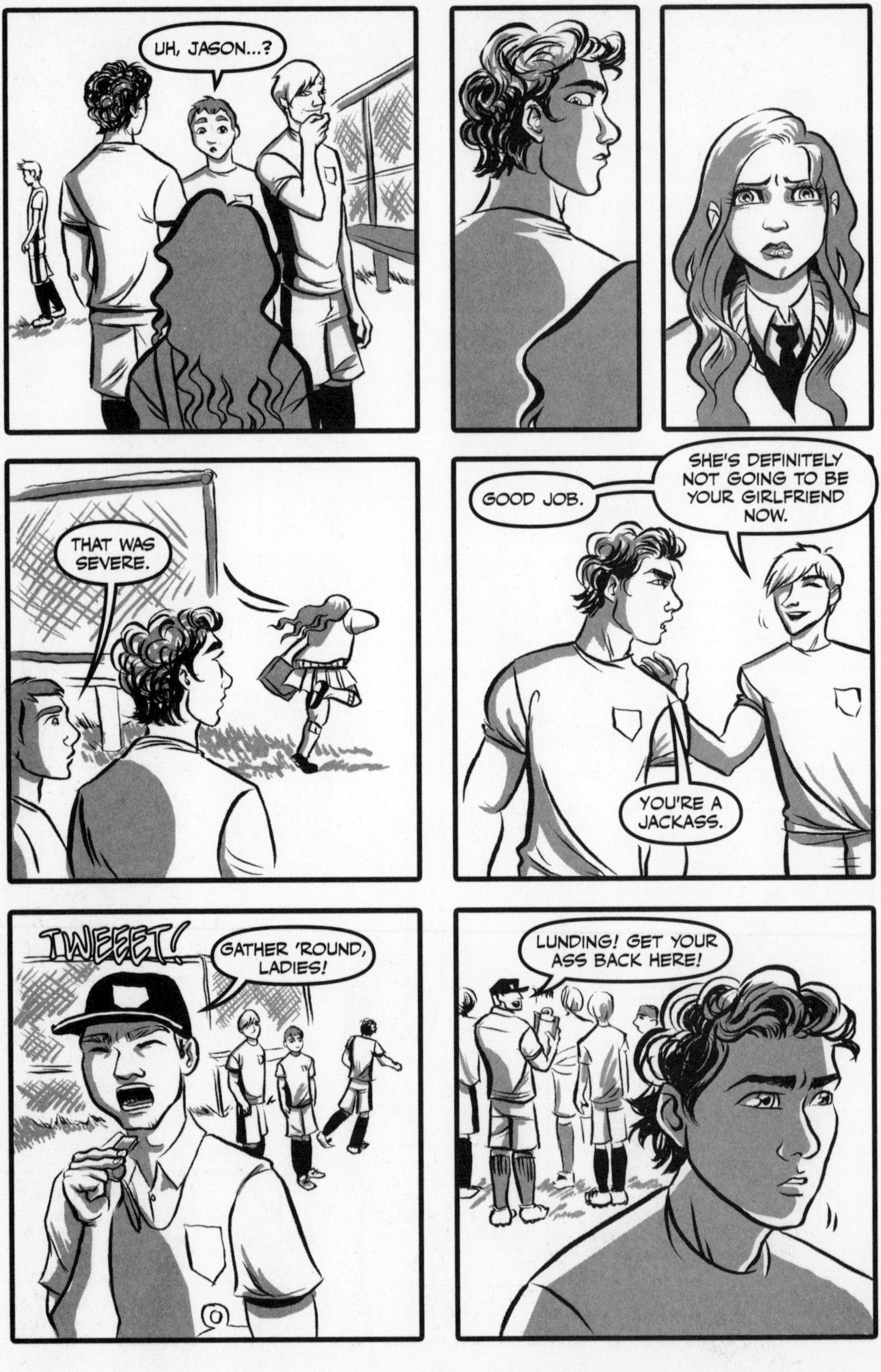
UH, JASON...?
THAT WAS SEVERE.
GOOD JOB.
SHE'S DEFINITELY NOT GOING TO BE YOUR GIRLFRIEND NOW.
YOU'RE A JACKASS.
TWEEET!
GATHER 'ROUND, LADIES!
LUNDING! GET YOUR ASS BACK HERE!

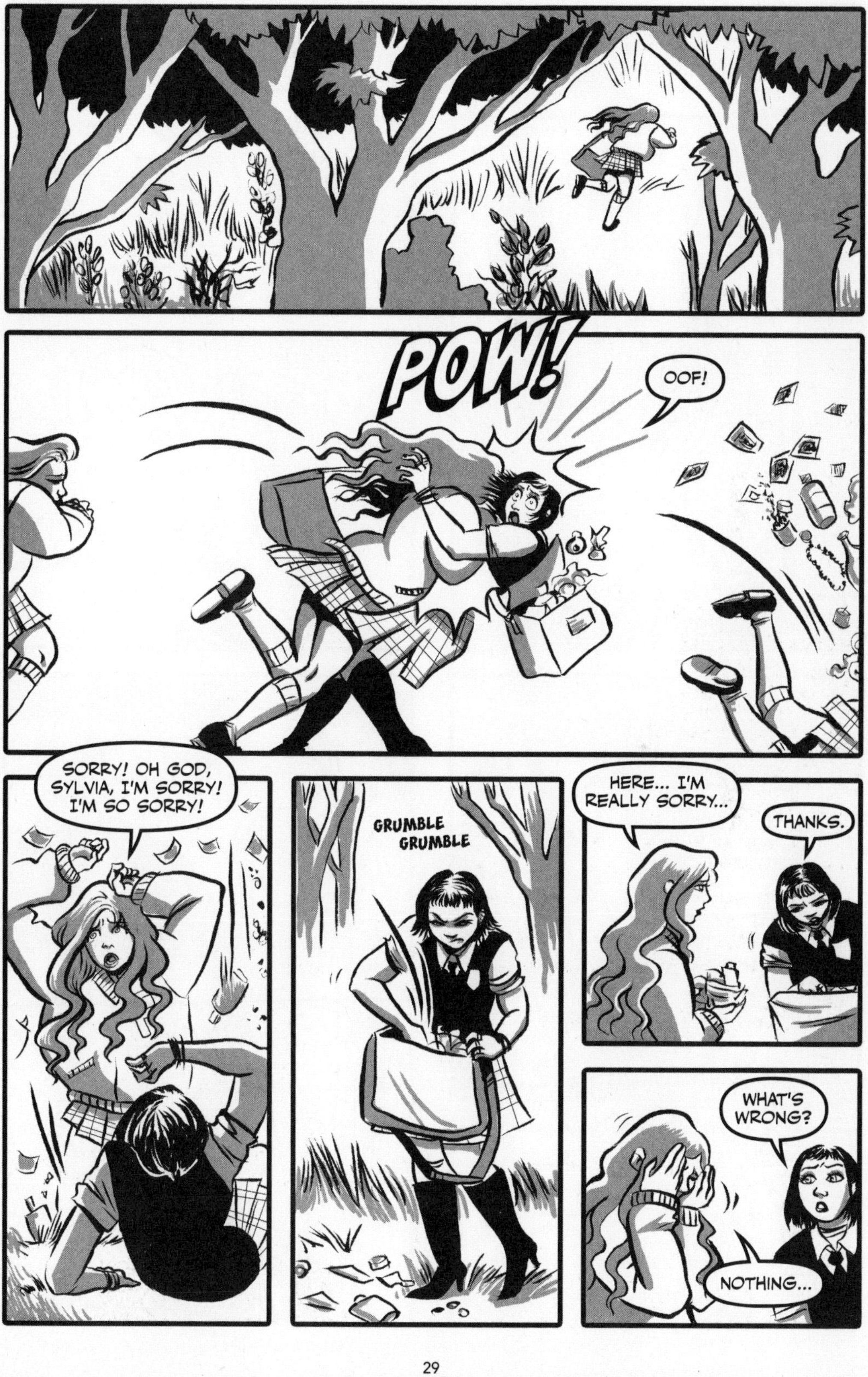
POW!
OOF!
SORRY! OH GOD, SYLVIA, I'M SORRY! I'M SO SORRY!
GRUMBLE GRUMBLE
HERE... I'M REALLY SORRY...
THANKS.
WHAT'S WRONG?
NOTHING...

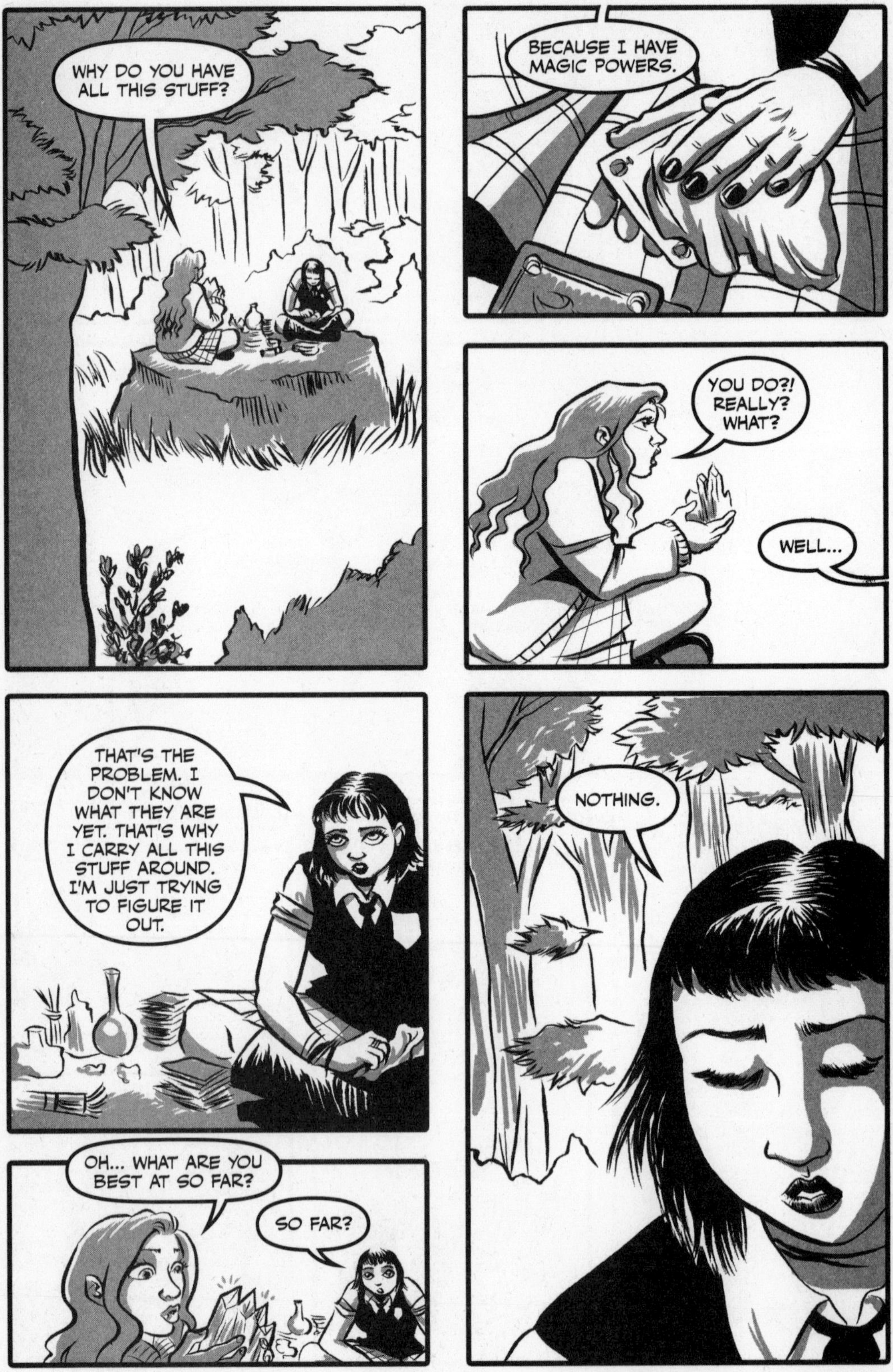
WHY DO YOU HAVE ALL THIS STUFF?
BECAUSE I HAVE MAGIC POWERS.
YOU DO?! REALLY? WHAT?
WELL...
THAT'S THE PROBLEM. I DON'T KNOW WHAT THEY ARE YET. THAT'S WHY I CARRY ALL THIS STUFF AROUND. I'M JUST TRYING TO FIGURE IT OUT.
OH... WHAT ARE YOU BEST AT SO FAR?
SO FAR?
NOTHING.

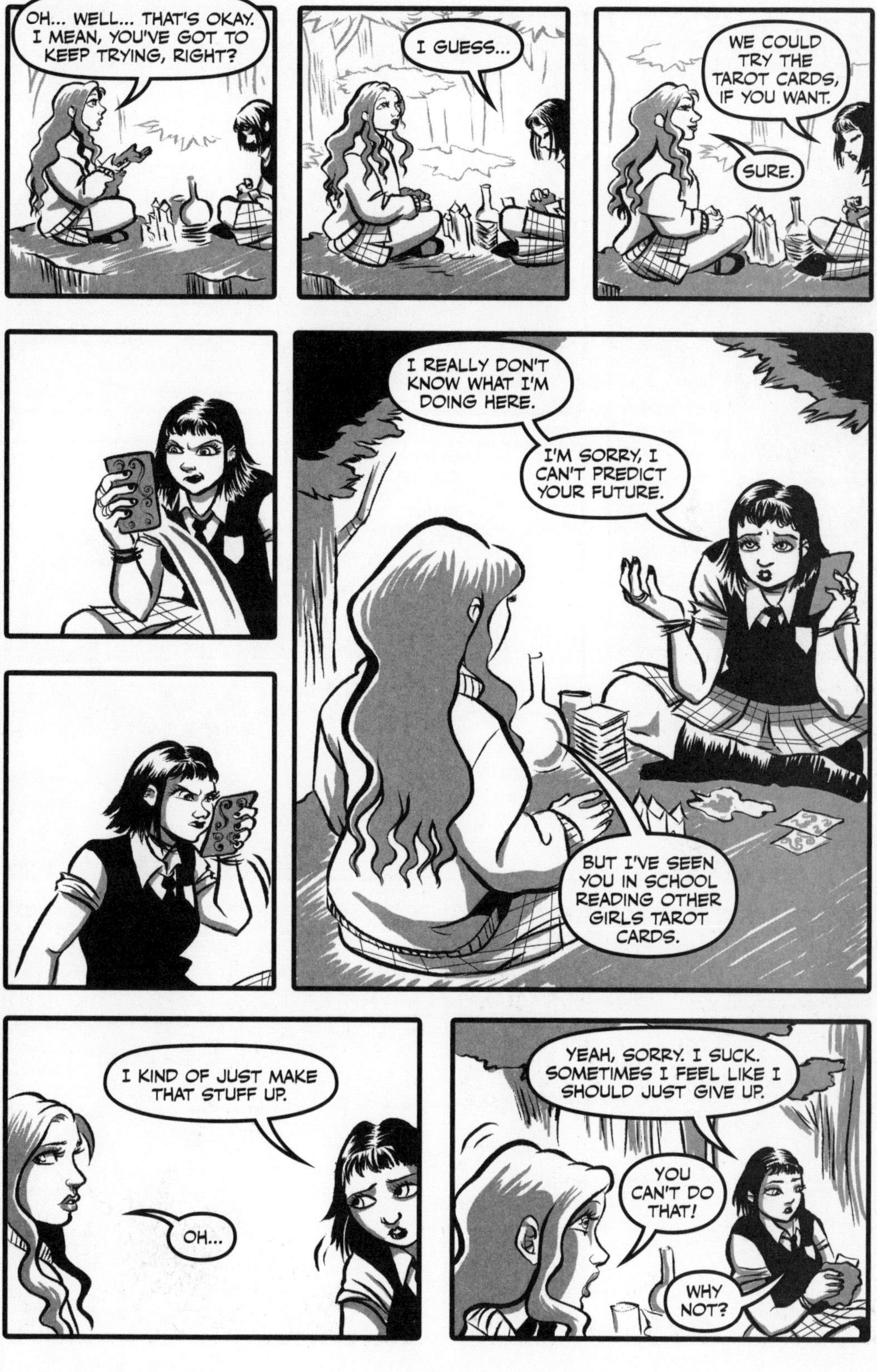
OH... WELL... THAT'S OKAY. I MEAN, YOU'VE GOT TO KEEP TRYING, RIGHT?
I GUESS...
WE COULD TRY THE TAROT CARDS, IF YOU WANT.
SURE.
I REALLY DON'T KNOW WHAT I'M DOING HERE.
I'M SORRY, I CAN'T PREDICT YOUR FUTURE.
BUT I'VE SEEN YOU IN SCHOOL READING OTHER GIRLS TAROT CARDS.
I KIND OF JUST MAKE THAT STUFF UP.
OH...
YEAH, SORRY. I SUCK. SOMETIMES I FEEL LIKE I SHOULD JUST GIVE UP.
YOU CAN'T DO THAT!
WHY NOT?

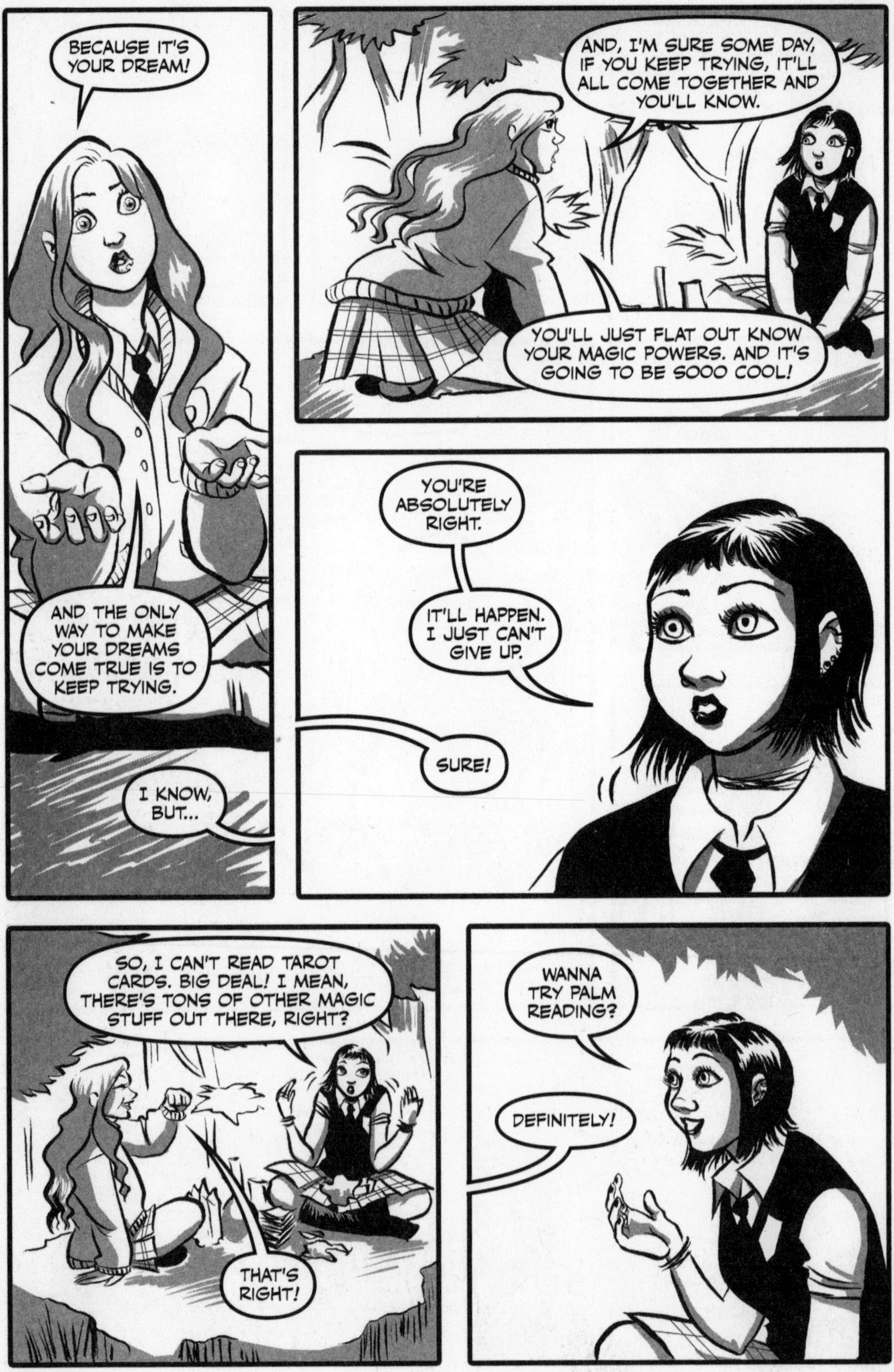
BECAUSE IT'S YOUR DREAM!
AND THE ONLY WAY TO MAKE YOUR DREAMS COME TRUE IS TO KEEP TRYING.
I KNOW, BUT...
AND, I'M SURE SOME DAY, IF YOU KEEP TRYING, IT'LL ALL COME TOGETHER AND YOU'LL KNOW.
YOU'LL JUST FLAT OUT KNOW YOUR MAGIC POWERS. AND IT'S GOING TO BE SOOO COOL!
YOU'RE ABSOLUTELY RIGHT.
IT'LL HAPPEN. I JUST CAN'T GIVE UP.
SURE!
SO, I CAN'T READ TAROT CARDS. BIG DEAL! I MEAN, THERE'S TONS OF OTHER MAGIC STUFF OUT THERE, RIGHT?
THAT'S RIGHT!
WANNA TRY PALM READING?
DEFINITELY!

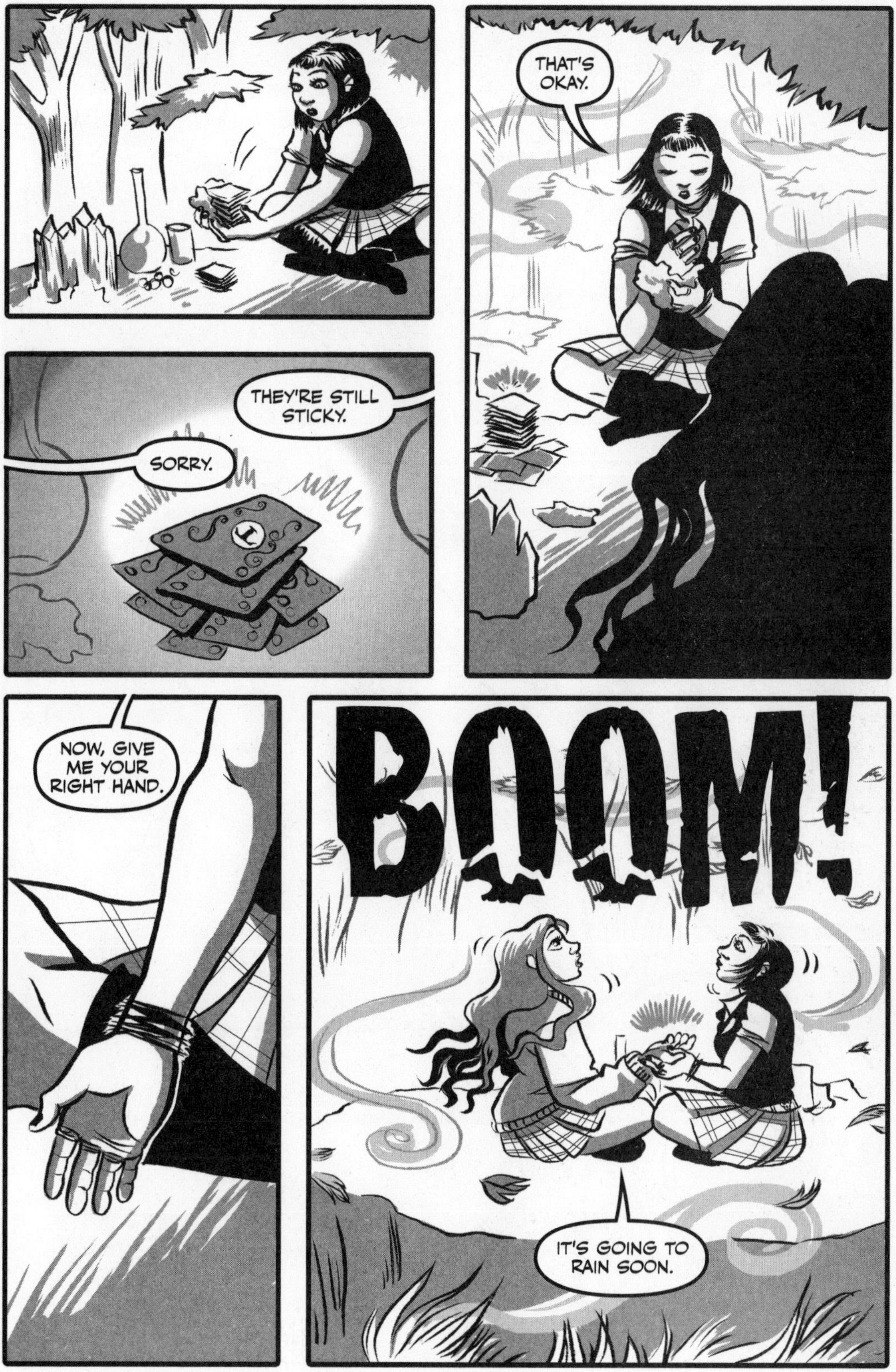
THAT'S OKAY.
THEY'RE STILL STICKY.
SORRY.
NOW, GIVE ME YOUR RIGHT HAND.
BOOM!
IT'S GOING TO RAIN SOON.

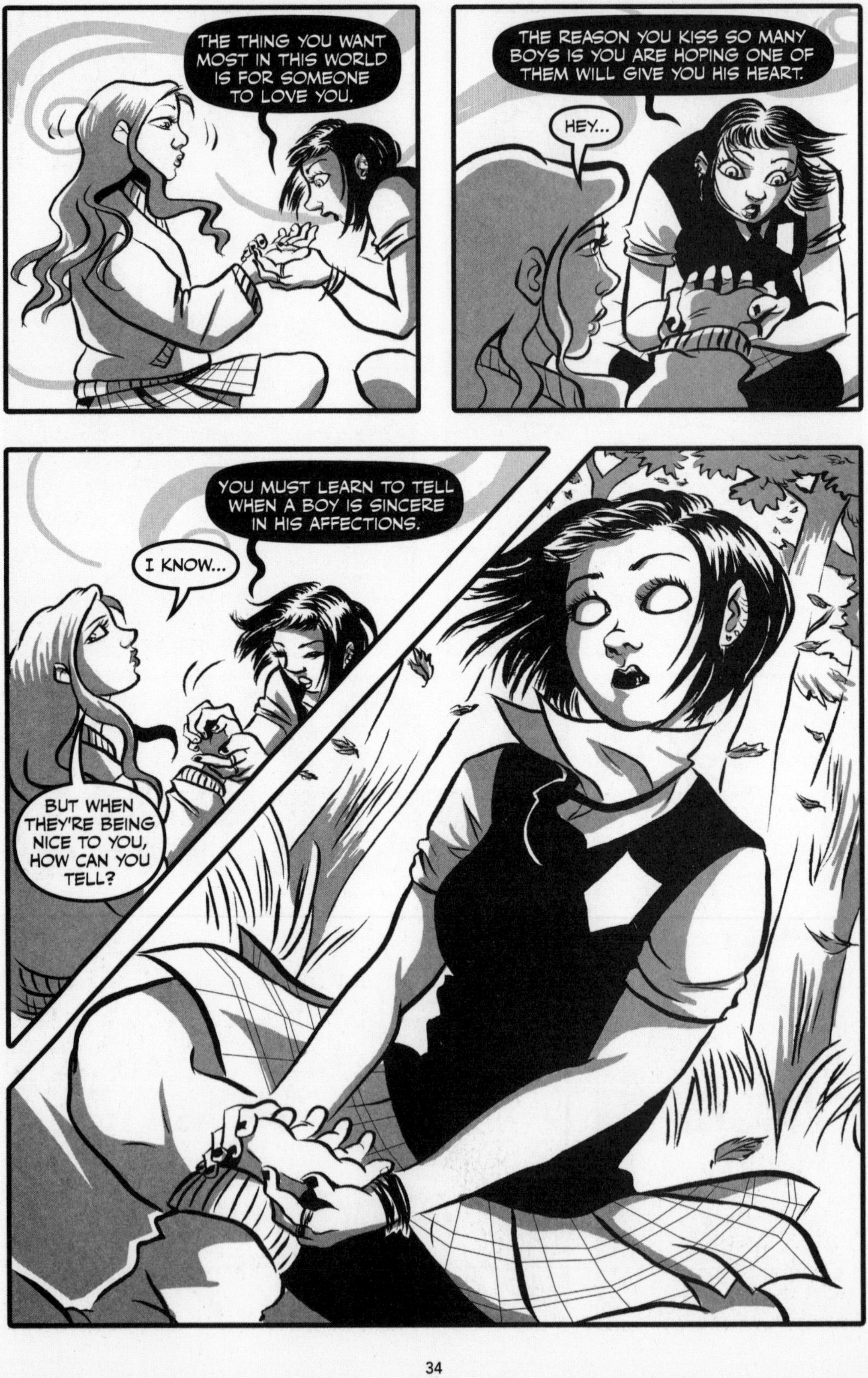
THE THING YOU WANT MOST IN THIS WORLD IS FOR SOMEONE TO LOVE YOU.
THE REASON YOU KISS SO MANY BOYS IS YOU ARE HOPING ONE OF THEM WILL GIVE YOU HIS HEART.
HEY...
YOU MUST LEARN TO TELL WHEN A BOY IS SINCERE IN HIS AFFECTIONS.
I KNOW...
BUT WHEN THEY'RE BEING NICE TO YOU, HOW CAN YOU TELL?

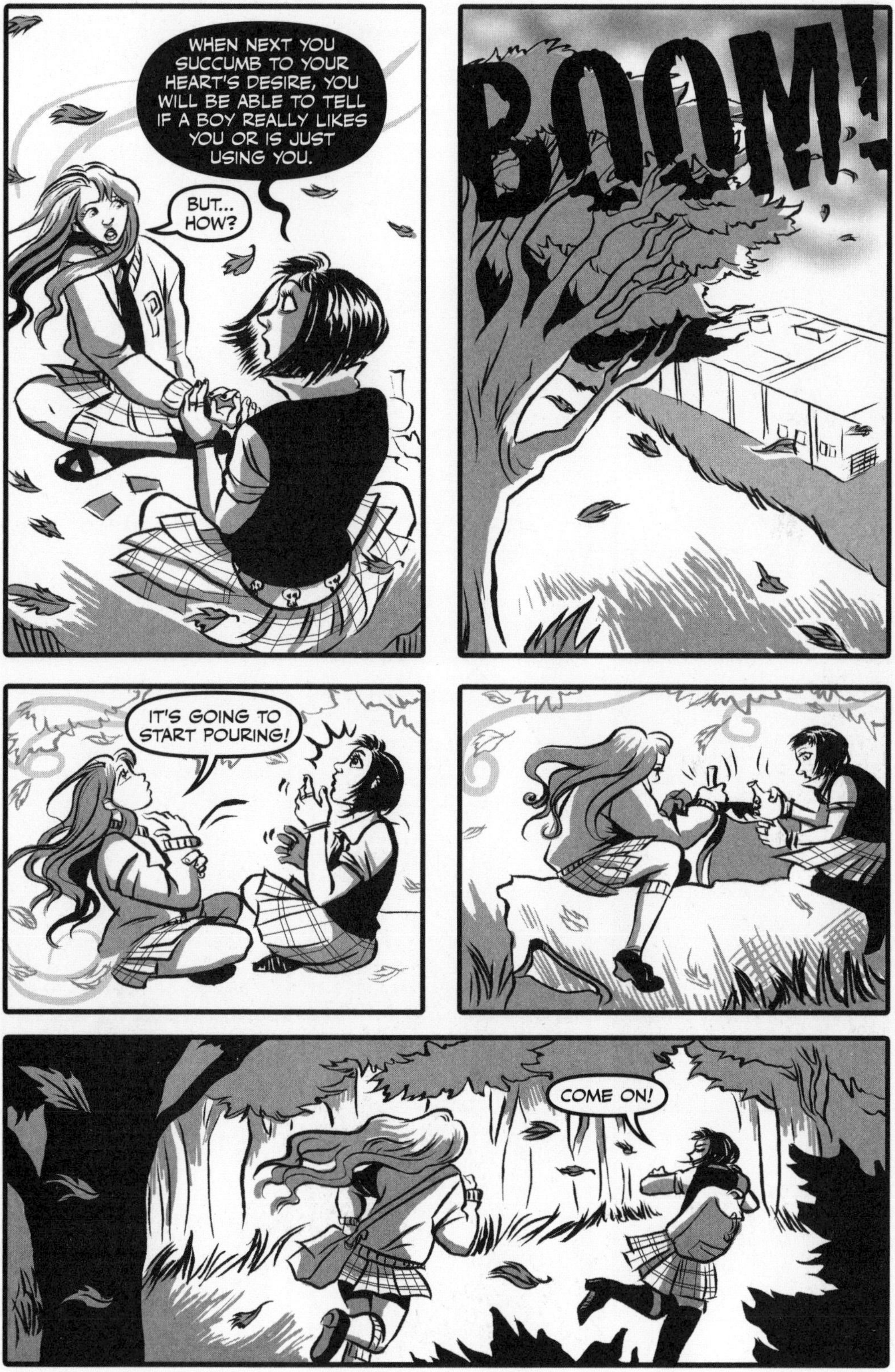
WHEN NEXT YOU SUCCUMB TO YOUR HEART'S DESIRE, YOU WILL BE ABLE TO TELL IF A BOY REALLY LIKES YOU OR IS JUST USING YOU.
BUT... HOW?
BOOM!
IT'S GOING TO START POURING!
COME ON!

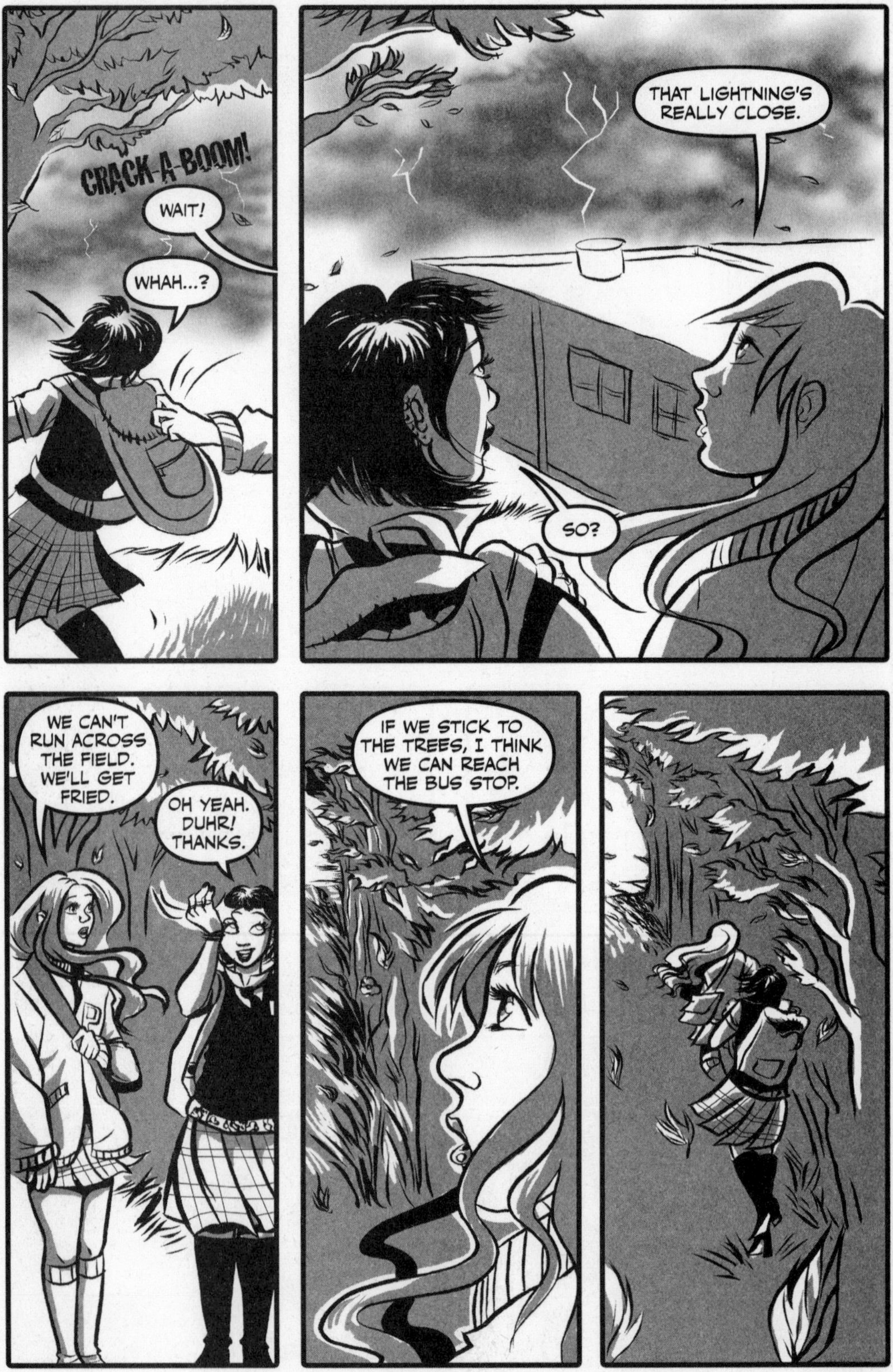
CRACK-A-BOOM!
WAIT!
WHAH...?
THAT LIGHTNING'S REALLY CLOSE.
SO?
WE CAN'T RUN ACROSS THE FIELD. WE'LL GET FRIED.
OH YEAH. DUHR! THANKS.
IF WE STICK TO THE TREES, I THINK WE CAN REACH THE BUS STOP.

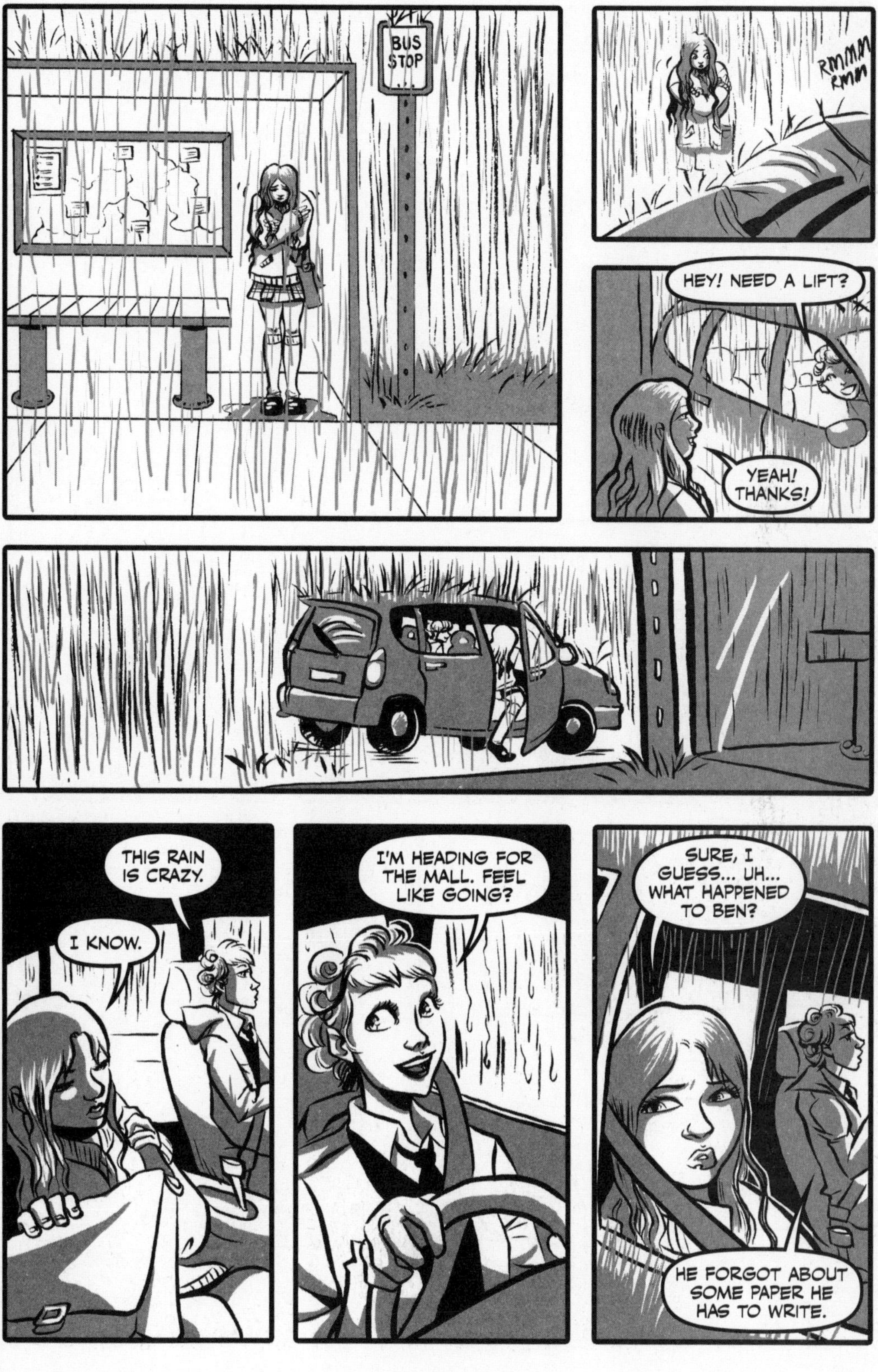
BUS STOP
RMMM RMM
HEY! NEED A LIFT?
YEAH! THANKS!
THIS RAIN IS CRAZY.
I KNOW.
I'M HEADING FOR THE MALL. FEEL LIKE GOING?
SURE, I GUESS... UH... WHAT HAPPENED TO BEN?
HE FORGOT ABOUT SOME PAPER HE HAS TO WRITE.

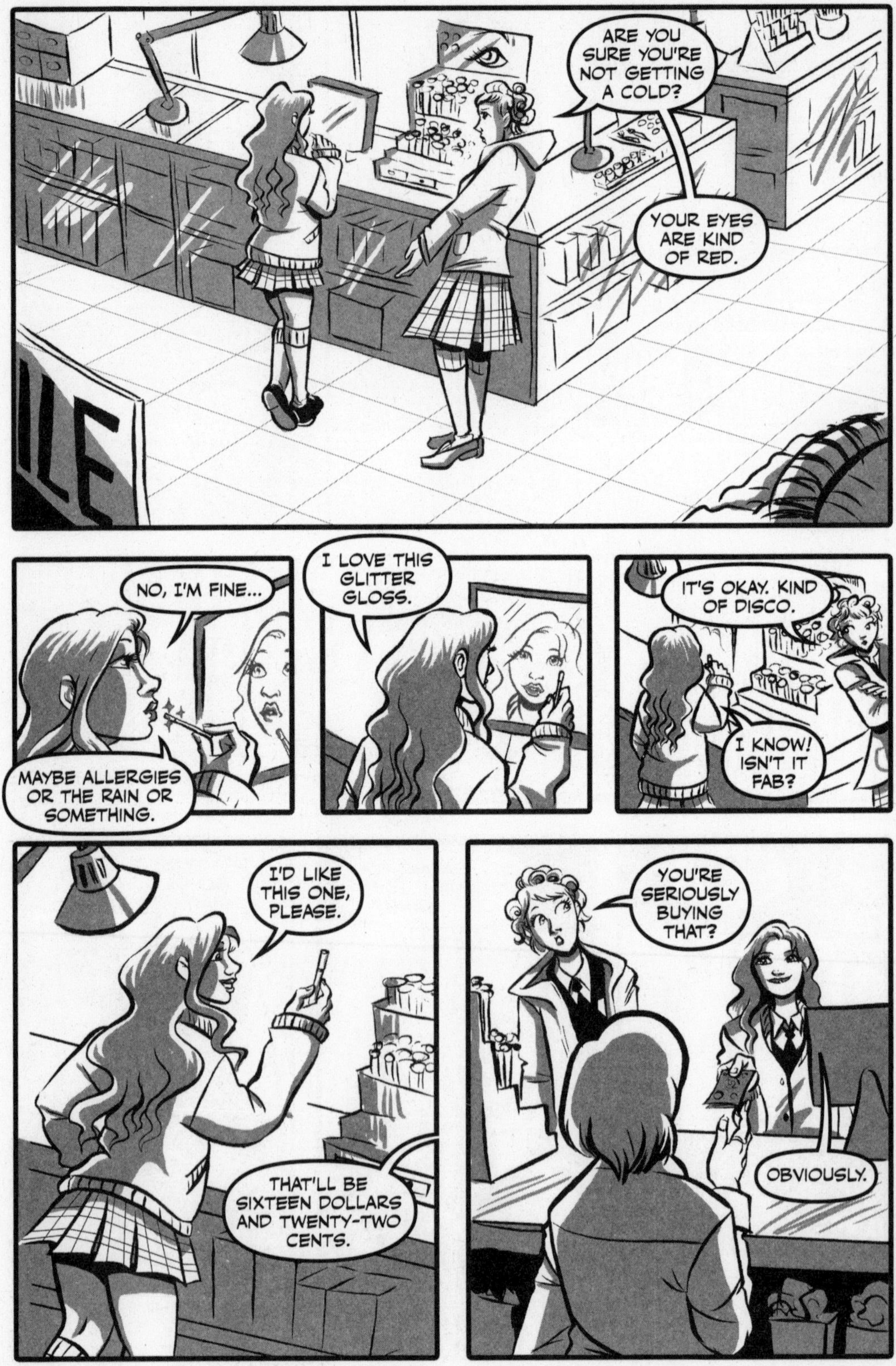

ILE
ARE YOU SURE YOU'RE NOT GETTING A COLD?
YOUR EYES ARE KIND OF RED.
NO, I'M FINE...
MAYBE ALLERGIES OR THE RAIN OR SOMETHING.
I LOVE THIS GLITTER GLOSS.
IT'S OKAY. KIND OF DISCO.
I KNOW! ISN'T IT FAB?
I'D LIKE THIS ONE, PLEASE.
THAT'LL BE SIXTEEN DOLLARS AND TWENTY-TWO CENTS.
YOU'RE SERIOUSLY BUYING THAT?
OBVIOUSLY.

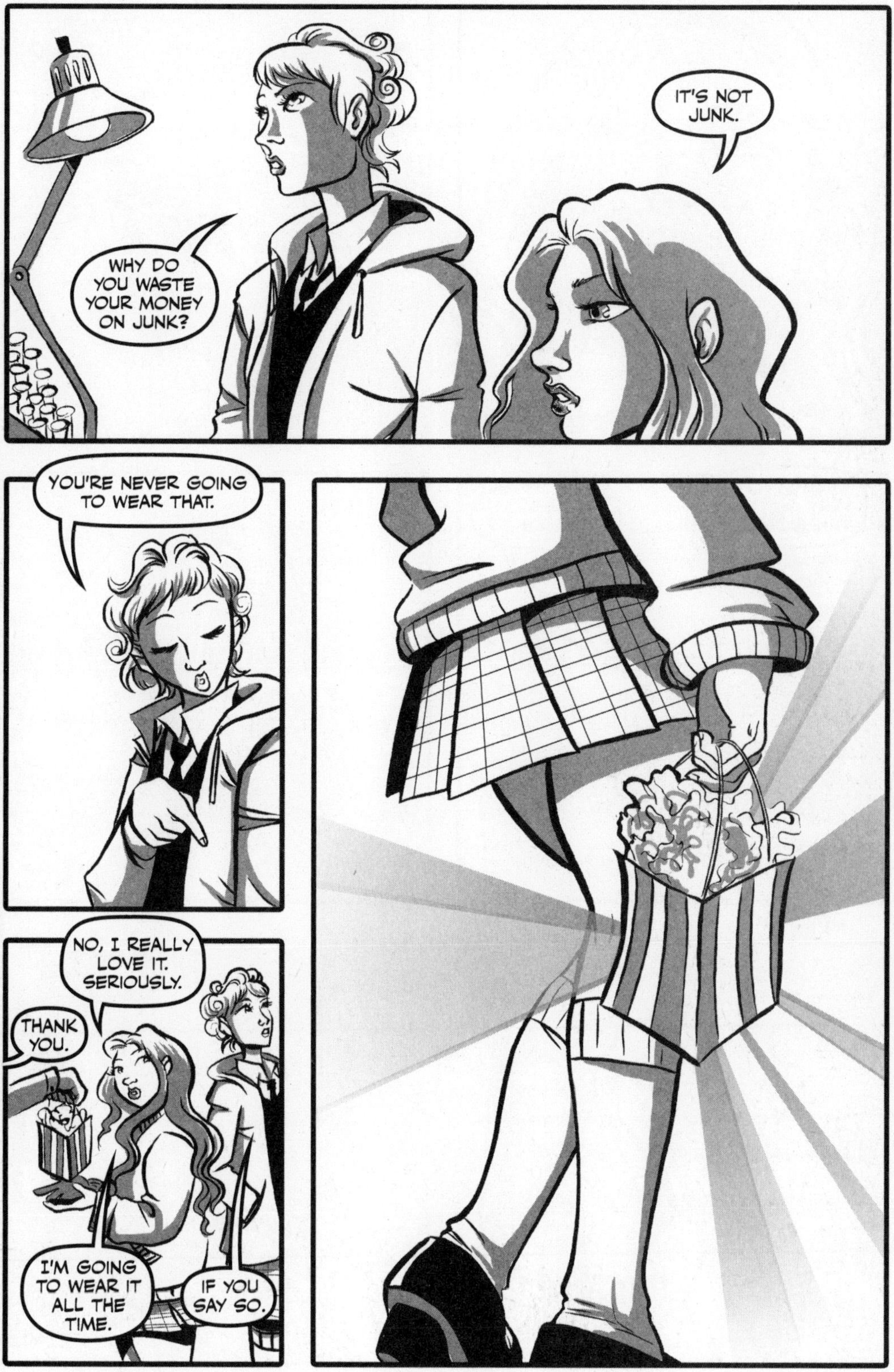

WHY DO YOU WASTE YOUR MONEY ON JUNK?
IT'S NOT JUNK.
YOU'RE NEVER GOING TO WEAR THAT.
NO, I REALLY LOVE IT. SERIOUSLY.
THANK YOU.
I'M GOING TO WEAR IT ALL THE TIME.
IF YOU SAY SO.

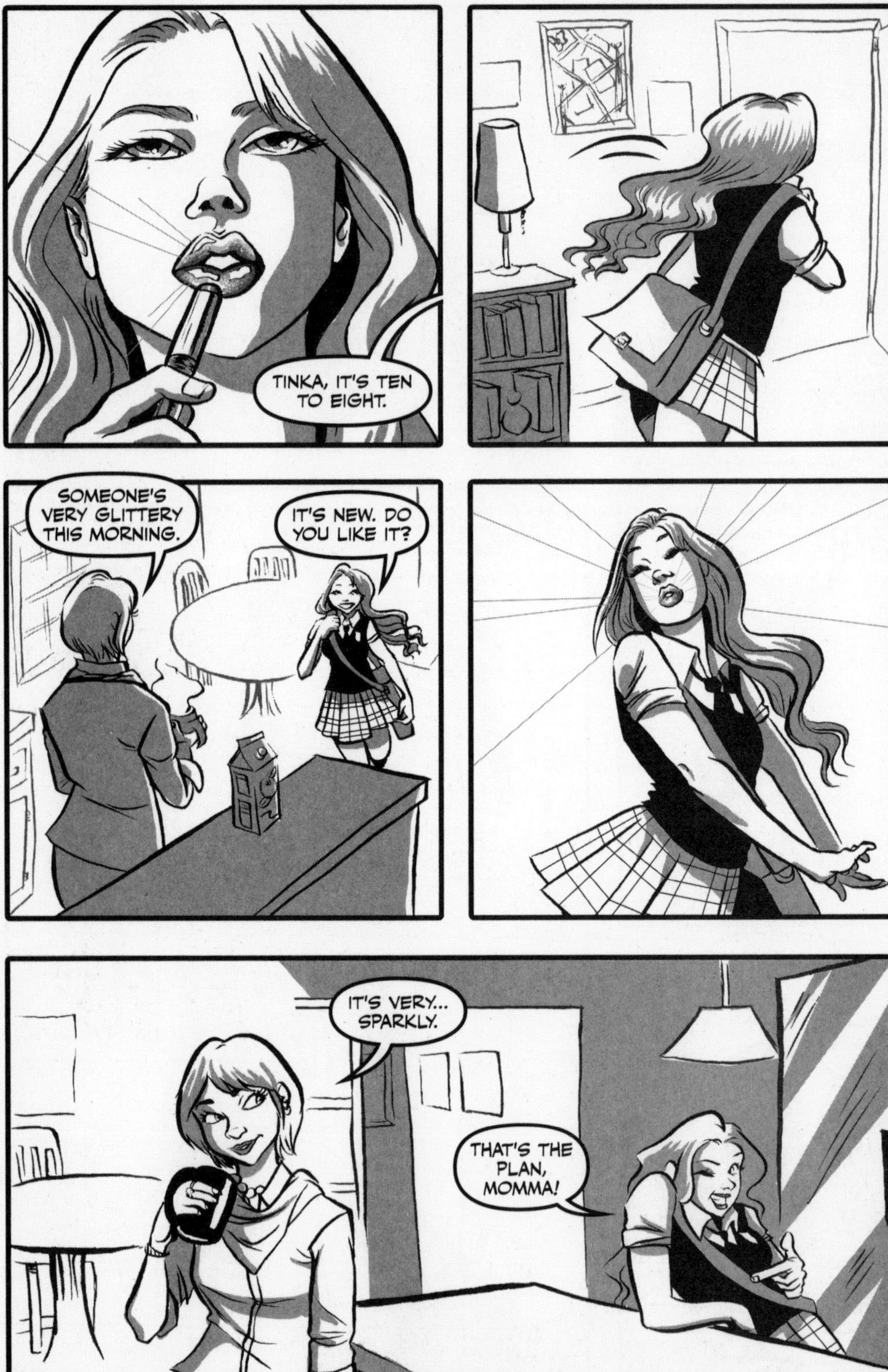
TINKA, IT'S TEN TO EIGHT.
SOMEONE'S VERY GLITTERY THIS MORNING.
IT'S NEW. DO YOU LIKE IT?
IT'S VERY... SPARKLY.
THAT'S THE PLAN, MOMMA!

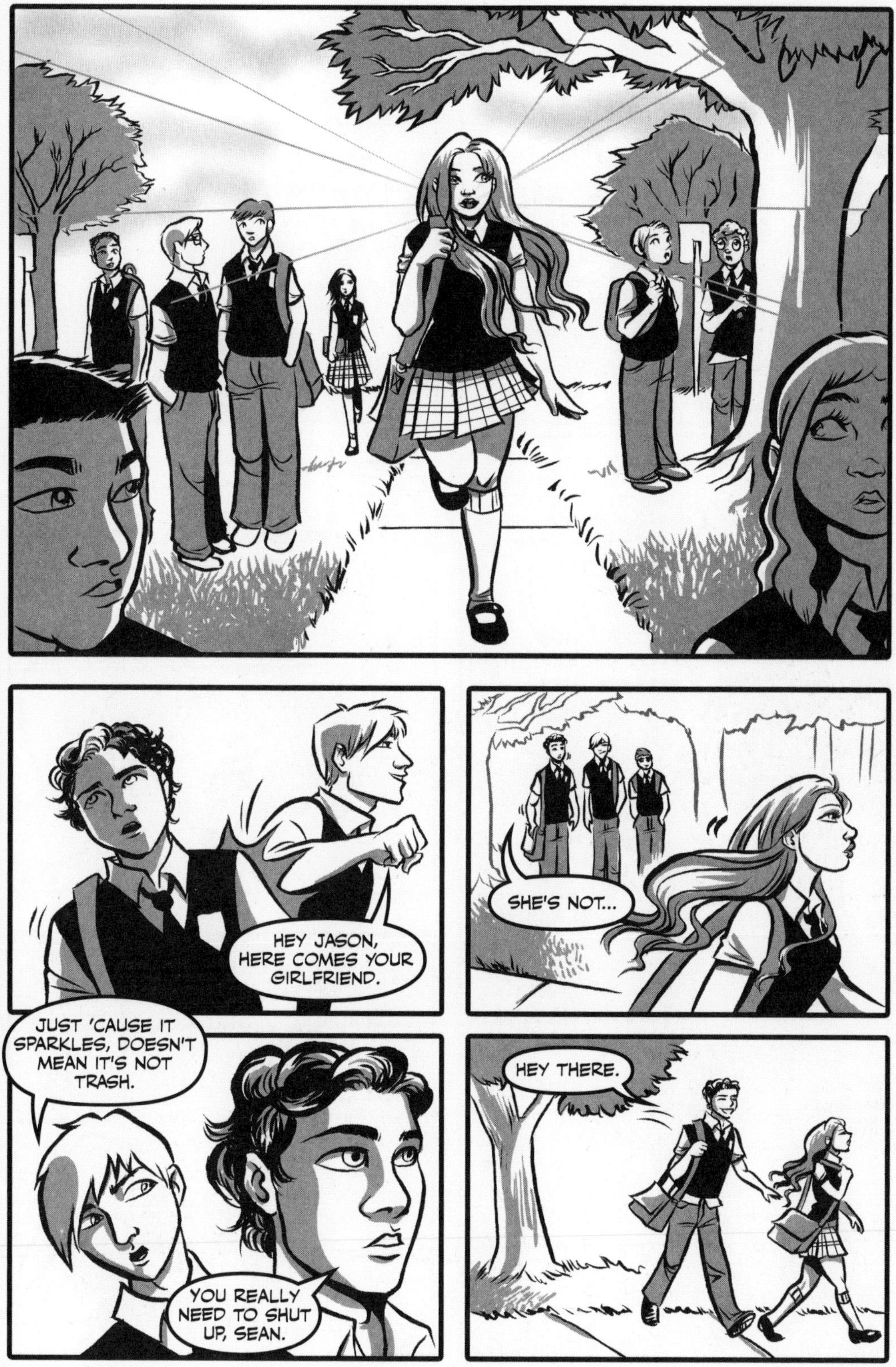
HEY JASON, HERE COMES YOUR GIRLFRIEND.
SHE'S NOT...
JUST 'CAUSE IT SPARKLES, DOESN'T MEAN IT'S NOT TRASH.
YOU REALLY NEED TO SHUT UP, SEAN.
HEY THERE.

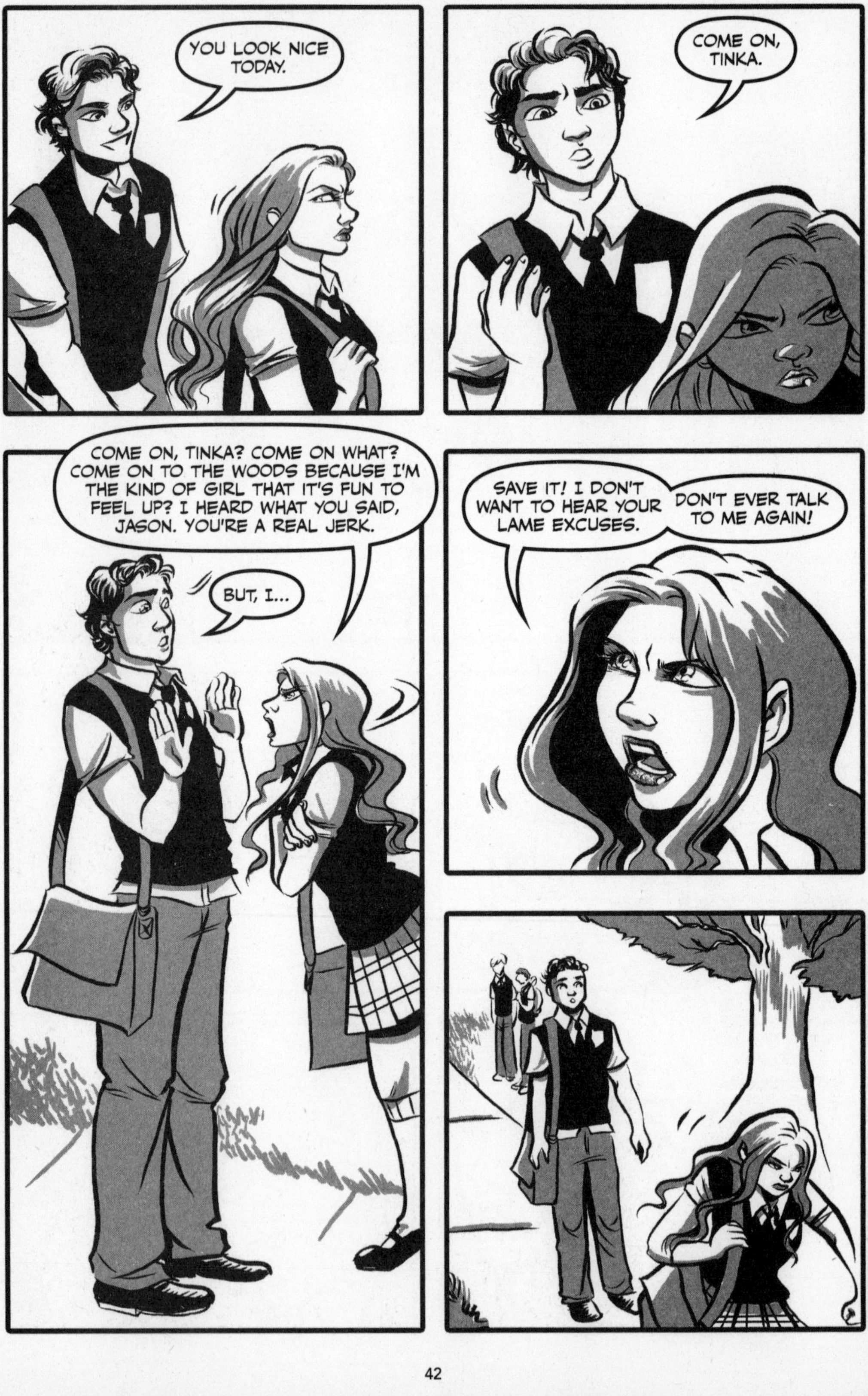
YOU LOOK NICE TODAY.
COME ON, TINKA.
COME ON, TINKA? COME ON WHAT? COME ON TO THE WOODS BECAUSE I'M THE KIND OF GIRL THAT IT'S FUN TO FEEL UP? I HEARD WHAT YOU SAID, JASON. YOU'RE A REAL JERK.
BUT, I...
SAVE IT! I DON'T WANT TO HEAR YOUR LAME EXCUSES.
DON'T EVER TALK TO ME AGAIN!

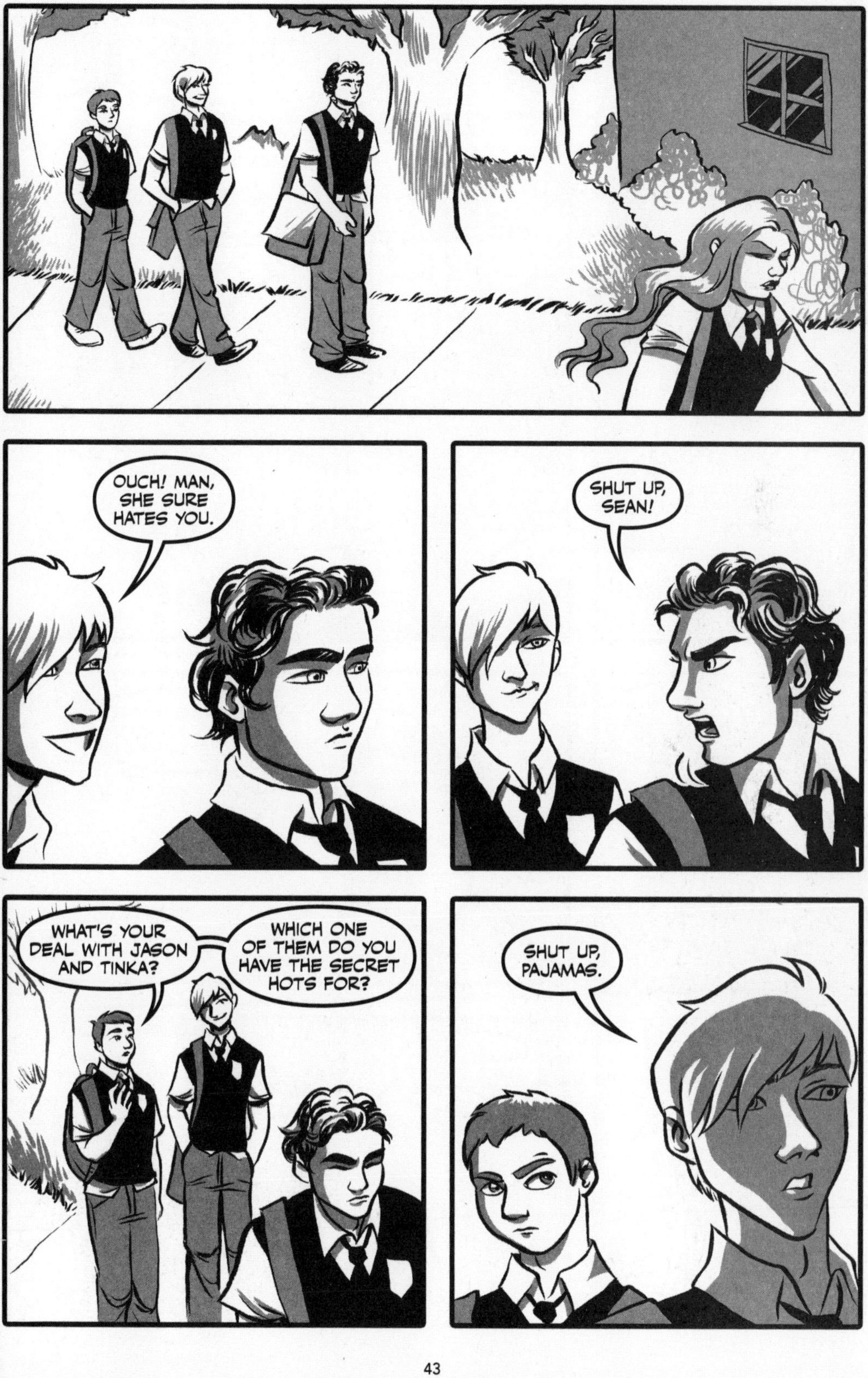
OUCH! MAN, SHE SURE HATES YOU.
SHUT UP, SEAN!
WHAT'S YOUR DEAL WITH JASON AND TINKA?
WHICH ONE OF THEM DO YOU HAVE THE SECRET HOTS FOR?
SHUT UP, PAJAMAS.

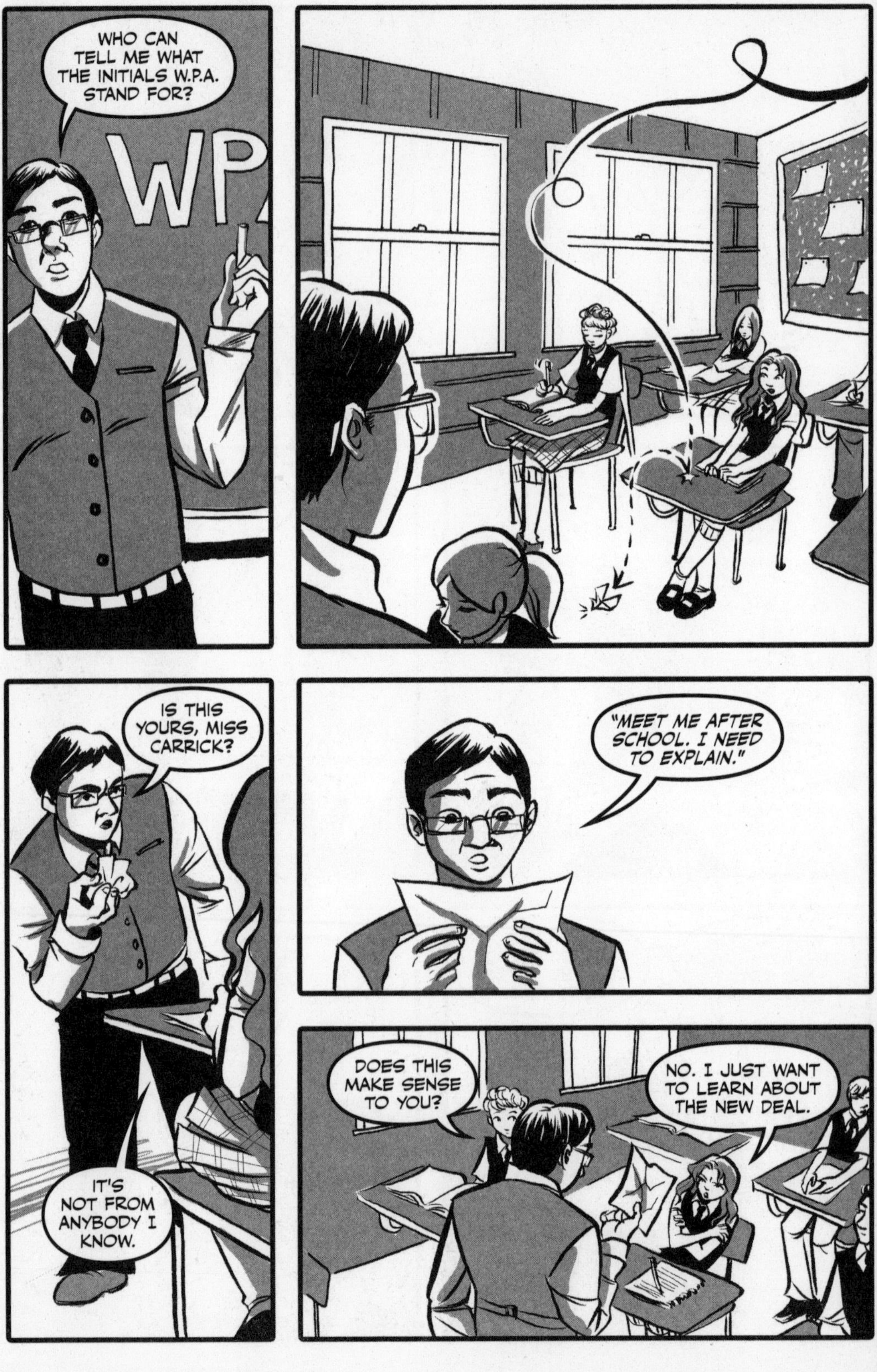
WHO CAN TELL ME WHAT THE INITIALS W.P.A. STAND FOR?
WP
IS THIS YOURS, MISS CARRICK?
IT'S NOT FROM ANYBODY I KNOW.
"MEET ME AFTER SCHOOL. I NEED TO EXPLAIN."
DOES THIS MAKE SENSE TO YOU?
NO. I JUST WANT TO LEARN ABOUT THE NEW DEAL.

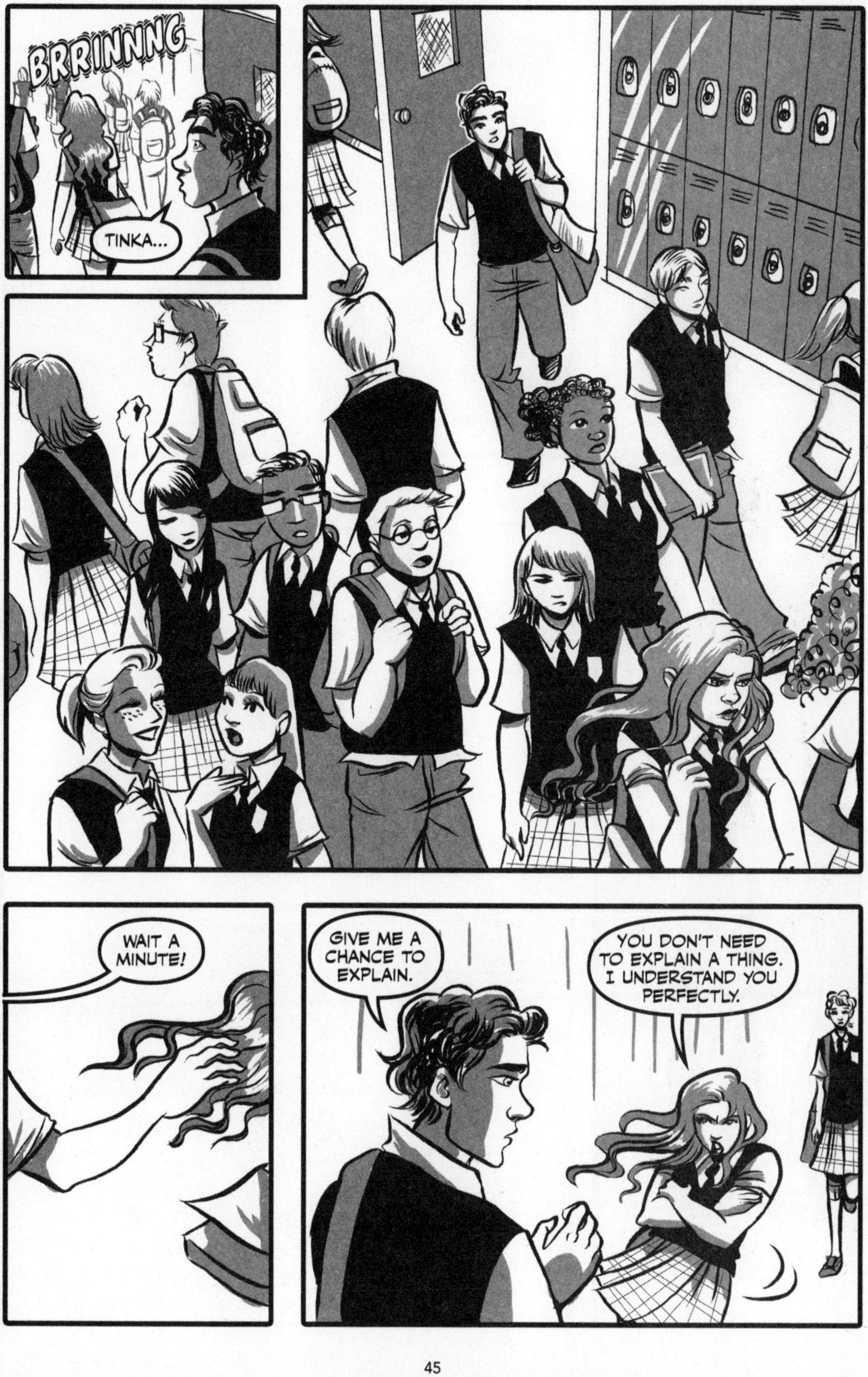
BRRINNNG
TINKA...
WAIT A MINUTE!
GIVE ME A CHANCE TO EXPLAIN.
YOU DON'T NEED TO EXPLAIN A THING. I UNDERSTAND YOU PERFECTLY.

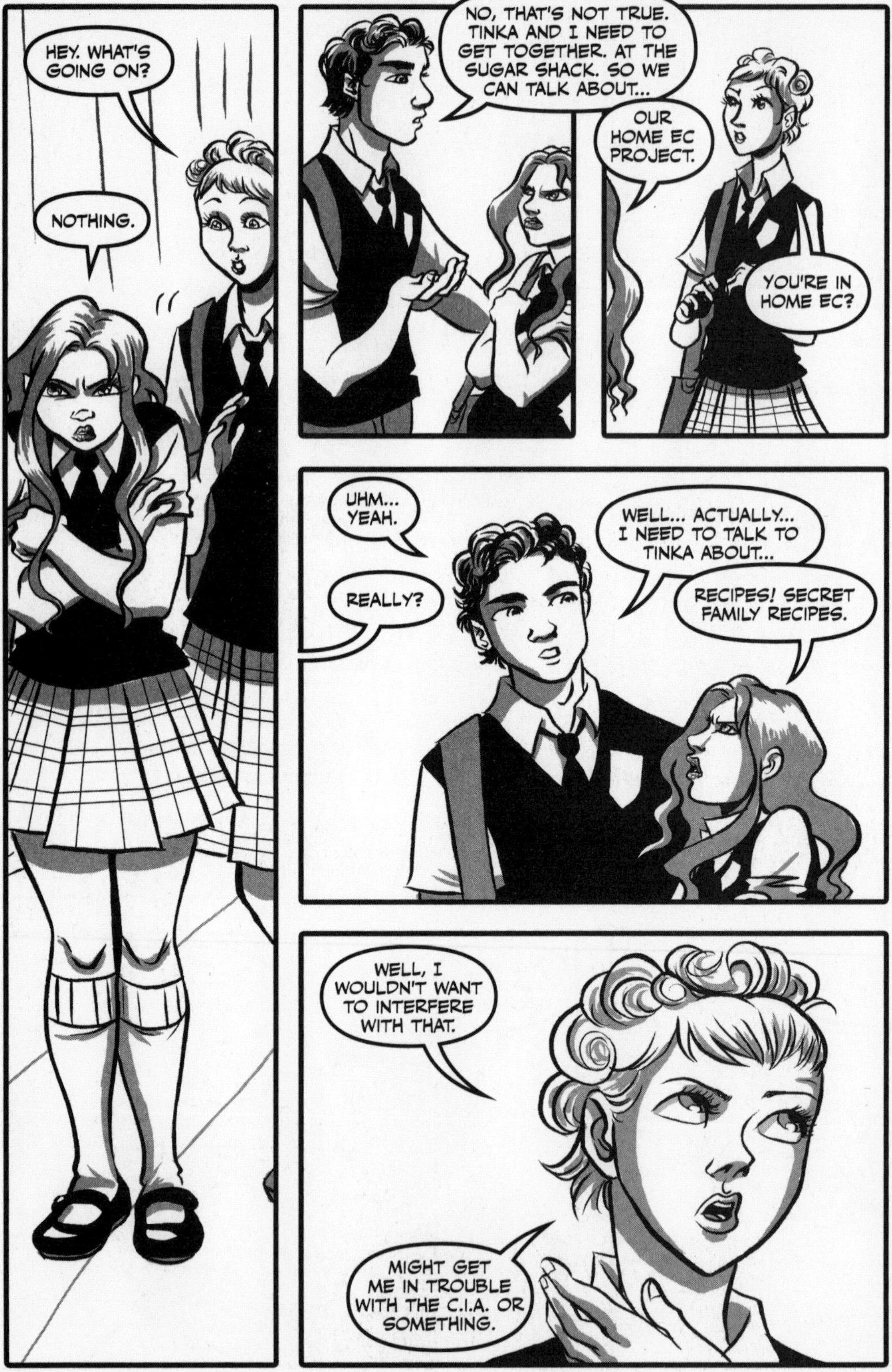
HEY. WHAT'S GOING ON?
NOTHING.
NO, THAT'S NOT TRUE. TINKA AND I NEED TO GET TOGETHER. AT THE SUGAR SHACK. SO WE CAN TALK ABOUT...
OUR HOME EC PROJECT.
YOU'RE IN HOME EC?
UHM... YEAH.
REALLY?
WELL... ACTUALLY... I NEED TO TALK TO TINKA ABOUT...
RECIPES! SECRET FAMILY RECIPES.
WELL, I WOULDN'T WANT TO INTERFERE WITH THAT.
MIGHT GET ME IN TROUBLE WITH THE C.I.A. OR SOMETHING.

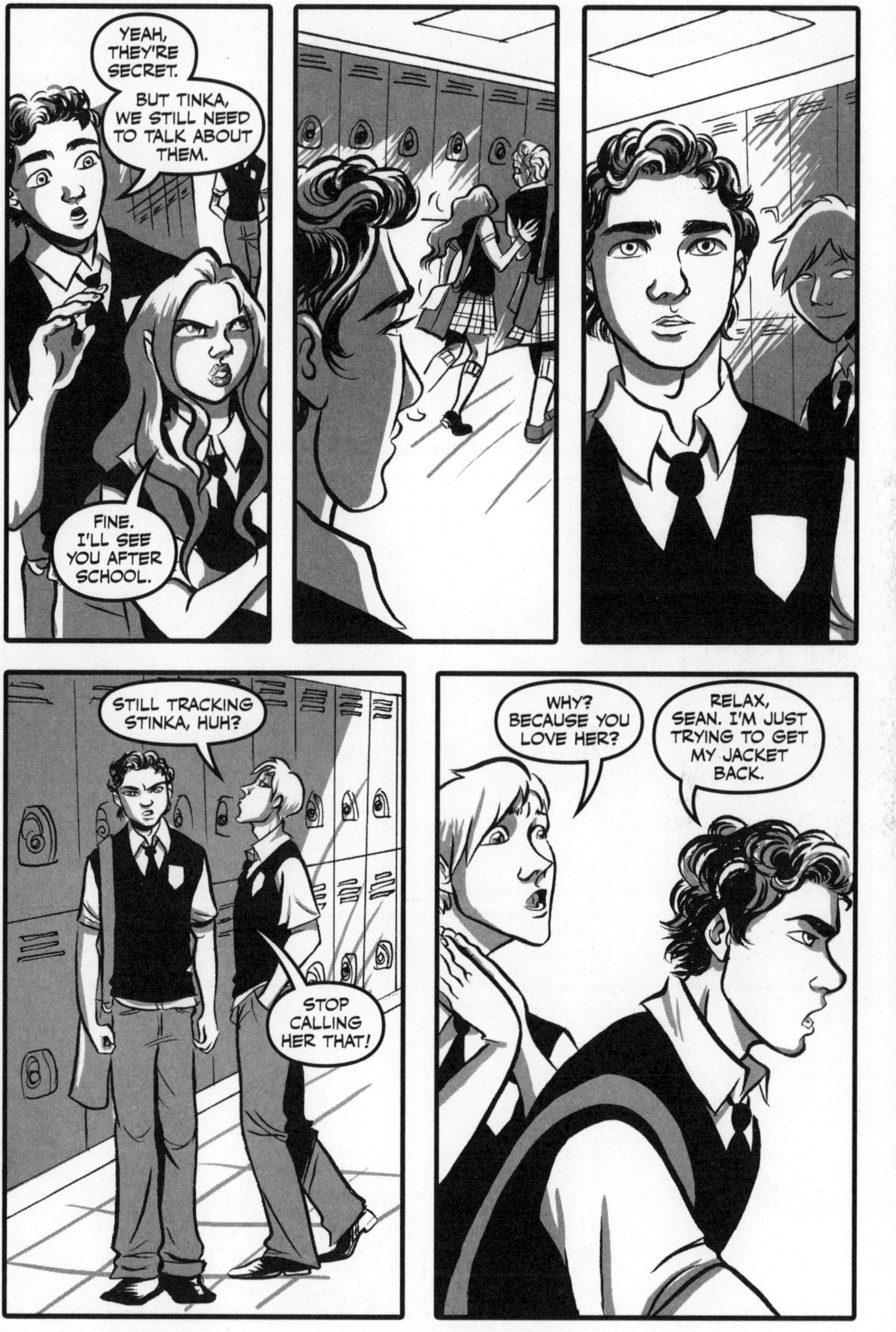
YEAH, THEY'RE SECRET.
BUT TINKA, WE STILL NEED TO TALK ABOUT THEM.
FINE. I'LL SEE YOU AFTER SCHOOL.
STILL TRACKING STINKA, HUH?
STOP CALLING HER THAT!
WHY? BECAUSE YOU LOVE HER?
RELAX, SEAN. I'M JUST TRYING TO GET MY JACKET BACK.

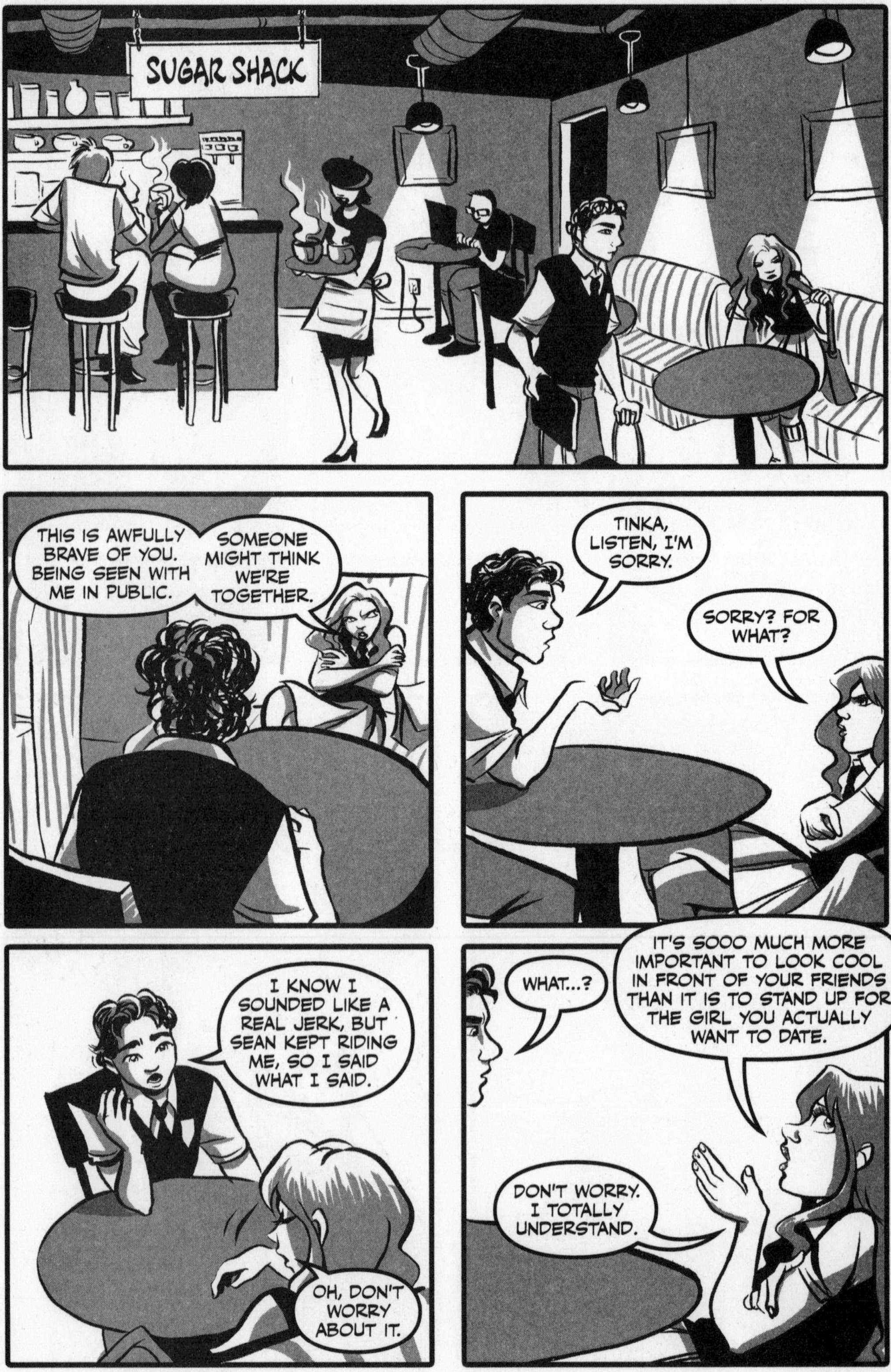
SUGAR SHACK
THIS IS AWFULLY BRAVE OF YOU. BEING SEEN WITH ME IN PUBLIC.
SOMEONE MIGHT THINK WE'RE TOGETHER.
TINKA, LISTEN, I'M SORRY.
SORRY? FOR WHAT?
I KNOW I SOUNDED LIKE A REAL JERK, BUT SEAN KEPT RIDING ME, SO I SAID WHAT I SAID.
OH, DON'T WORRY ABOUT IT.
WHAT...?
IT'S SOOO MUCH MORE IMPORTANT TO LOOK COOL IN FRONT OF YOUR FRIENDS THAN IT IS TO STAND UP FOR THE GIRL YOU ACTUALLY WANT TO DATE.
DON'T WORRY. I TOTALLY UNDERSTAND.

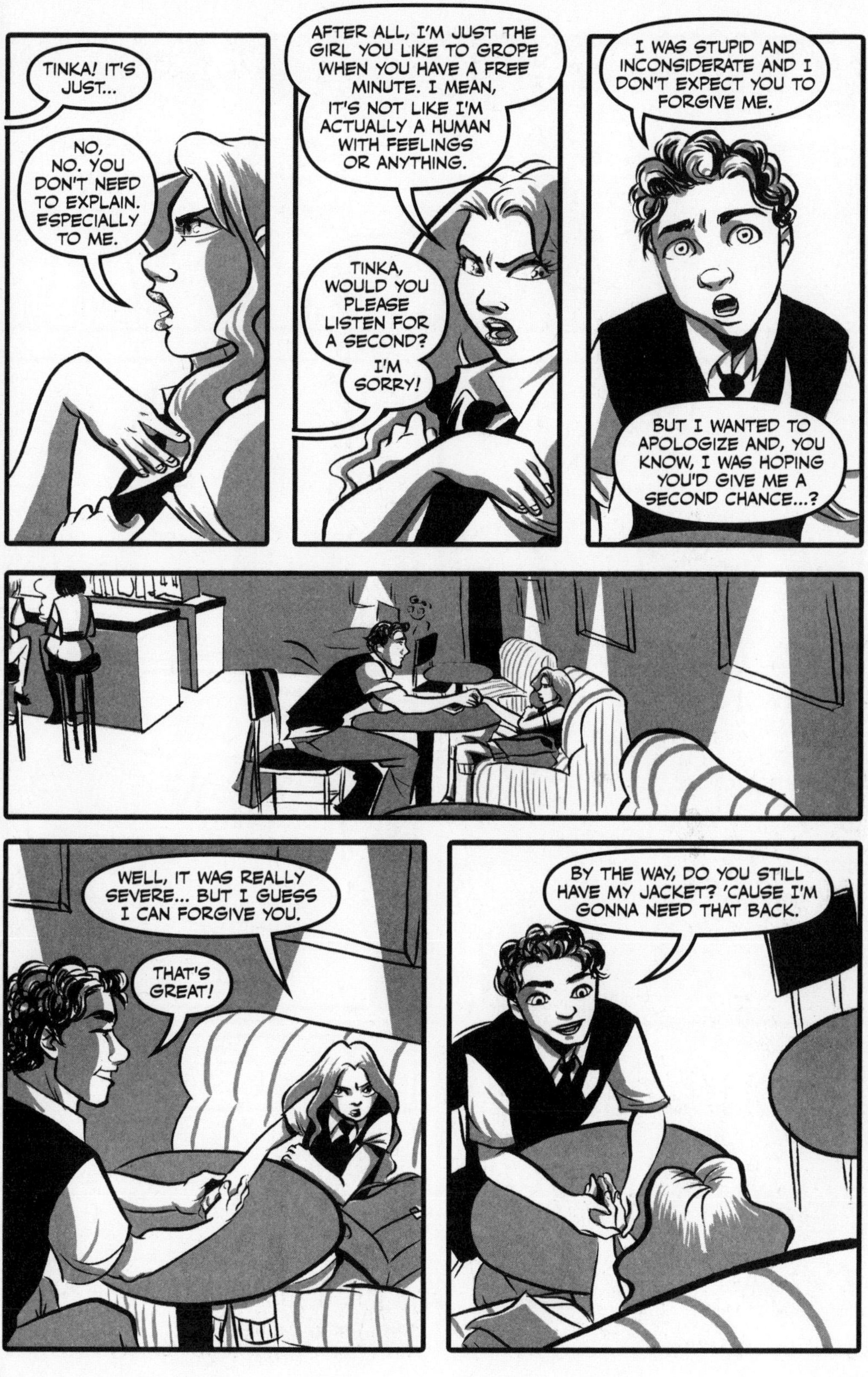
TINKA! IT'S JUST...
NO, NO. YOU DON'T NEED TO EXPLAIN. ESPECIALLY TO ME.
AFTER ALL, I'M JUST THE GIRL YOU LIKE TO GROPE WHEN YOU HAVE A FREE MINUTE. I MEAN, IT'S NOT LIKE I'M ACTUALLY A HUMAN WITH FEELINGS OR ANYTHING.
TINKA, WOULD YOU PLEASE LISTEN FOR A SECOND?
I'M SORRY!
I WAS STUPID AND INCONSIDERATE AND I DON'T EXPECT YOU TO FORGIVE ME.
BUT I WANTED TO APOLOGIZE AND, YOU KNOW, I WAS HOPING YOU'D GIVE ME A SECOND CHANCE...?
WELL, IT WAS REALLY SEVERE... BUT I GUESS I CAN FORGIVE YOU.
THAT'S GREAT!
BY THE WAY, DO YOU STILL HAVE MY JACKET? 'CAUSE I'M GONNA NEED THAT BACK.

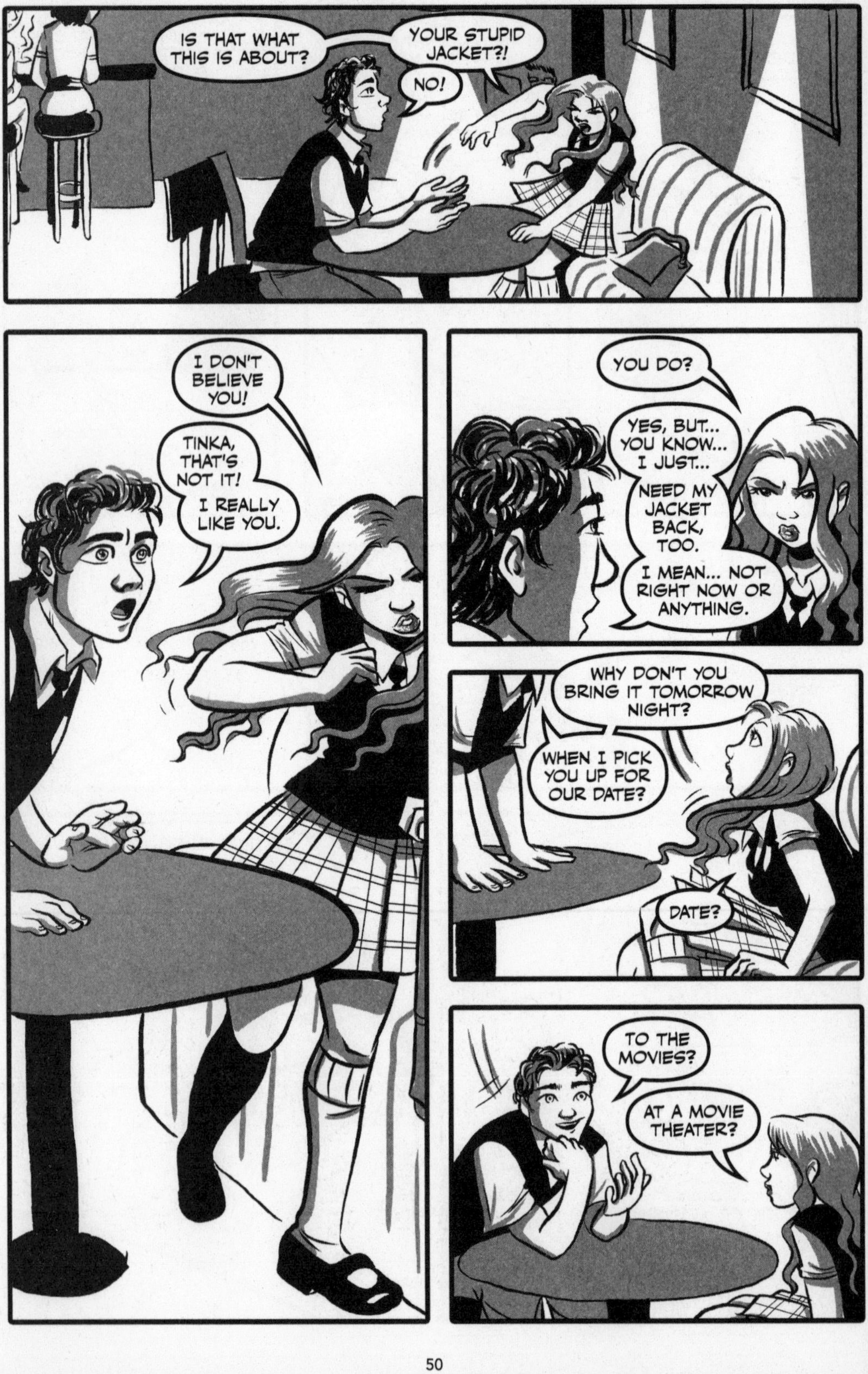
IS THAT WHAT THIS IS ABOUT?
YOUR STUPID JACKET?!
NO!
I DON'T BELIEVE YOU!
TINKA, THAT'S NOT IT!
I REALLY LIKE YOU.
YOU DO?
YES, BUT... YOU KNOW... I JUST...
NEED MY JACKET BACK, TOO.
I MEAN... NOT RIGHT NOW OR ANYTHING.
WHY DON'T YOU BRING IT TOMORROW NIGHT?
WHEN I PICK YOU UP FOR OUR DATE?
DATE?
TO THE MOVIES?
AT A MOVIE THEATER?

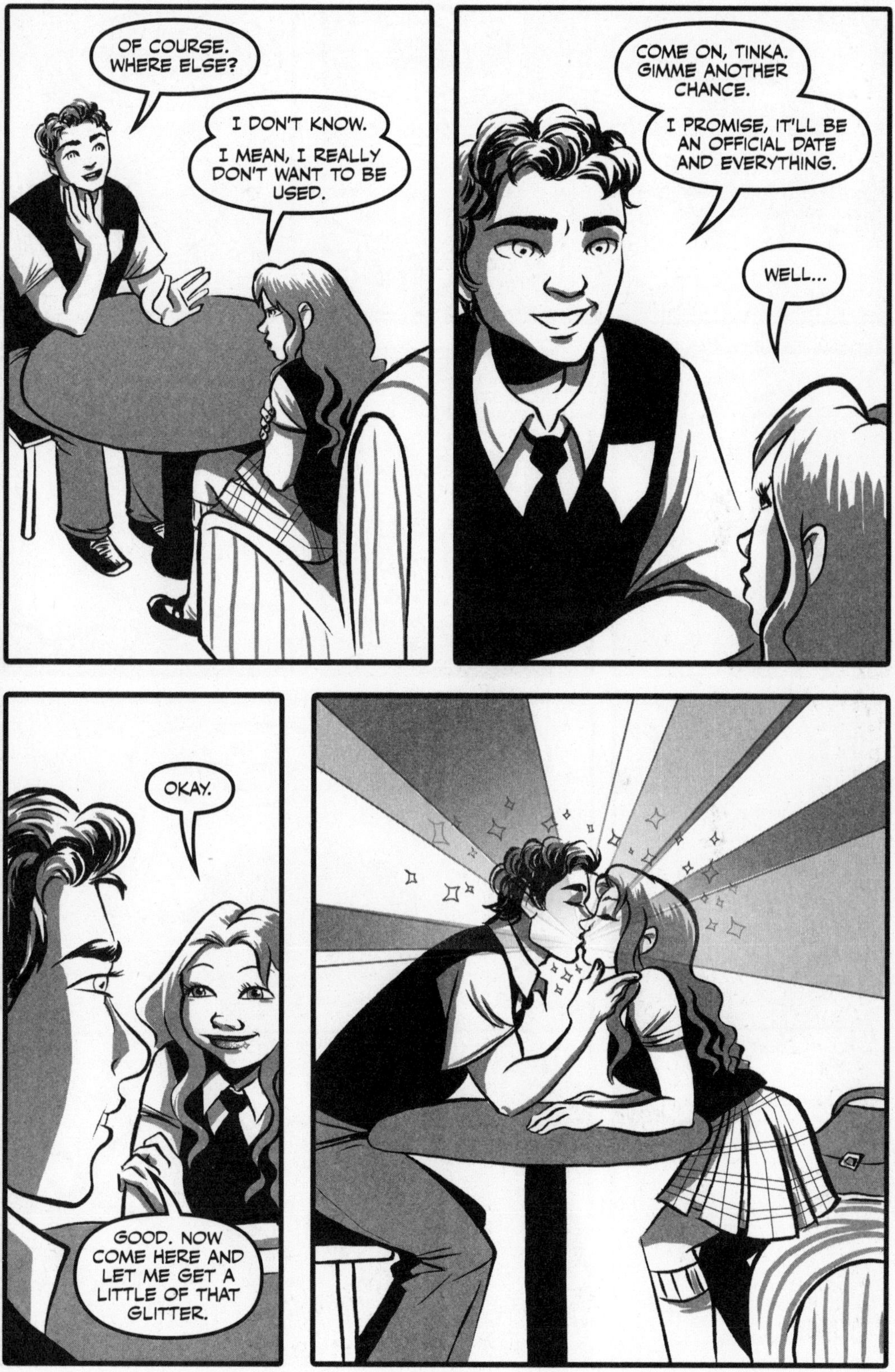
OF COURSE. WHERE ELSE?
I DON'T KNOW.
I MEAN, I REALLY DON'T WANT TO BE USED.
COME ON, TINKA. GIMME ANOTHER CHANCE.
I PROMISE, IT'LL BE AN OFFICIAL DATE AND EVERYTHING.
WELL...
OKAY.
GOOD. NOW COME HERE AND LET ME GET A LITTLE OF THAT GLITTER.

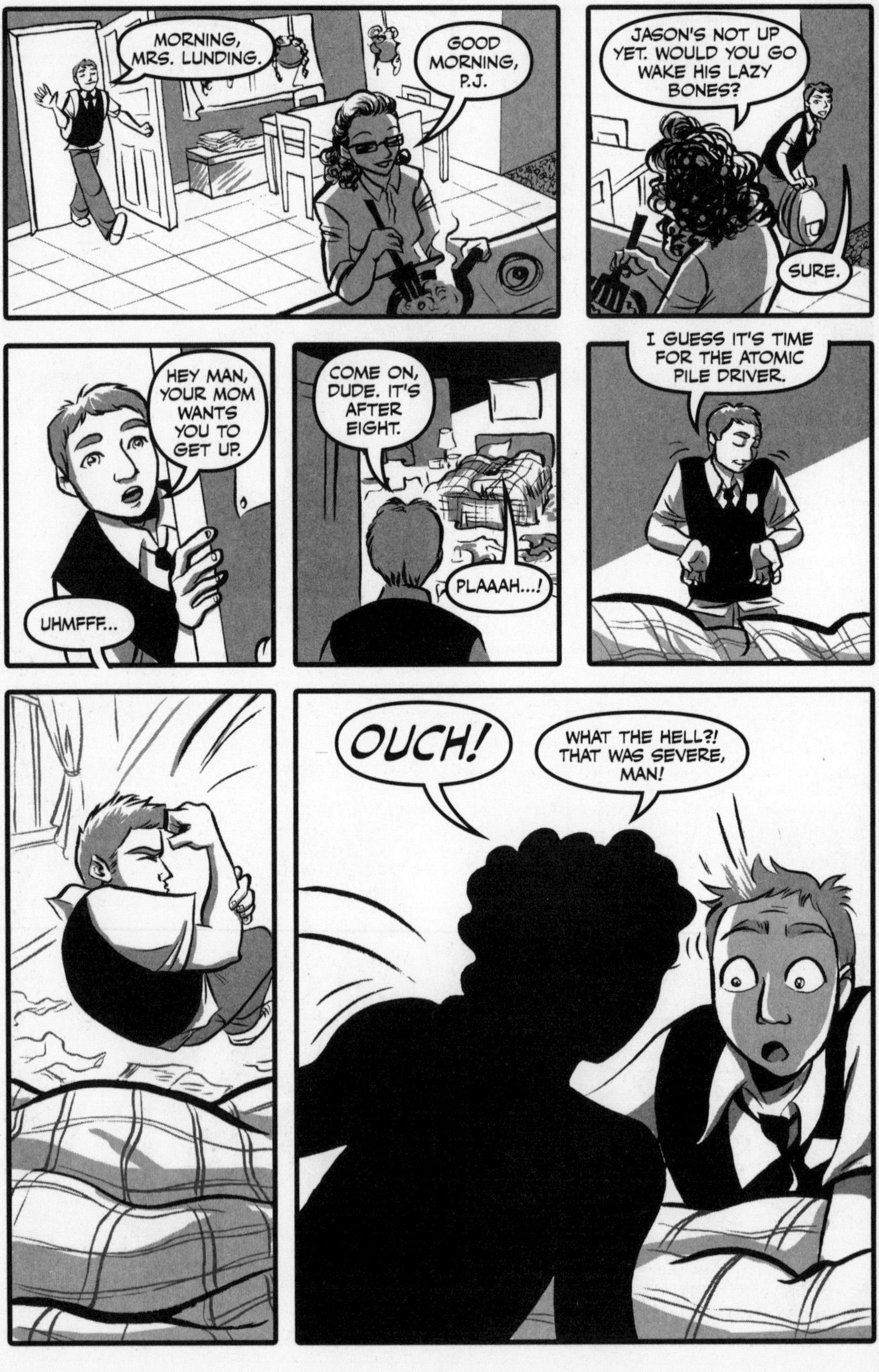
MORNING, MRS. LUNDING.
GOOD MORNING, P.J.
JASON'S NOT UP YET. WOULD YOU GO WAKE HIS LAZY BONES?
SURE.
HEY MAN, YOUR MOM WANTS YOU TO GET UP.
UHMFFF...
COME ON, DUDE. IT'S AFTER EIGHT.
PLAAAH...!
I GUESS IT'S TIME FOR THE ATOMIC PILE DRIVER.
OUCH!
WHAT THE HELL?! THAT WAS SEVERE, MAN!

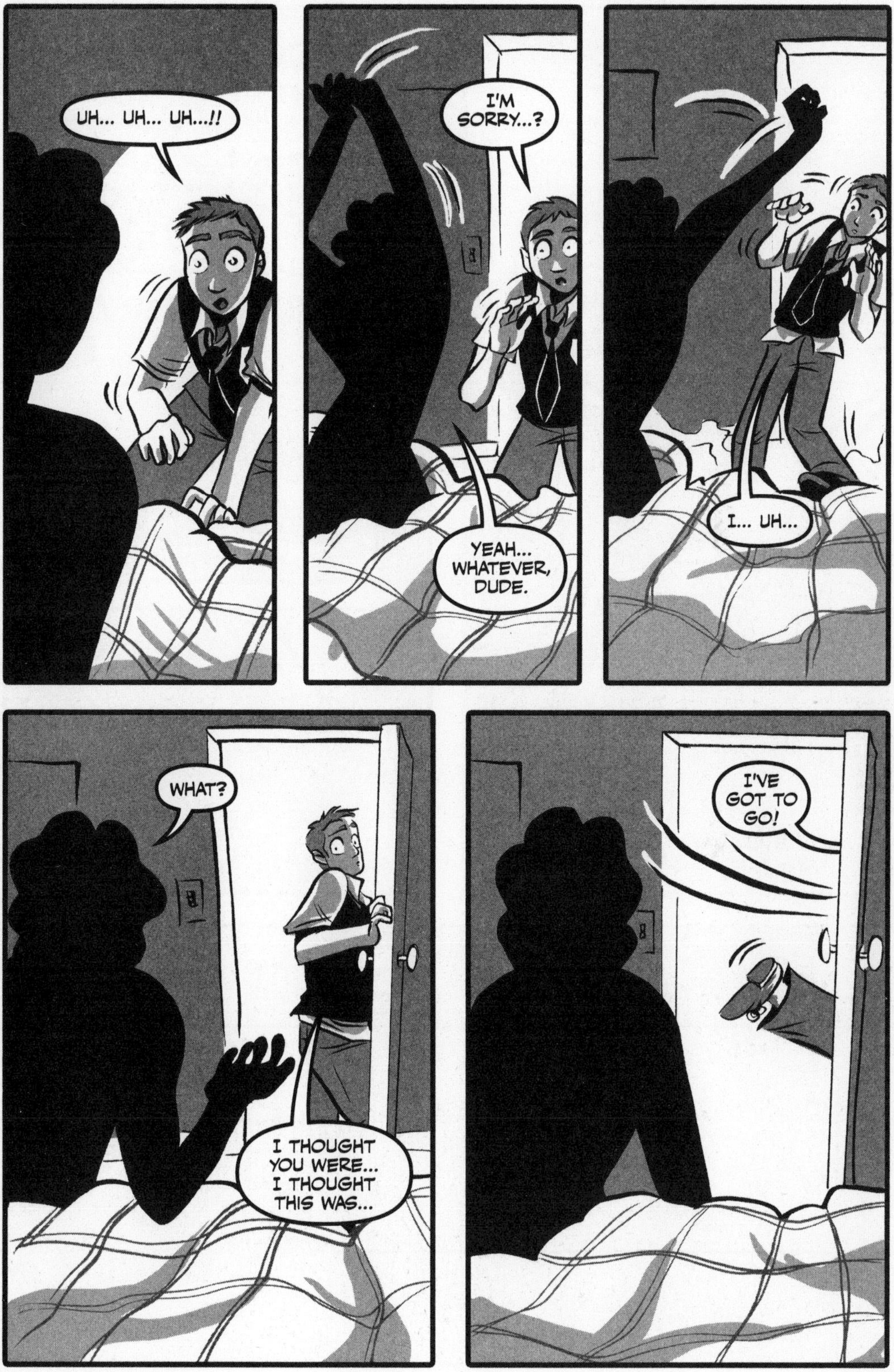
UH... UH... UH...!!
I'M SORRY...?
YEAH... WHATEVER, DUDE.
I... UH...
WHAT?
I THOUGHT YOU WERE... I THOUGHT THIS WAS...
I'VE GOT TO GO!

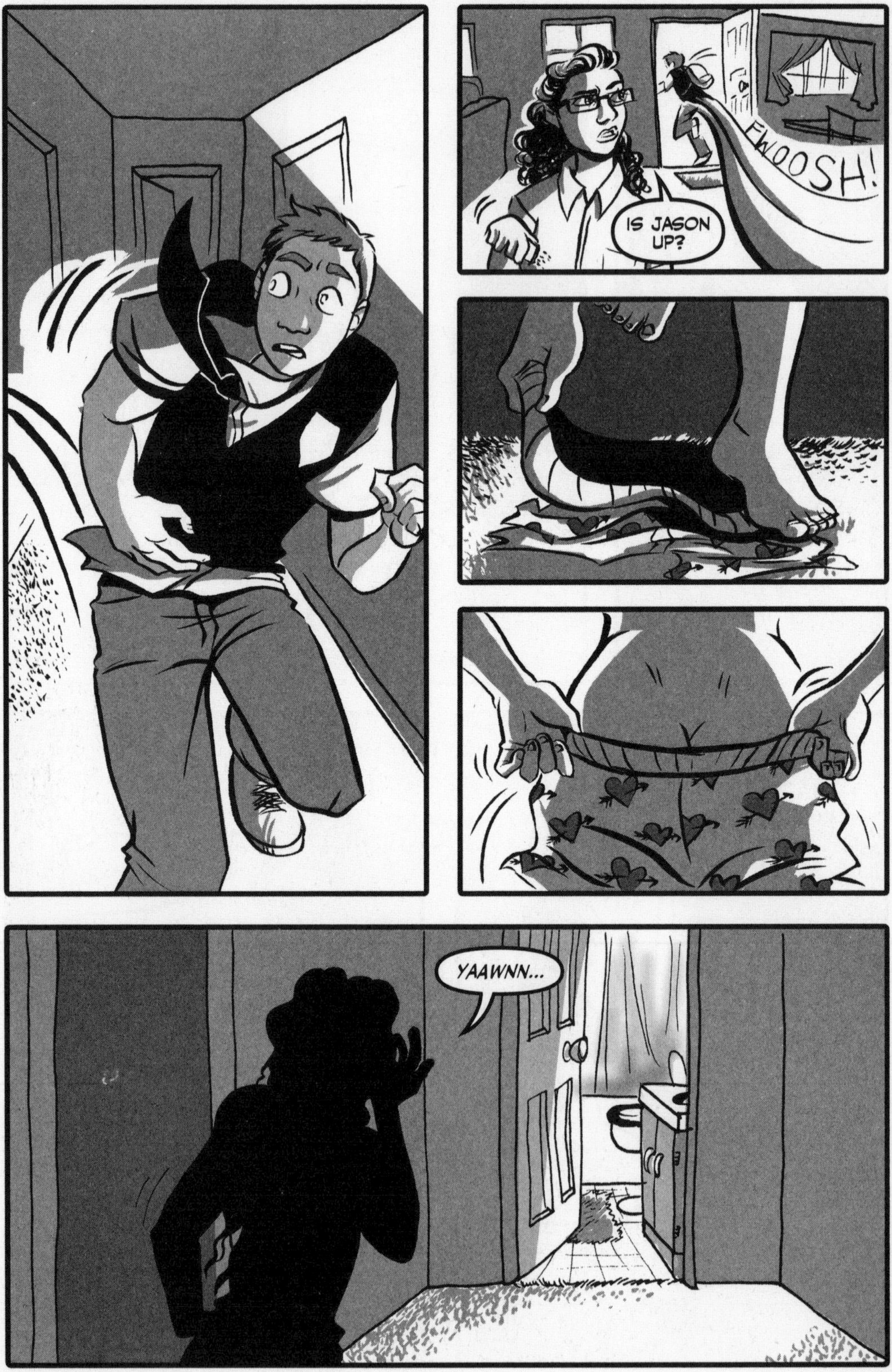
IS JASON UP?
FWOOSH!
YAAWNN...

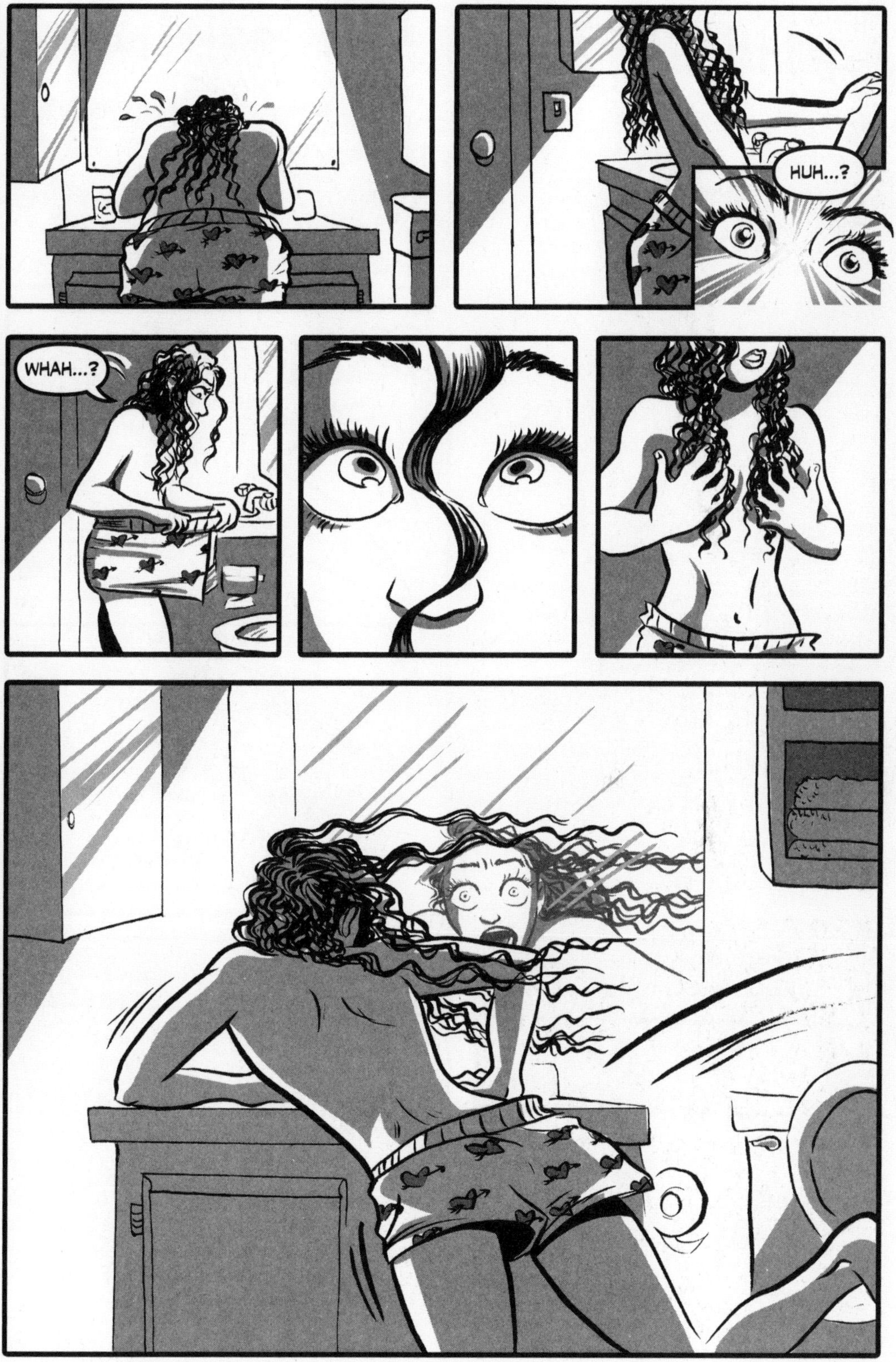
HUH...?
WHAH...?

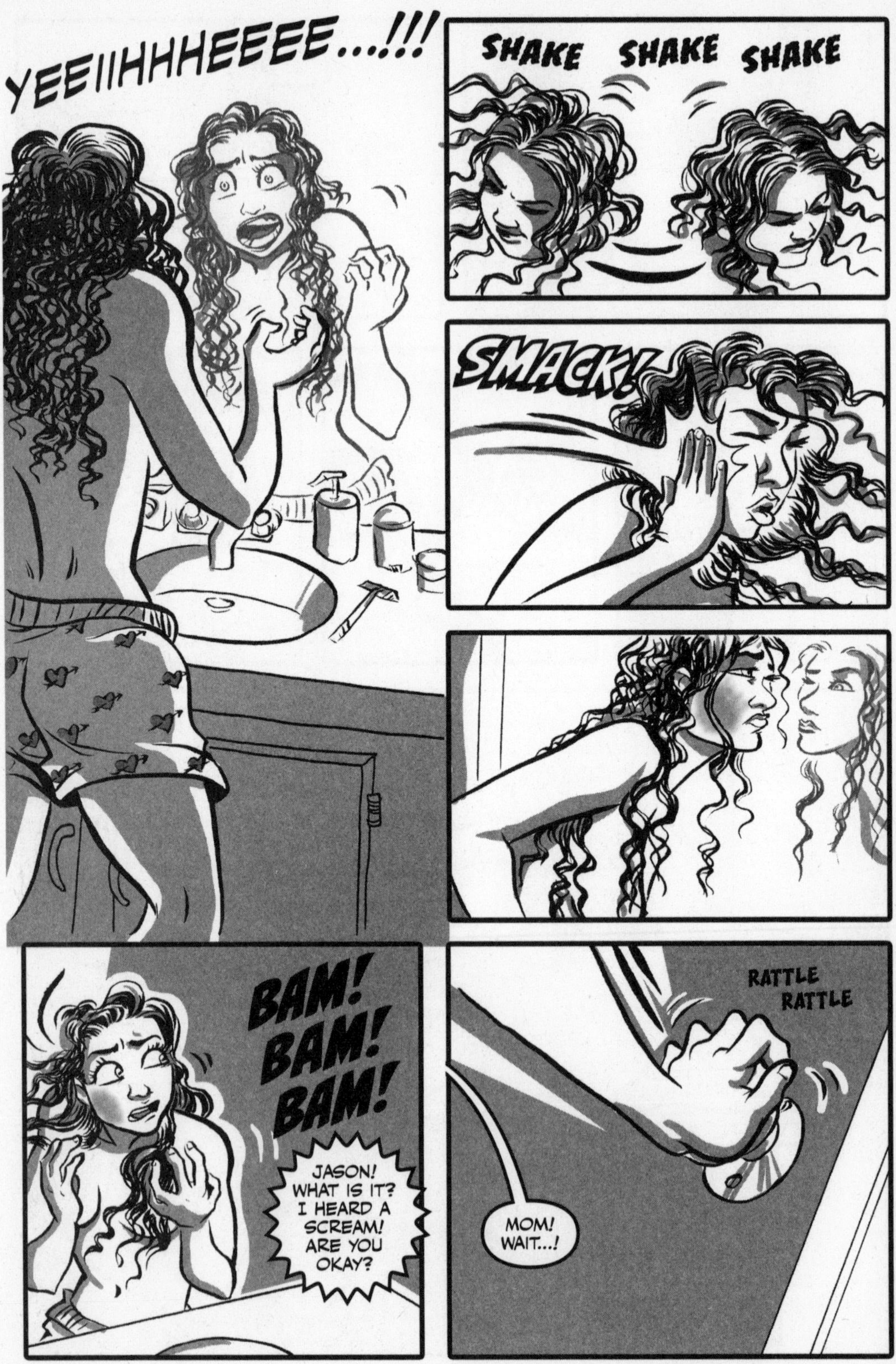
YEEIIHHHEEEEE...!!!
SHAKE SHAKE SHAKE
SMACK!
BAM! BAM! BAM!
JASON! WHAT IS IT? I HEARD A SCREAM! ARE YOU OKAY?
RATTLE RATTLE
MOM! WAIT...!

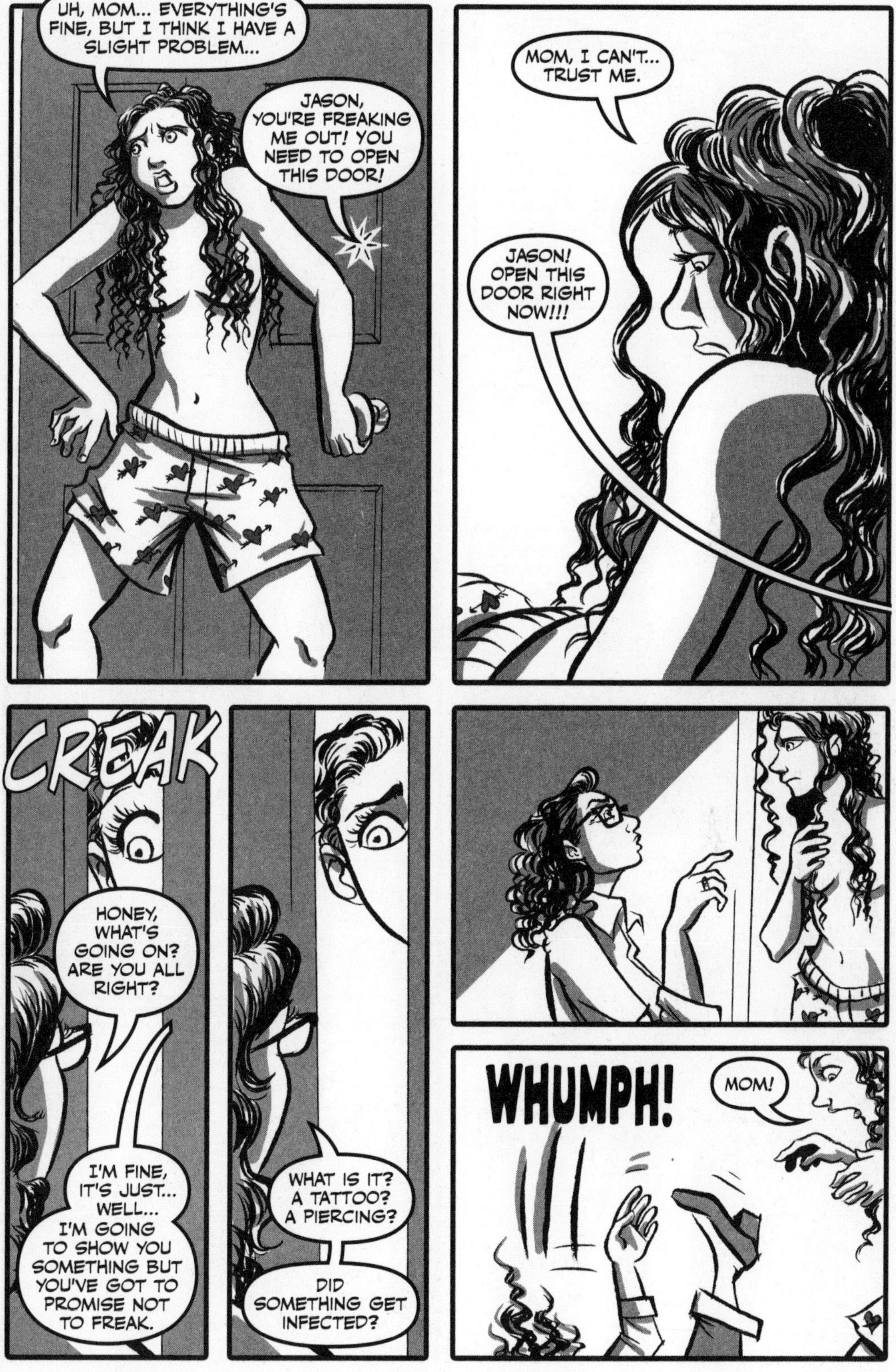
UH, MOM... EVERYTHING'S FINE, BUT I THINK I HAVE A SLIGHT PROBLEM...
JASON, YOU'RE FREAKING ME OUT! YOU NEED TO OPEN THIS DOOR!
MOM, I CAN'T... TRUST ME.
JASON! OPEN THIS DOOR RIGHT NOW!!!
CREAK
HONEY, WHAT'S GOING ON? ARE YOU ALL RIGHT?
I'M FINE, IT'S JUST... WELL... I'M GOING TO SHOW YOU SOMETHING BUT YOU'VE GOT TO PROMISE NOT TO FREAK.
WHAT IS IT? A TATTOO? A PIERCING?
DID SOMETHING GET INFECTED?
WHUMPH!
MOM!

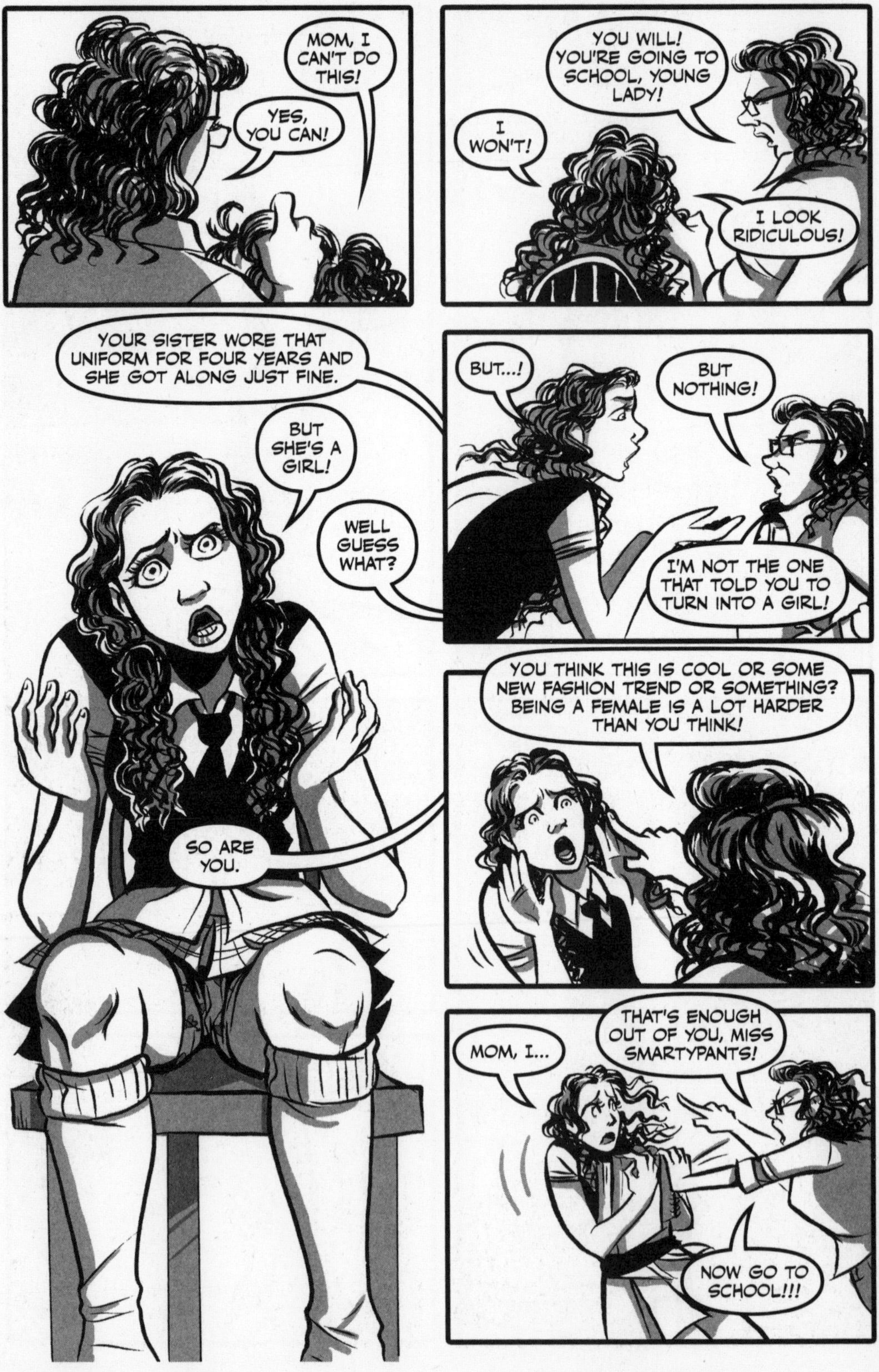
MOM, I CAN'T DO THIS!
YES, YOU CAN!
YOU WILL! YOU'RE GOING TO SCHOOL, YOUNG LADY!
I WON'T!
I LOOK RIDICULOUS!
YOUR SISTER WORE THAT UNIFORM FOR FOUR YEARS AND SHE GOT ALONG JUST FINE.
BUT SHE'S A GIRL!
WELL GUESS WHAT?
SO ARE YOU.
BUT...!
BUT NOTHING!
I'M NOT THE ONE THAT TOLD YOU TO TURN INTO A GIRL!
YOU THINK THIS IS COOL OR SOME NEW FASHION TREND OR SOMETHING? BEING A FEMALE IS A LOT HARDER THAN YOU THINK!
MOM, I...
THAT'S ENOUGH OUT OF YOU, MISS SMARTYPANTS!
NOW GO TO SCHOOL!!!

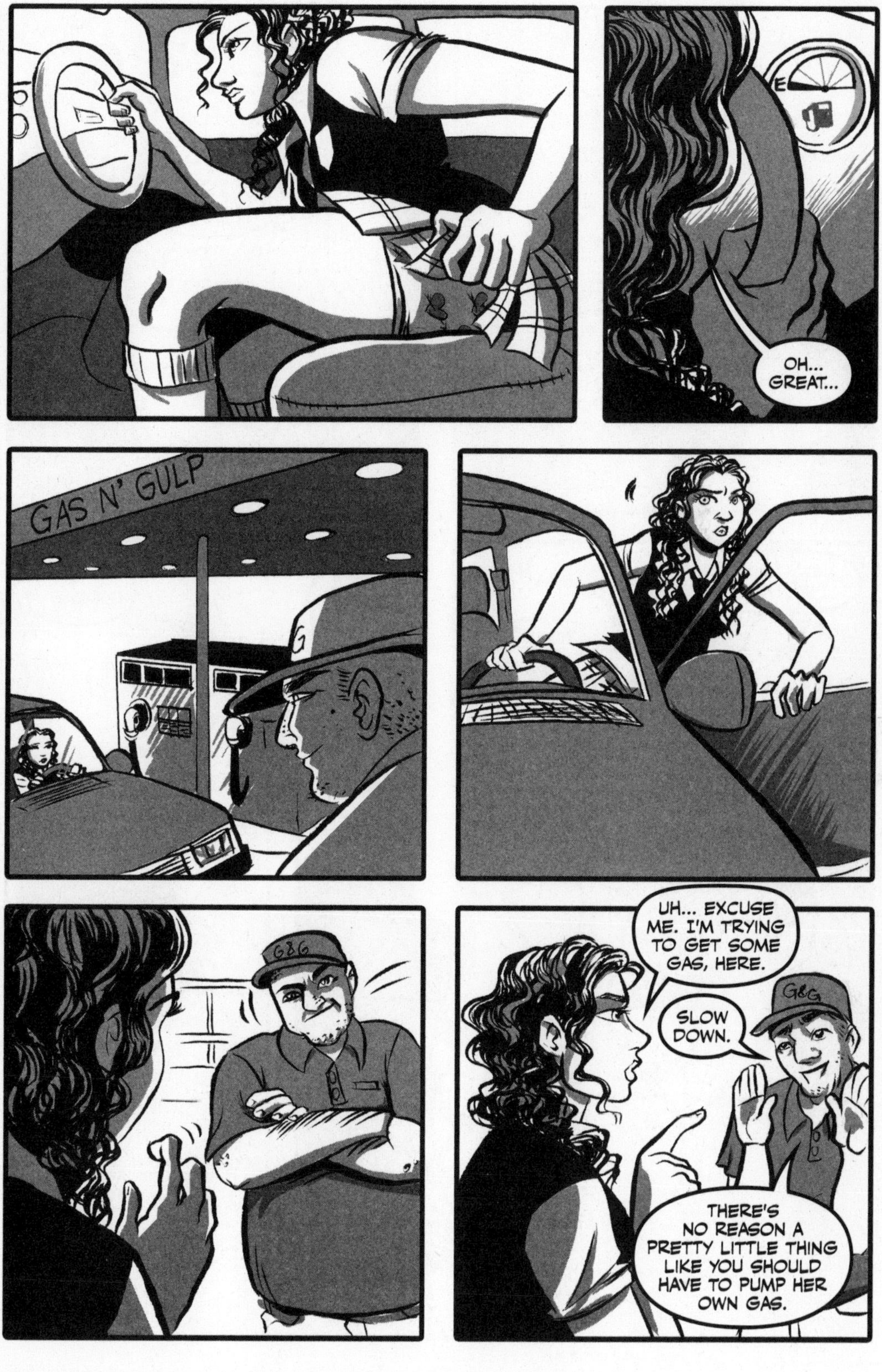
OH... GREAT...
GAS N' GULP
G&G
UH... EXCUSE ME. I'M TRYING TO GET SOME GAS, HERE.
SLOW DOWN.
THERE'S NO REASON A PRETTY LITTLE THING LIKE YOU SHOULD HAVE TO PUMP HER OWN GAS.

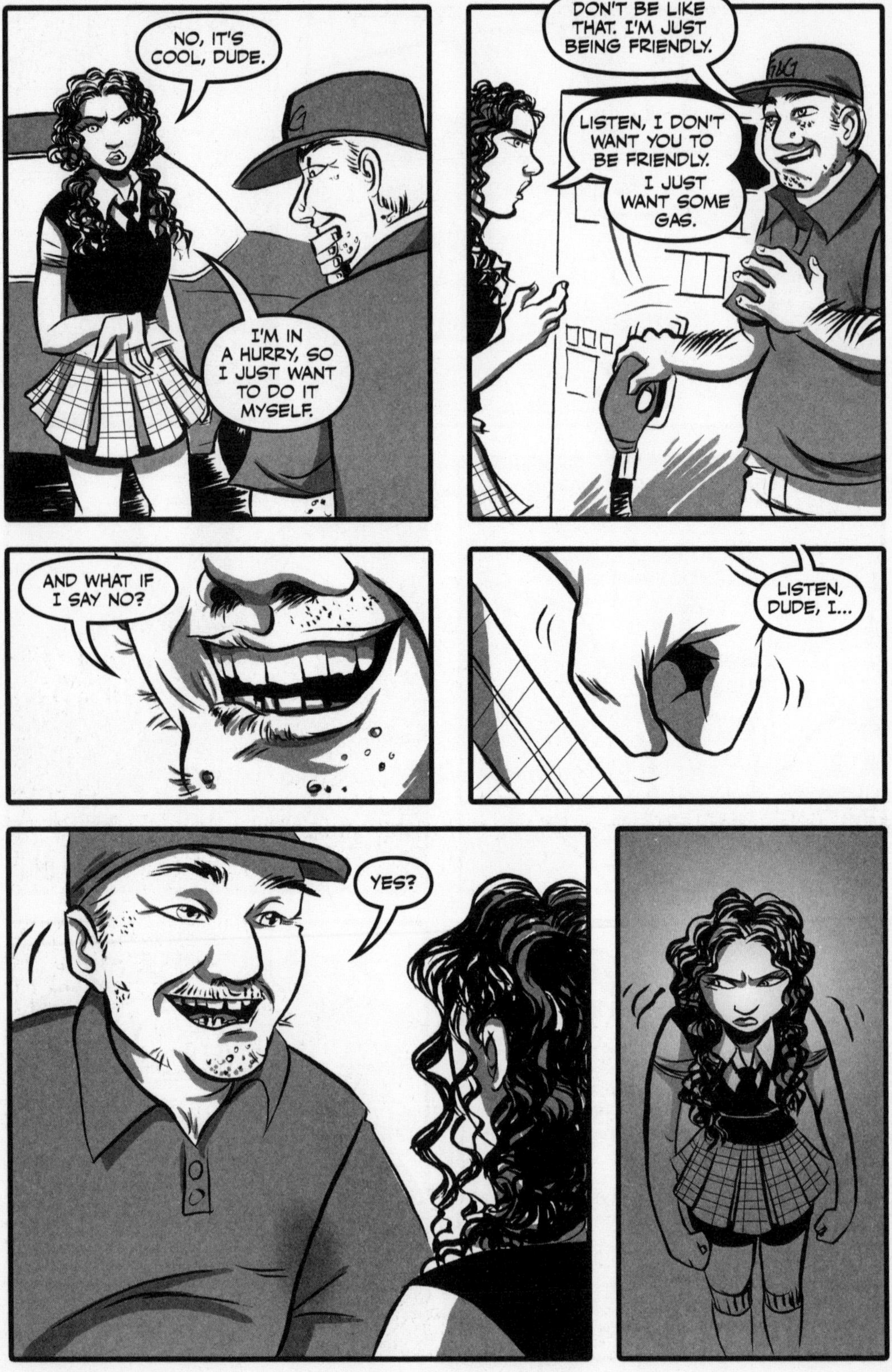
NO, IT'S COOL, DUDE.
I'M IN A HURRY, SO I JUST WANT TO DO IT MYSELF.
DON'T BE LIKE THAT. I'M JUST BEING FRIENDLY.
LISTEN, I DON'T WANT YOU TO BE FRIENDLY.
I JUST WANT SOME GAS.
AND WHAT IF I SAY NO?
LISTEN, DUDE, I...
YES?

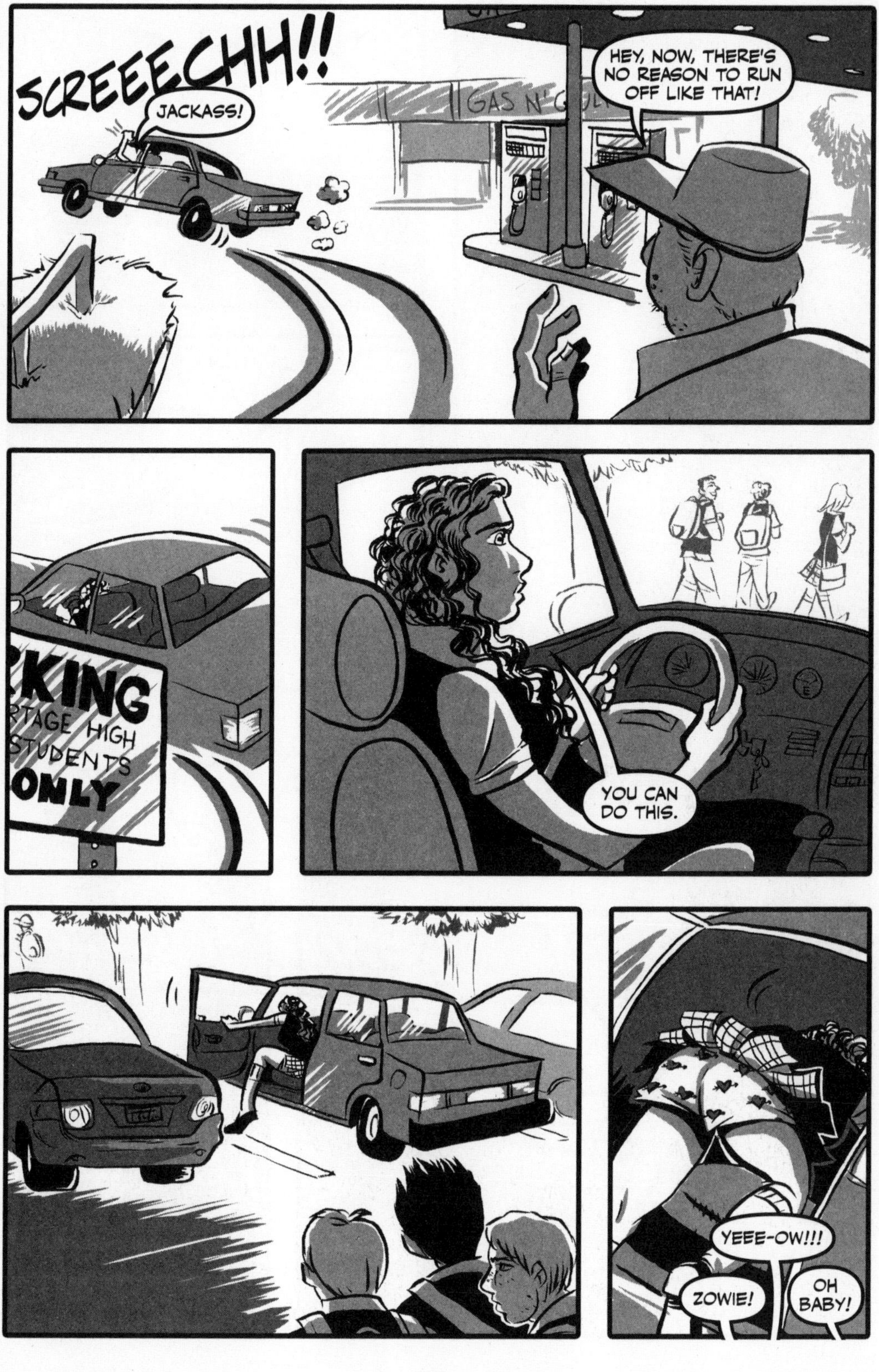
SCREEECHH!!
JACKASS!
GAS N' GULP
HEY, NOW, THERE'S NO REASON TO RUN OFF LIKE THAT!
KING
RTAGE HIGH
STUDENTS
ONLY
YOU CAN DO THIS.
YEEE-OW!!!
ZOWIE!
OH BABY!

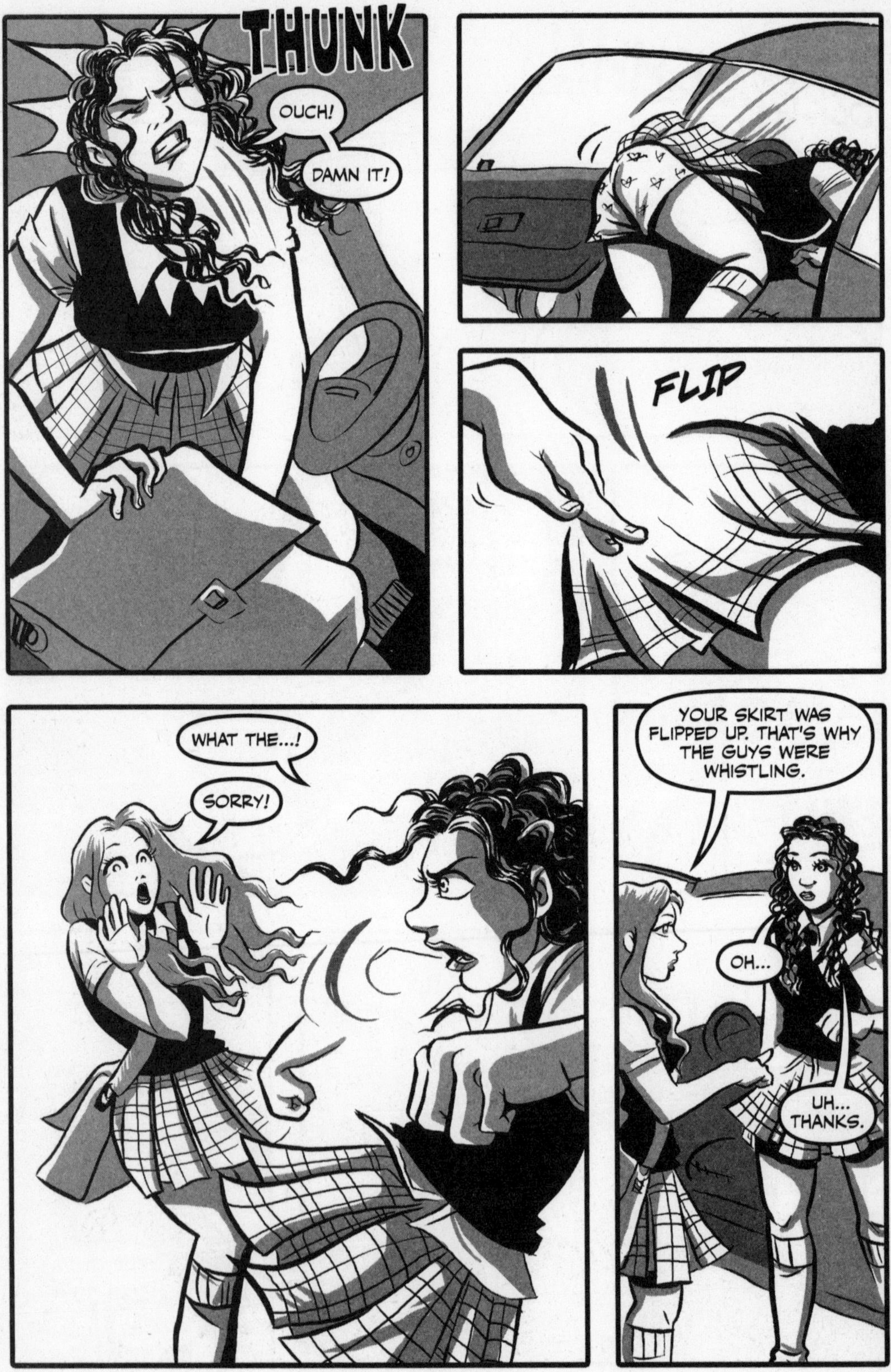
THUNK
OUCH!
DAMN IT!
FLIP
WHAT THE...!
SORRY!
YOUR SKIRT WAS FLIPPED UP. THAT'S WHY THE GUYS WERE WHISTLING.
OH...
UH... THANKS.

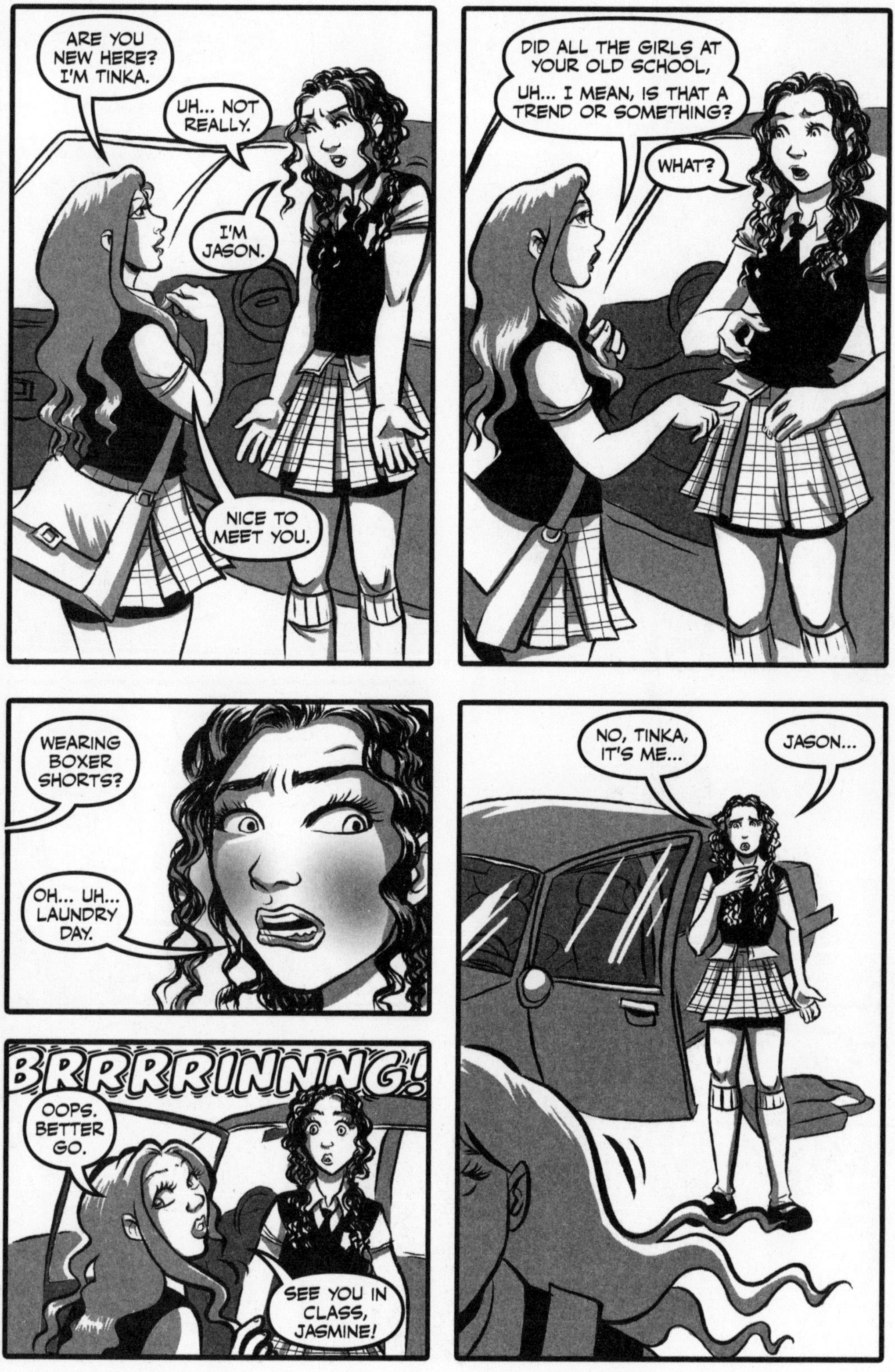
ARE YOU NEW HERE? I'M TINKA.
UH... NOT REALLY.
I'M JASON.
NICE TO MEET YOU.
DID ALL THE GIRLS AT YOUR OLD SCHOOL,
UH... I MEAN, IS THAT A TREND OR SOMETHING?
WHAT?
WEARING BOXER SHORTS?
OH... UH... LAUNDRY DAY.
BRRRRINNNG!
OOPS. BETTER GO.
SEE YOU IN CLASS, JASMINE!
NO, TINKA, IT'S ME...
JASON...

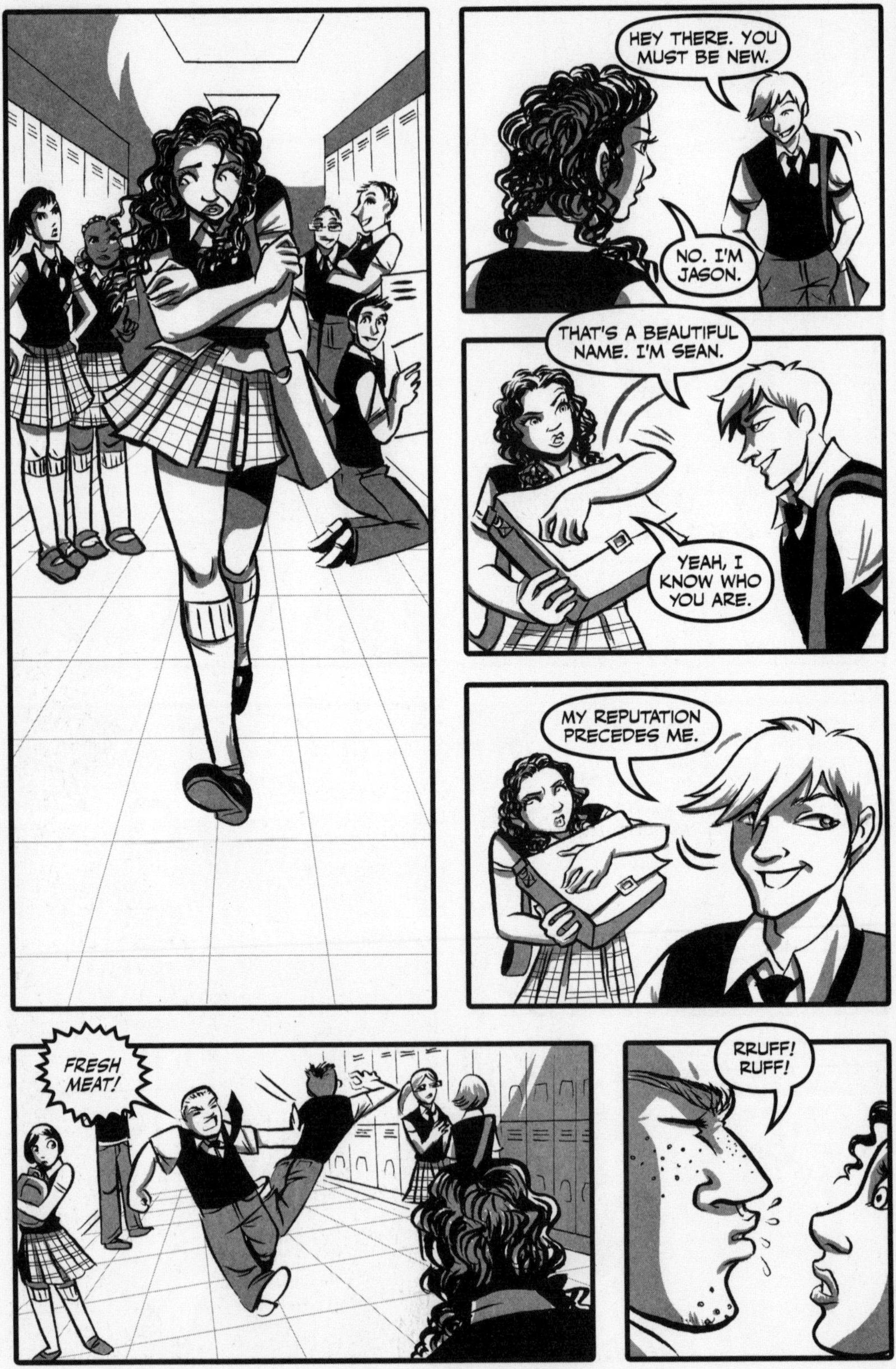
HEY THERE. YOU MUST BE NEW.
NO. I'M JASON.
THAT'S A BEAUTIFUL NAME. I'M SEAN.
YEAH, I KNOW WHO YOU ARE.
MY REPUTATION PRECEDES ME.
FRESH MEAT!
RRUFF! RUFF!

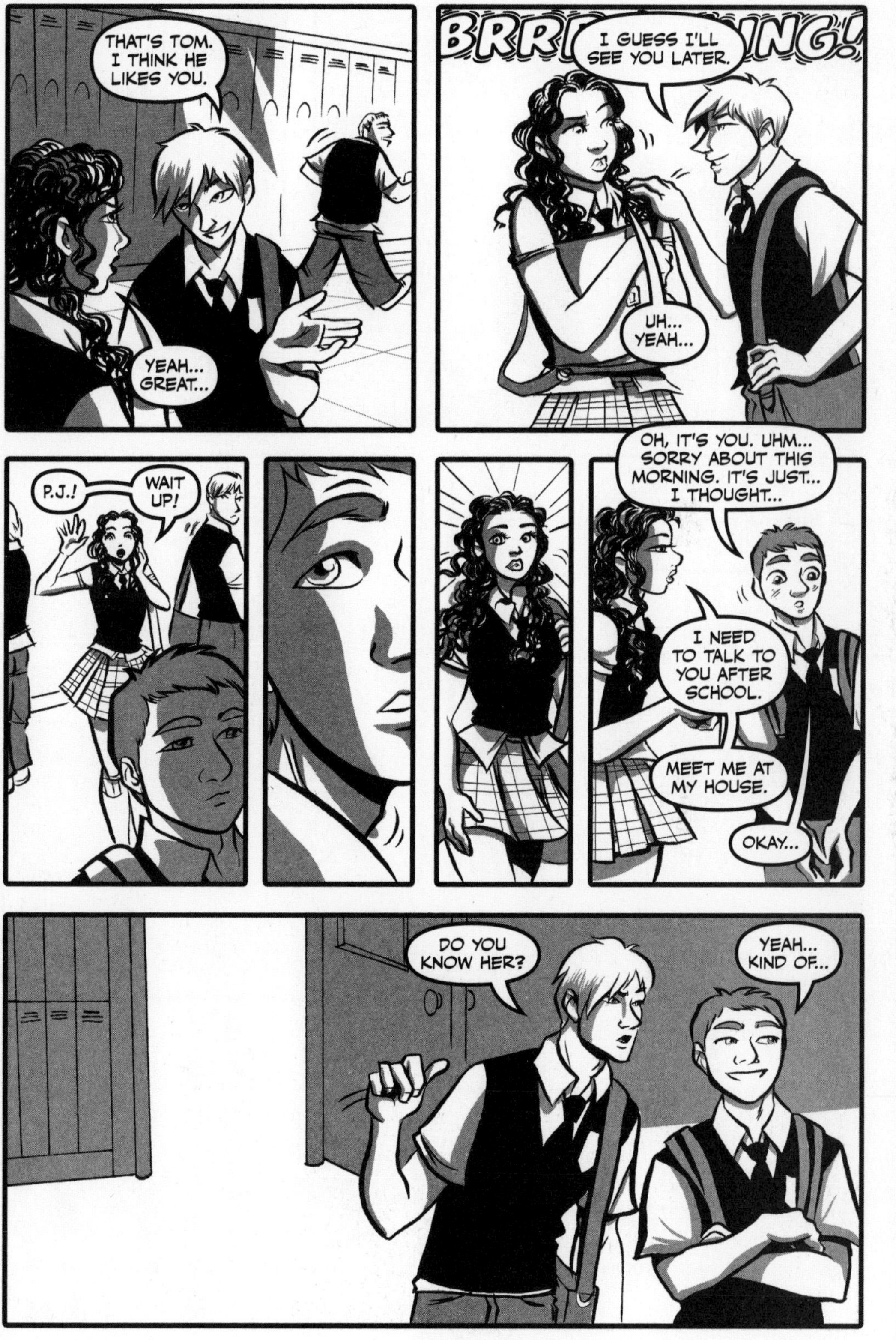
THAT'S TOM. I THINK HE LIKES YOU.
YEAH... GREAT...
BRRRING!
I GUESS I'LL SEE YOU LATER.
UH... YEAH...
P.J.!
WAIT UP!
OH, IT'S YOU. UHM... SORRY ABOUT THIS MORNING. IT'S JUST... I THOUGHT...
I NEED TO TALK TO YOU AFTER SCHOOL.
MEET ME AT MY HOUSE.
OKAY...
DO YOU KNOW HER?
YEAH... KIND OF...

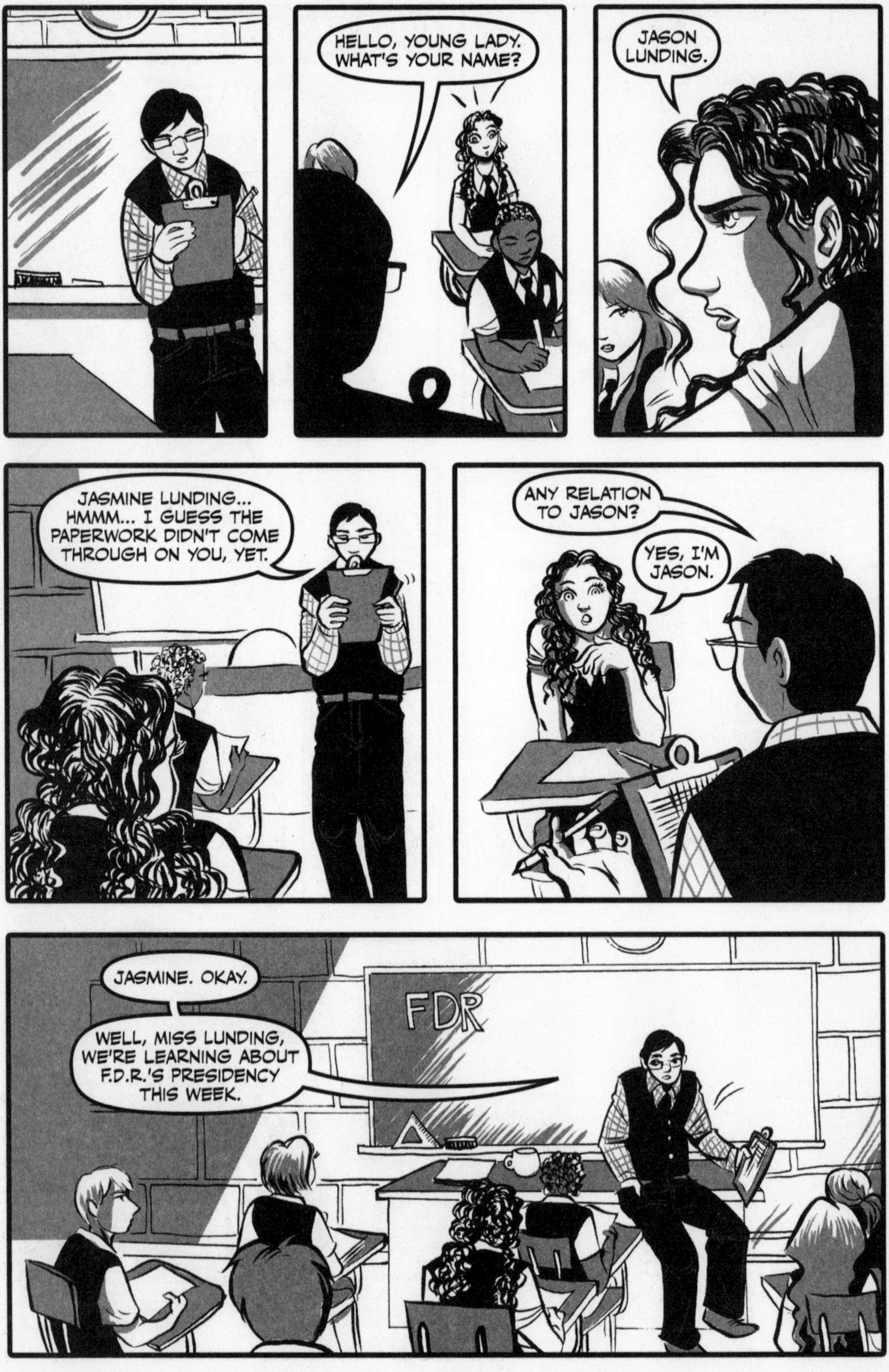
HELLO, YOUNG LADY. WHAT'S YOUR NAME?
JASON LUNDING.
JASMINE LUNDING... HMMM... I GUESS THE PAPERWORK DIDN'T COME THROUGH ON YOU, YET.
ANY RELATION TO JASON?
YES, I'M JASON.
JASMINE. OKAY.
WELL, MISS LUNDING, WE'RE LEARNING ABOUT F.D.R.'S PRESIDENCY THIS WEEK.
FDR

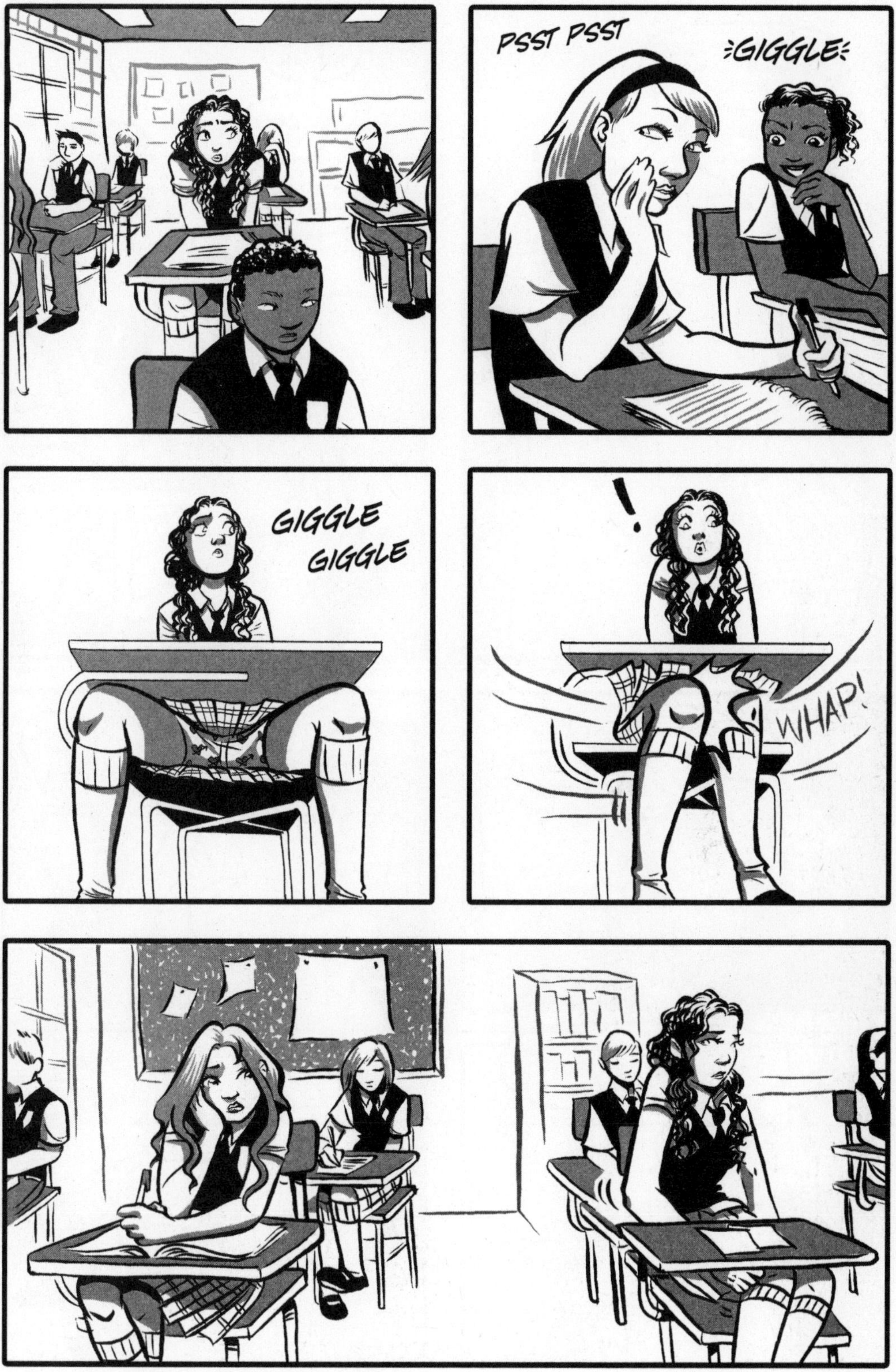
PSST PSST
GIGGLE
GIGGLE
GIGGLE
!
WHAP!

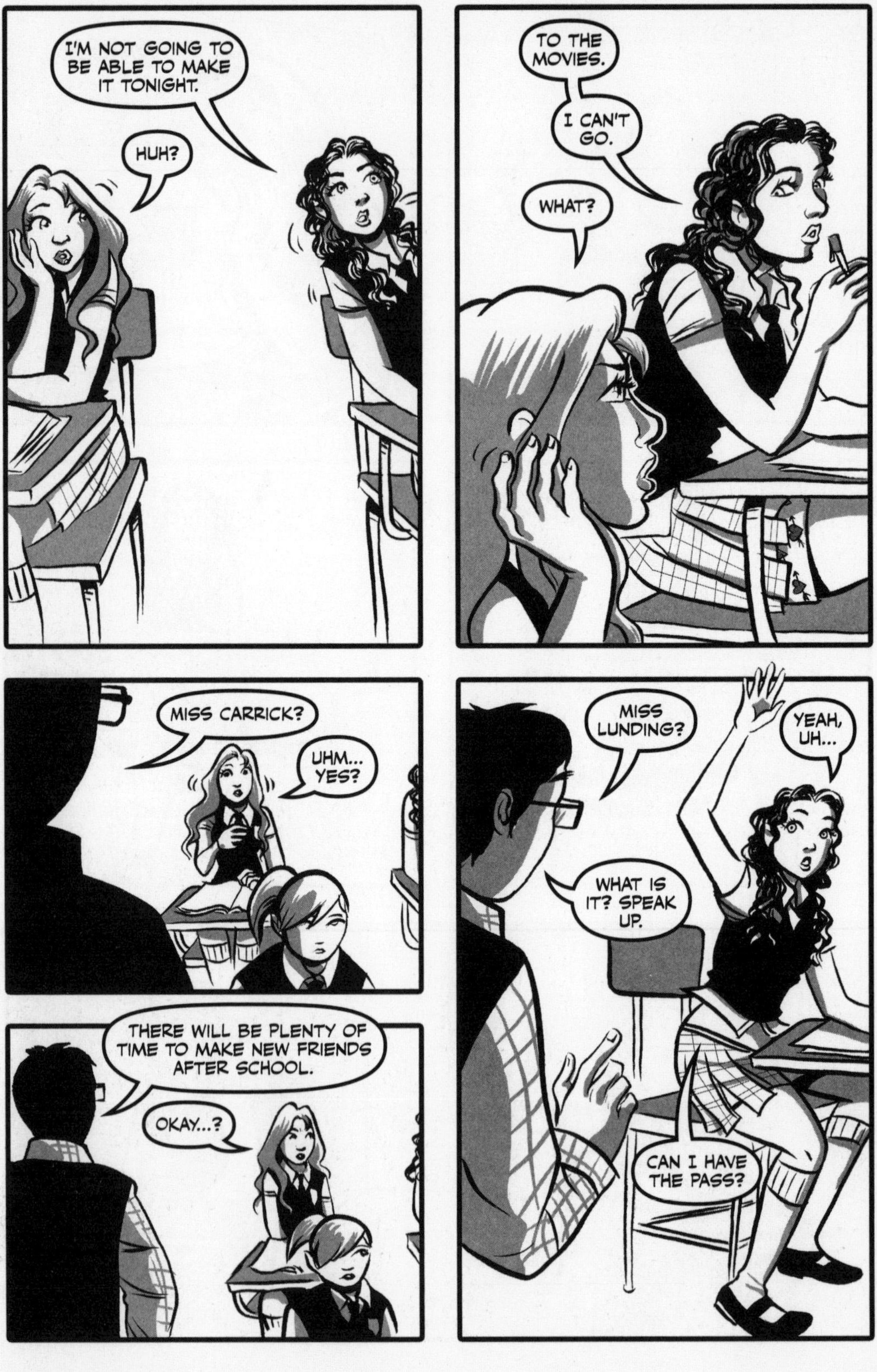
I'M NOT GOING TO BE ABLE TO MAKE IT TONIGHT.
HUH?
TO THE MOVIES.
I CAN'T GO.
WHAT?
MISS CARRICK?
UHM... YES?
THERE WILL BE PLENTY OF TIME TO MAKE NEW FRIENDS AFTER SCHOOL.
OKAY...?
MISS LUNDING?
YEAH, UH...
WHAT IS IT? SPEAK UP.
CAN I HAVE THE PASS?

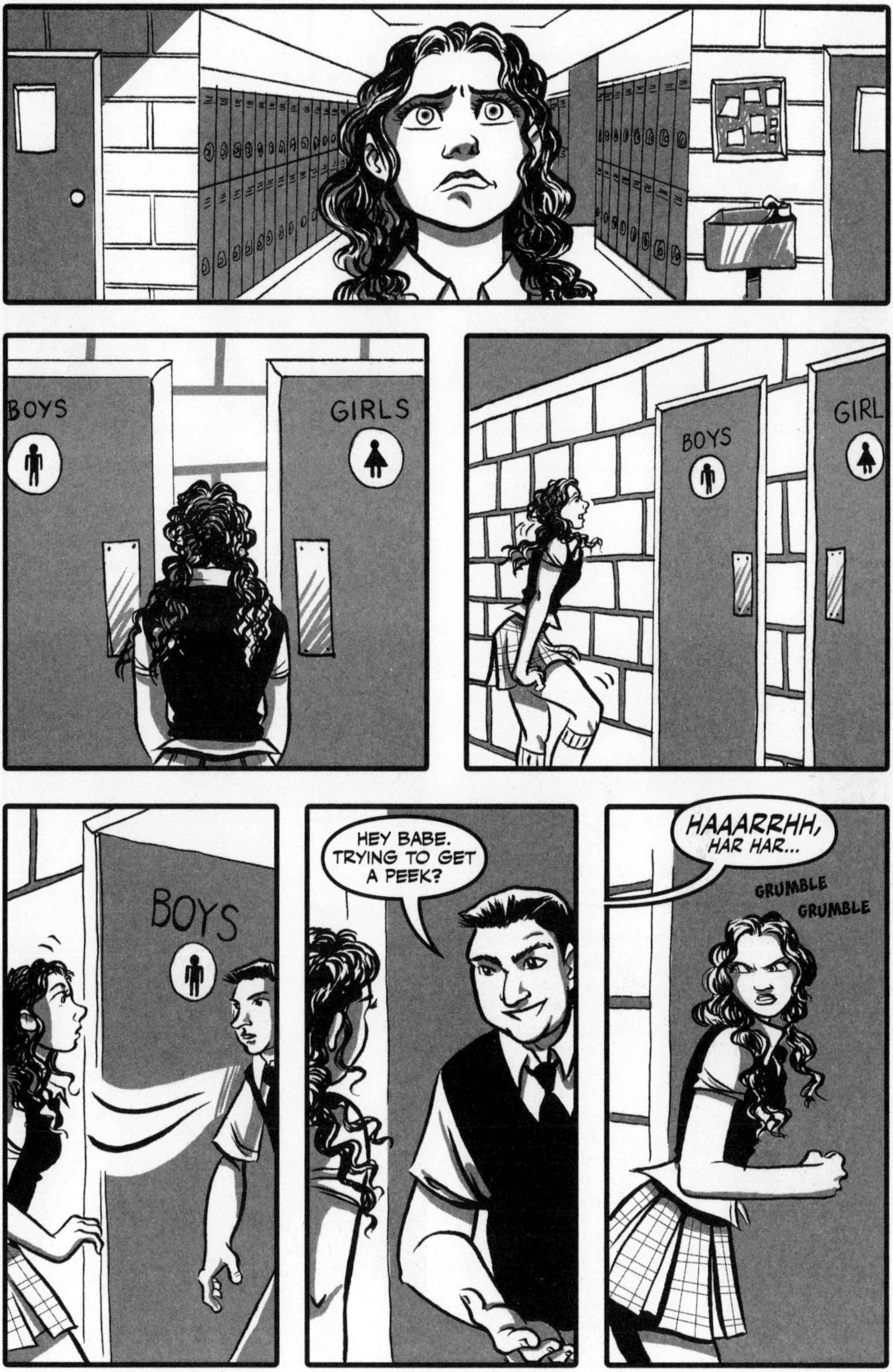
BOYS
GIRLS
BOYS
GIRL
BOYS
HEY BABE. TRYING TO GET A PEEK?
HAAARRHH, HAR HAR...
GRUMBLE
GRUMBLE

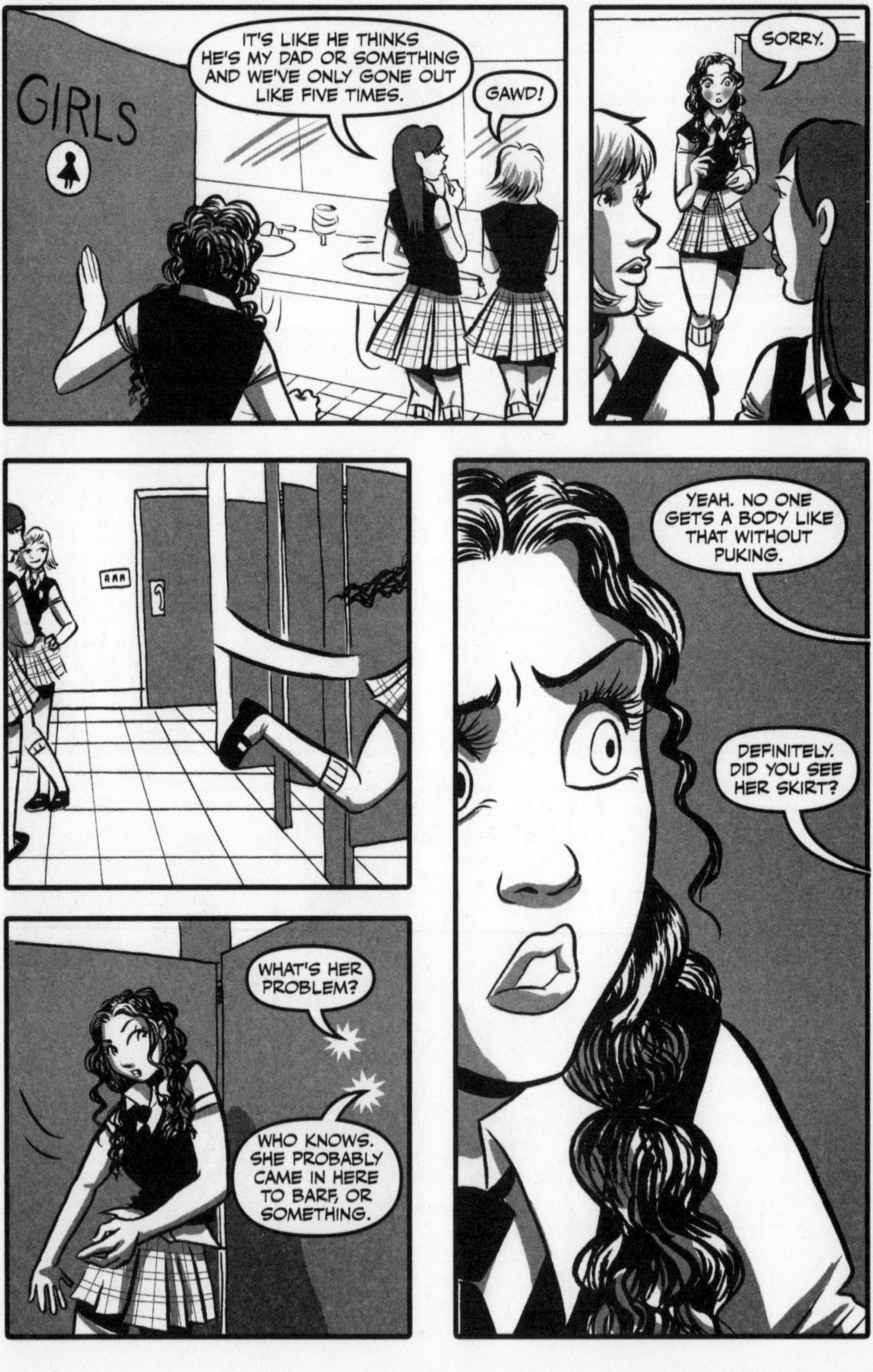
GIRLS
IT'S LIKE HE THINKS HE'S MY DAD OR SOMETHING AND WE'VE ONLY GONE OUT LIKE FIVE TIMES.
GAWD!
SORRY.
YEAH. NO ONE GETS A BODY LIKE THAT WITHOUT PUKING.
DEFINITELY. DID YOU SEE HER SKIRT?
WHAT'S HER PROBLEM?
WHO KNOWS. SHE PROBABLY CAME IN HERE TO BARF, OR SOMETHING.

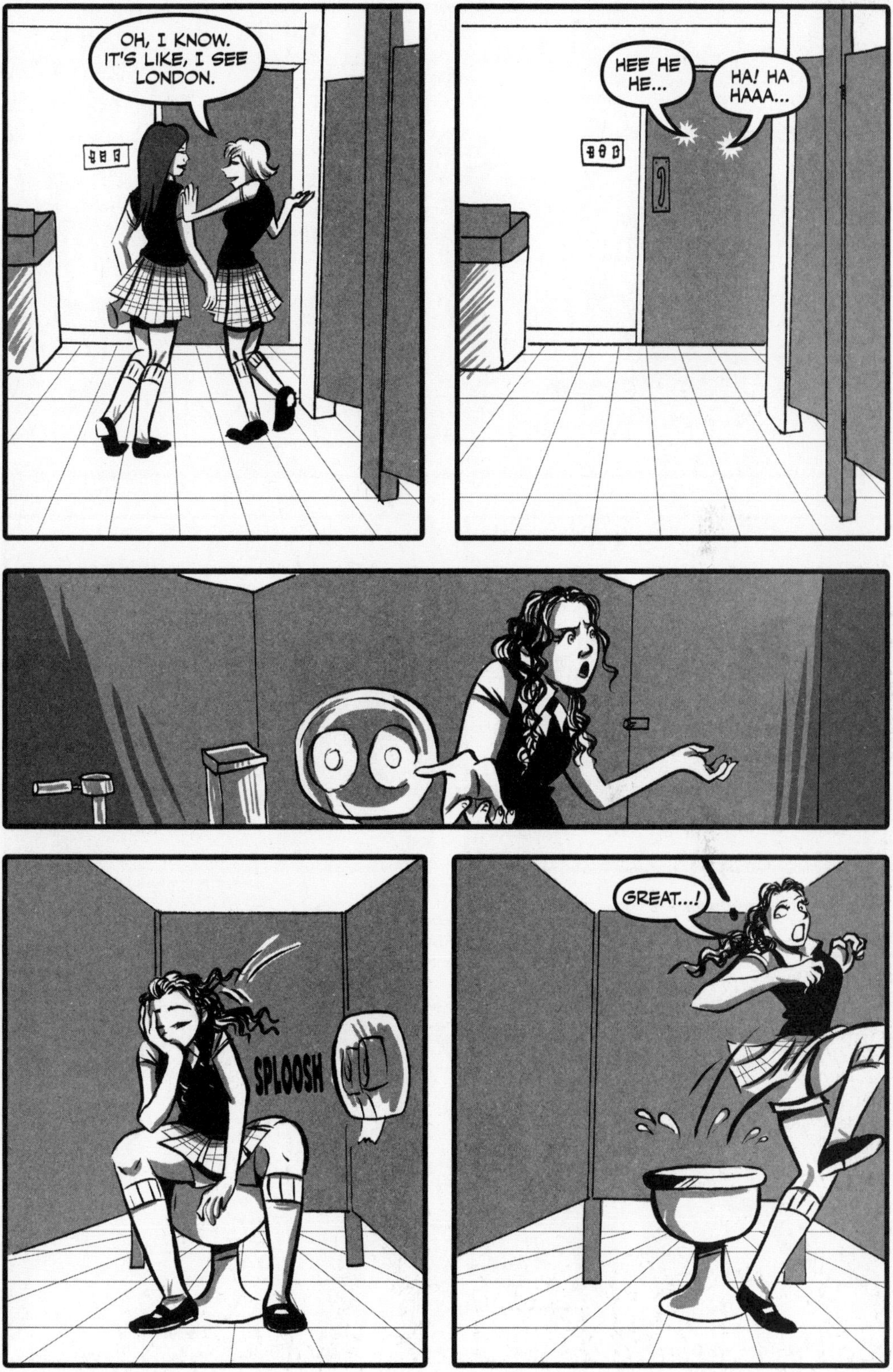
OH, I KNOW. IT'S LIKE, I SEE LONDON.
HEE HE HE...
HA! HA HAAA...
SPLOOSH
GREAT...!

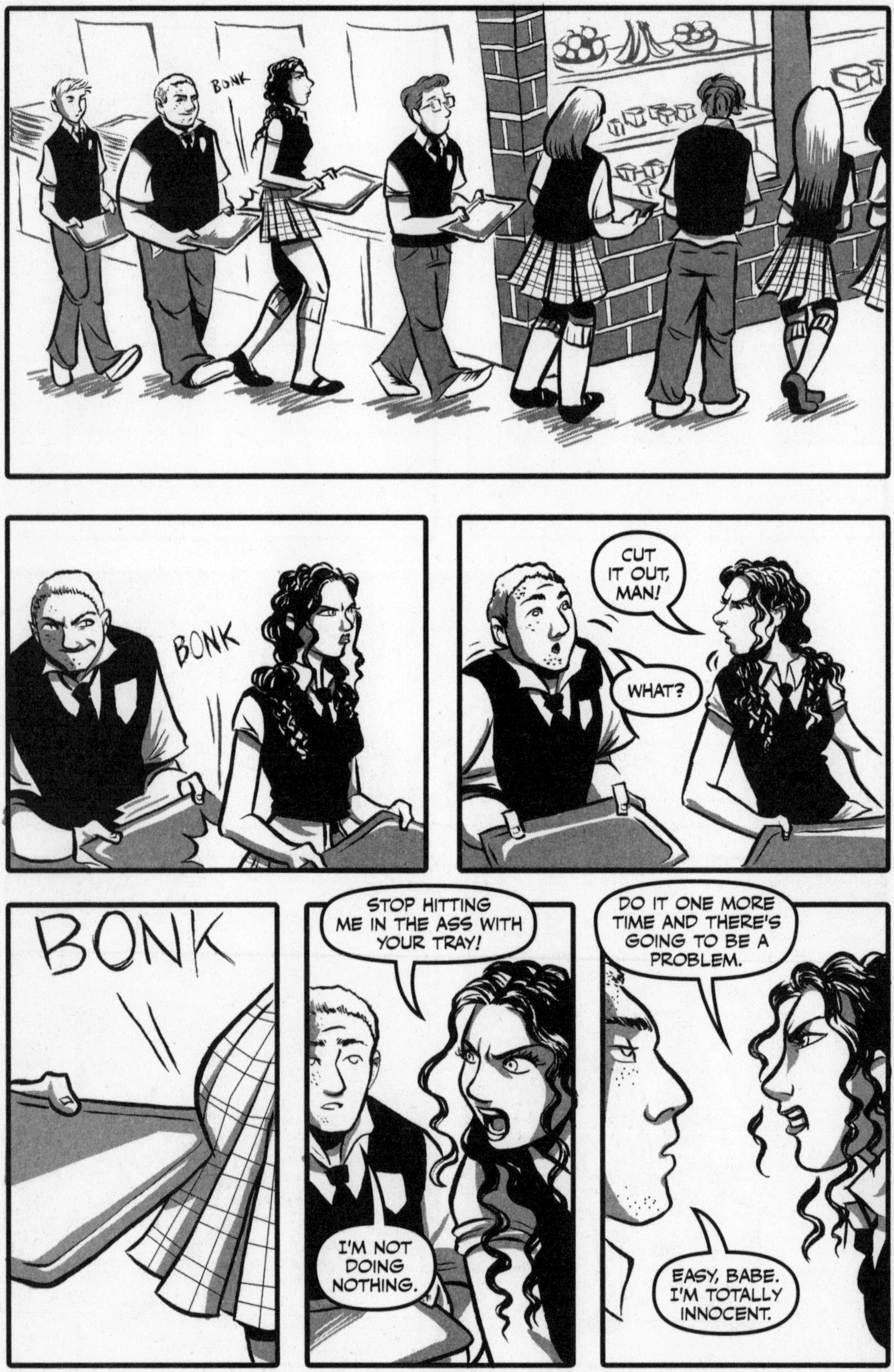
BONK
BONK
CUT IT OUT, MAN!
WHAT?
BONK
STOP HITTING ME IN THE ASS WITH YOUR TRAY!
I'M NOT DOING NOTHING.
DO IT ONE MORE TIME AND THERE'S GOING TO BE A PROBLEM.
EASY, BABE. I'M TOTALLY INNOCENT.

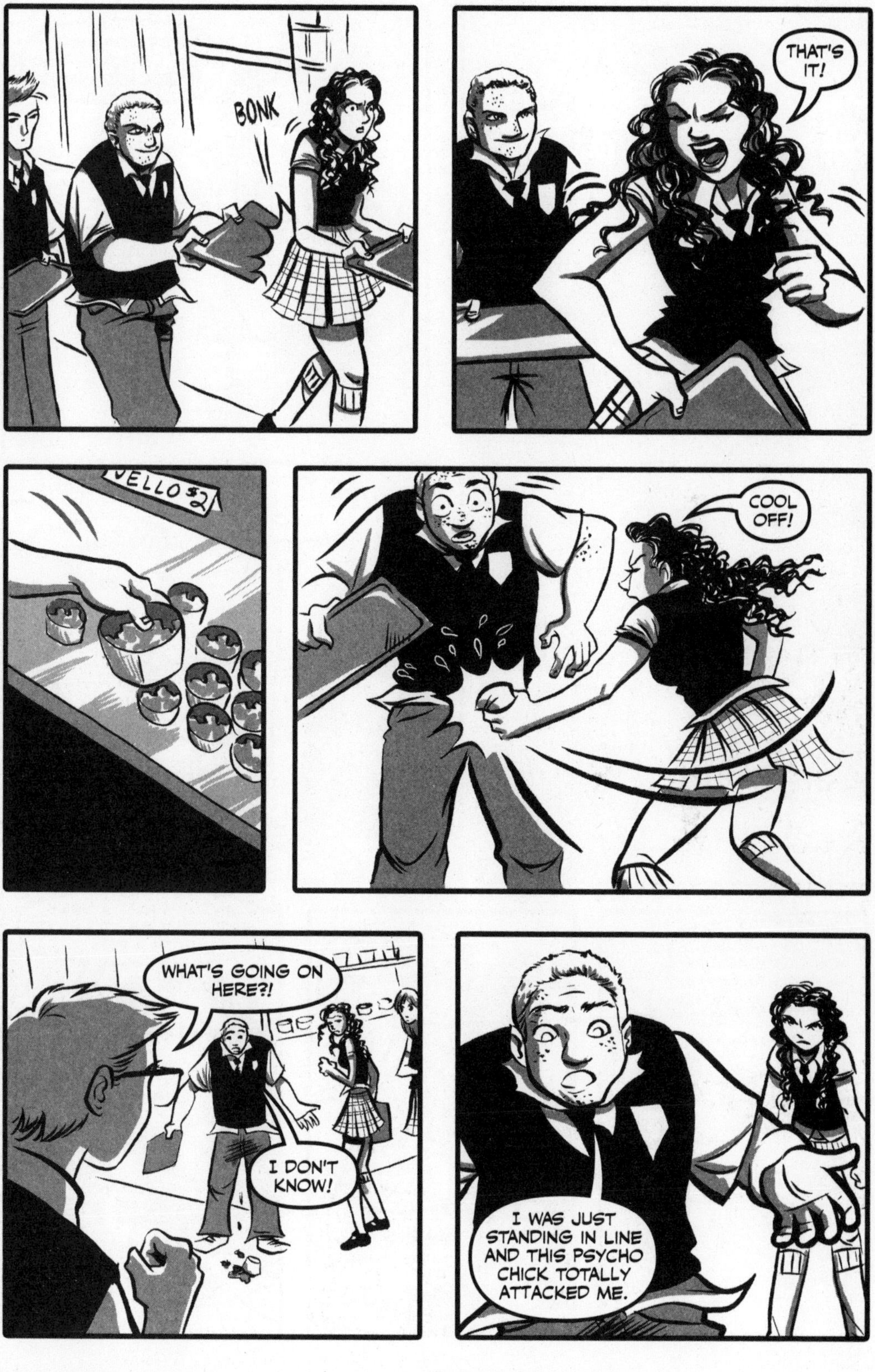
BONK
THAT'S IT!
JELLO $2
COOL OFF!
WHAT'S GOING ON HERE?!
I DON'T KNOW!
I WAS JUST STANDING IN LINE AND THIS PSYCHO CHICK TOTALLY ATTACKED ME.

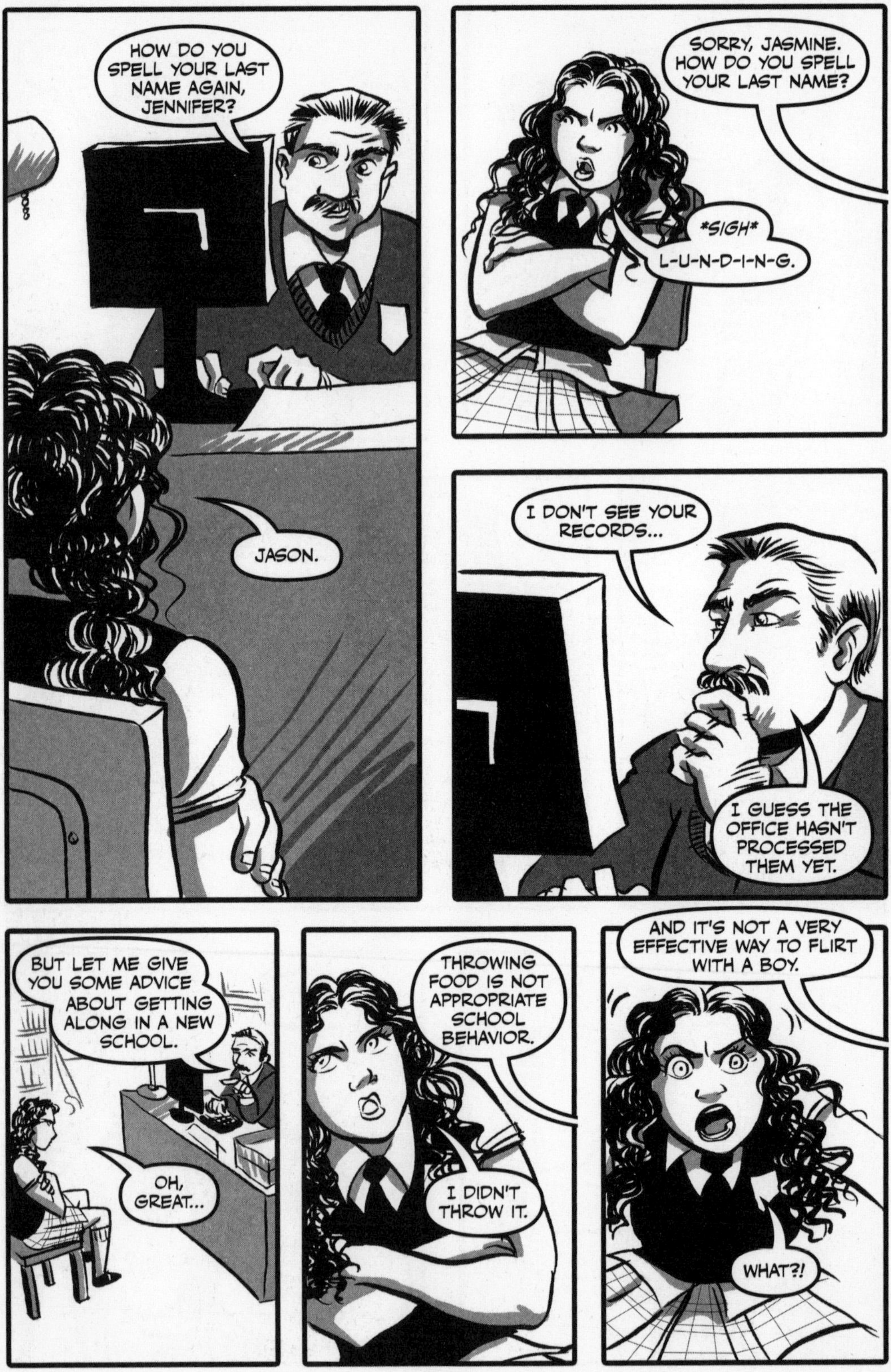
HOW DO YOU SPELL YOUR LAST NAME AGAIN, JENNIFER?
JASON.
SORRY, JASMINE. HOW DO YOU SPELL YOUR LAST NAME?
*SIGH*
L-U-N-D-I-N-G.
I DON'T SEE YOUR RECORDS...
I GUESS THE OFFICE HASN'T PROCESSED THEM YET.
BUT LET ME GIVE YOU SOME ADVICE ABOUT GETTING ALONG IN A NEW SCHOOL.
OH, GREAT...
THROWING FOOD IS NOT APPROPRIATE SCHOOL BEHAVIOR.
I DIDN'T THROW IT.
AND IT'S NOT A VERY EFFECTIVE WAY TO FLIRT WITH A BOY.
WHAT?!

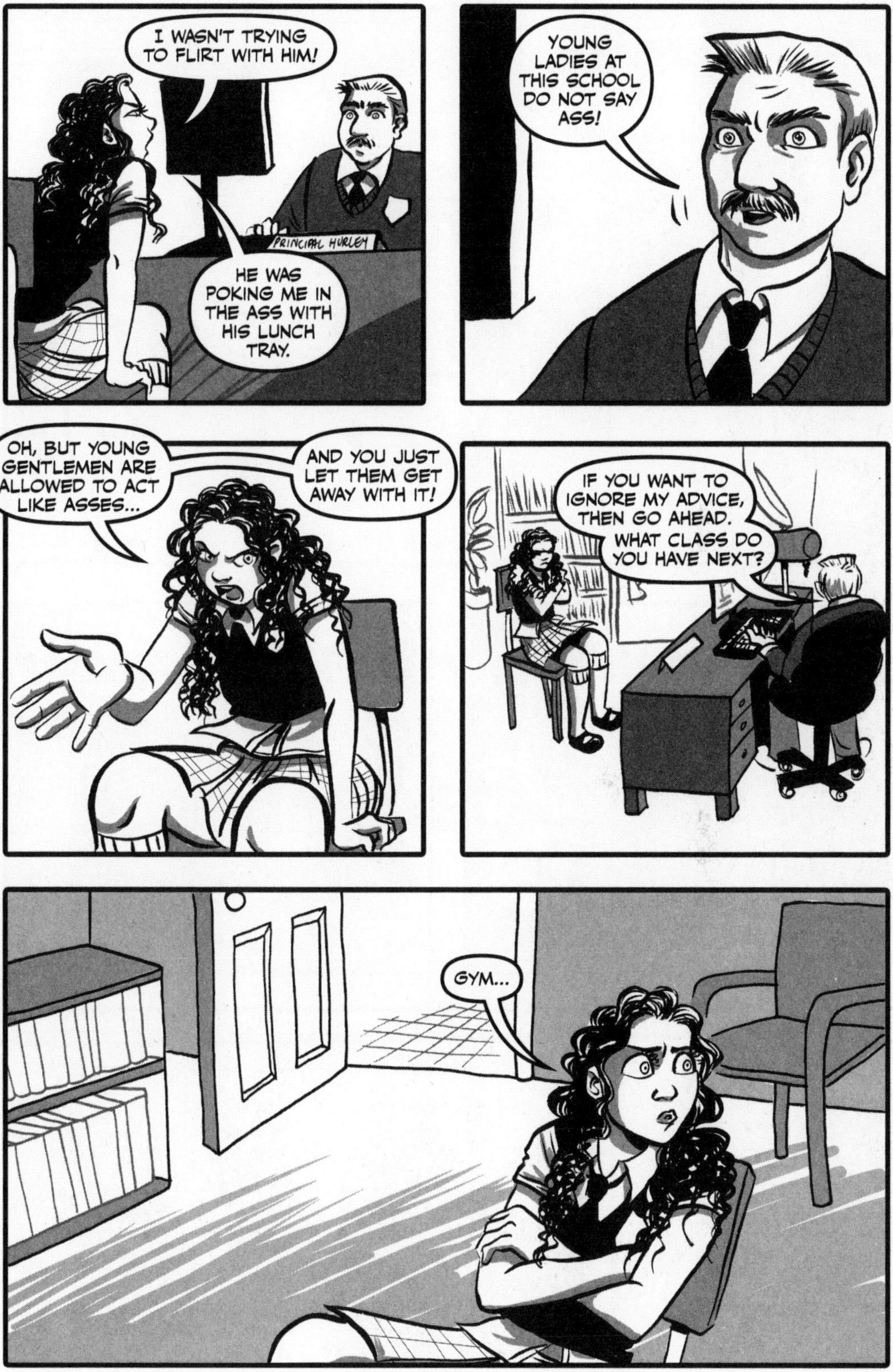
I WASN'T TRYING TO FLIRT WITH HIM!
PRINCIPAL HURLEY
HE WAS POKING ME IN THE ASS WITH HIS LUNCH TRAY.
YOUNG LADIES AT THIS SCHOOL DO NOT SAY ASS!
OH, BUT YOUNG GENTLEMEN ARE ALLOWED TO ACT LIKE ASSES...
AND YOU JUST LET THEM GET AWAY WITH IT!
IF YOU WANT TO IGNORE MY ADVICE, THEN GO AHEAD.
WHAT CLASS DO YOU HAVE NEXT?
GYM...

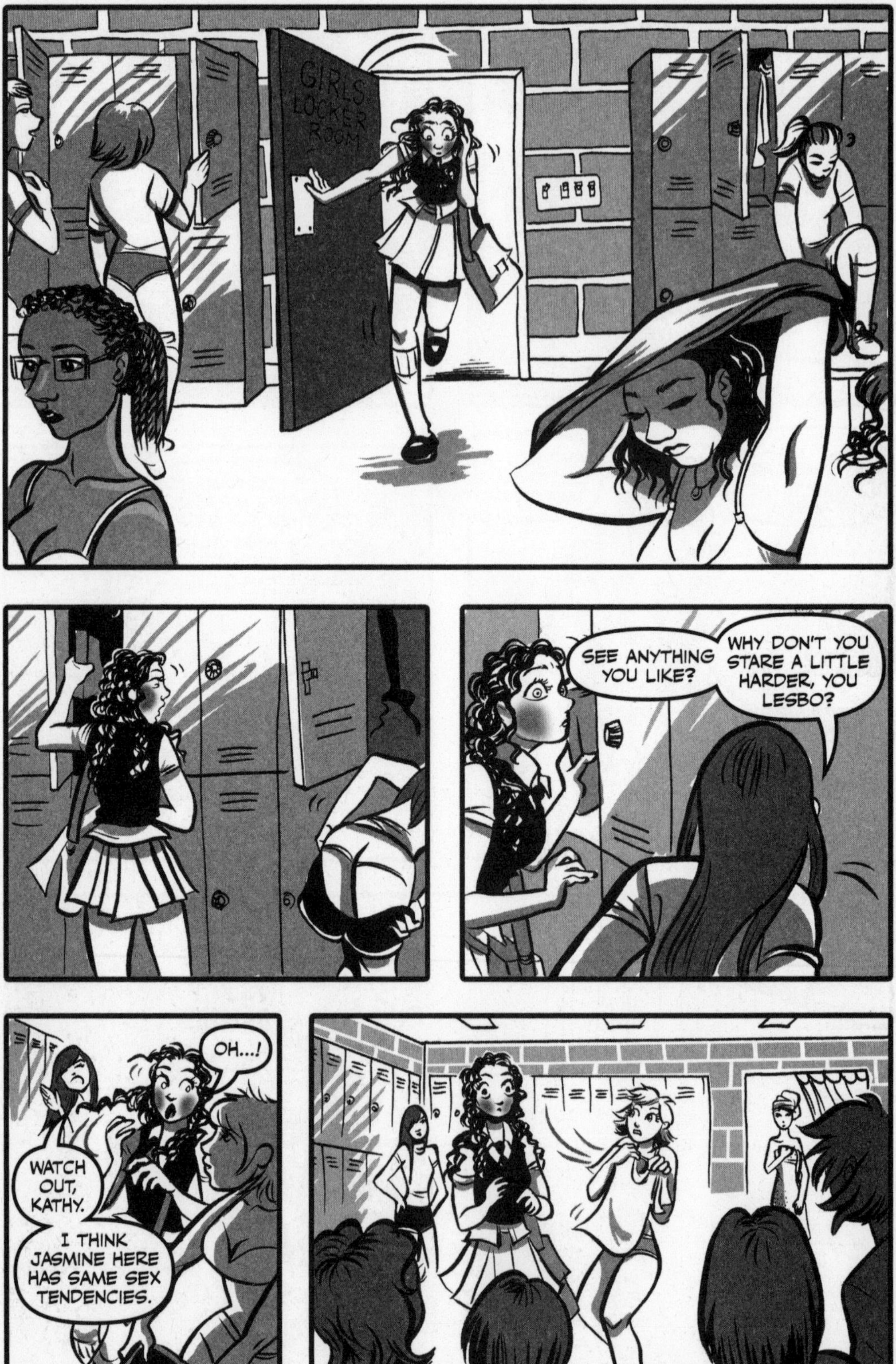
GIRLS LOCKER ROOM
SEE ANYTHING YOU LIKE?
WHY DON'T YOU STARE A LITTLE HARDER, YOU LESBO?
OH...!
WATCH OUT, KATHY.
I THINK JASMINE HERE HAS SAME SEX TENDENCIES.

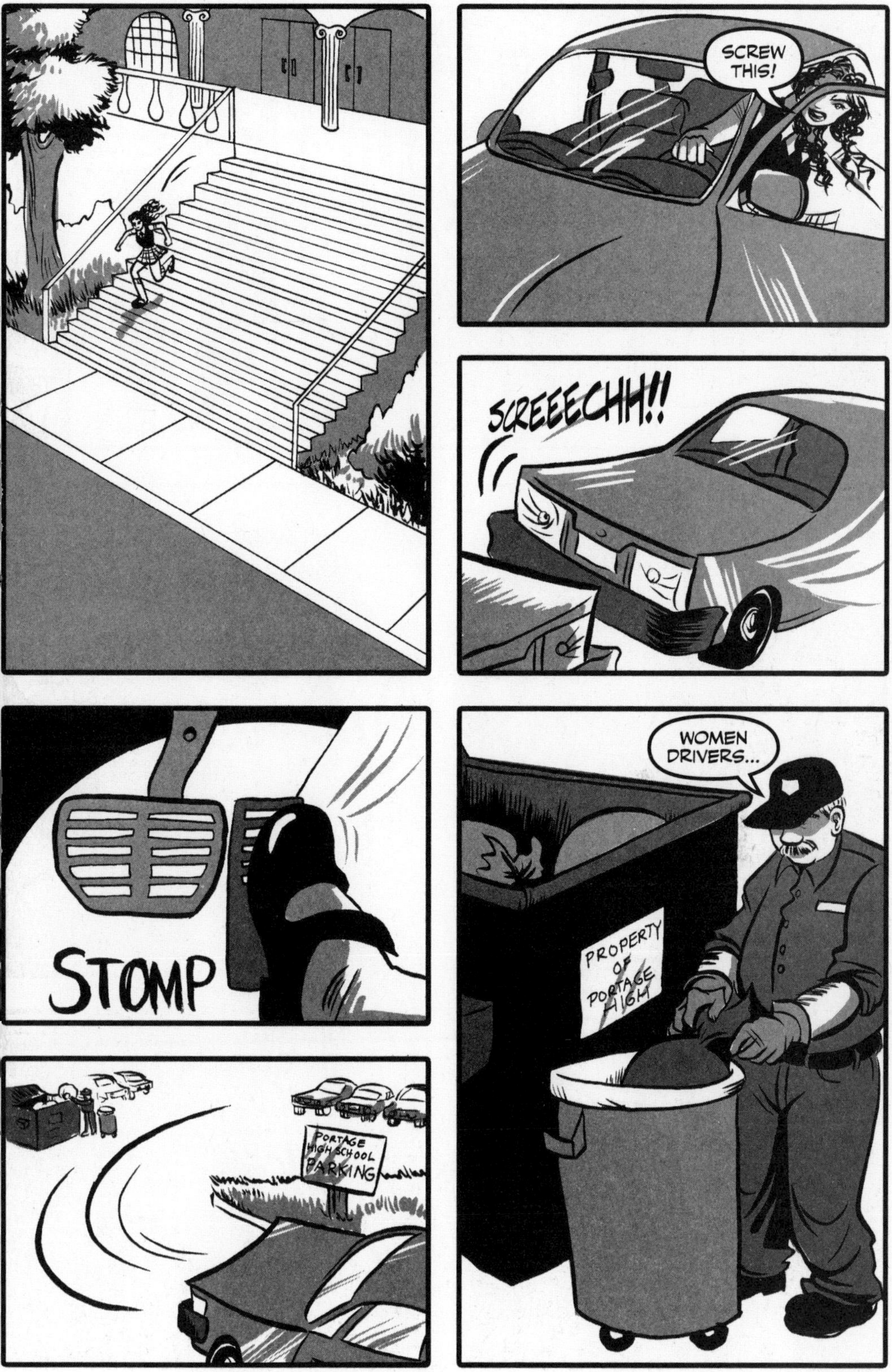
SCREW THIS!
SCREEECHH!!
STOMP
PORTAGE HIGH SCHOOL PARKING
WOMEN DRIVERS...
PROPERTY OF PORTAGE HIGH

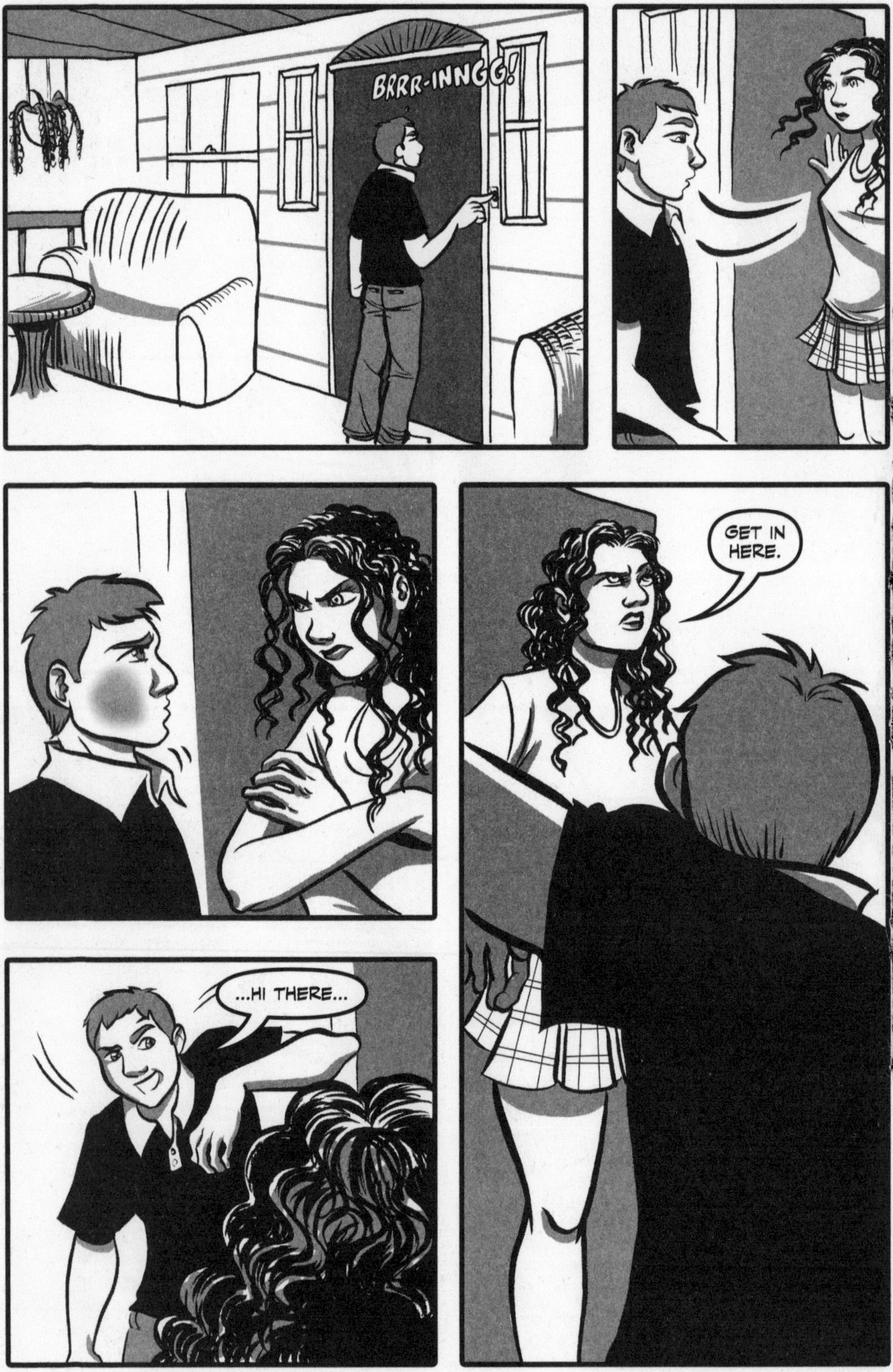
BRRR-INNGG!
GET IN HERE.
...HI THERE...

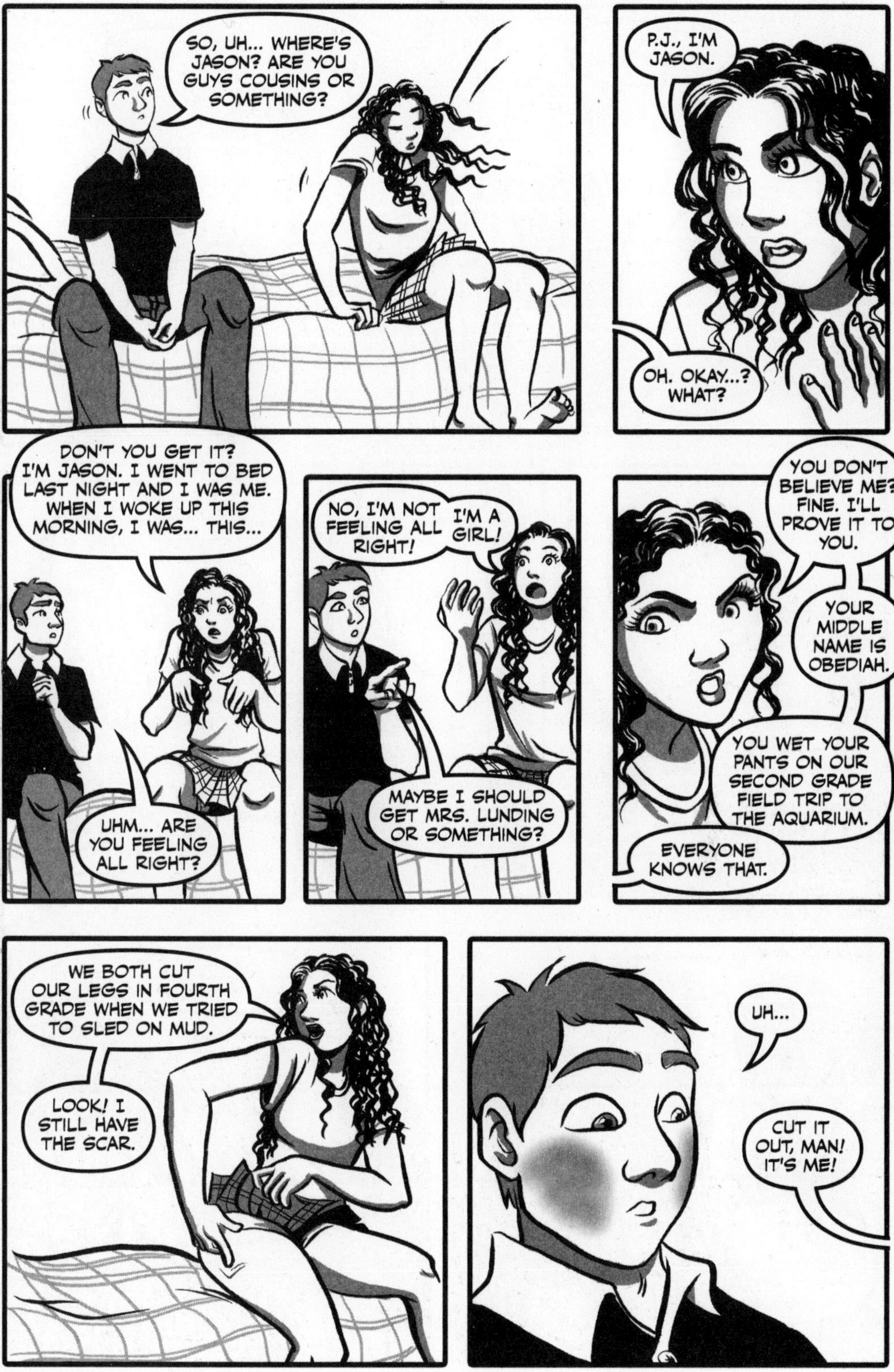
SO, UH... WHERE'S JASON? ARE YOU GUYS COUSINS OR SOMETHING?
P.J., I'M JASON.
OH. OKAY...? WHAT?
DON'T YOU GET IT? I'M JASON. I WENT TO BED LAST NIGHT AND I WAS ME. WHEN I WOKE UP THIS MORNING, I WAS... THIS...
UHM... ARE YOU FEELING ALL RIGHT?
NO, I'M NOT FEELING ALL RIGHT!
I'M A GIRL!
MAYBE I SHOULD GET MRS. LUNDING OR SOMETHING?
YOU DON'T BELIEVE ME? FINE. I'LL PROVE IT TO YOU.
YOUR MIDDLE NAME IS OBEDIAH.
YOU WET YOUR PANTS ON OUR SECOND GRADE FIELD TRIP TO THE AQUARIUM.
EVERYONE KNOWS THAT.
WE BOTH CUT OUR LEGS IN FOURTH GRADE WHEN WE TRIED TO SLED ON MUD.
LOOK! I STILL HAVE THE SCAR.
UH...
CUT IT OUT, MAN! IT'S ME!

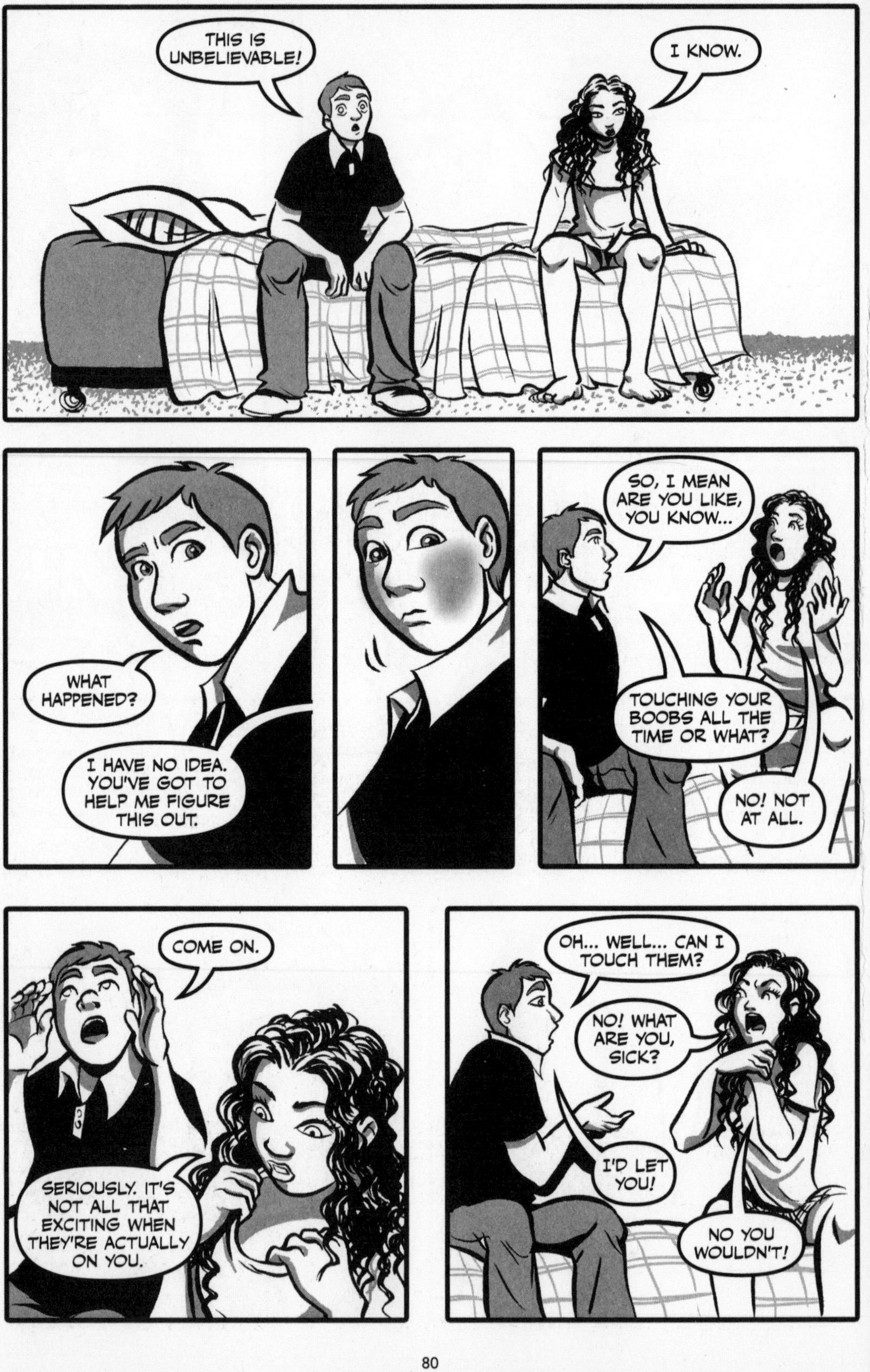
THIS IS UNBELIEVABLE!
I KNOW.
WHAT HAPPENED?
I HAVE NO IDEA. YOU'VE GOT TO HELP ME FIGURE THIS OUT.
SO, I MEAN ARE YOU LIKE, YOU KNOW...
TOUCHING YOUR BOOBS ALL THE TIME OR WHAT?
NO! NOT AT ALL.
COME ON.
SERIOUSLY. IT'S NOT ALL THAT EXCITING WHEN THEY'RE ACTUALLY ON YOU.
OH... WELL... CAN I TOUCH THEM?
NO! WHAT ARE YOU, SICK?
I'D LET YOU!
NO YOU WOULDN'T!

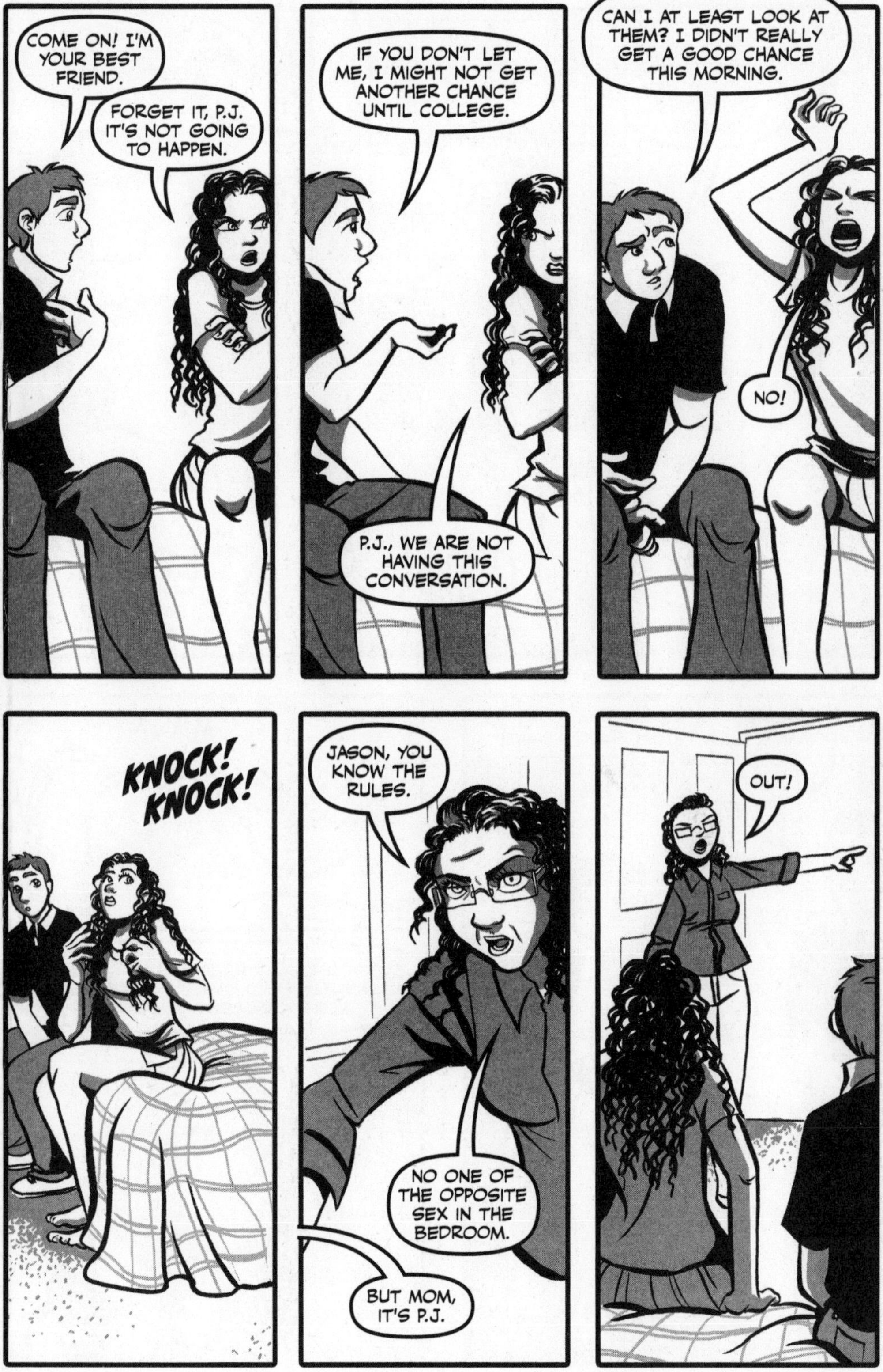
COME ON! I'M YOUR BEST FRIEND.
FORGET IT, P.J. IT'S NOT GOING TO HAPPEN.
IF YOU DON'T LET ME, I MIGHT NOT GET ANOTHER CHANCE UNTIL COLLEGE.
P.J., WE ARE NOT HAVING THIS CONVERSATION.
CAN I AT LEAST LOOK AT THEM? I DIDN'T REALLY GET A GOOD CHANCE THIS MORNING.
NO!
KNOCK! KNOCK!
JASON, YOU KNOW THE RULES.
NO ONE OF THE OPPOSITE SEX IN THE BEDROOM.
BUT MOM, IT'S P.J.
OUT!

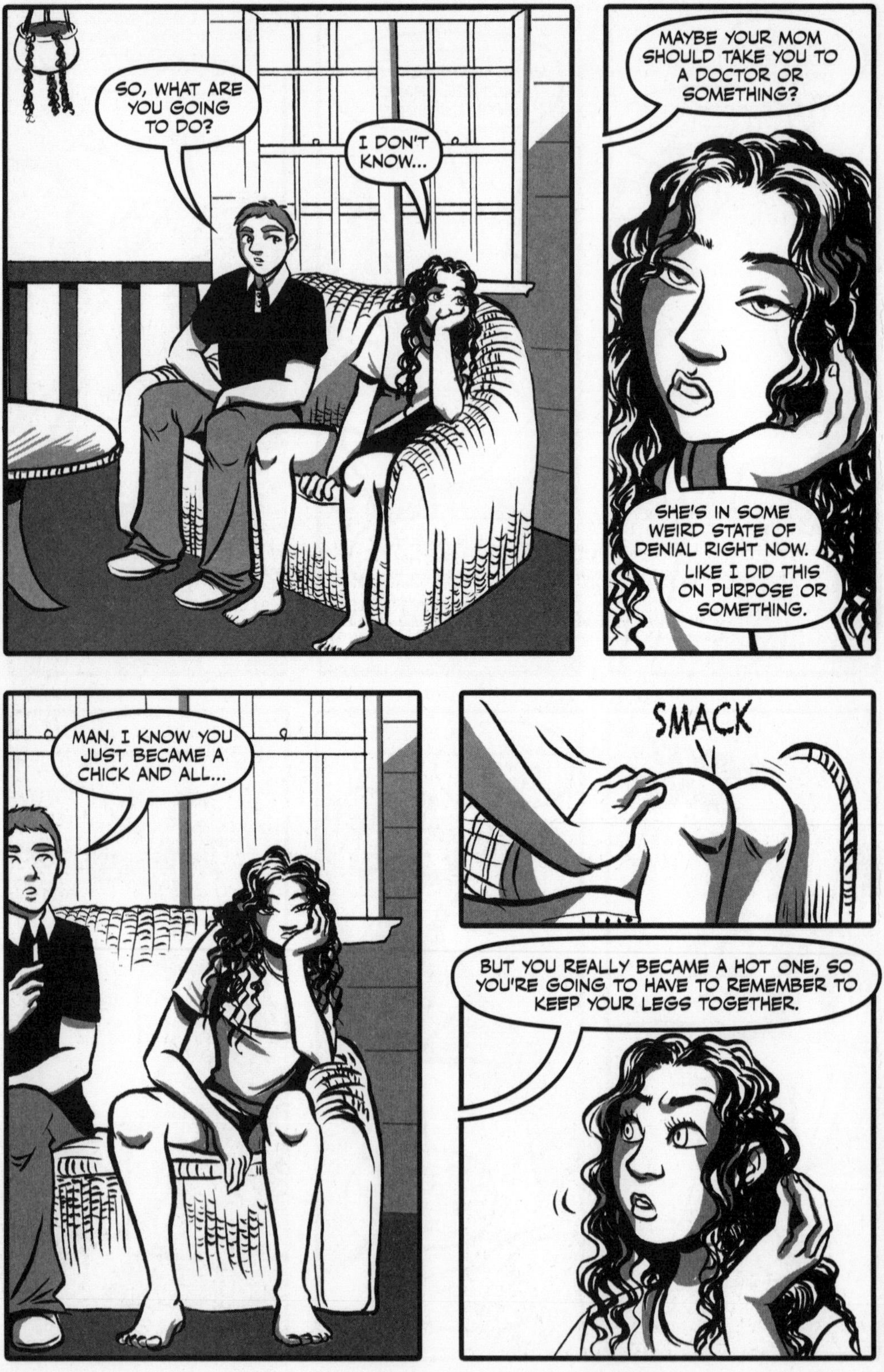
SO, WHAT ARE YOU GOING TO DO?
I DON'T KNOW...
MAYBE YOUR MOM SHOULD TAKE YOU TO A DOCTOR OR SOMETHING?
SHE'S IN SOME WEIRD STATE OF DENIAL RIGHT NOW.
LIKE I DID THIS ON PURPOSE OR SOMETHING.
MAN, I KNOW YOU JUST BECAME A CHICK AND ALL...
SMACK
BUT YOU REALLY BECAME A HOT ONE, SO YOU'RE GOING TO HAVE TO REMEMBER TO KEEP YOUR LEGS TOGETHER.

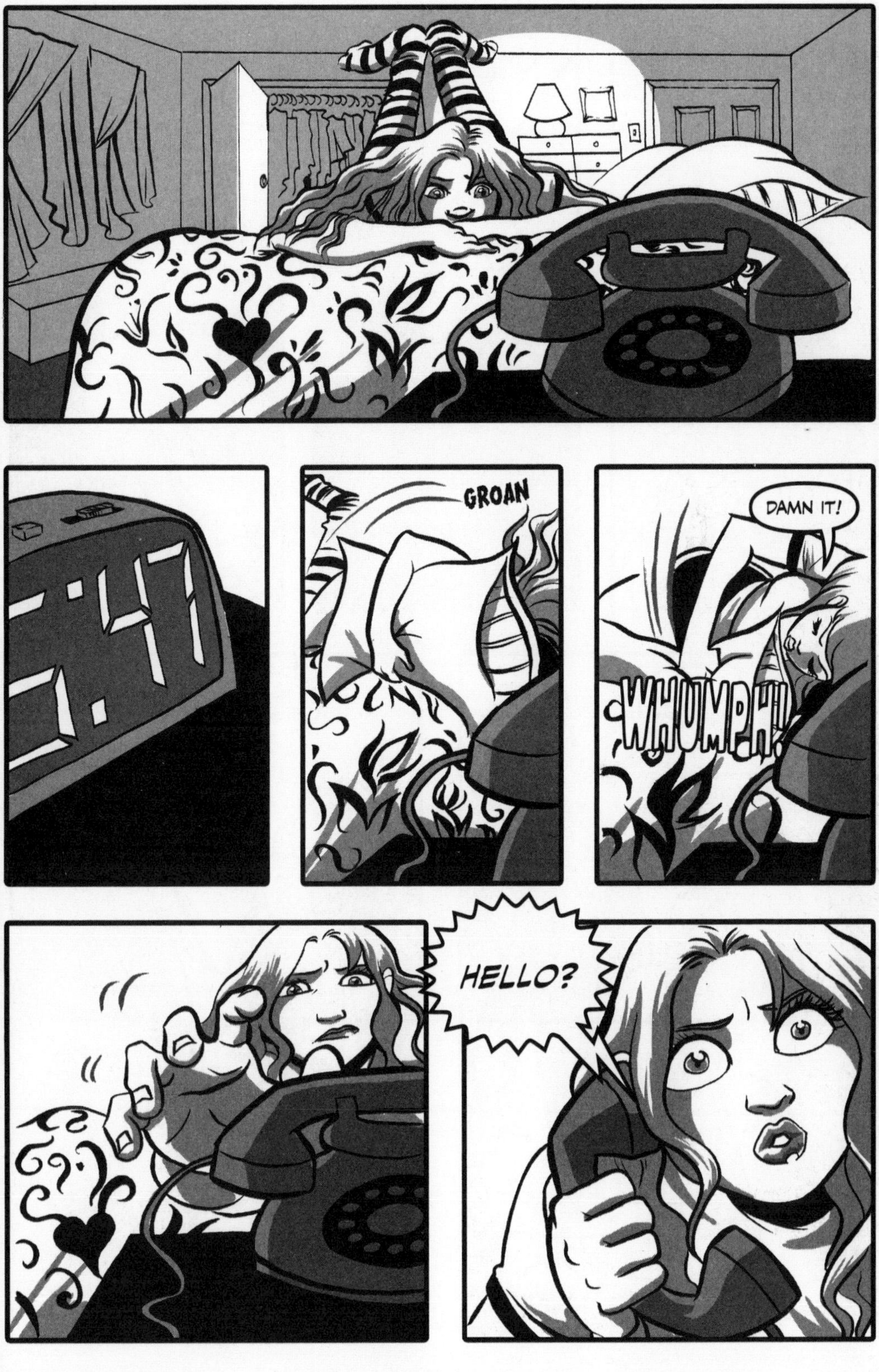
GROAN
DAMN IT!
WHUMPH!
HELLO?

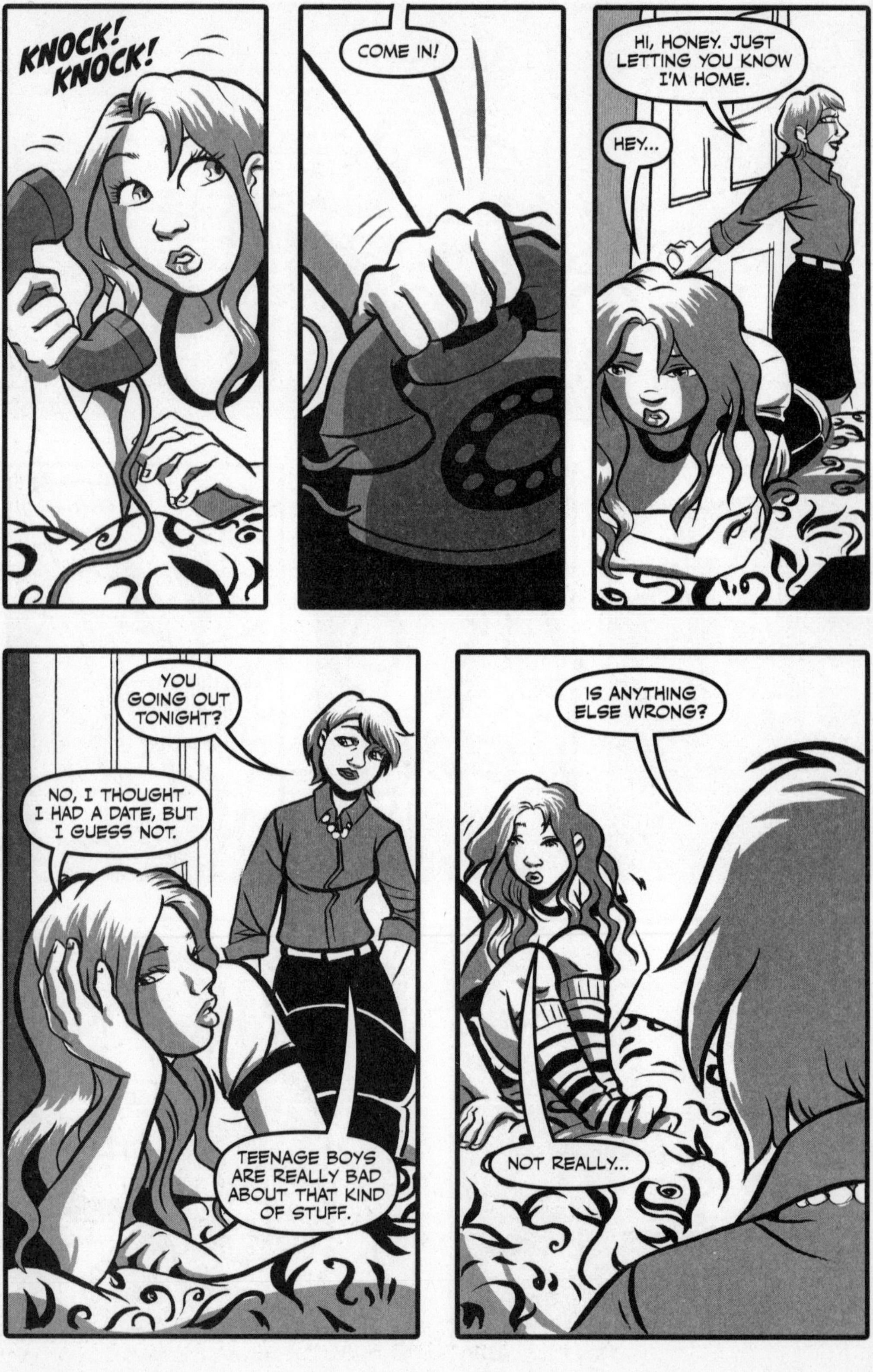
KNOCK! KNOCK!
COME IN!
HI, HONEY. JUST LETTING YOU KNOW I'M HOME.
HEY...
YOU GOING OUT TONIGHT?
NO, I THOUGHT I HAD A DATE, BUT I GUESS NOT.
TEENAGE BOYS ARE REALLY BAD ABOUT THAT KIND OF STUFF.
IS ANYTHING ELSE WRONG?
NOT REALLY...

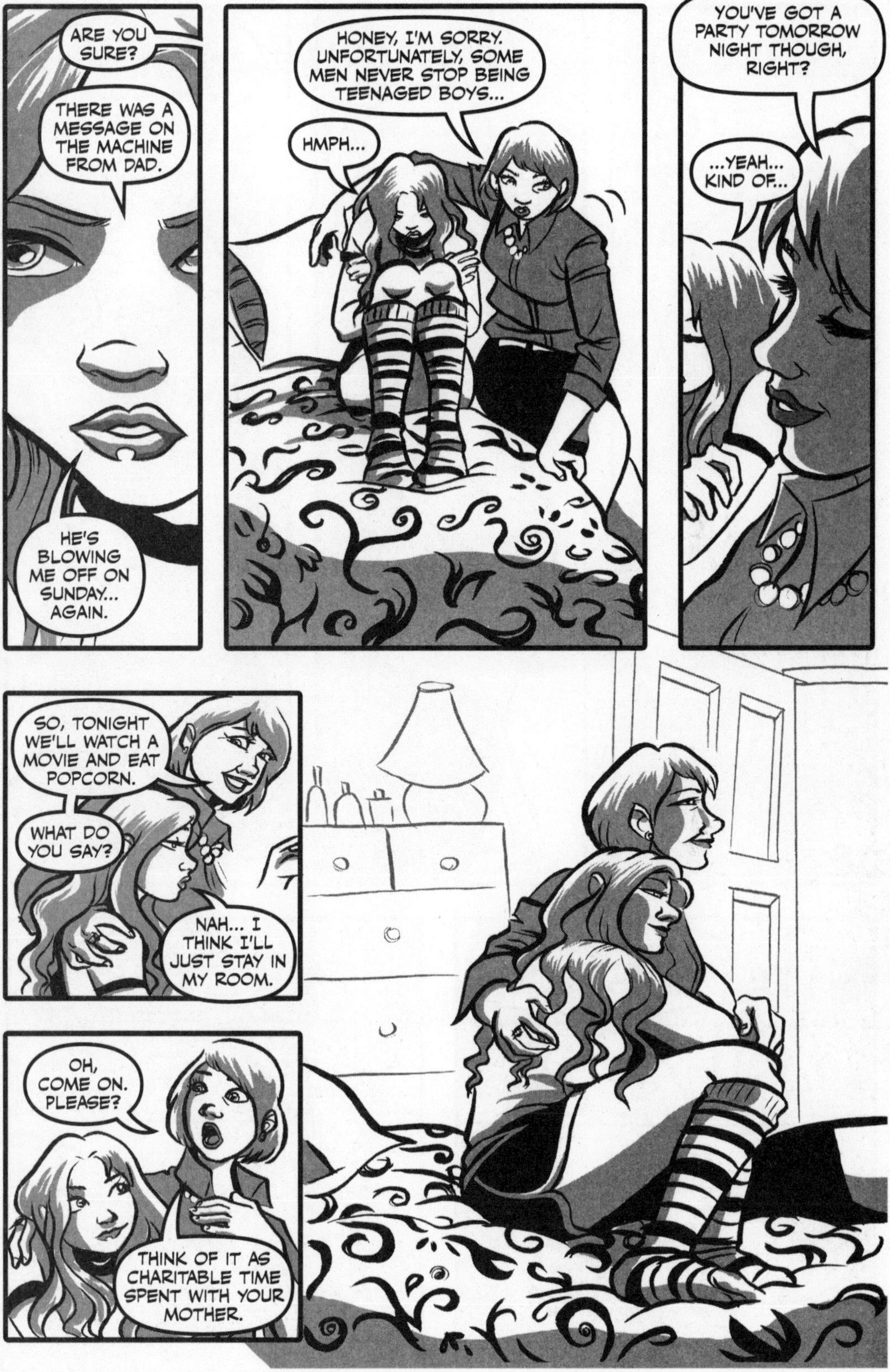

ARE YOU SURE?
THERE WAS A MESSAGE ON THE MACHINE FROM DAD.
HE'S BLOWING ME OFF ON SUNDAY... AGAIN.
HONEY, I'M SORRY. UNFORTUNATELY, SOME MEN NEVER STOP BEING TEENAGED BOYS...
HMPH...
YOU'VE GOT A PARTY TOMORROW NIGHT THOUGH, RIGHT?
...YEAH... KIND OF...
SO, TONIGHT WE'LL WATCH A MOVIE AND EAT POPCORN.
WHAT DO YOU SAY?
NAH... I THINK I'LL JUST STAY IN MY ROOM.
OH, COME ON. PLEASE?
THINK OF IT AS CHARITABLE TIME SPENT WITH YOUR MOTHER.

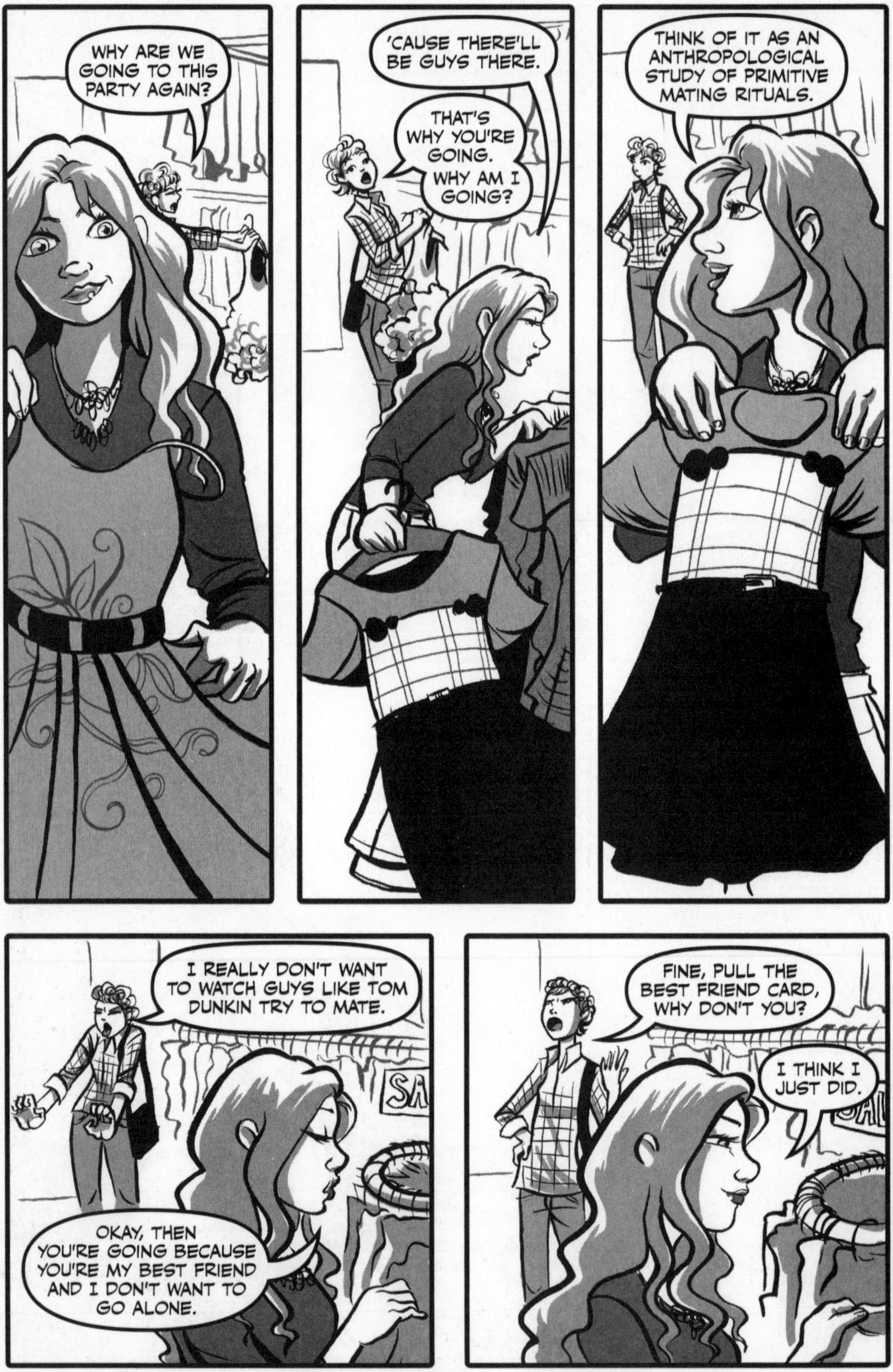
WHY ARE WE GOING TO THIS PARTY AGAIN?
'CAUSE THERE'LL BE GUYS THERE.
THAT'S WHY YOU'RE GOING.
WHY AM I GOING?
THINK OF IT AS AN ANTHROPOLOGICAL STUDY OF PRIMITIVE MATING RITUALS.
I REALLY DON'T WANT TO WATCH GUYS LIKE TOM DUNKIN TRY TO MATE.
OKAY, THEN YOU'RE GOING BECAUSE YOU'RE MY BEST FRIEND AND I DON'T WANT TO GO ALONE.
FINE, PULL THE BEST FRIEND CARD, WHY DON'T YOU?
I THINK I JUST DID.

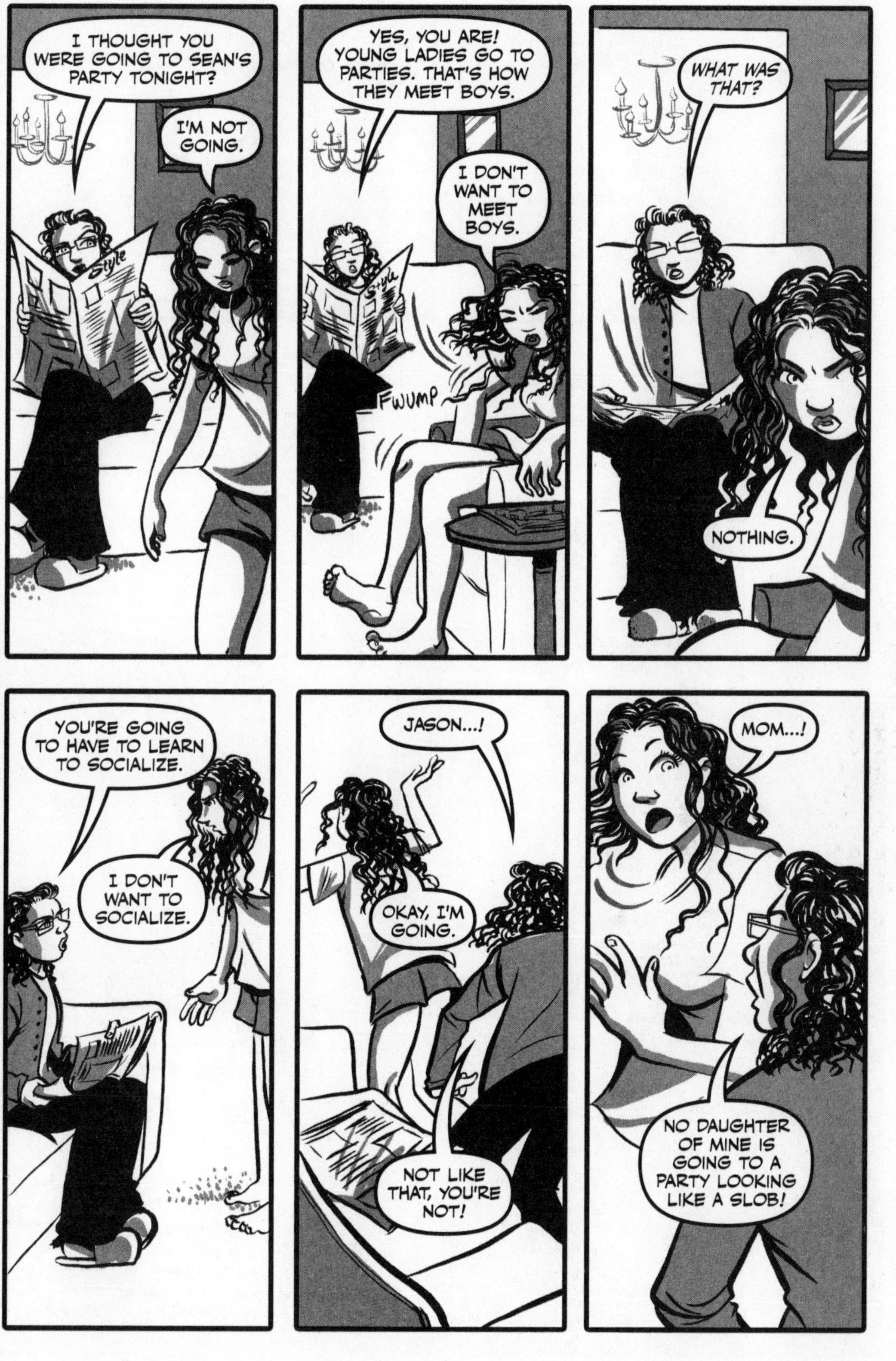
I THOUGHT YOU WERE GOING TO SEAN'S PARTY TONIGHT?
I'M NOT GOING.
YES, YOU ARE! YOUNG LADIES GO TO PARTIES. THAT'S HOW THEY MEET BOYS.
I DON'T WANT TO MEET BOYS.
FWUMP
WHAT WAS THAT?
NOTHING.
YOU'RE GOING TO HAVE TO LEARN TO SOCIALIZE.
I DON'T WANT TO SOCIALIZE.
JASON...!
OKAY, I'M GOING.
NOT LIKE THAT, YOU'RE NOT!
MOM...!
NO DAUGHTER OF MINE IS GOING TO A PARTY LOOKING LIKE A SLOB!

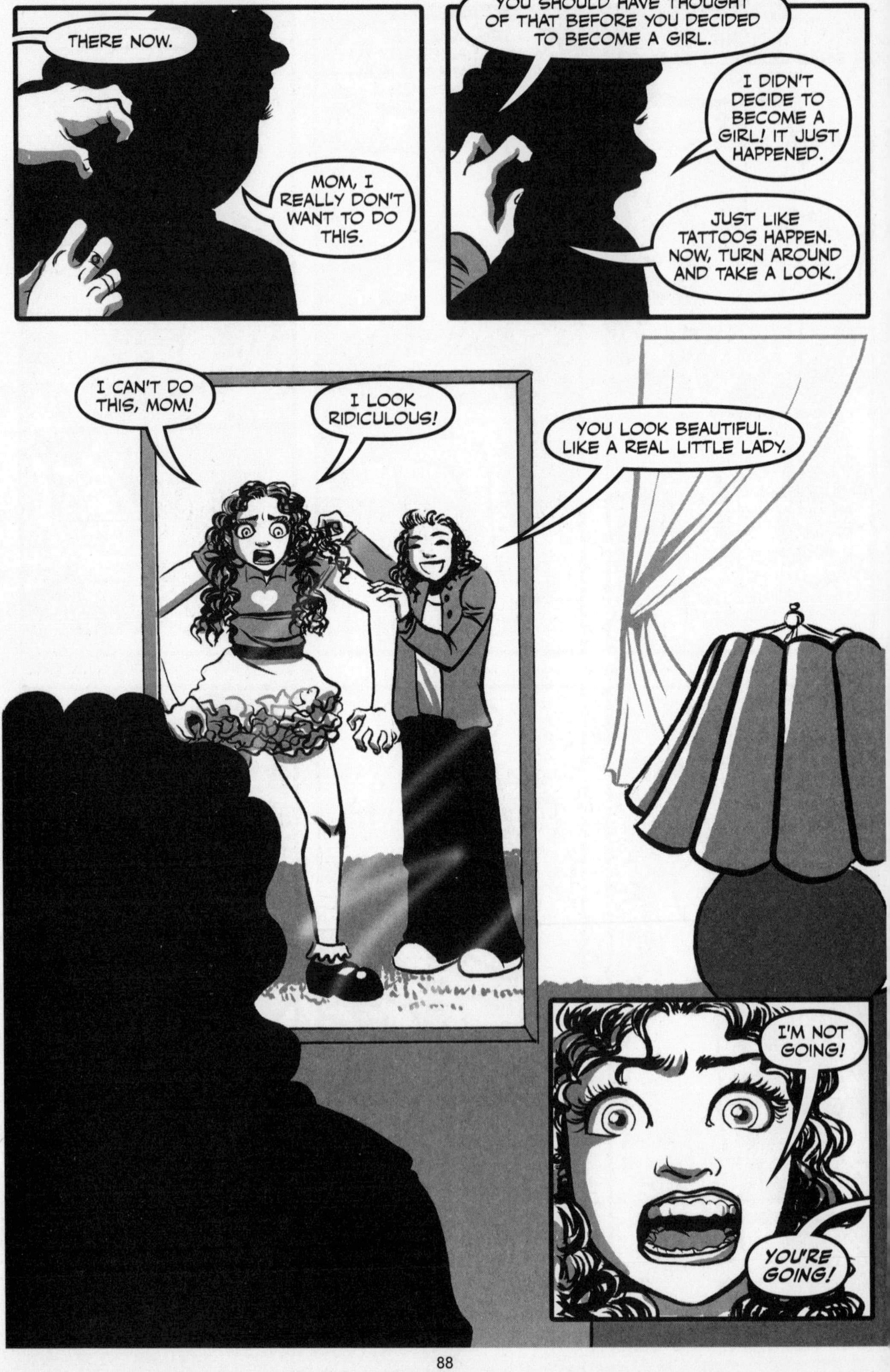
THERE NOW.
MOM, I REALLY DON'T WANT TO DO THIS.
YOU SHOULD HAVE THOUGHT OF THAT BEFORE YOU DECIDED TO BECOME A GIRL.
I DIDN'T DECIDE TO BECOME A GIRL! IT JUST HAPPENED.
JUST LIKE TATTOOS HAPPEN. NOW, TURN AROUND AND TAKE A LOOK.
I CAN'T DO THIS, MOM!
I LOOK RIDICULOUS!
YOU LOOK BEAUTIFUL. LIKE A REAL LITTLE LADY.
I'M NOT GOING!
YOU'RE GOING!

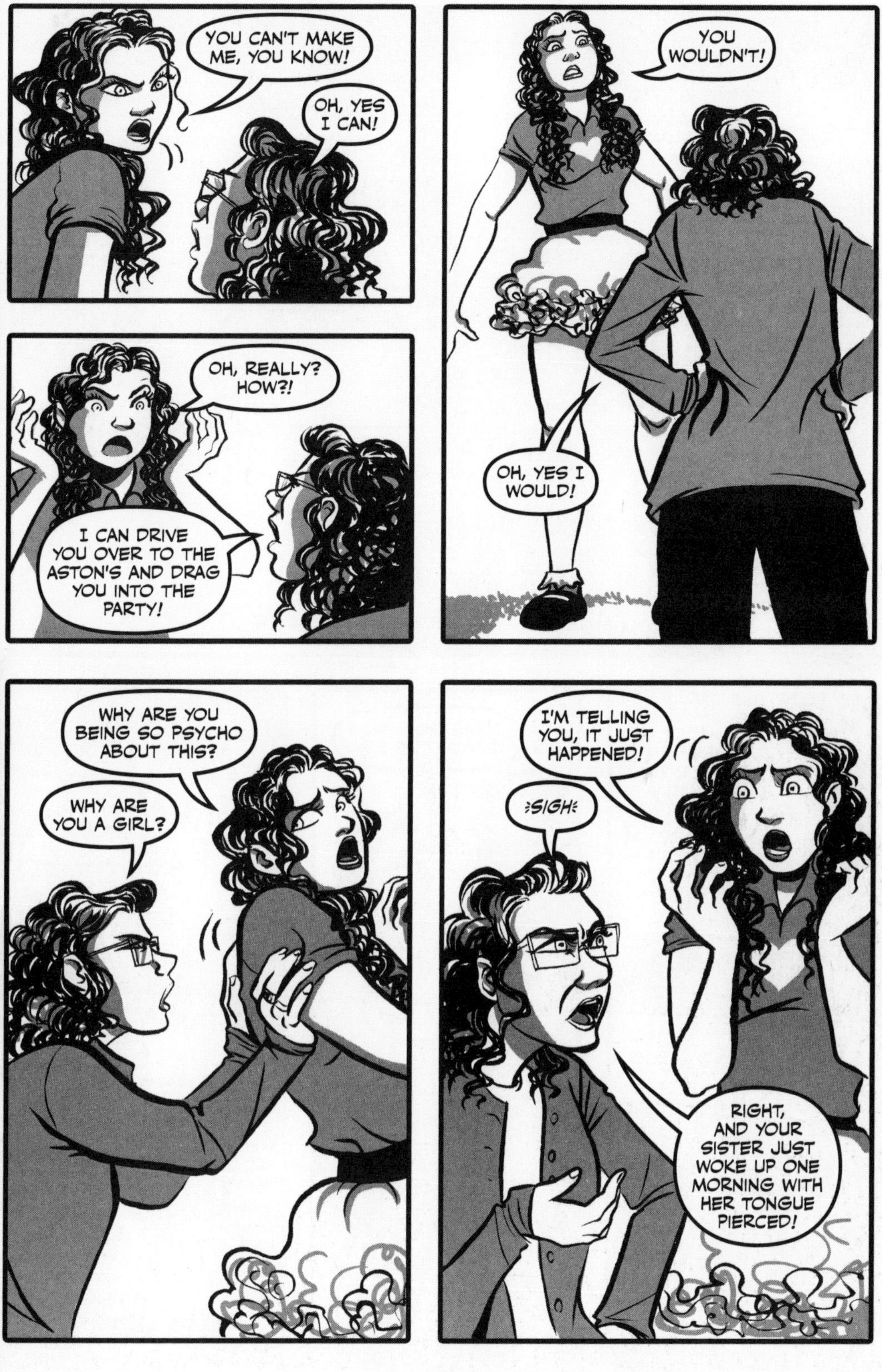
YOU CAN'T MAKE ME, YOU KNOW!
OH, YES I CAN!
OH, REALLY? HOW?!
I CAN DRIVE YOU OVER TO THE ASTON'S AND DRAG YOU INTO THE PARTY!
YOU WOULDN'T!
OH, YES I WOULD!
WHY ARE YOU BEING SO PSYCHO ABOUT THIS?
WHY ARE YOU A GIRL?
I'M TELLING YOU, IT JUST HAPPENED!
SIGH
RIGHT, AND YOUR SISTER JUST WOKE UP ONE MORNING WITH HER TONGUE PIERCED!

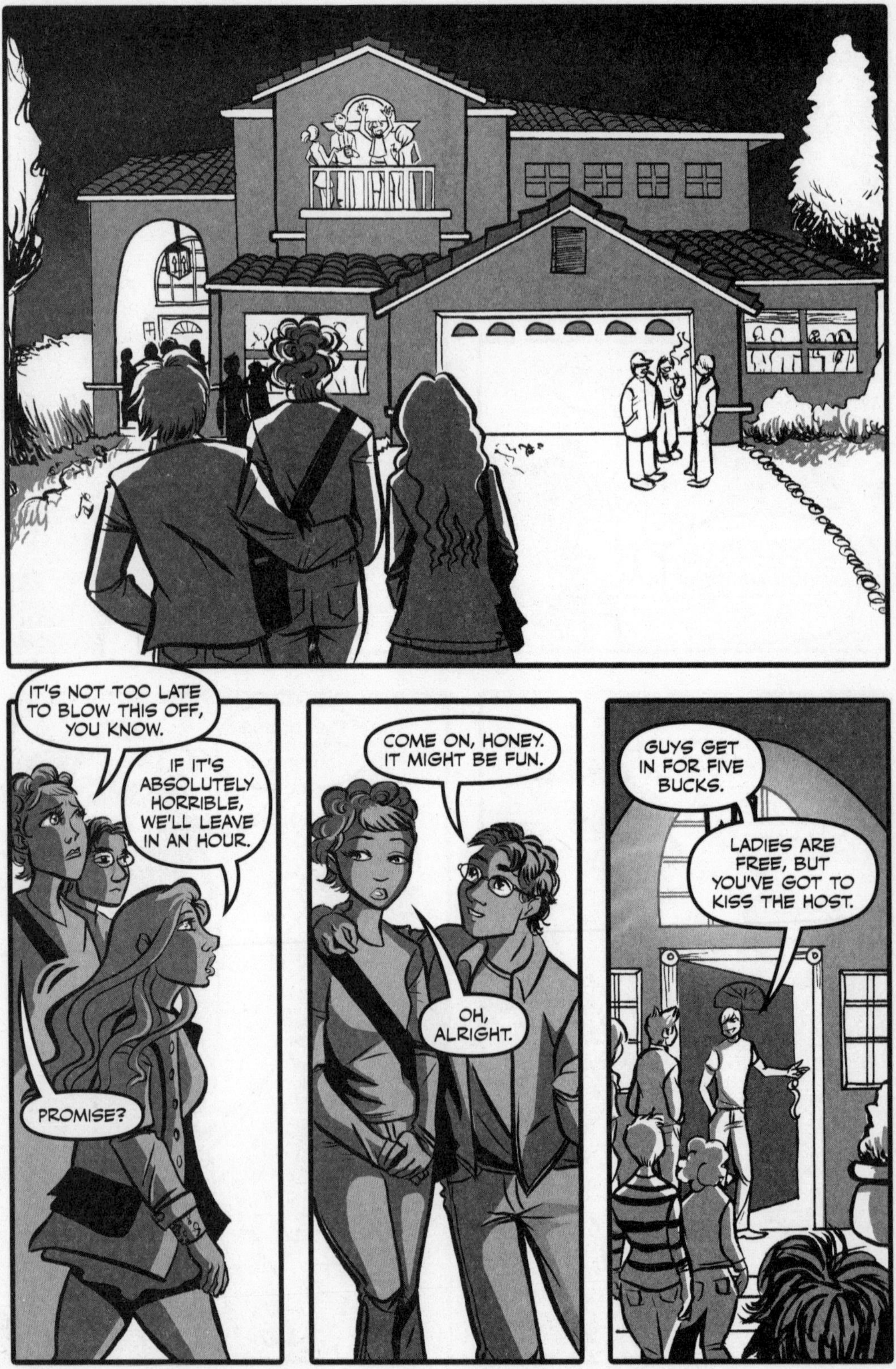
IT'S NOT TOO LATE TO BLOW THIS OFF, YOU KNOW.
IF IT'S ABSOLUTELY HORRIBLE, WE'LL LEAVE IN AN HOUR.
PROMISE?
COME ON, HONEY. IT MIGHT BE FUN.
OH, ALRIGHT.
GUYS GET IN FOR FIVE BUCKS.
LADIES ARE FREE, BUT YOU'VE GOT TO KISS THE HOST.

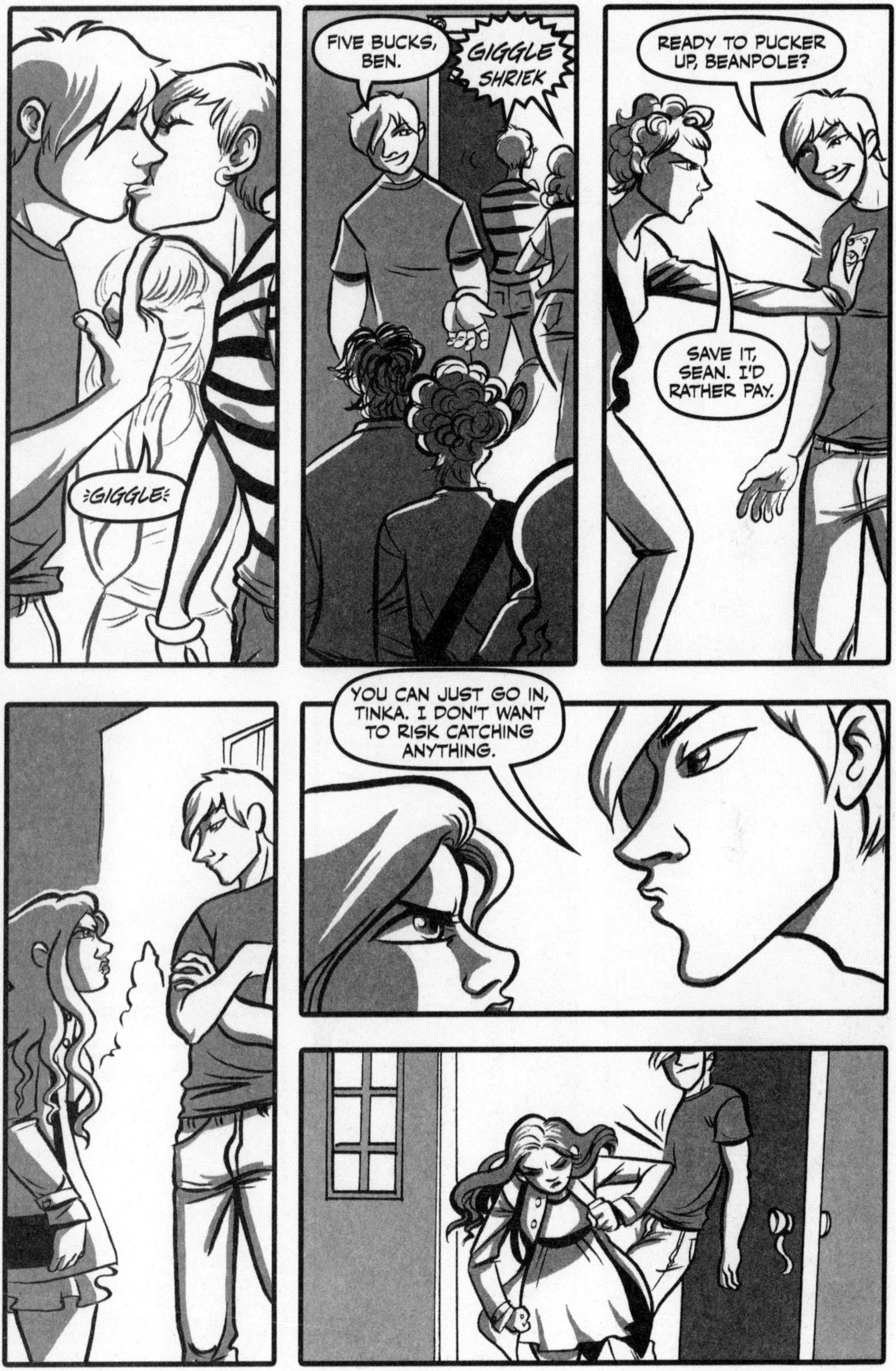
GIGGLE
FIVE BUCKS, BEN.
GIGGLE SHRIEK
READY TO PUCKER UP, BEANPOLE?
SAVE IT, SEAN. I'D RATHER PAY.
YOU CAN JUST GO IN, TINKA. I DON'T WANT TO RISK CATCHING ANYTHING.

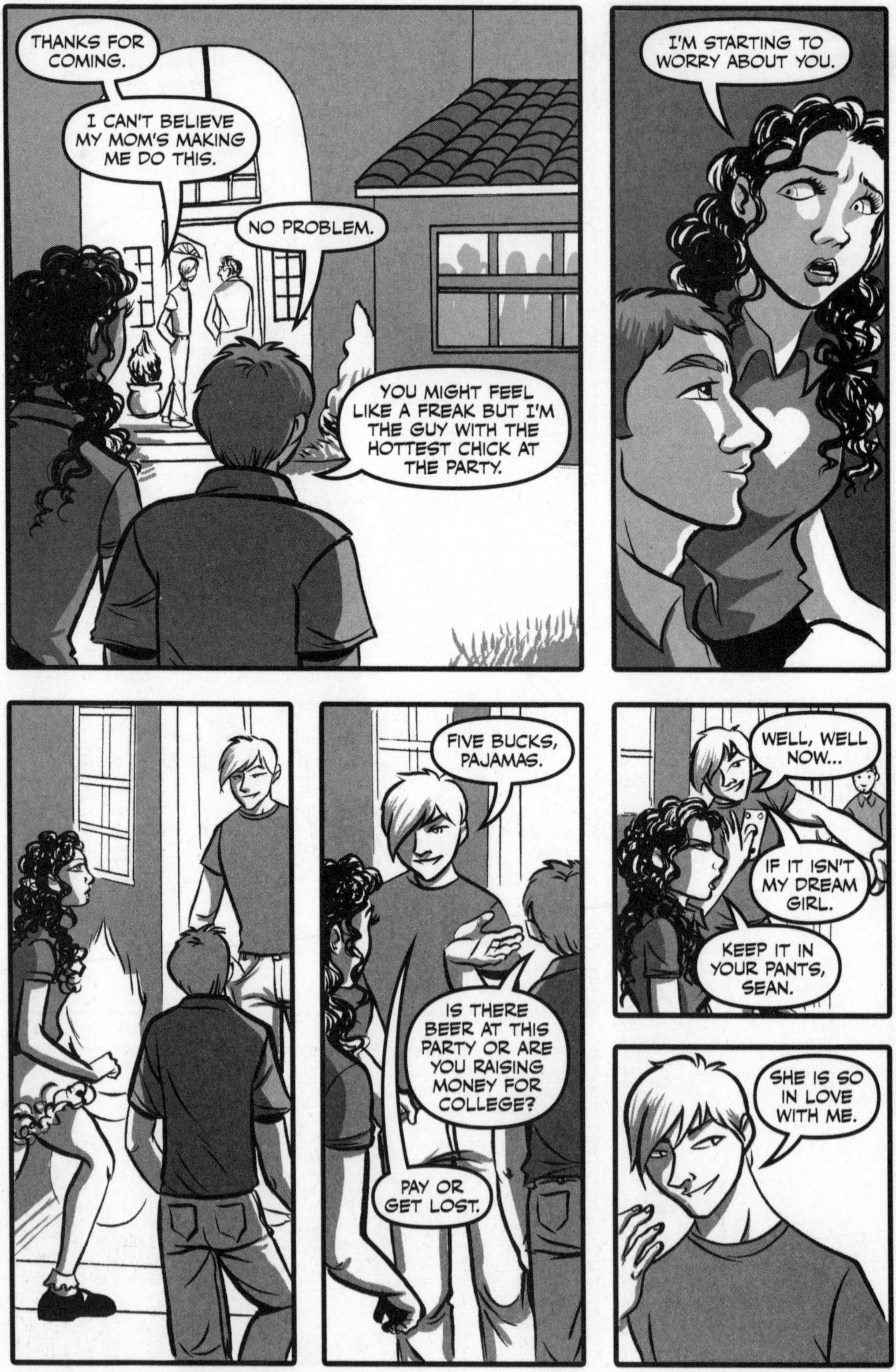
THANKS FOR COMING.
I CAN'T BELIEVE MY MOM'S MAKING ME DO THIS.
NO PROBLEM.
YOU MIGHT FEEL LIKE A FREAK BUT I'M THE GUY WITH THE HOTTEST CHICK AT THE PARTY.
I'M STARTING TO WORRY ABOUT YOU.
FIVE BUCKS, PAJAMAS.
IS THERE BEER AT THIS PARTY OR ARE YOU RAISING MONEY FOR COLLEGE?
PAY OR GET LOST.
WELL, WELL NOW...
IF IT ISN'T MY DREAM GIRL.
KEEP IT IN YOUR PANTS, SEAN.
SHE IS SO IN LOVE WITH ME.

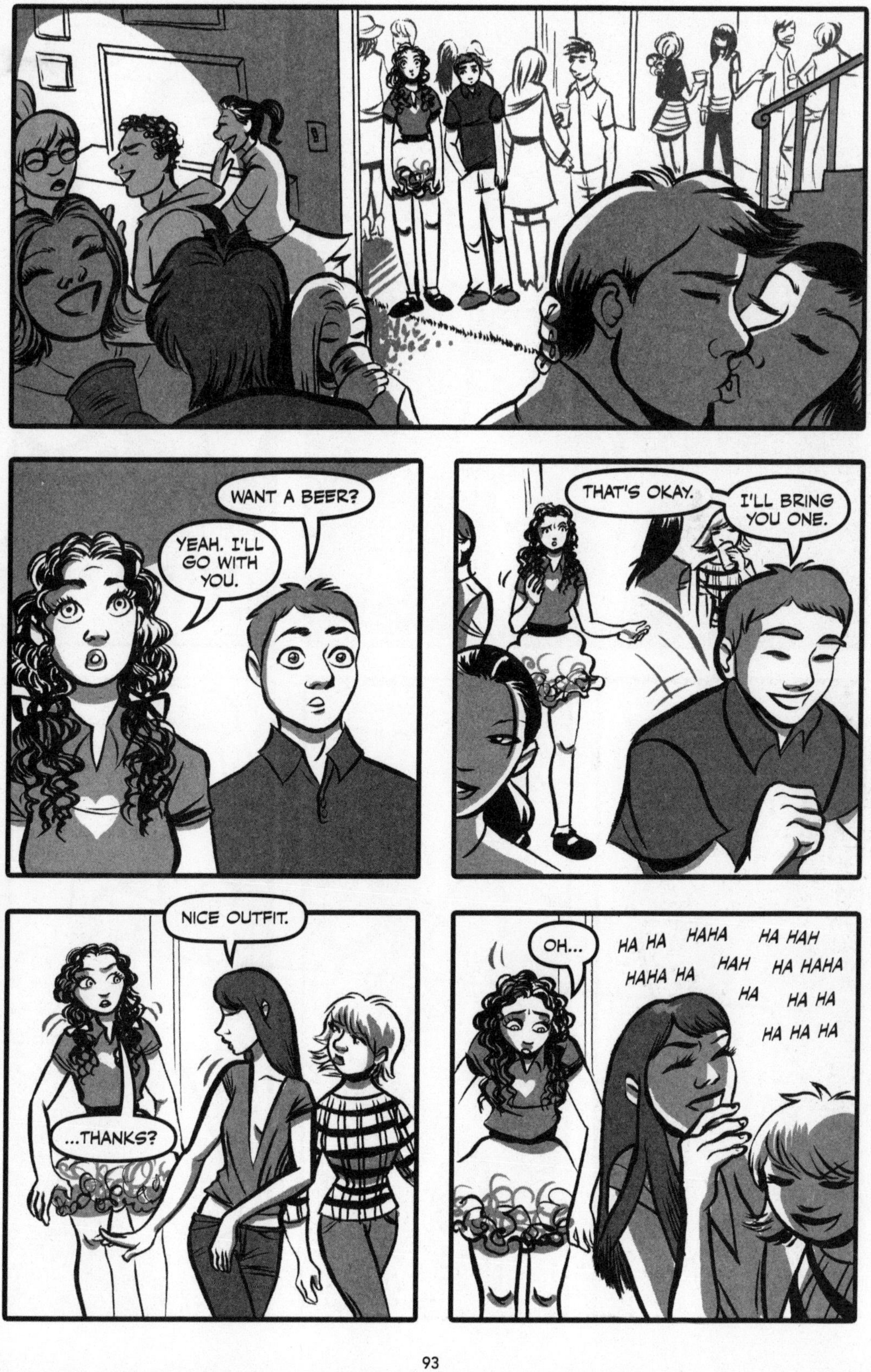
WANT A BEER?
YEAH. I'LL GO WITH YOU.
THAT'S OKAY.
I'LL BRING YOU ONE.
NICE OUTFIT.
...THANKS?
OH...
HA HA HAHA HA HAH
HAHA HA HAH HA HAHA
HA HA HA
HA HA HA

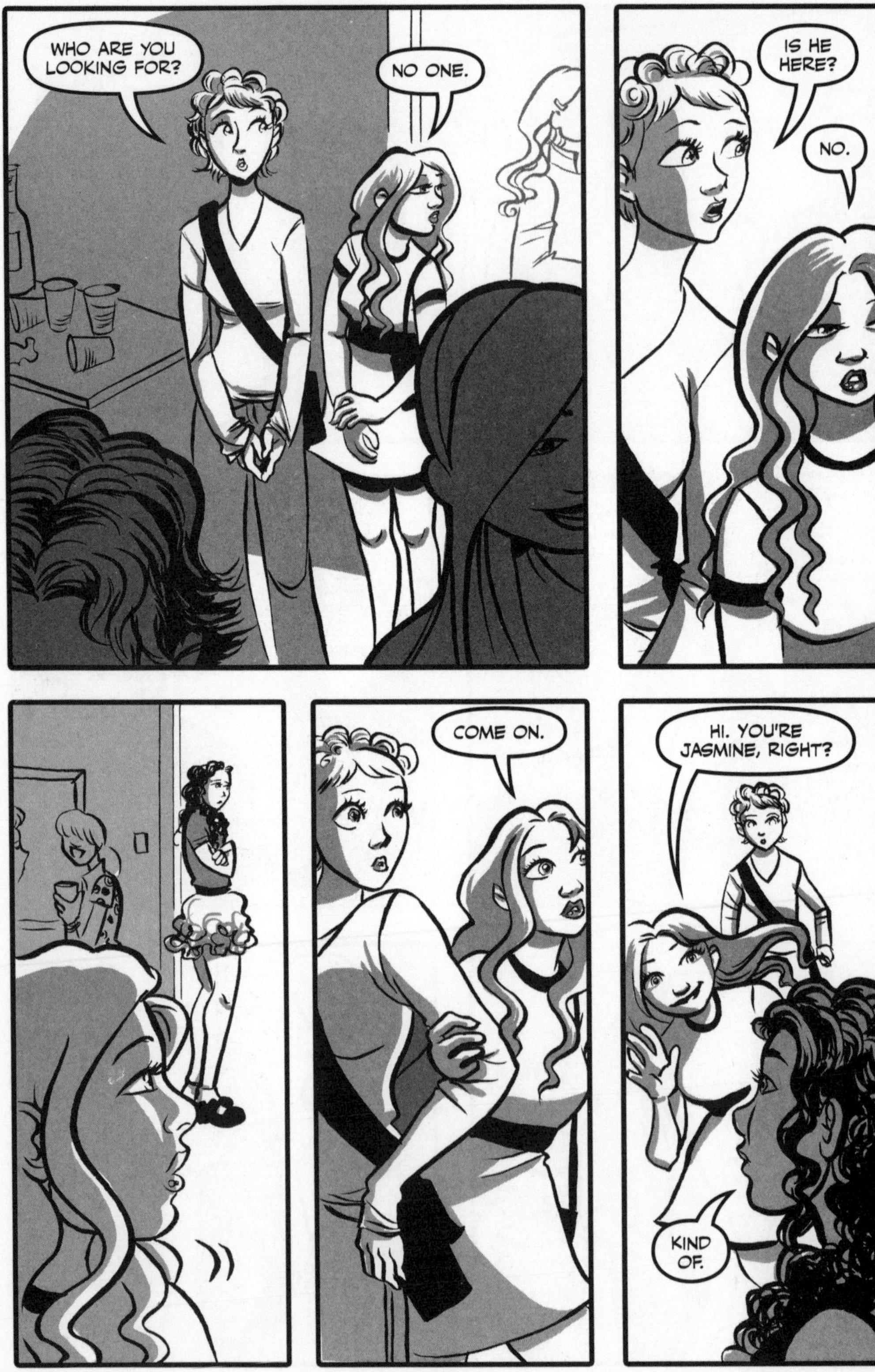
WHO ARE YOU LOOKING FOR?
NO ONE.
IS HE HERE?
NO.
COME ON.
HI. YOU'RE JASMINE, RIGHT?
KIND OF.

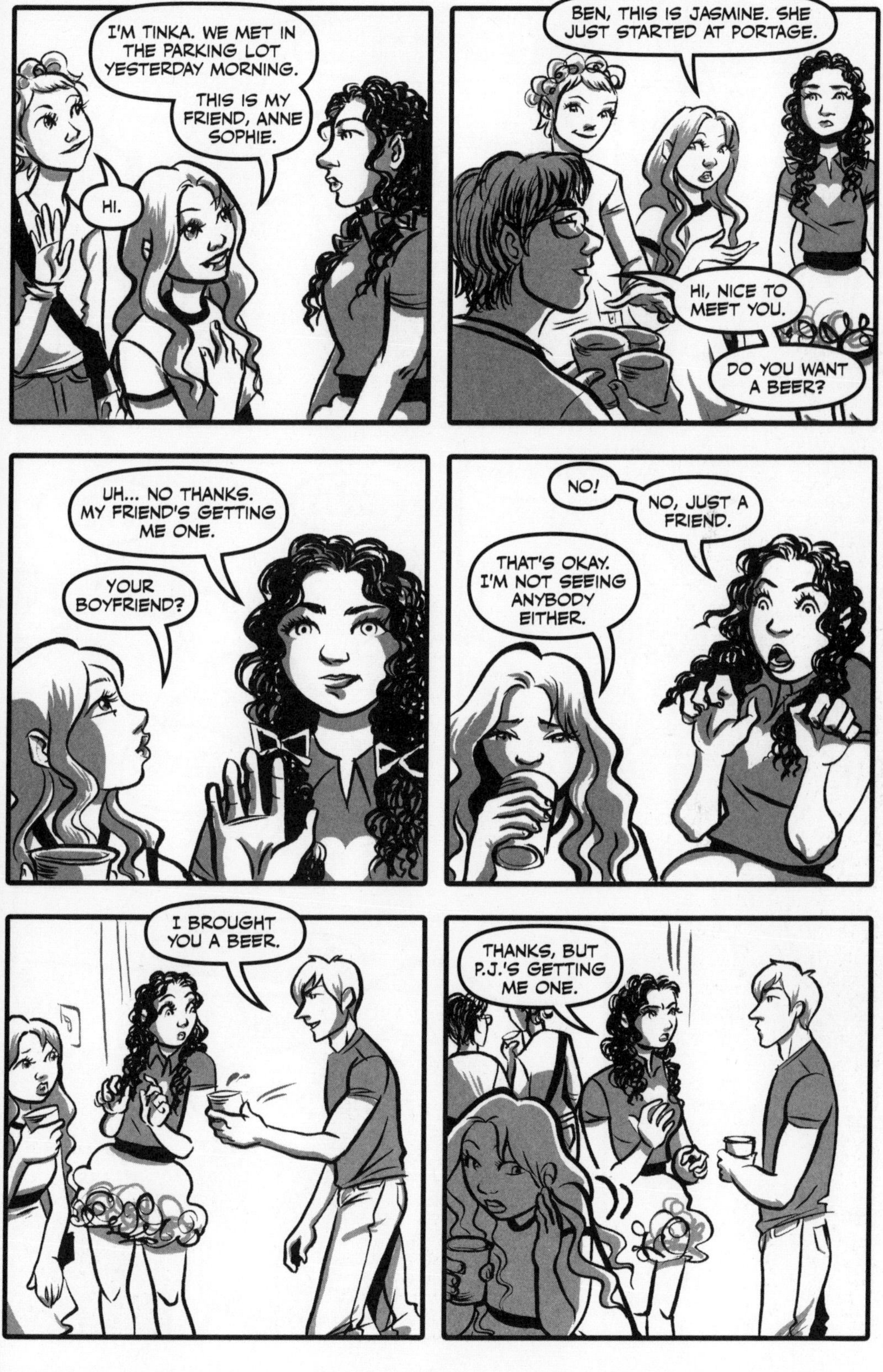
I'M TINKA. WE MET IN THE PARKING LOT YESTERDAY MORNING.
THIS IS MY FRIEND, ANNE SOPHIE.
HI.
BEN, THIS IS JASMINE. SHE JUST STARTED AT PORTAGE.
HI, NICE TO MEET YOU.
DO YOU WANT A BEER?
UH... NO THANKS. MY FRIEND'S GETTING ME ONE.
YOUR BOYFRIEND?
NO!
NO, JUST A FRIEND.
THAT'S OKAY. I'M NOT SEEING ANYBODY EITHER.
I BROUGHT YOU A BEER.
THANKS, BUT P.J.'S GETTING ME ONE.

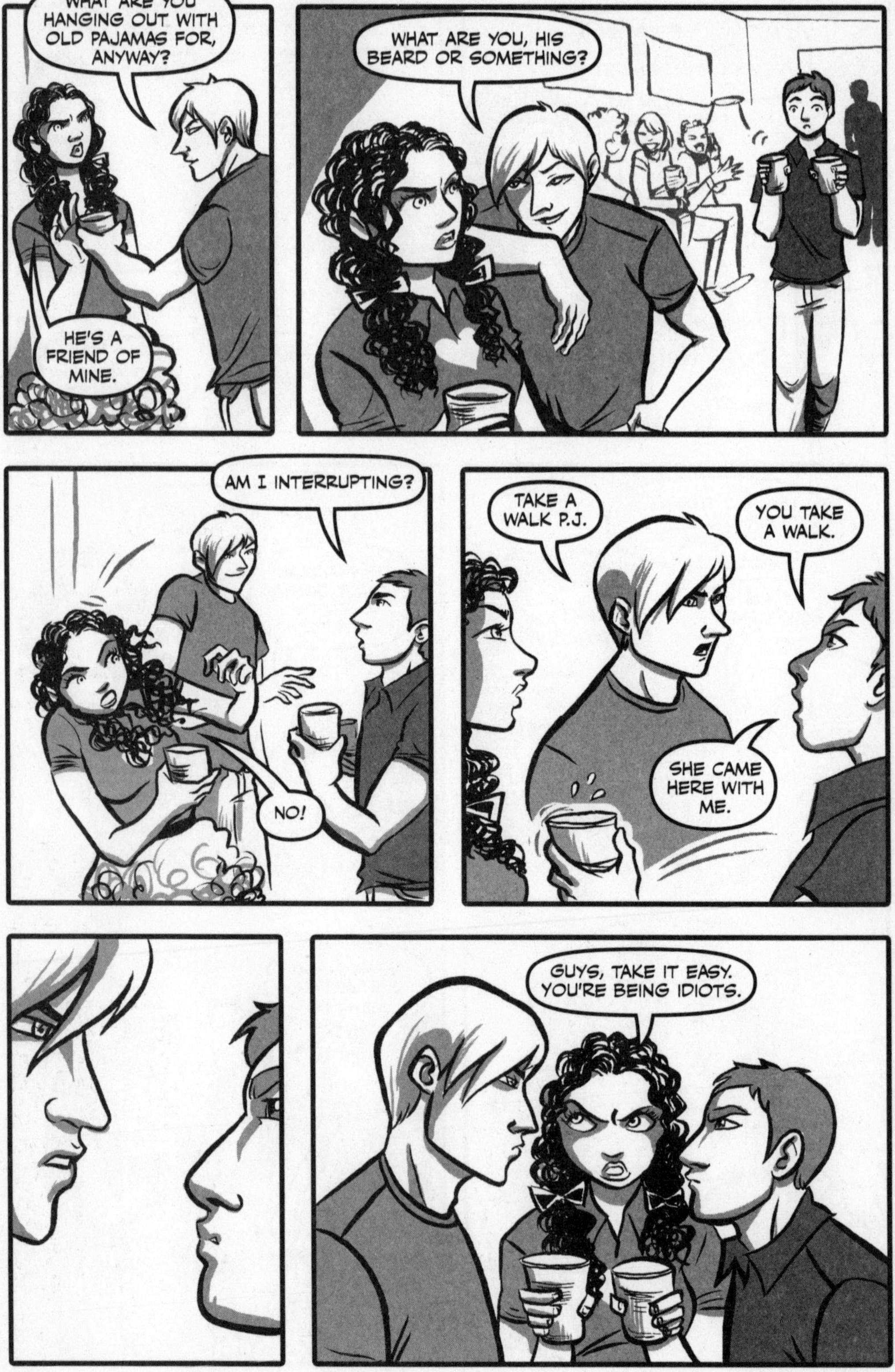
WHAT ARE YOU HANGING OUT WITH OLD PAJAMAS FOR, ANYWAY?
HE'S A FRIEND OF MINE.
WHAT ARE YOU, HIS BEARD OR SOMETHING?
AM I INTERRUPTING?
NO!
TAKE A WALK P.J.
YOU TAKE A WALK.
SHE CAME HERE WITH ME.
GUYS, TAKE IT EASY. YOU'RE BEING IDIOTS.

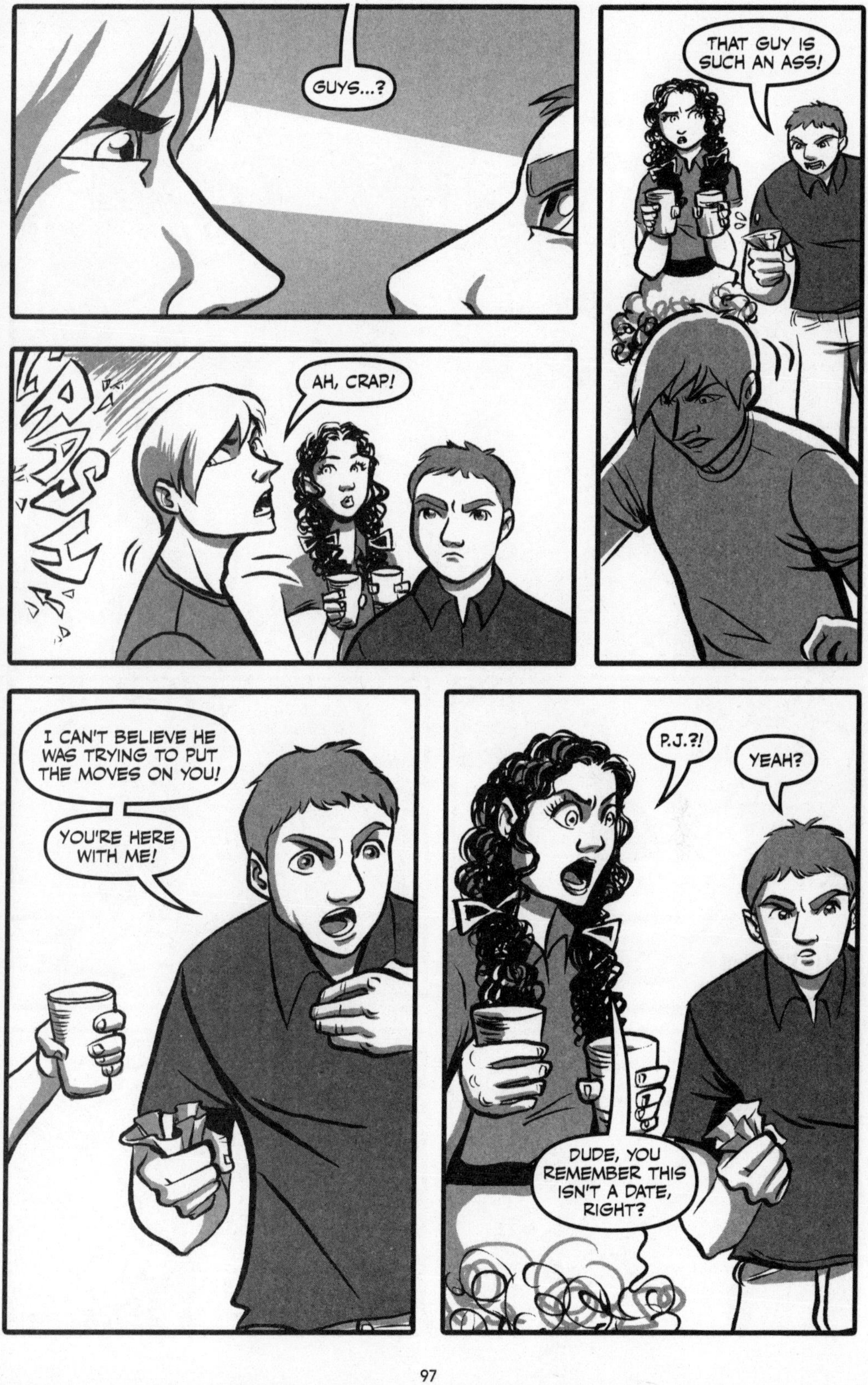

GUYS...?
THAT GUY IS SUCH AN ASS!
AH, CRAP!
I CAN'T BELIEVE HE WAS TRYING TO PUT THE MOVES ON YOU!
YOU'RE HERE WITH ME!
P.J.?!
YEAH?
DUDE, YOU REMEMBER THIS ISN'T A DATE, RIGHT?

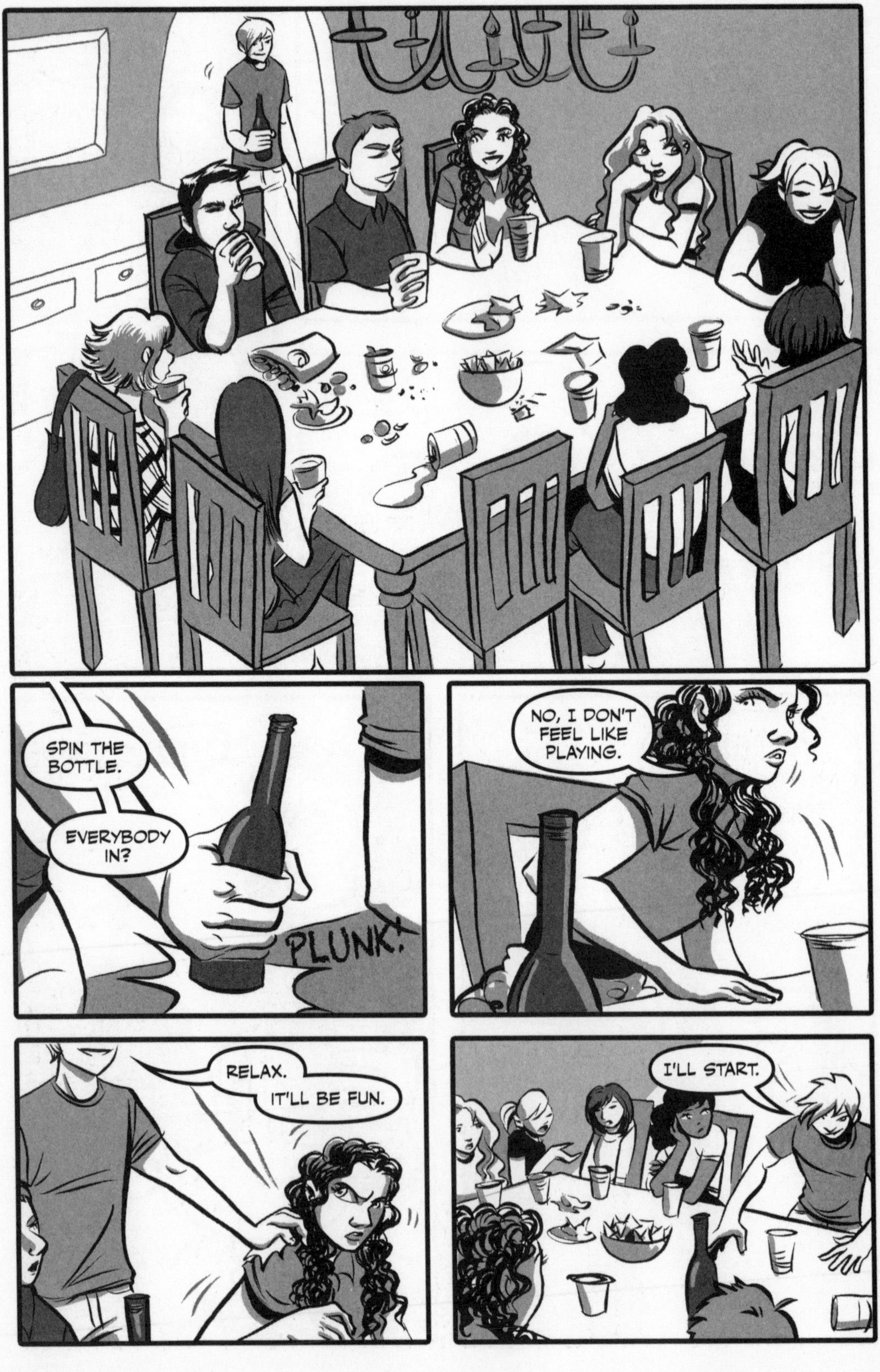
SPIN THE BOTTLE.
EVERYBODY IN?
PLUNK!
NO, I DON'T FEEL LIKE PLAYING.
RELAX.
IT'LL BE FUN.
I'LL START.

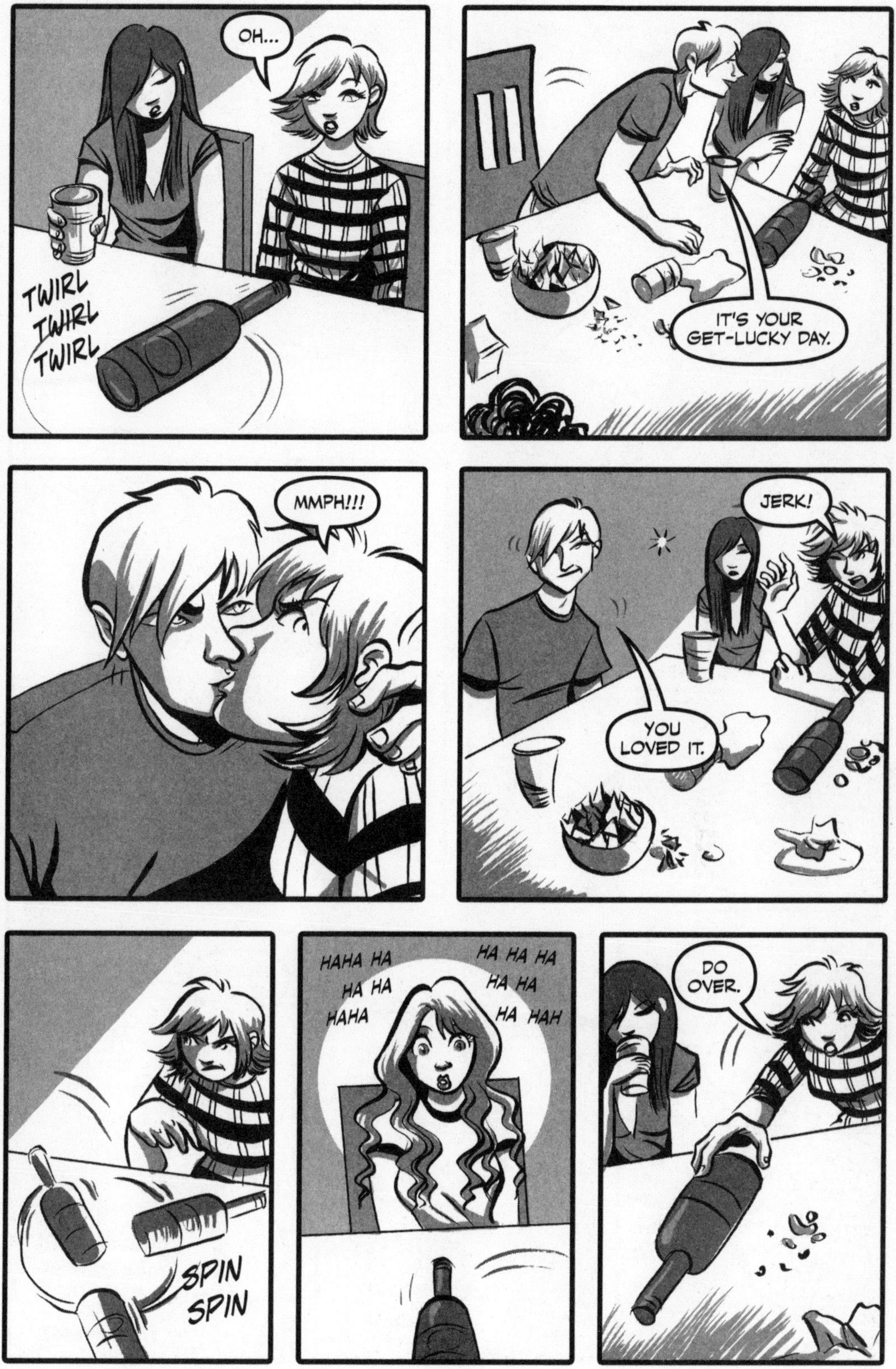
OH...
TWIRL
TWIRL
TWIRL
IT'S YOUR GET-LUCKY DAY.
MMPH!!!
JERK!
YOU LOVED IT.
SPIN
SPIN
HAHA HA
HA HA
HAHA
HA HA HA
HA HA
HA HAH
DO OVER.

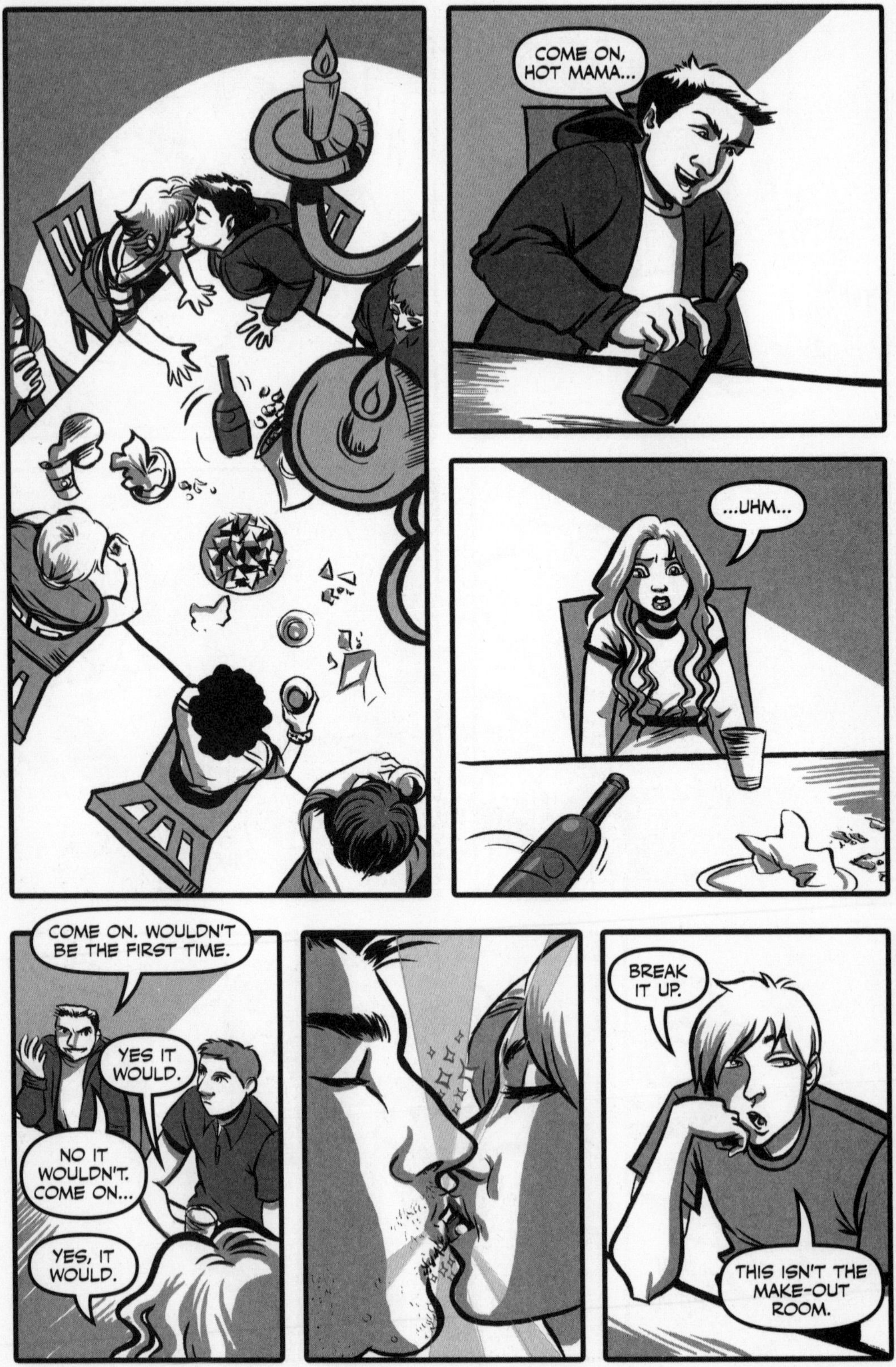
COME ON, HOT MAMA...
...UHM...
COME ON. WOULDN'T BE THE FIRST TIME.
YES IT WOULD.
NO IT WOULDN'T. COME ON...
YES, IT WOULD.
BREAK IT UP.
THIS ISN'T THE MAKE-OUT ROOM.

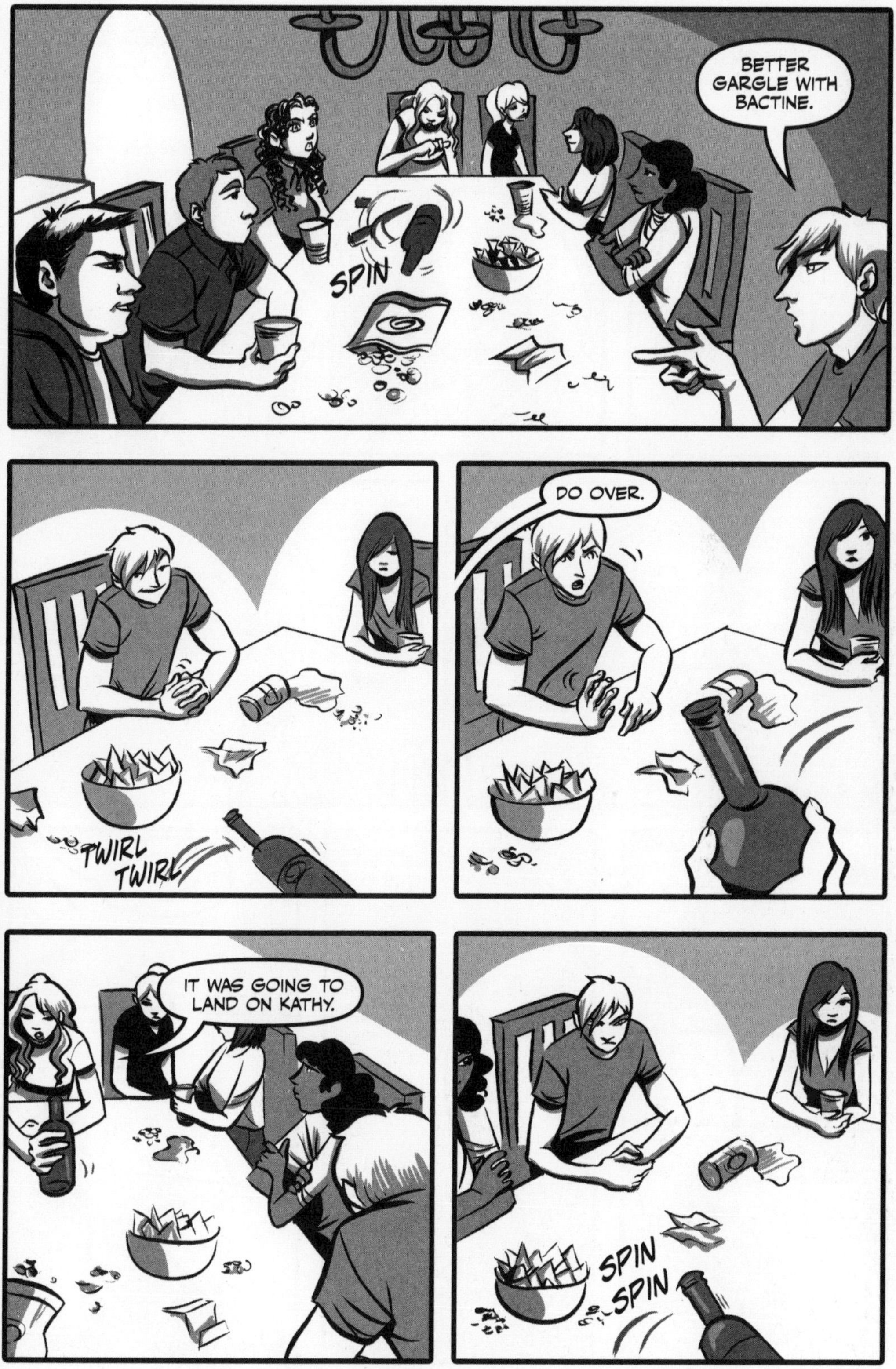
BETTER GARGLE WITH BACTINE.
SPIN
TWIRL TWIRL
DO OVER.
IT WAS GOING TO LAND ON KATHY.
SPIN SPIN

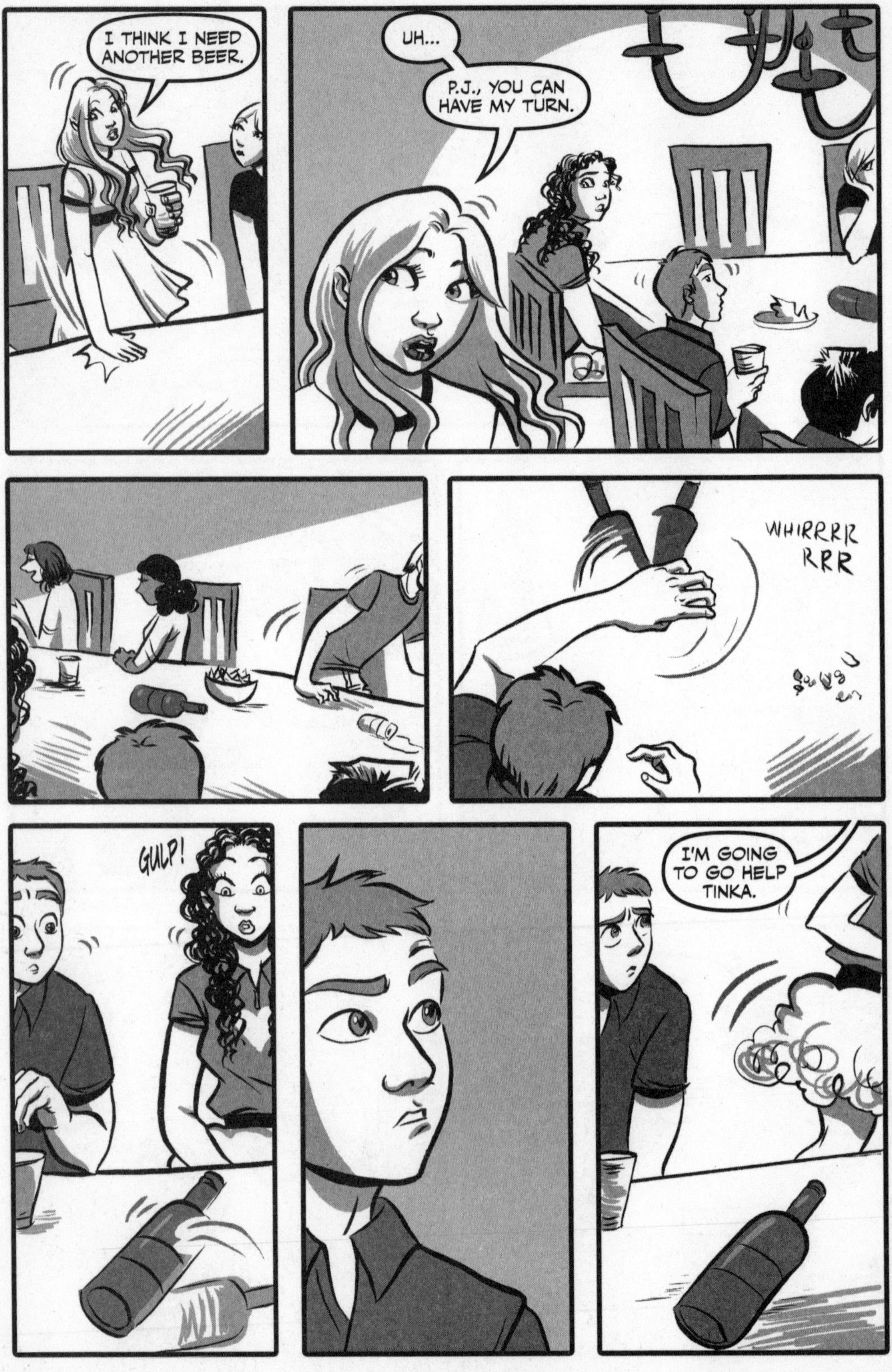
I THINK I NEED ANOTHER BEER.
UH...
P.J., YOU CAN HAVE MY TURN.
WHIRRRR RRR
GULP!
I'M GOING TO GO HELP TINKA.

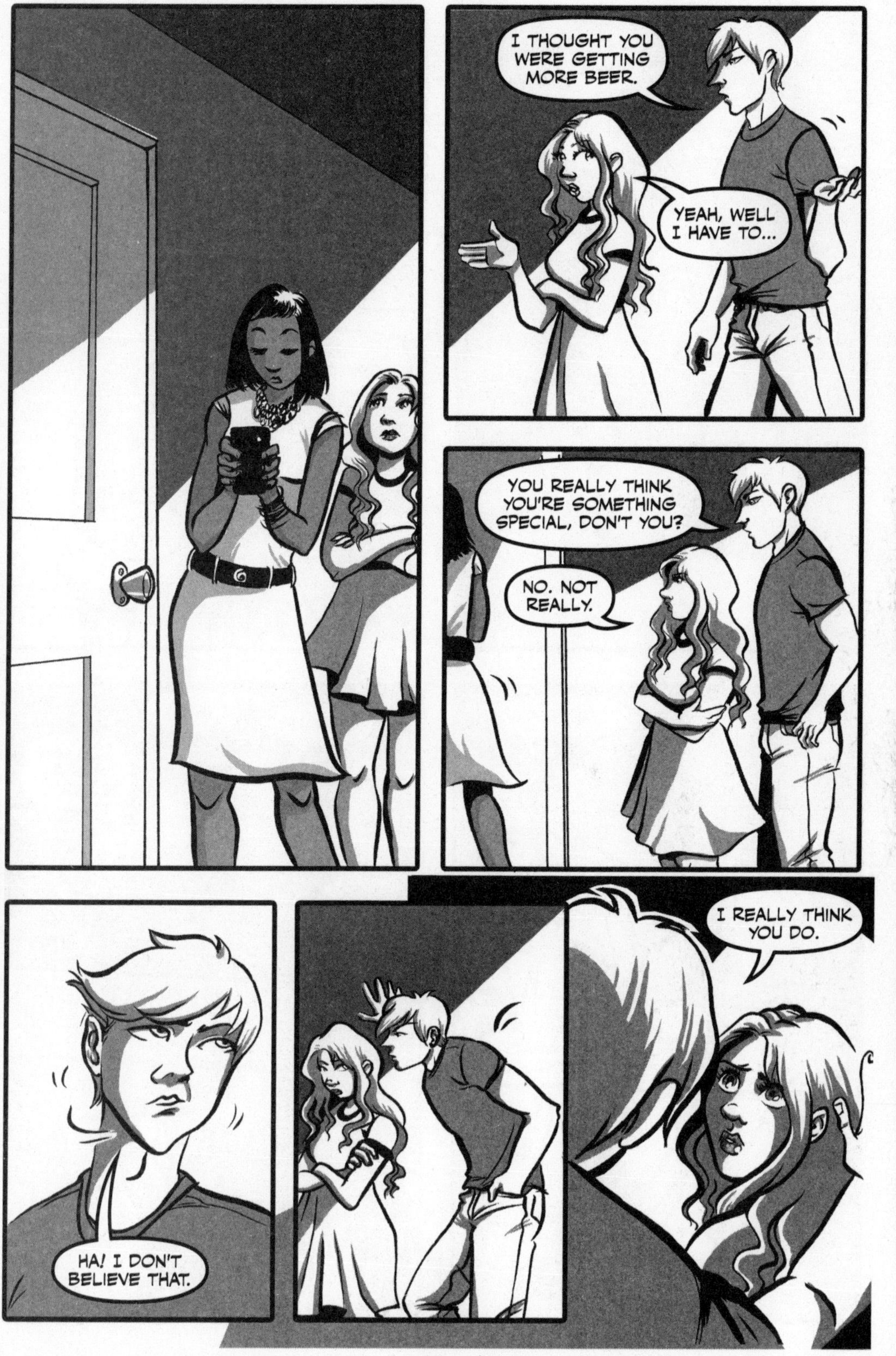
I THOUGHT YOU WERE GETTING MORE BEER.
YEAH, WELL I HAVE TO...
YOU REALLY THINK YOU'RE SOMETHING SPECIAL, DON'T YOU?
NO. NOT REALLY.
HA! I DON'T BELIEVE THAT.
I REALLY THINK YOU DO.

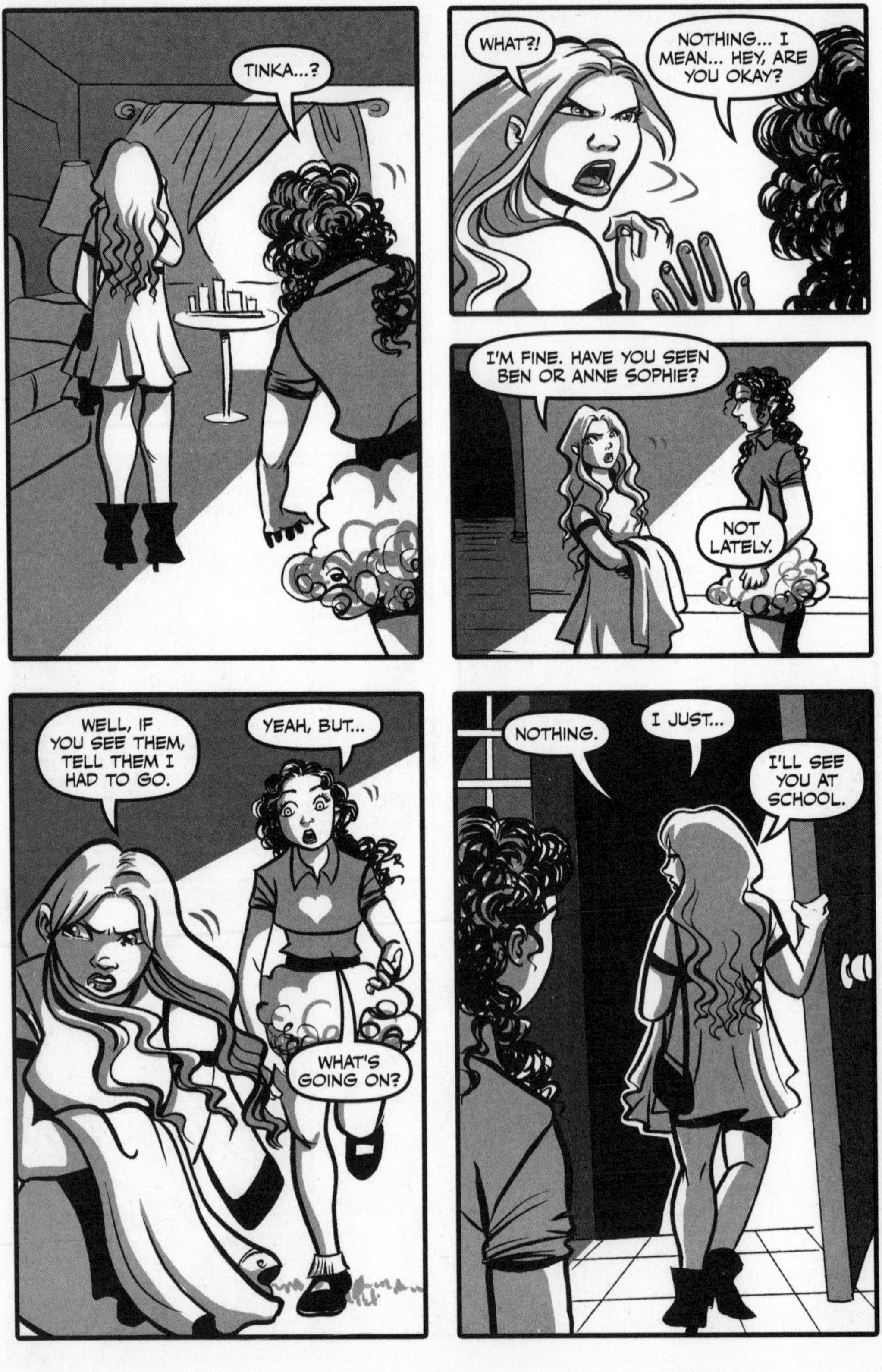
TINKA...?
WHAT?!
NOTHING... I MEAN... HEY, ARE YOU OKAY?
I'M FINE. HAVE YOU SEEN BEN OR ANNE SOPHIE?
NOT LATELY.
WELL, IF YOU SEE THEM, TELL THEM I HAD TO GO.
YEAH, BUT...
WHAT'S GOING ON?
NOTHING.
I JUST...
I'LL SEE YOU AT SCHOOL.

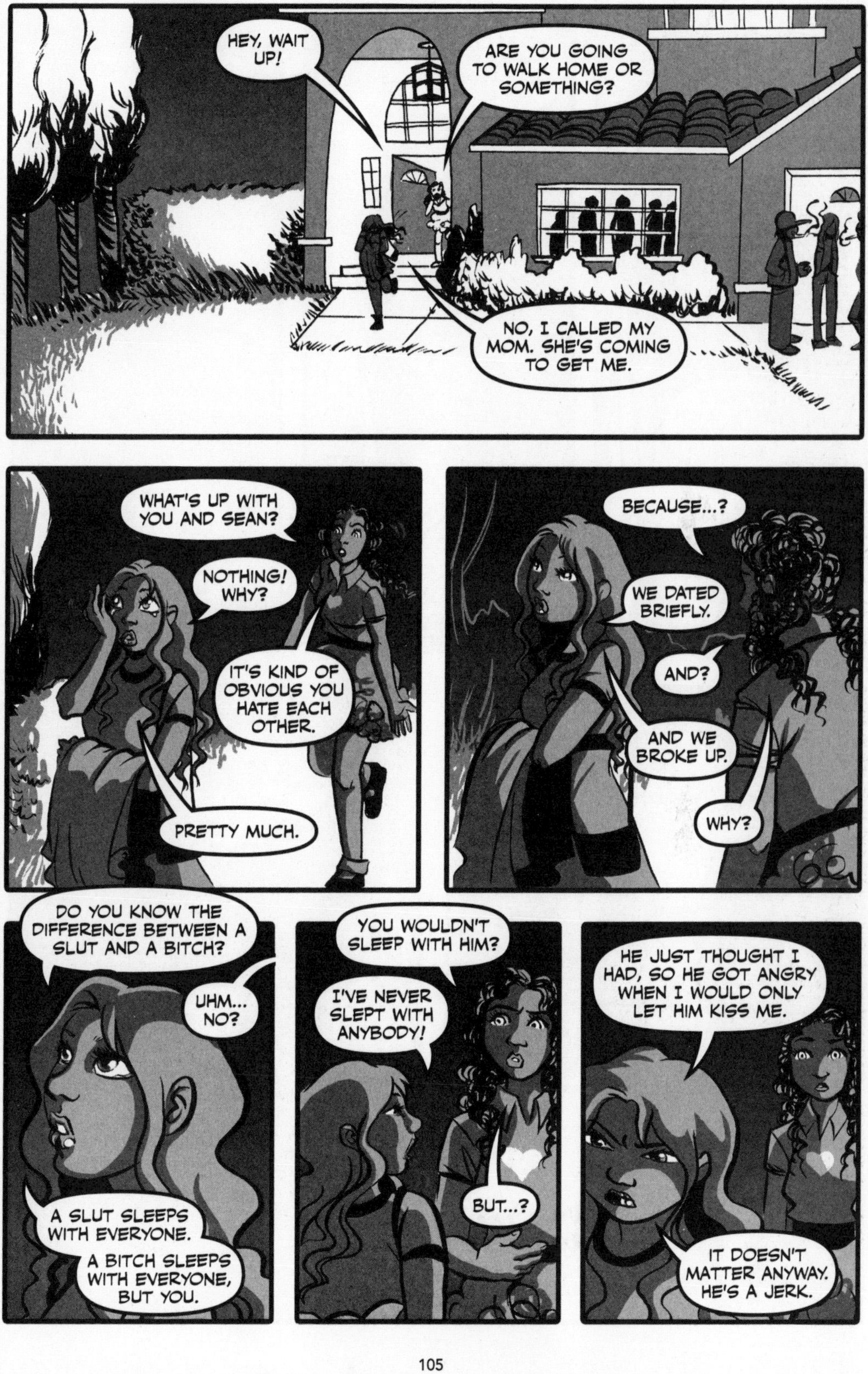
HEY, WAIT UP!
ARE YOU GOING TO WALK HOME OR SOMETHING?
NO, I CALLED MY MOM. SHE'S COMING TO GET ME.
WHAT'S UP WITH YOU AND SEAN?
NOTHING! WHY?
IT'S KIND OF OBVIOUS YOU HATE EACH OTHER.
PRETTY MUCH.
BECAUSE...?
WE DATED BRIEFLY.
AND?
AND WE BROKE UP.
WHY?
DO YOU KNOW THE DIFFERENCE BETWEEN A SLUT AND A BITCH?
UHM... NO?
A SLUT SLEEPS WITH EVERYONE.
A BITCH SLEEPS WITH EVERYONE, BUT YOU.
YOU WOULDN'T SLEEP WITH HIM?
I'VE NEVER SLEPT WITH ANYBODY!
BUT...?
HE JUST THOUGHT I HAD, SO HE GOT ANGRY WHEN I WOULD ONLY LET HIM KISS ME.
IT DOESN'T MATTER ANYWAY. HE'S A JERK.

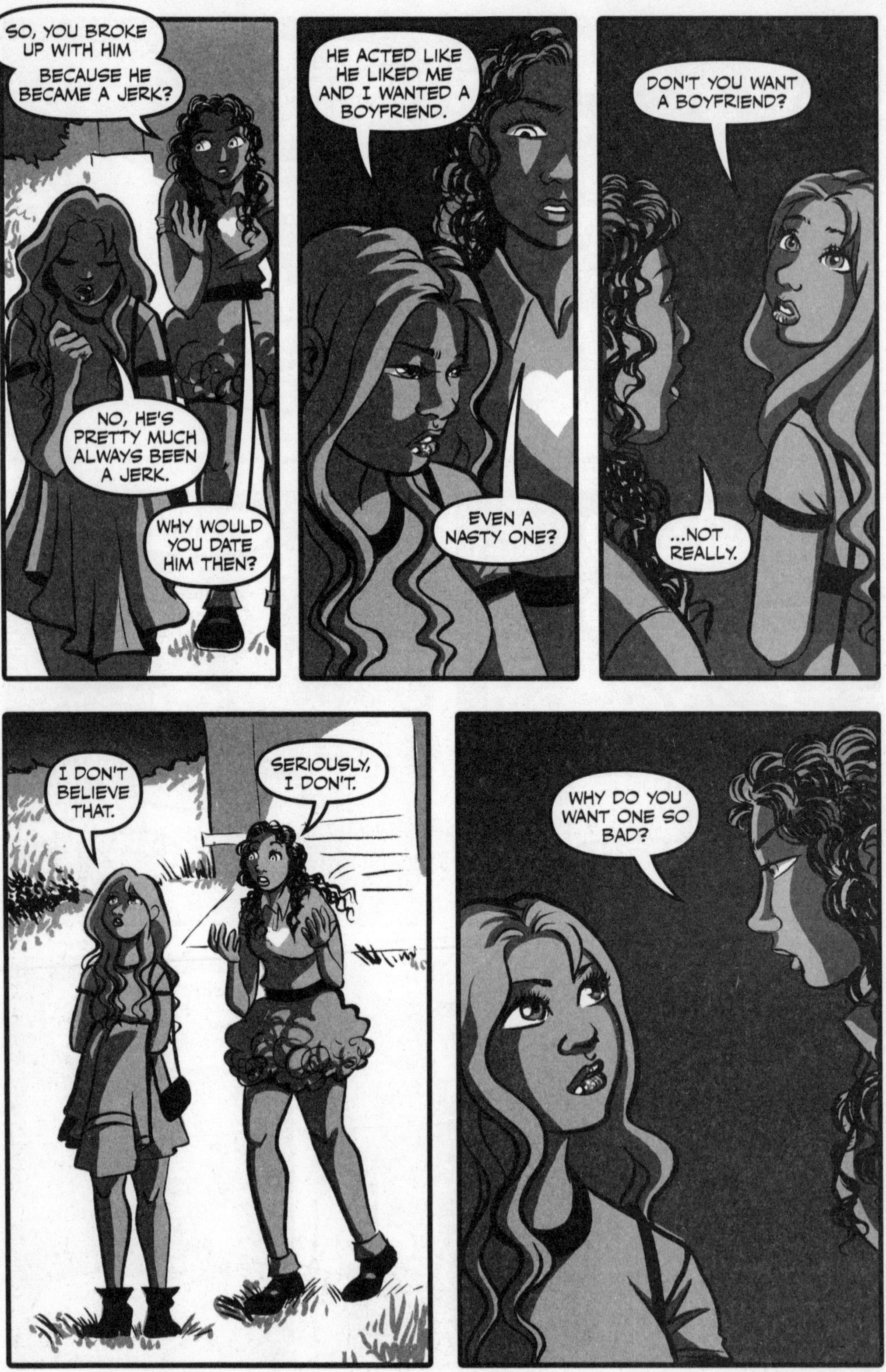
SO, YOU BROKE UP WITH HIM BECAUSE HE BECAME A JERK?
NO, HE'S PRETTY MUCH ALWAYS BEEN A JERK.
WHY WOULD YOU DATE HIM THEN?
HE ACTED LIKE HE LIKED ME AND I WANTED A BOYFRIEND.
EVEN A NASTY ONE?
DON'T YOU WANT A BOYFRIEND?
...NOT REALLY.
I DON'T BELIEVE THAT.
SERIOUSLY, I DON'T.
WHY DO YOU WANT ONE SO BAD?

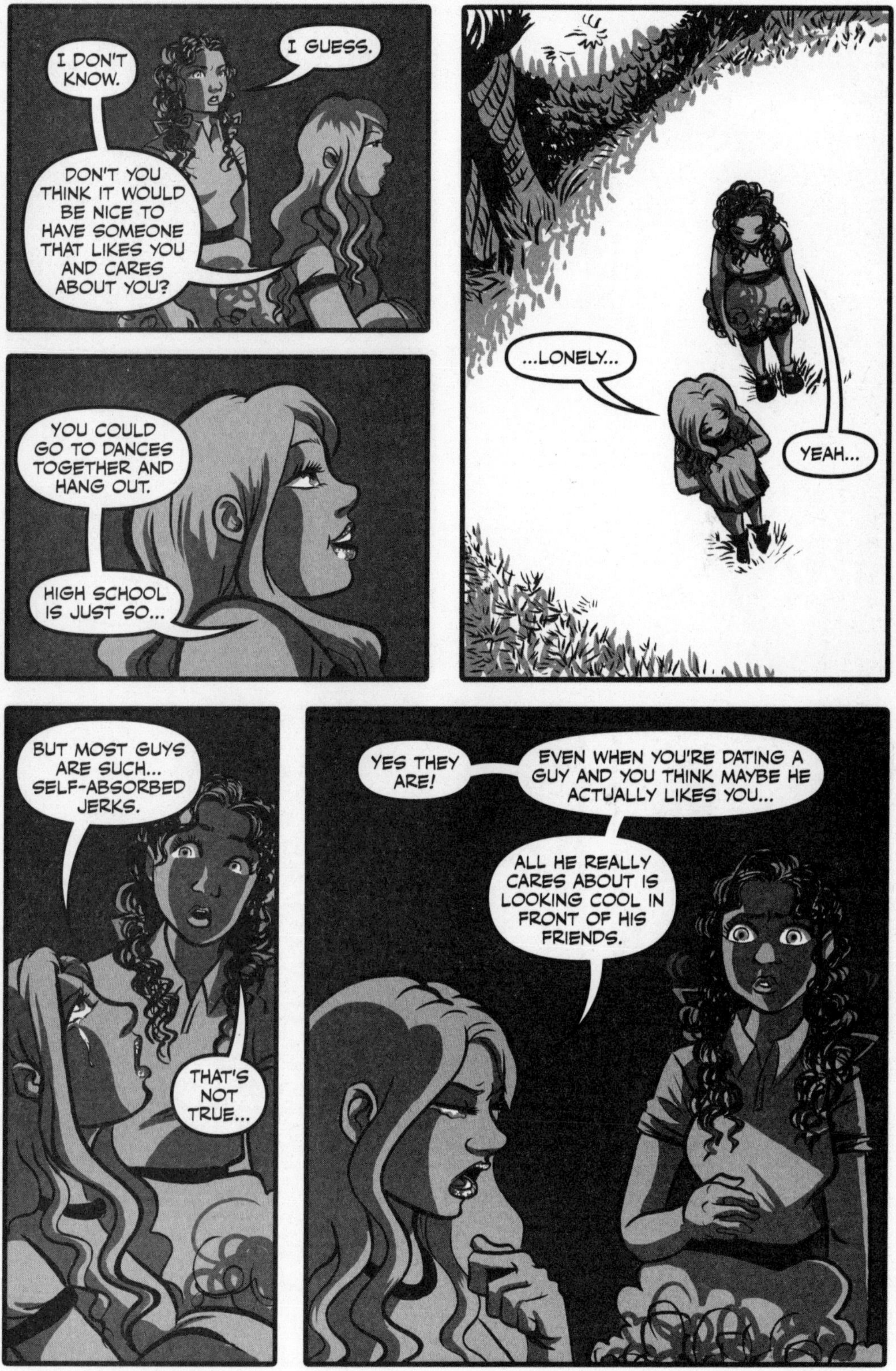

I DON'T KNOW.
I GUESS.
DON'T YOU THINK IT WOULD BE NICE TO HAVE SOMEONE THAT LIKES YOU AND CARES ABOUT YOU?
YOU COULD GO TO DANCES TOGETHER AND HANG OUT.
HIGH SCHOOL IS JUST SO...
...LONELY...
YEAH...
BUT MOST GUYS ARE SUCH... SELF-ABSORBED JERKS.
THAT'S NOT TRUE...
YES THEY ARE!
EVEN WHEN YOU'RE DATING A GUY AND YOU THINK MAYBE HE ACTUALLY LIKES YOU...
ALL HE REALLY CARES ABOUT IS LOOKING COOL IN FRONT OF HIS FRIENDS.

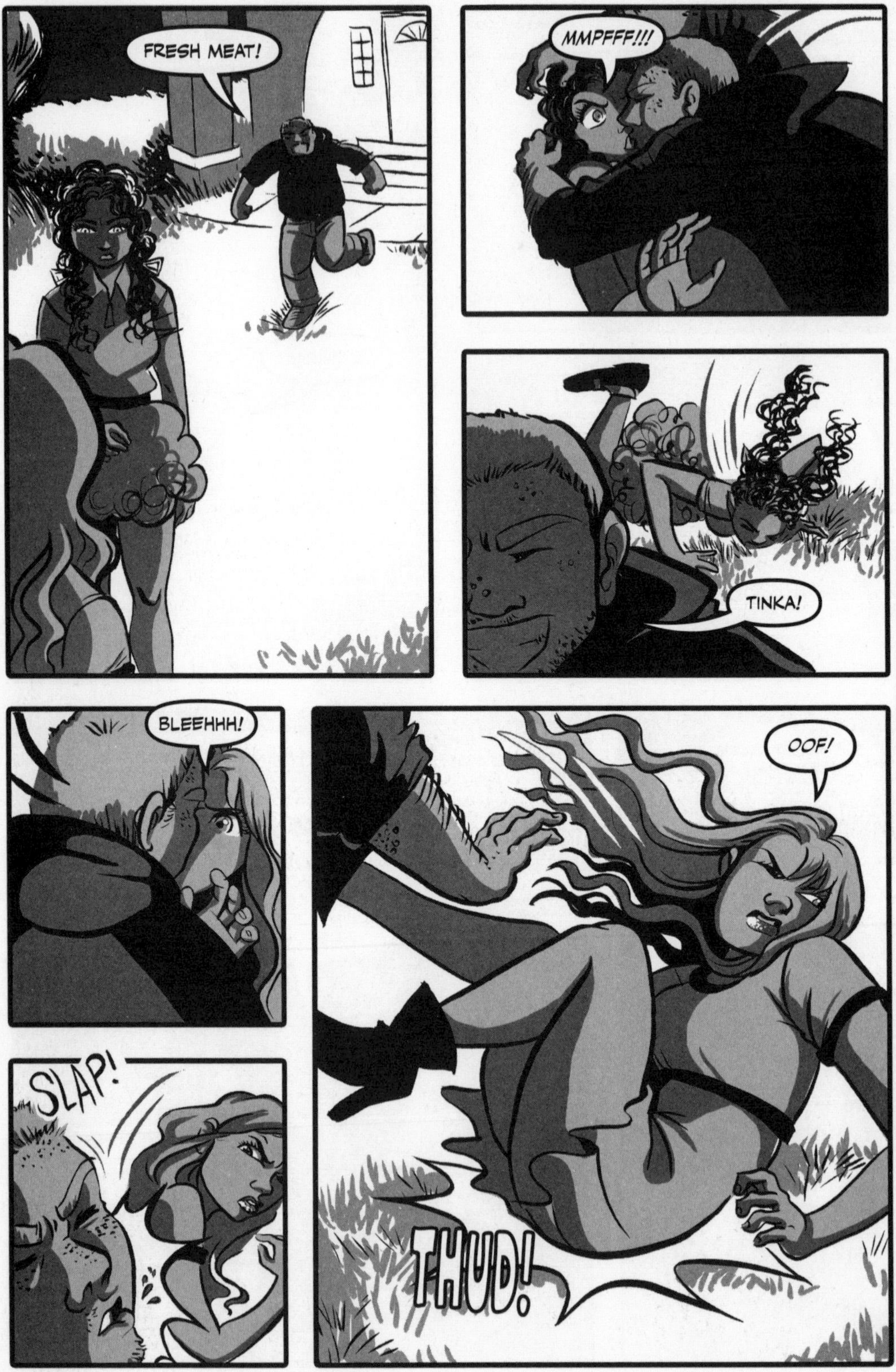
FRESH MEAT!
MMPFFF!!!
TINKA!
BLEEHHH!
SLAP!
OOF!
THUD!

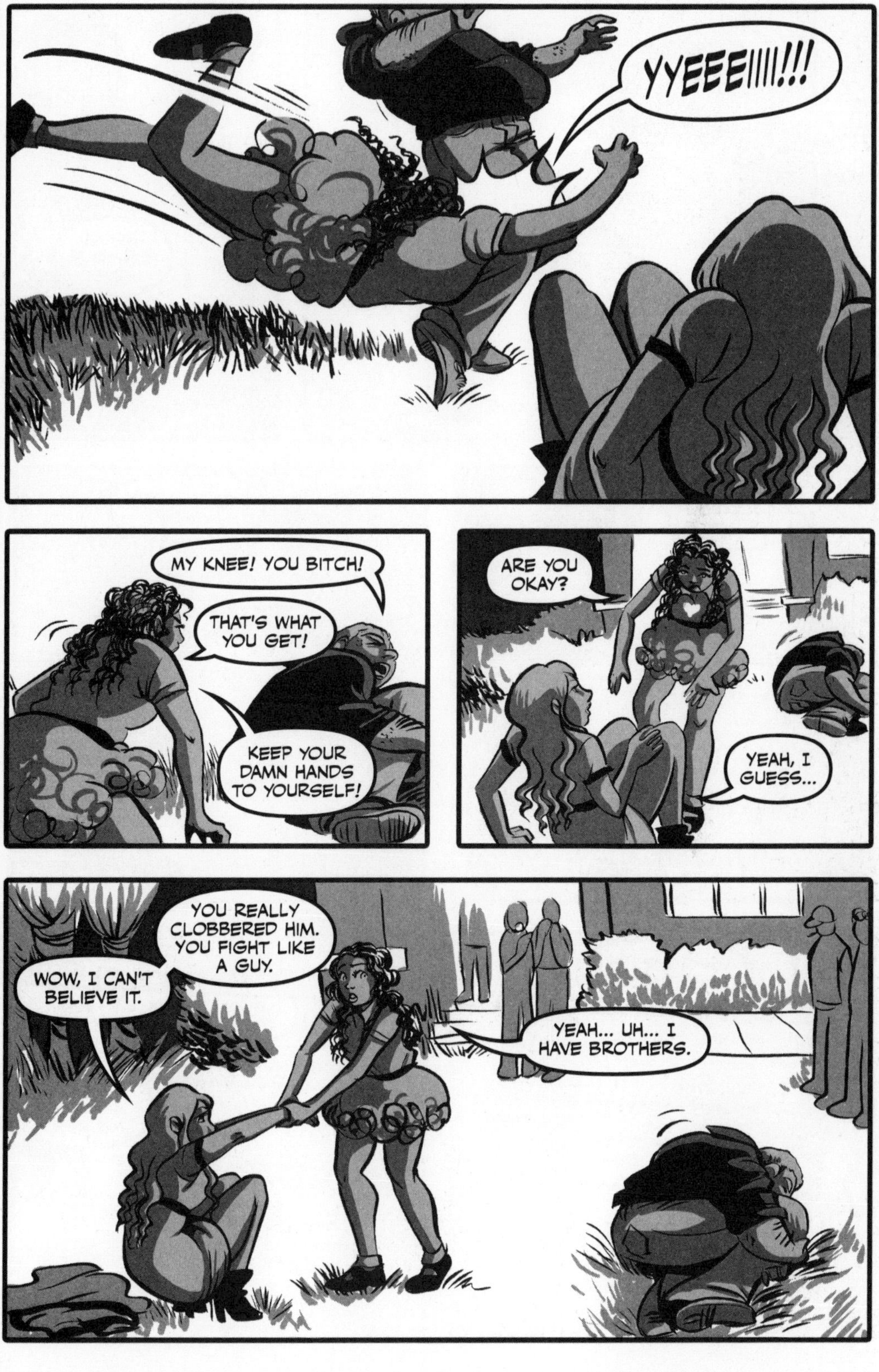
YYEEEIIIII!!!
MY KNEE! YOU BITCH!
THAT'S WHAT YOU GET!
KEEP YOUR DAMN HANDS TO YOURSELF!
ARE YOU OKAY?
YEAH, I GUESS...
WOW, I CAN'T BELIEVE IT.
YOU REALLY CLOBBERED HIM. YOU FIGHT LIKE A GUY.
YEAH... UH... I HAVE BROTHERS.

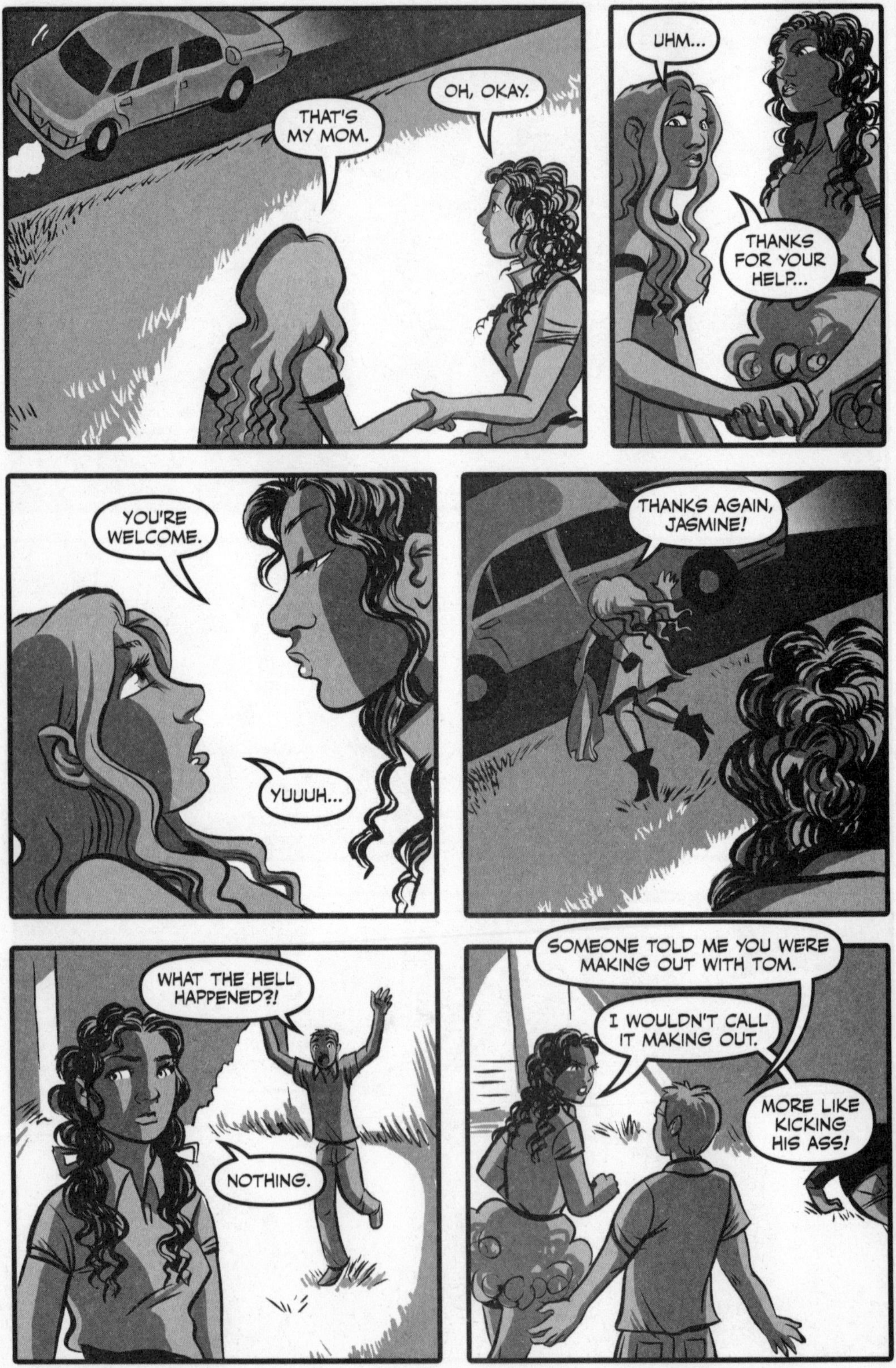
THAT'S MY MOM.
OH, OKAY.
UHM...
THANKS FOR YOUR HELP...
YOU'RE WELCOME.
YUUUH...
THANKS AGAIN, JASMINE!
WHAT THE HELL HAPPENED?!
NOTHING.
SOMEONE TOLD ME YOU WERE MAKING OUT WITH TOM.
I WOULDN'T CALL IT MAKING OUT.
MORE LIKE KICKING HIS ASS!

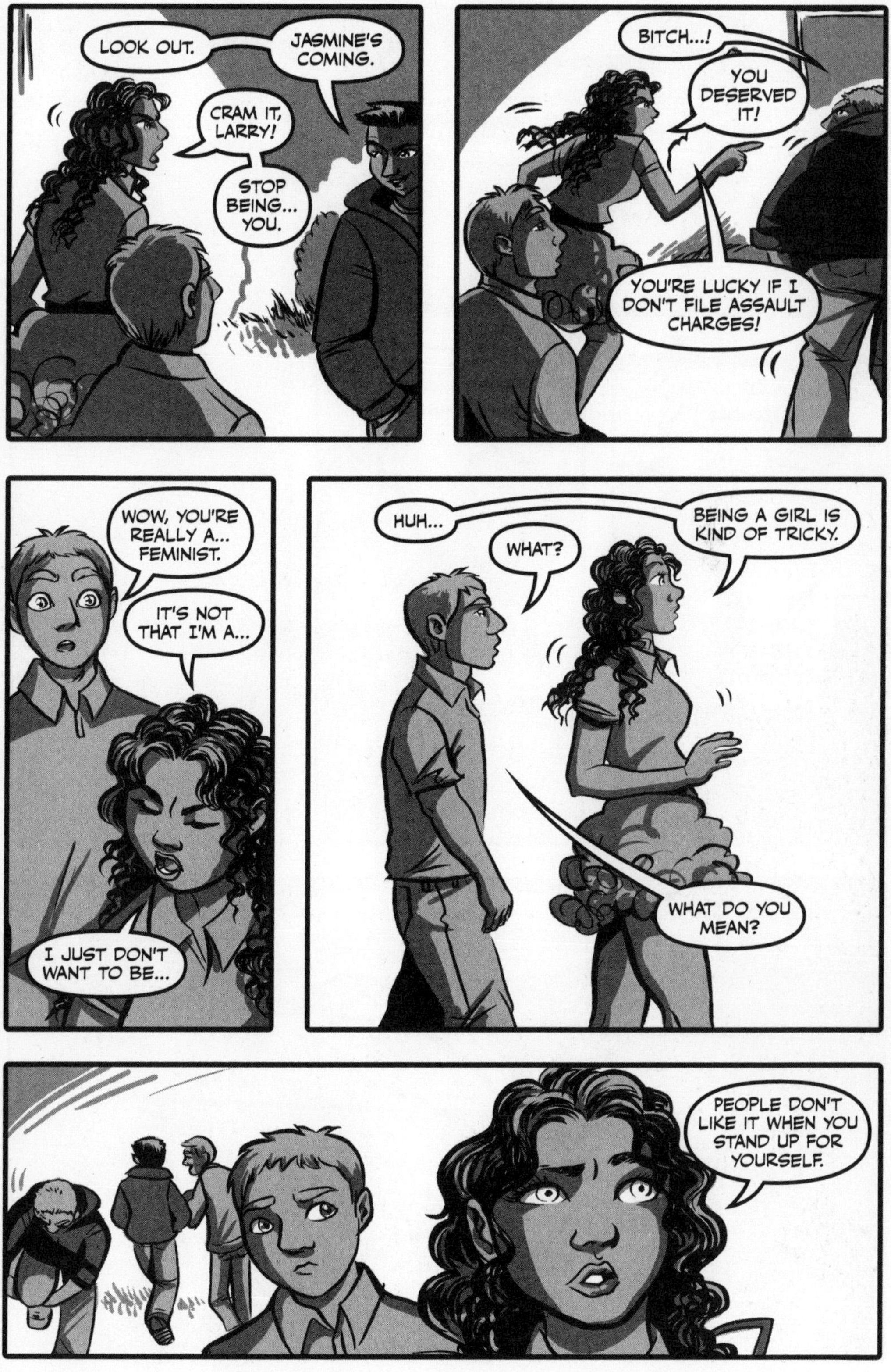
LOOK OUT.
JASMINE'S COMING.
CRAM IT, LARRY!
STOP BEING... YOU.
BITCH...!
YOU DESERVED IT!
YOU'RE LUCKY IF I DON'T FILE ASSAULT CHARGES!
WOW, YOU'RE REALLY A... FEMINIST.
IT'S NOT THAT I'M A...
I JUST DON'T WANT TO BE...
HUH...
BEING A GIRL IS KIND OF TRICKY.
WHAT?
WHAT DO YOU MEAN?
PEOPLE DON'T LIKE IT WHEN YOU STAND UP FOR YOURSELF.

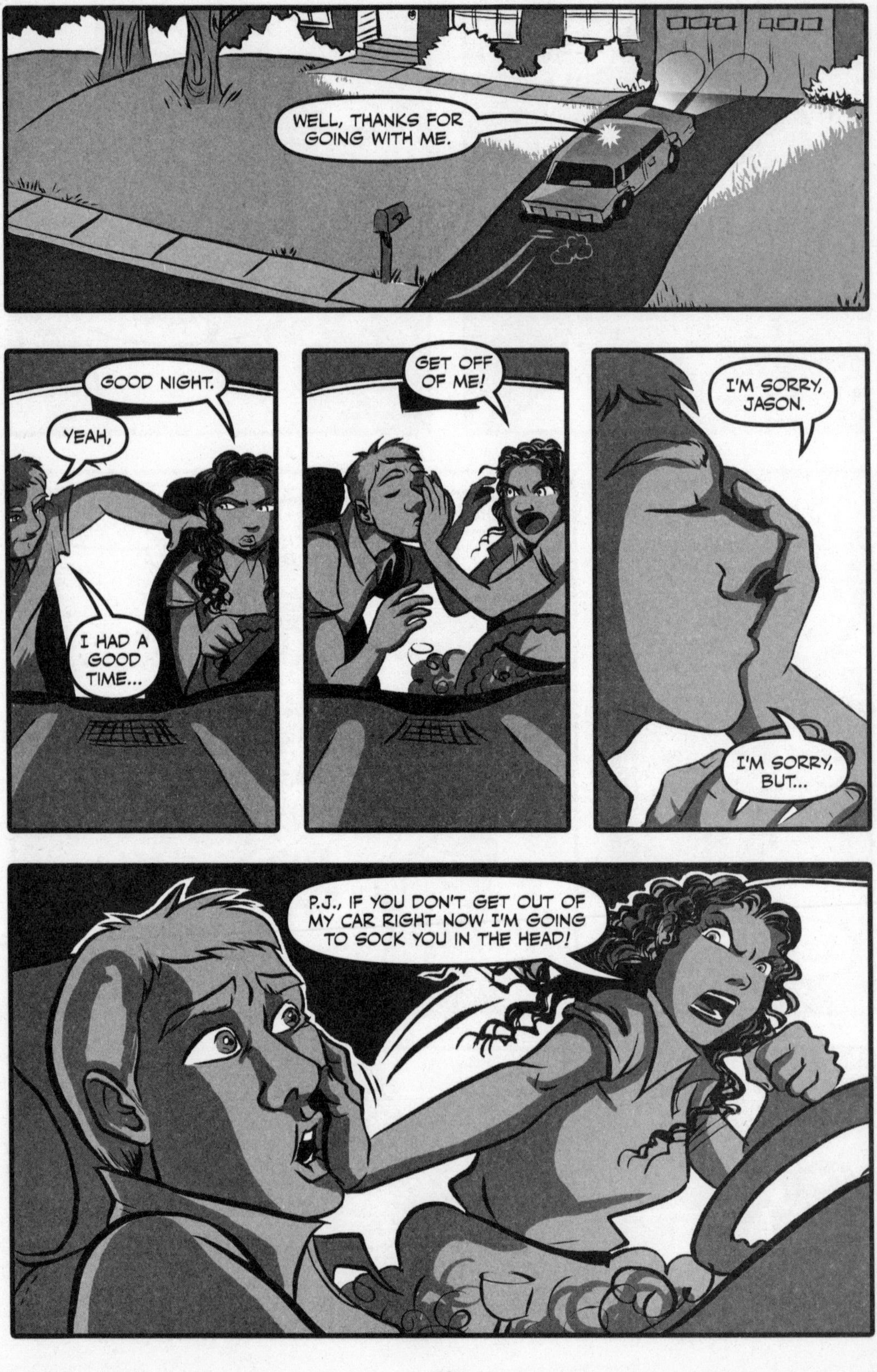
WELL, THANKS FOR GOING WITH ME.
GOOD NIGHT.
YEAH,
I HAD A GOOD TIME...
GET OFF OF ME!
I'M SORRY, JASON.
I'M SORRY, BUT...
P.J., IF YOU DON'T GET OUT OF MY CAR RIGHT NOW I'M GOING TO SOCK YOU IN THE HEAD!

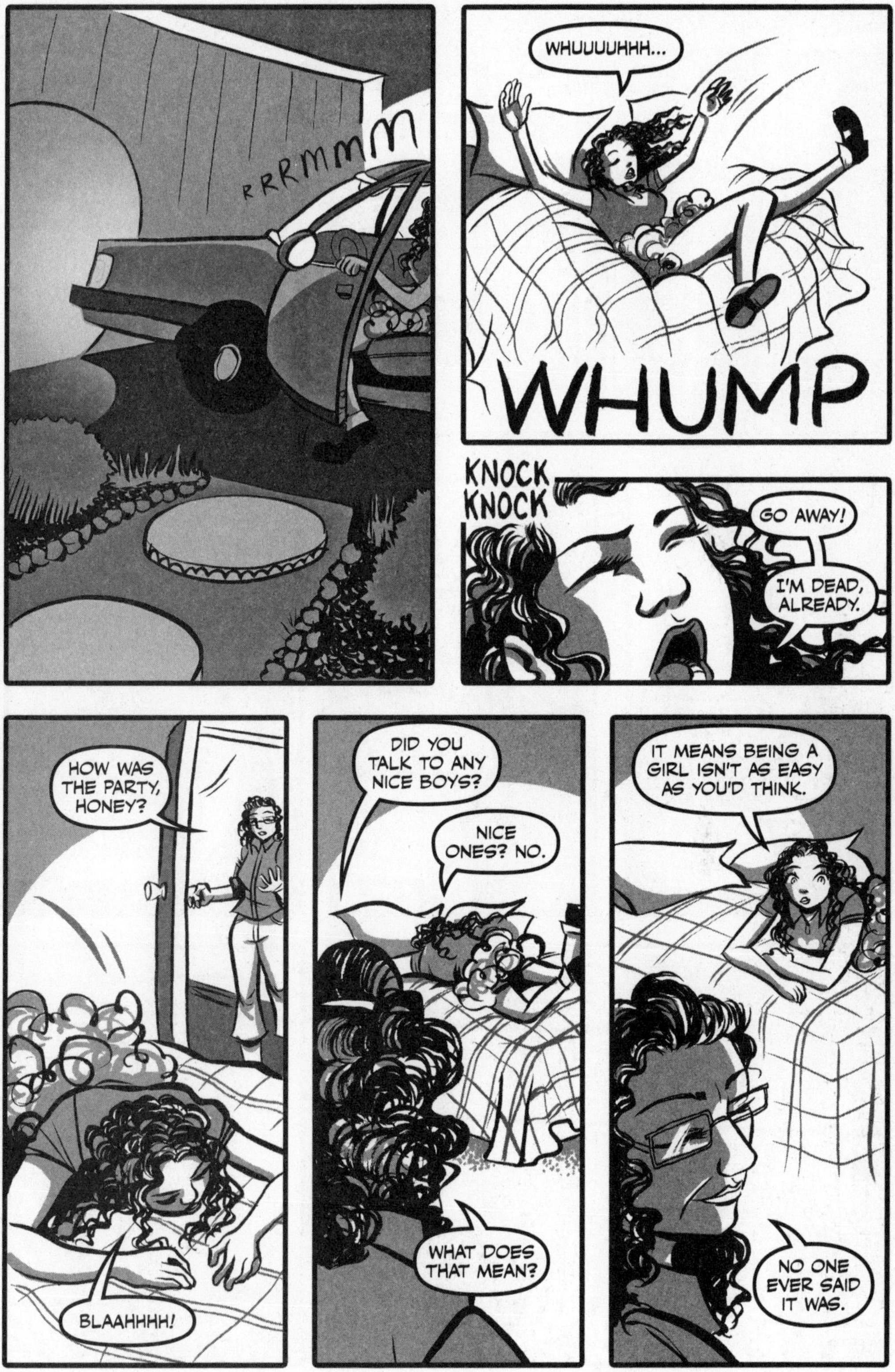

RRRMMMM
WHUUUUHHH...
WHUMP
KNOCK KNOCK
GO AWAY!
I'M DEAD, ALREADY.
HOW WAS THE PARTY, HONEY?
BLAAHHHH!
DID YOU TALK TO ANY NICE BOYS?
NICE ONES? NO.
WHAT DOES THAT MEAN?
IT MEANS BEING A GIRL ISN'T AS EASY AS YOU'D THINK.
NO ONE EVER SAID IT WAS.

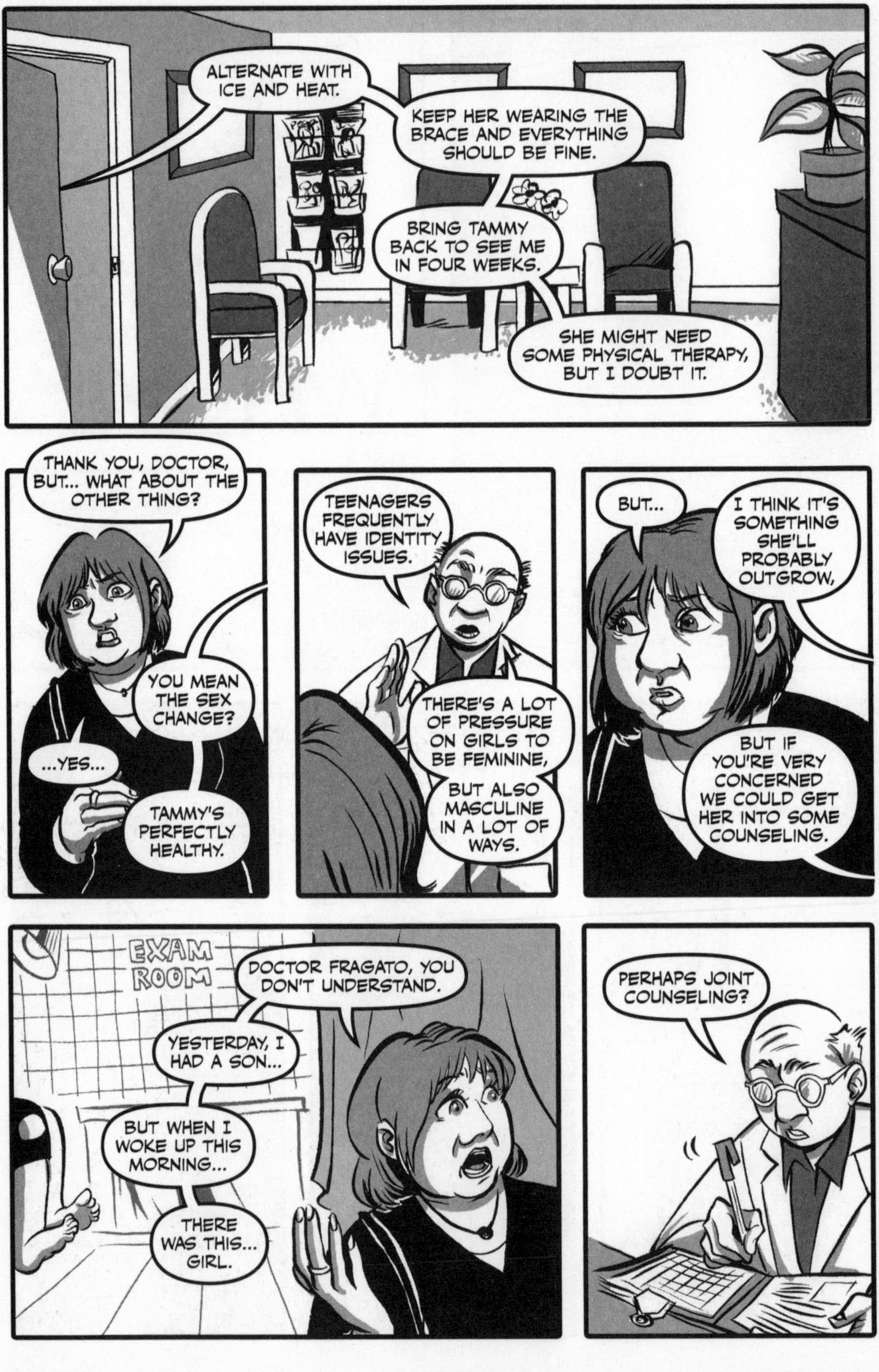
ALTERNATE WITH ICE AND HEAT.
KEEP HER WEARING THE BRACE AND EVERYTHING SHOULD BE FINE.
BRING TAMMY BACK TO SEE ME IN FOUR WEEKS.
SHE MIGHT NEED SOME PHYSICAL THERAPY, BUT I DOUBT IT.
THANK YOU, DOCTOR, BUT... WHAT ABOUT THE OTHER THING?
YOU MEAN THE SEX CHANGE?
...YES...
TAMMY'S PERFECTLY HEALTHY.
TEENAGERS FREQUENTLY HAVE IDENTITY ISSUES.
THERE'S A LOT OF PRESSURE ON GIRLS TO BE FEMININE,
BUT ALSO MASCULINE IN A LOT OF WAYS.
BUT...
I THINK IT'S SOMETHING SHE'LL PROBABLY OUTGROW,
BUT IF YOU'RE VERY CONCERNED WE COULD GET HER INTO SOME COUNSELING.
EXAM ROOM
DOCTOR FRAGATO, YOU DON'T UNDERSTAND.
YESTERDAY, I HAD A SON...
BUT WHEN I WOKE UP THIS MORNING...
THERE WAS THIS... GIRL.
PERHAPS JOINT COUNSELING?

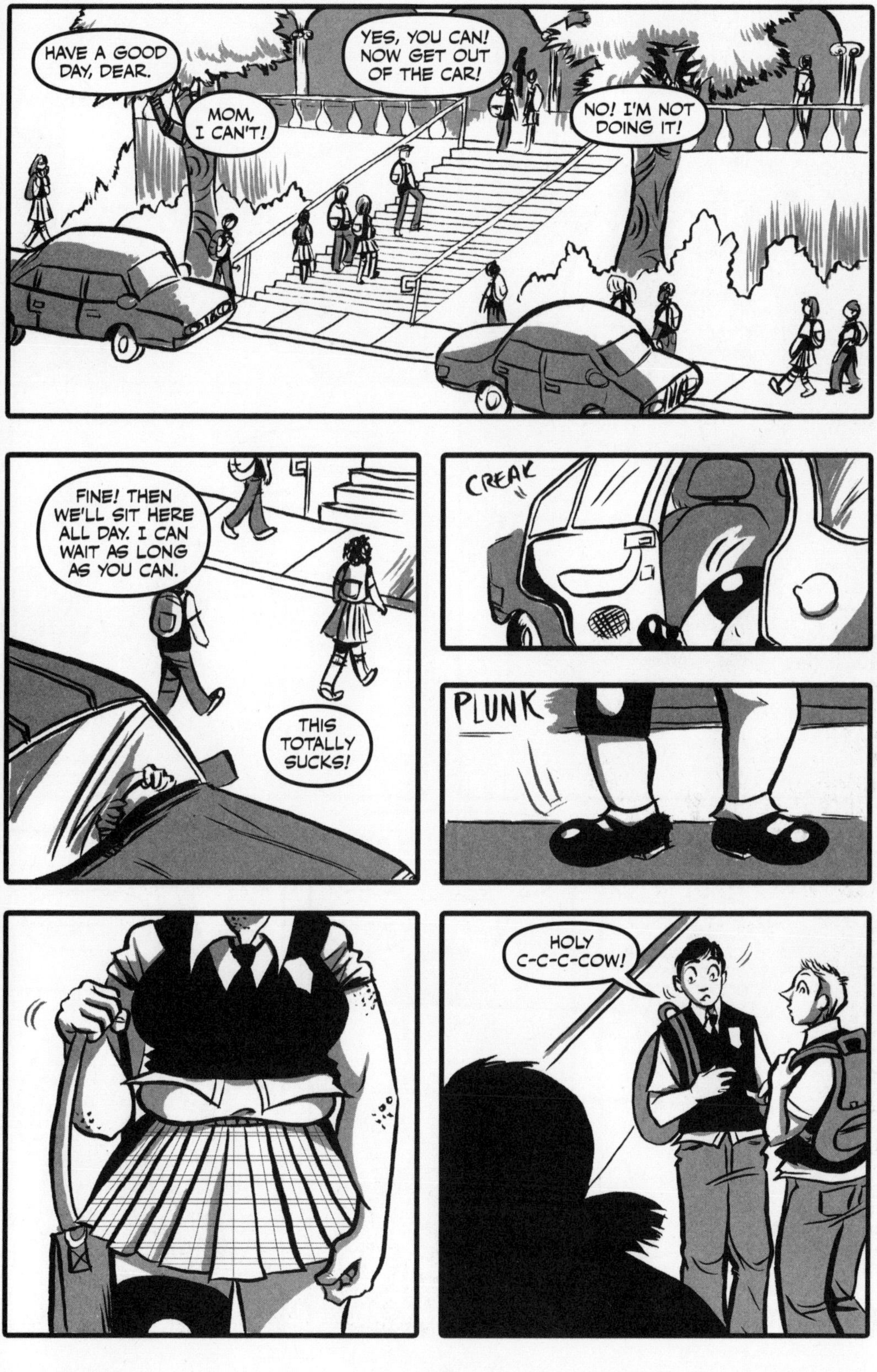
HAVE A GOOD DAY, DEAR.
MOM, I CAN'T!
YES, YOU CAN! NOW GET OUT OF THE CAR!
NO! I'M NOT DOING IT!
FINE! THEN WE'LL SIT HERE ALL DAY. I CAN WAIT AS LONG AS YOU CAN.
THIS TOTALLY SUCKS!
CREAK
PLUNK
HOLY C-C-C-COW!

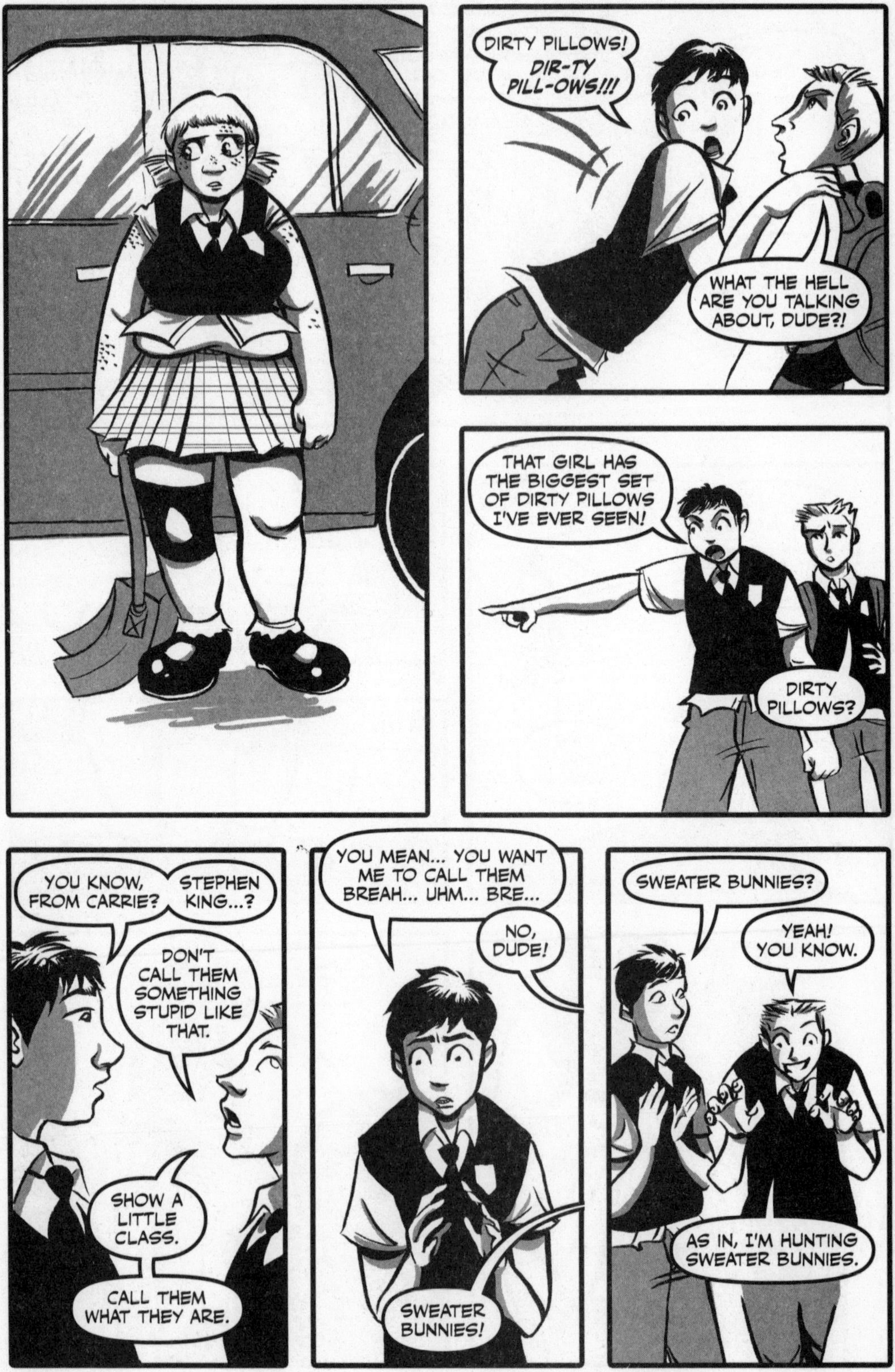
DIRTY PILLOWS! DIR-TY PILL-OWS!!!
WHAT THE HELL ARE YOU TALKING ABOUT, DUDE?!
THAT GIRL HAS THE BIGGEST SET OF DIRTY PILLOWS I'VE EVER SEEN!
DIRTY PILLOWS?
YOU KNOW, FROM CARRIE?
STEPHEN KING...?
DON'T CALL THEM SOMETHING STUPID LIKE THAT.
SHOW A LITTLE CLASS.
CALL THEM WHAT THEY ARE.
YOU MEAN... YOU WANT ME TO CALL THEM BREAH... UHM... BRE...
NO, DUDE!
SWEATER BUNNIES!
SWEATER BUNNIES?
YEAH! YOU KNOW.
AS IN, I'M HUNTING SWEATER BUNNIES.

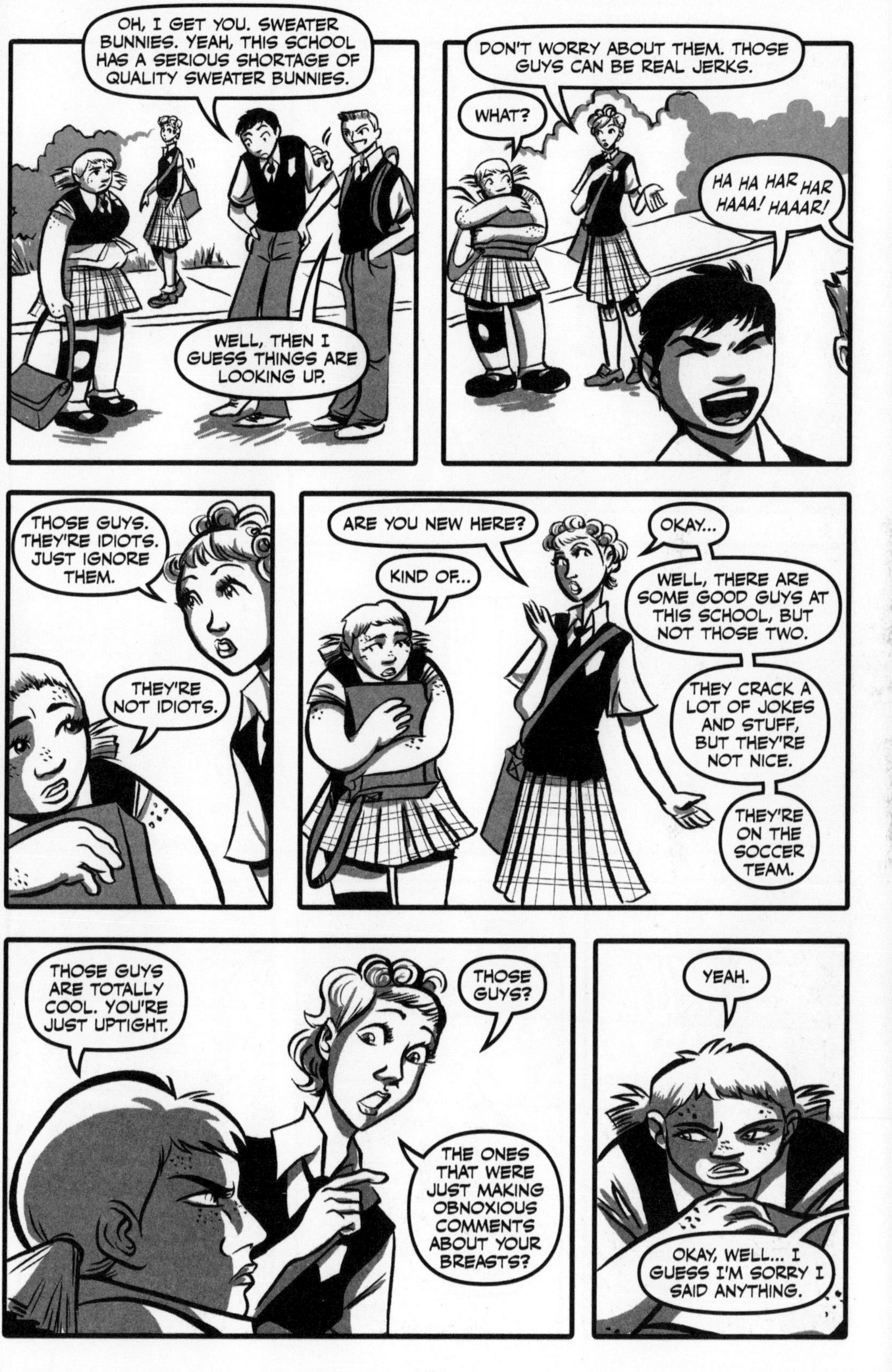

OH, I GET YOU. SWEATER BUNNIES. YEAH, THIS SCHOOL HAS A SERIOUS SHORTAGE OF QUALITY SWEATER BUNNIES.
WELL, THEN I GUESS THINGS ARE LOOKING UP.
DON'T WORRY ABOUT THEM. THOSE GUYS CAN BE REAL JERKS.
WHAT?
HA HA HAR HAR HAAA! HAAAR!
THOSE GUYS. THEY'RE IDIOTS. JUST IGNORE THEM.
THEY'RE NOT IDIOTS.
ARE YOU NEW HERE?
KIND OF...
OKAY...
WELL, THERE ARE SOME GOOD GUYS AT THIS SCHOOL, BUT NOT THOSE TWO.
THEY CRACK A LOT OF JOKES AND STUFF, BUT THEY'RE NOT NICE.
THEY'RE ON THE SOCCER TEAM.
THOSE GUYS ARE TOTALLY COOL. YOU'RE JUST UPTIGHT.
THOSE GUYS?
THE ONES THAT WERE JUST MAKING OBNOXIOUS COMMENTS ABOUT YOUR BREASTS?
YEAH.
OKAY, WELL... I GUESS I'M SORRY I SAID ANYTHING.

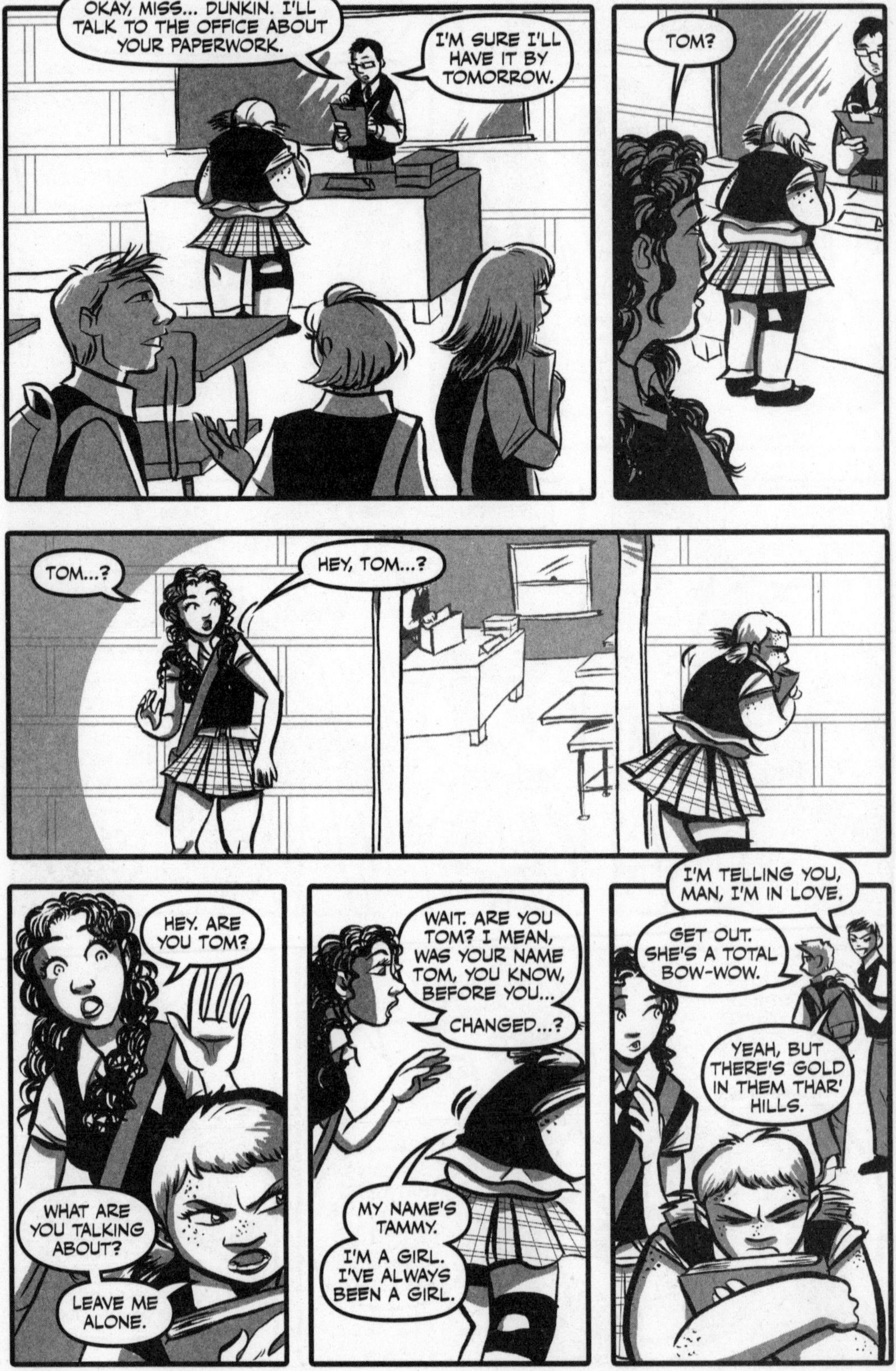
OKAY, MISS... DUNKIN. I'LL TALK TO THE OFFICE ABOUT YOUR PAPERWORK.
I'M SURE I'LL HAVE IT BY TOMORROW.
TOM?
TOM...?
HEY, TOM...?
HEY. ARE YOU TOM?
WHAT ARE YOU TALKING ABOUT?
LEAVE ME ALONE.
WAIT. ARE YOU TOM? I MEAN, WAS YOUR NAME TOM, YOU KNOW, BEFORE YOU...
CHANGED...?
MY NAME'S TAMMY.
I'M A GIRL. I'VE ALWAYS BEEN A GIRL.
I'M TELLING YOU, MAN, I'M IN LOVE.
GET OUT. SHE'S A TOTAL BOW-WOW.
YEAH, BUT THERE'S GOLD IN THEM THAR' HILLS.

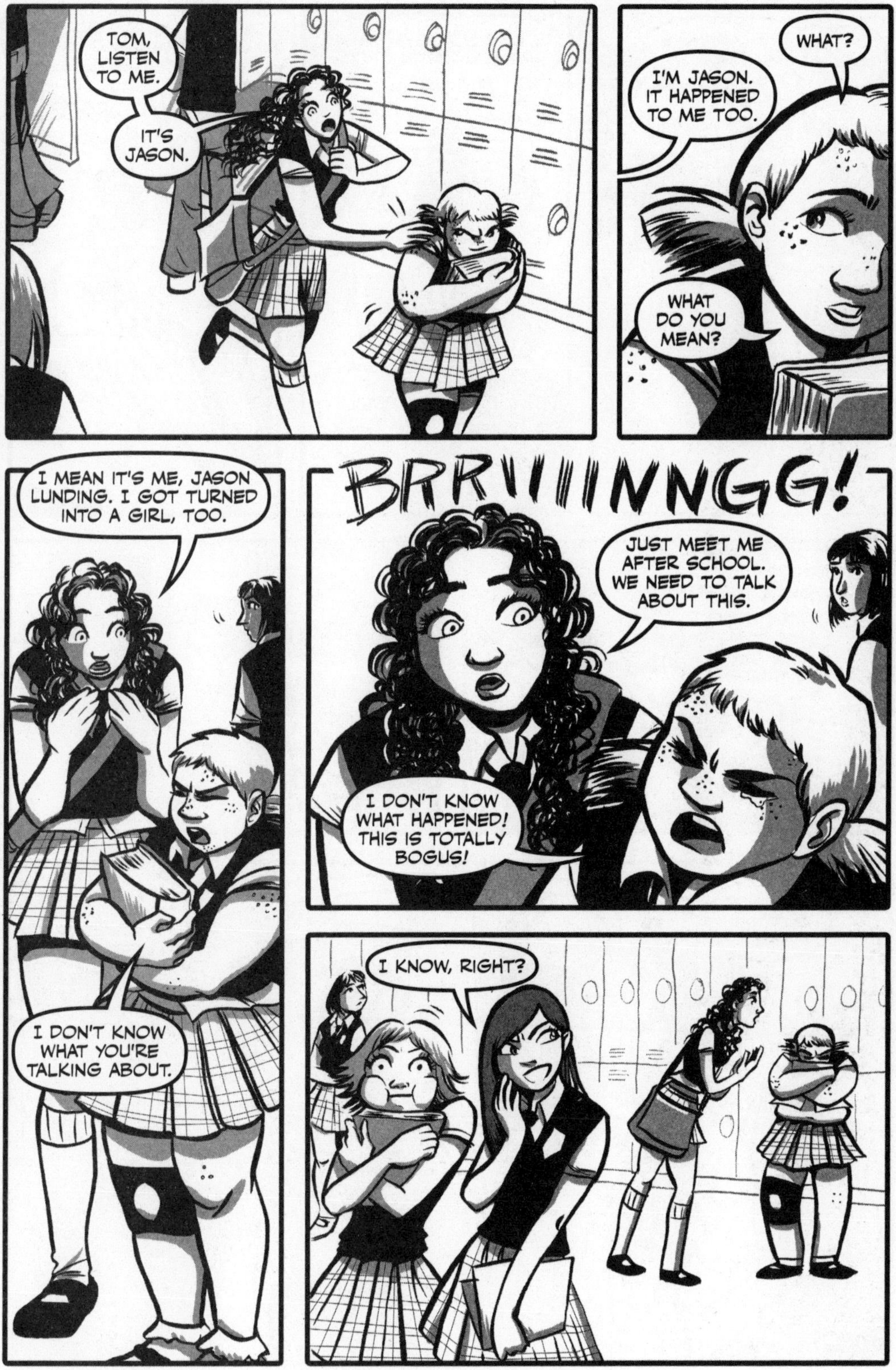
TOM, LISTEN TO ME.
IT'S JASON.
WHAT?
I'M JASON. IT HAPPENED TO ME TOO.
WHAT DO YOU MEAN?
I MEAN IT'S ME, JASON LUNDING. I GOT TURNED INTO A GIRL, TOO.
I DON'T KNOW WHAT YOU'RE TALKING ABOUT.
BRRIIIINNGG!
JUST MEET ME AFTER SCHOOL. WE NEED TO TALK ABOUT THIS.
I DON'T KNOW WHAT HAPPENED! THIS IS TOTALLY BOGUS!
I KNOW, RIGHT?

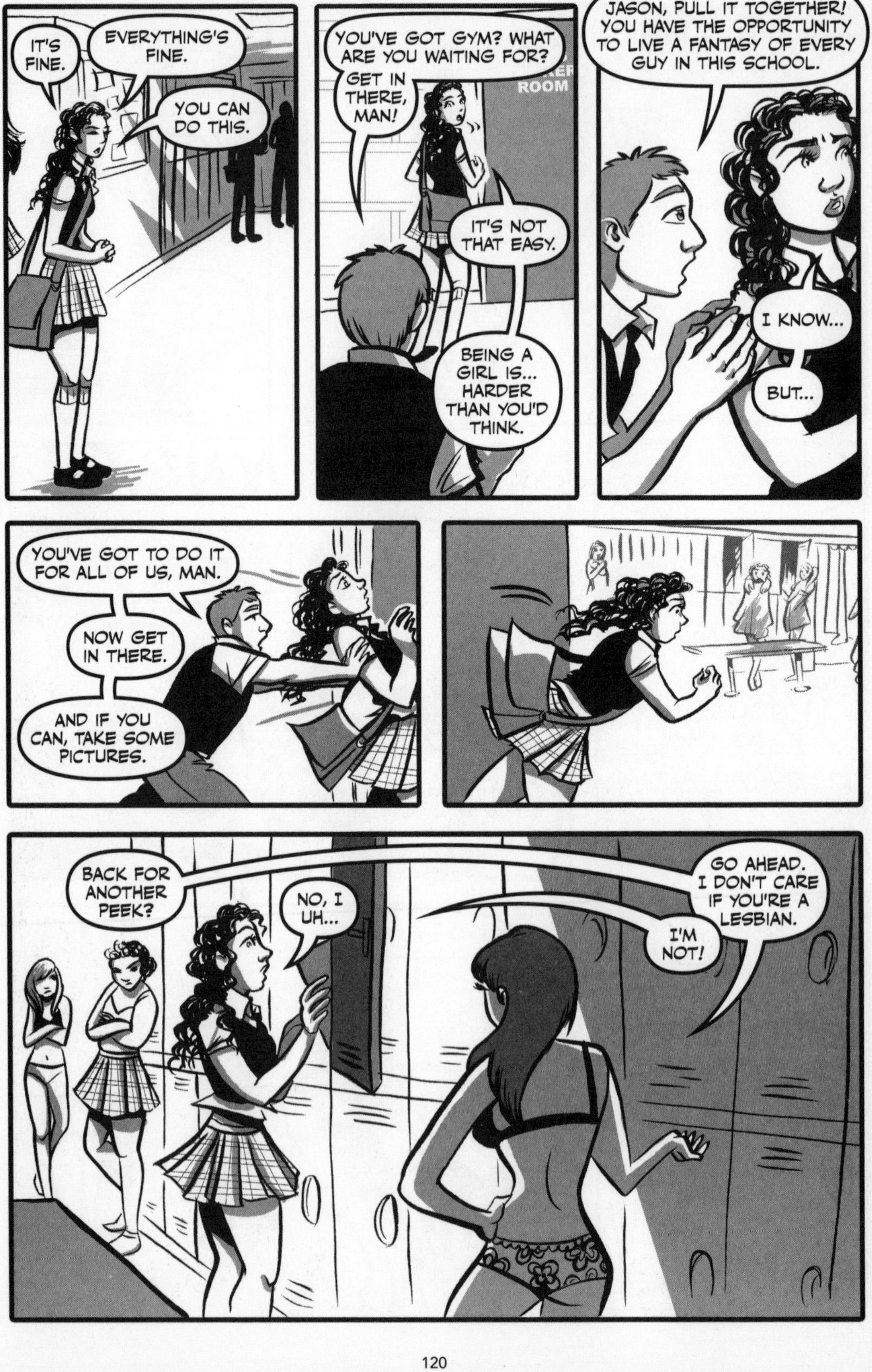
IT'S FINE.
EVERYTHING'S FINE.
YOU CAN DO THIS.
ROOM
YOU'VE GOT GYM? WHAT ARE YOU WAITING FOR?
GET IN THERE, MAN!
IT'S NOT THAT EASY.
BEING A GIRL IS... HARDER THAN YOU'D THINK.
JASON, PULL IT TOGETHER! YOU HAVE THE OPPORTUNITY TO LIVE A FANTASY OF EVERY GUY IN THIS SCHOOL.
I KNOW...
BUT...
YOU'VE GOT TO DO IT FOR ALL OF US, MAN.
NOW GET IN THERE.
AND IF YOU CAN, TAKE SOME PICTURES.
BACK FOR ANOTHER PEEK?
NO, I UH...
GO AHEAD. I DON'T CARE IF YOU'RE A LESBIAN.
I'M NOT!

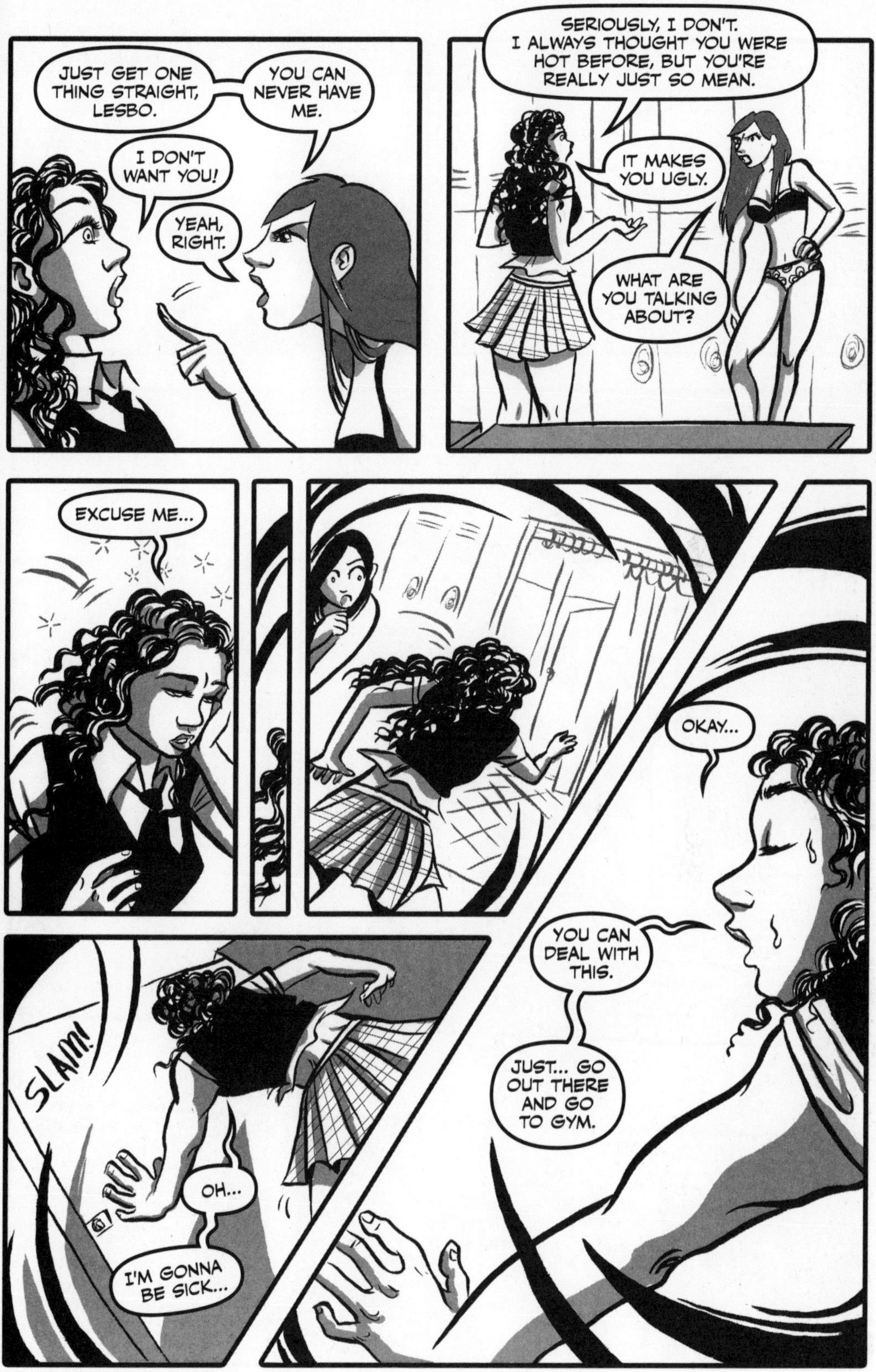
JUST GET ONE THING STRAIGHT, LESBO.
YOU CAN NEVER HAVE ME.
I DON'T WANT YOU!
YEAH, RIGHT.
SERIOUSLY, I DON'T. I ALWAYS THOUGHT YOU WERE HOT BEFORE, BUT YOU'RE REALLY JUST SO MEAN.
IT MAKES YOU UGLY.
WHAT ARE YOU TALKING ABOUT?
EXCUSE ME...
OKAY...
YOU CAN DEAL WITH THIS.
JUST... GO OUT THERE AND GO TO GYM.
SLAM!
OH...
I'M GONNA BE SICK...

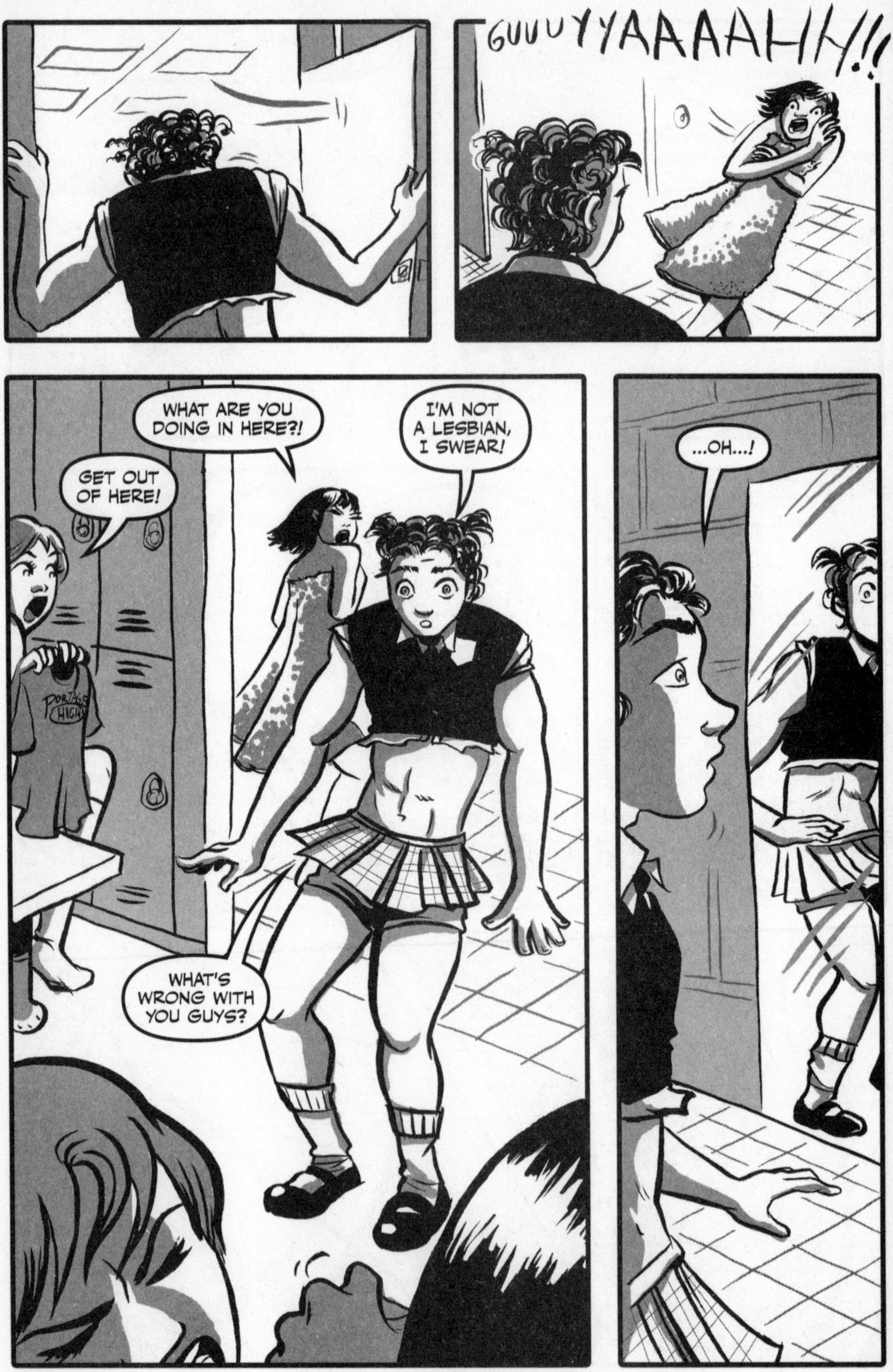
GUUUYYAAAAHH!!!
WHAT ARE YOU DOING IN HERE?!
GET OUT OF HERE!
I'M NOT A LESBIAN, I SWEAR!
PORTAGE HIGH
WHAT'S WRONG WITH YOU GUYS?
...OH...!

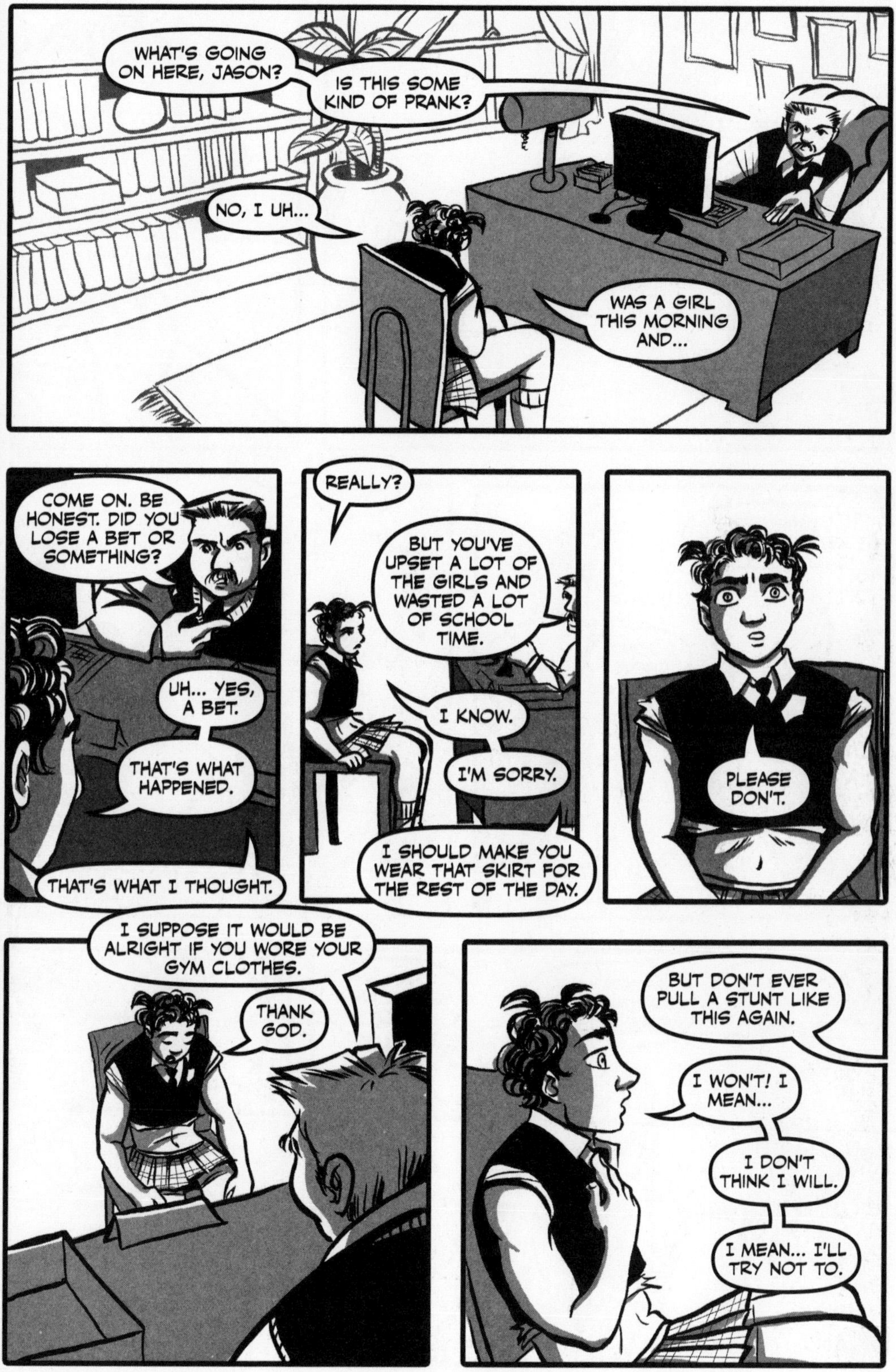
WHAT'S GOING ON HERE, JASON?
IS THIS SOME KIND OF PRANK?
NO, I UH...
WAS A GIRL THIS MORNING AND...
COME ON. BE HONEST. DID YOU LOSE A BET OR SOMETHING?
UH... YES, A BET.
THAT'S WHAT HAPPENED.
THAT'S WHAT I THOUGHT.
REALLY?
BUT YOU'VE UPSET A LOT OF THE GIRLS AND WASTED A LOT OF SCHOOL TIME.
I KNOW.
I'M SORRY.
I SHOULD MAKE YOU WEAR THAT SKIRT FOR THE REST OF THE DAY.
PLEASE DON'T.
I SUPPOSE IT WOULD BE ALRIGHT IF YOU WORE YOUR GYM CLOTHES.
THANK GOD.
BUT DON'T EVER PULL A STUNT LIKE THIS AGAIN.
I WON'T! I MEAN...
I DON'T THINK I WILL.
I MEAN... I'LL TRY NOT TO.

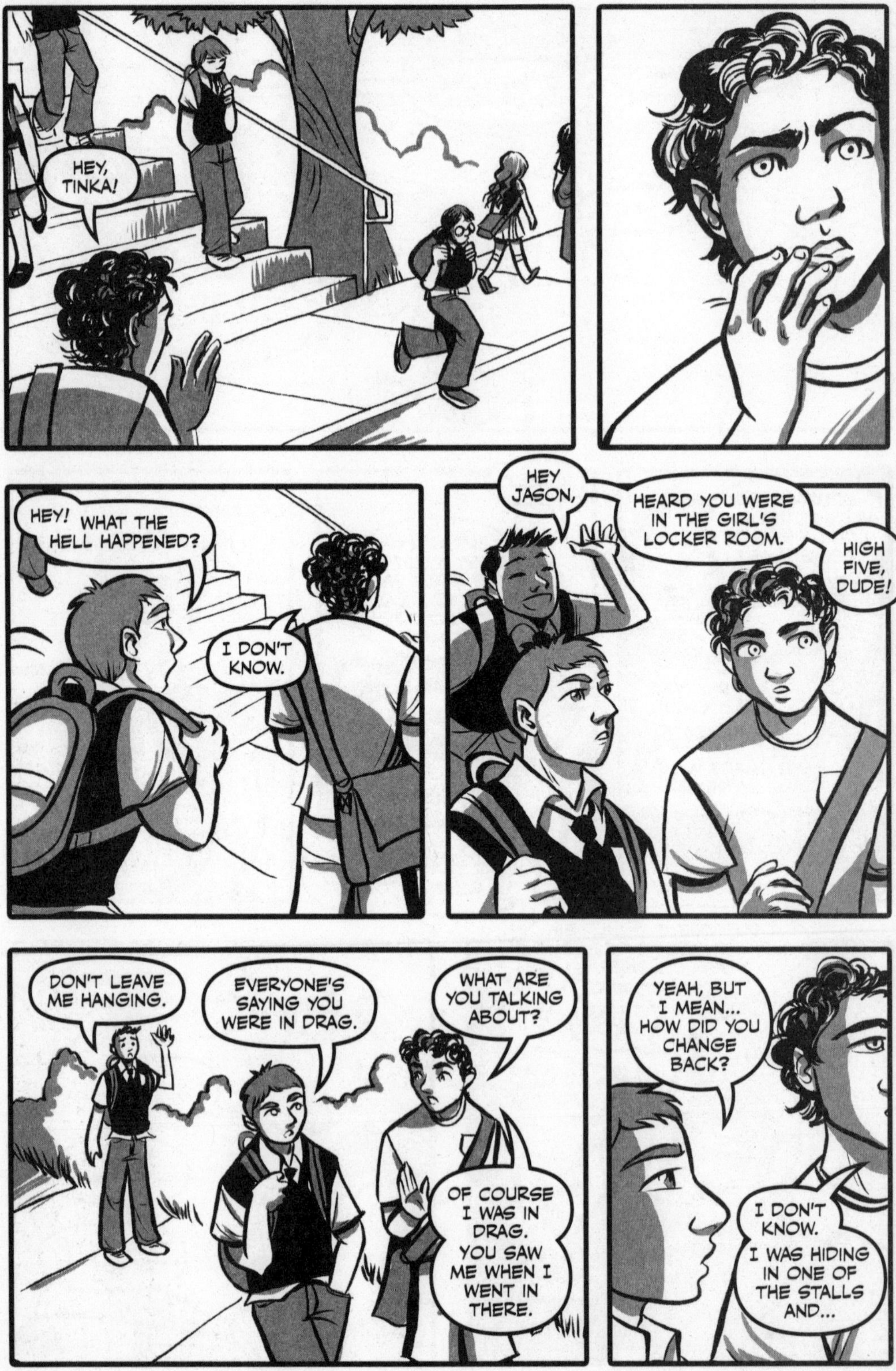
HEY, TINKA!
HEY! WHAT THE HELL HAPPENED?
I DON'T KNOW.
HEY JASON,
HEARD YOU WERE IN THE GIRL'S LOCKER ROOM.
HIGH FIVE, DUDE!
DON'T LEAVE ME HANGING.
EVERYONE'S SAYING YOU WERE IN DRAG.
WHAT ARE YOU TALKING ABOUT?
OF COURSE I WAS IN DRAG. YOU SAW ME WHEN I WENT IN THERE.
YEAH, BUT I MEAN... HOW DID YOU CHANGE BACK?
I DON'T KNOW. I WAS HIDING IN ONE OF THE STALLS AND...

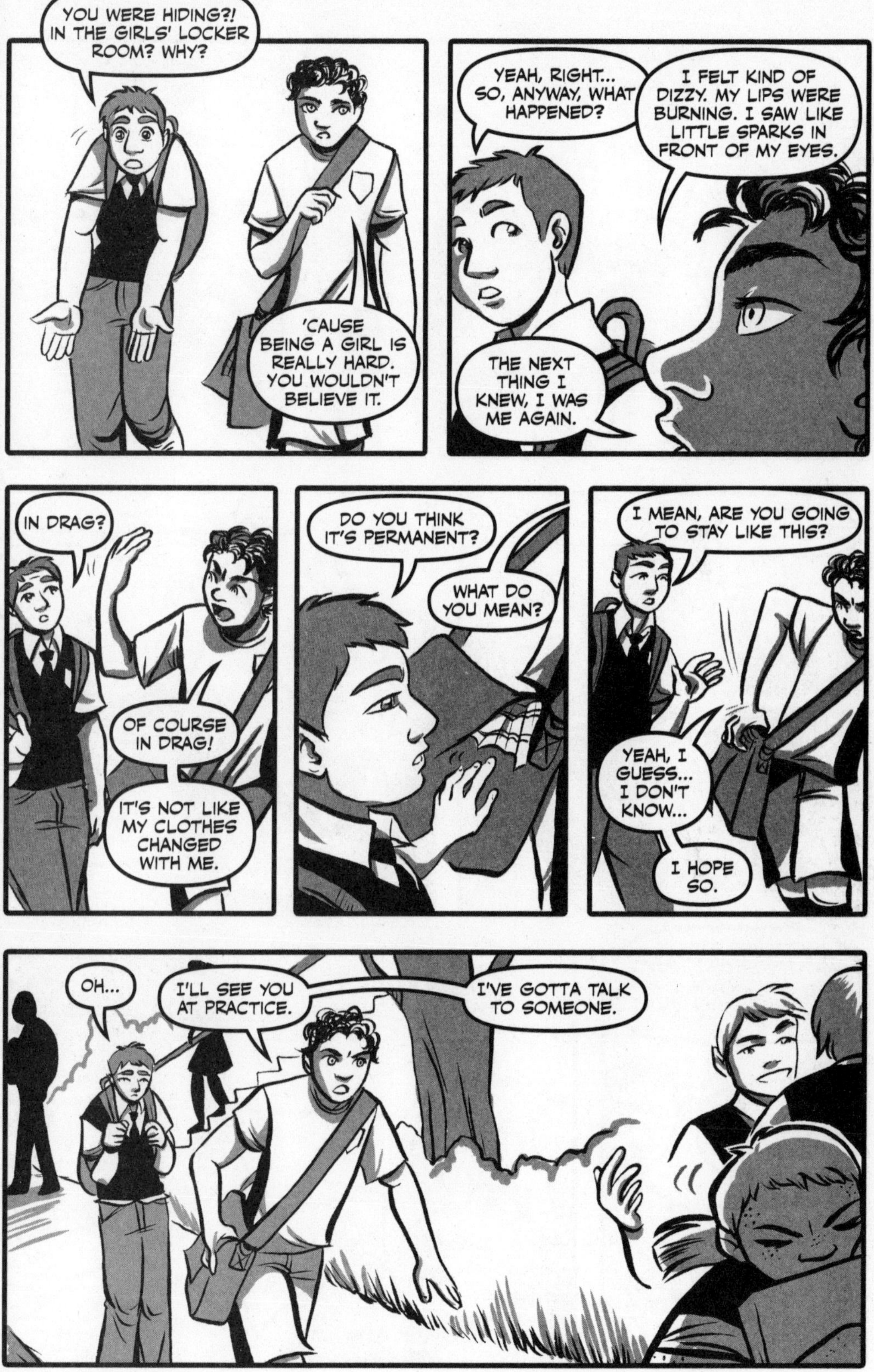
YOU WERE HIDING?! IN THE GIRLS' LOCKER ROOM? WHY?
'CAUSE BEING A GIRL IS REALLY HARD. YOU WOULDN'T BELIEVE IT.
YEAH, RIGHT... SO, ANYWAY, WHAT HAPPENED?
I FELT KIND OF DIZZY. MY LIPS WERE BURNING. I SAW LIKE LITTLE SPARKS IN FRONT OF MY EYES.
THE NEXT THING I KNEW, I WAS ME AGAIN.
IN DRAG?
OF COURSE IN DRAG!
IT'S NOT LIKE MY CLOTHES CHANGED WITH ME.
DO YOU THINK IT'S PERMANENT?
WHAT DO YOU MEAN?
I MEAN, ARE YOU GOING TO STAY LIKE THIS?
YEAH, I GUESS... I DON'T KNOW...
I HOPE SO.
OH...
I'LL SEE YOU AT PRACTICE.
I'VE GOTTA TALK TO SOMEONE.

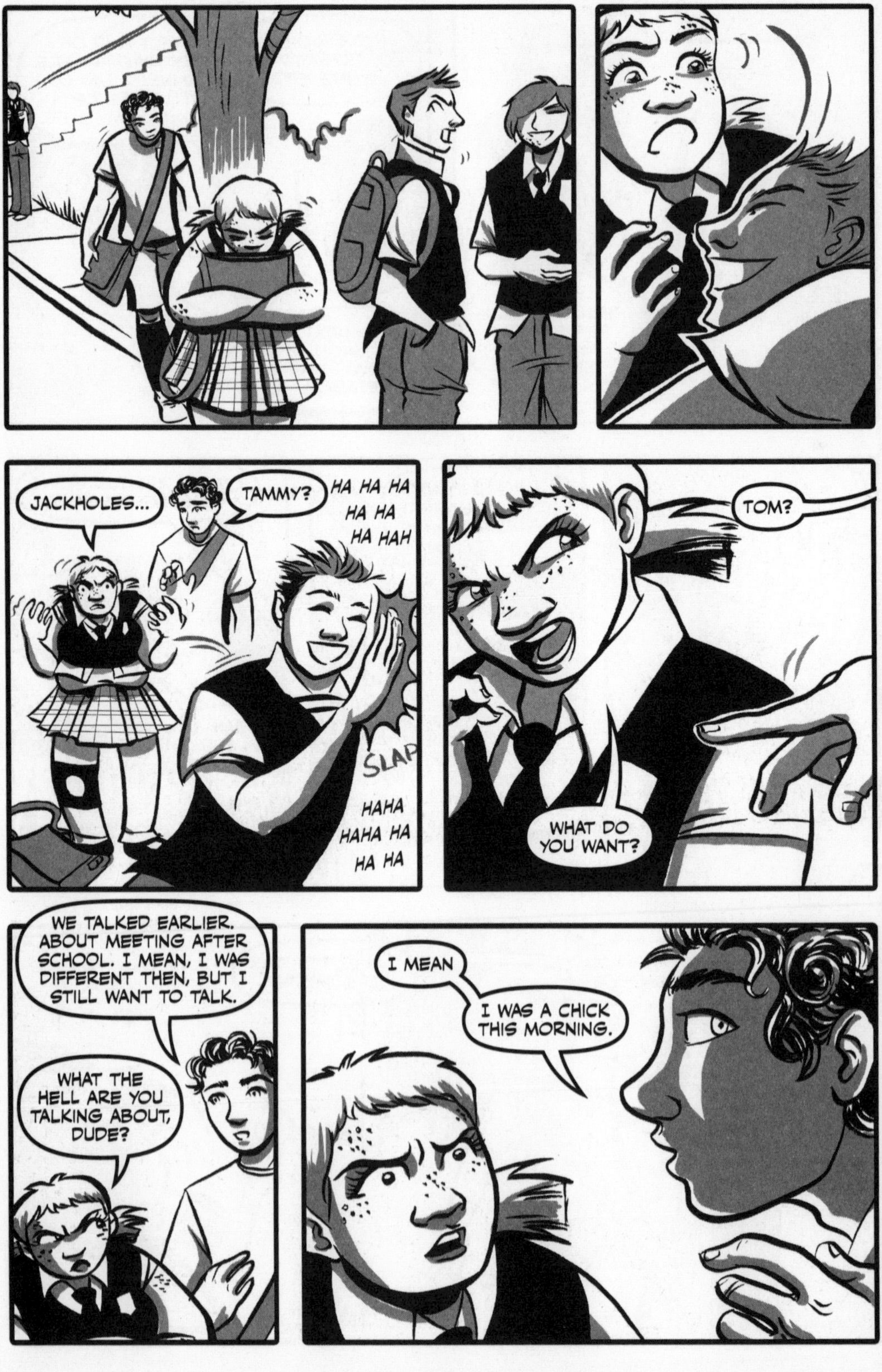

JACKHOLES...
TAMMY?
HA HA HA
HA HA
HA HAH
SLAP
HAHA
HAHA HA
HA HA
TOM?
WHAT DO YOU WANT?
WE TALKED EARLIER. ABOUT MEETING AFTER SCHOOL. I MEAN, I WAS DIFFERENT THEN, BUT I STILL WANT TO TALK.
WHAT THE HELL ARE YOU TALKING ABOUT, DUDE?
I MEAN
I WAS A CHICK THIS MORNING.

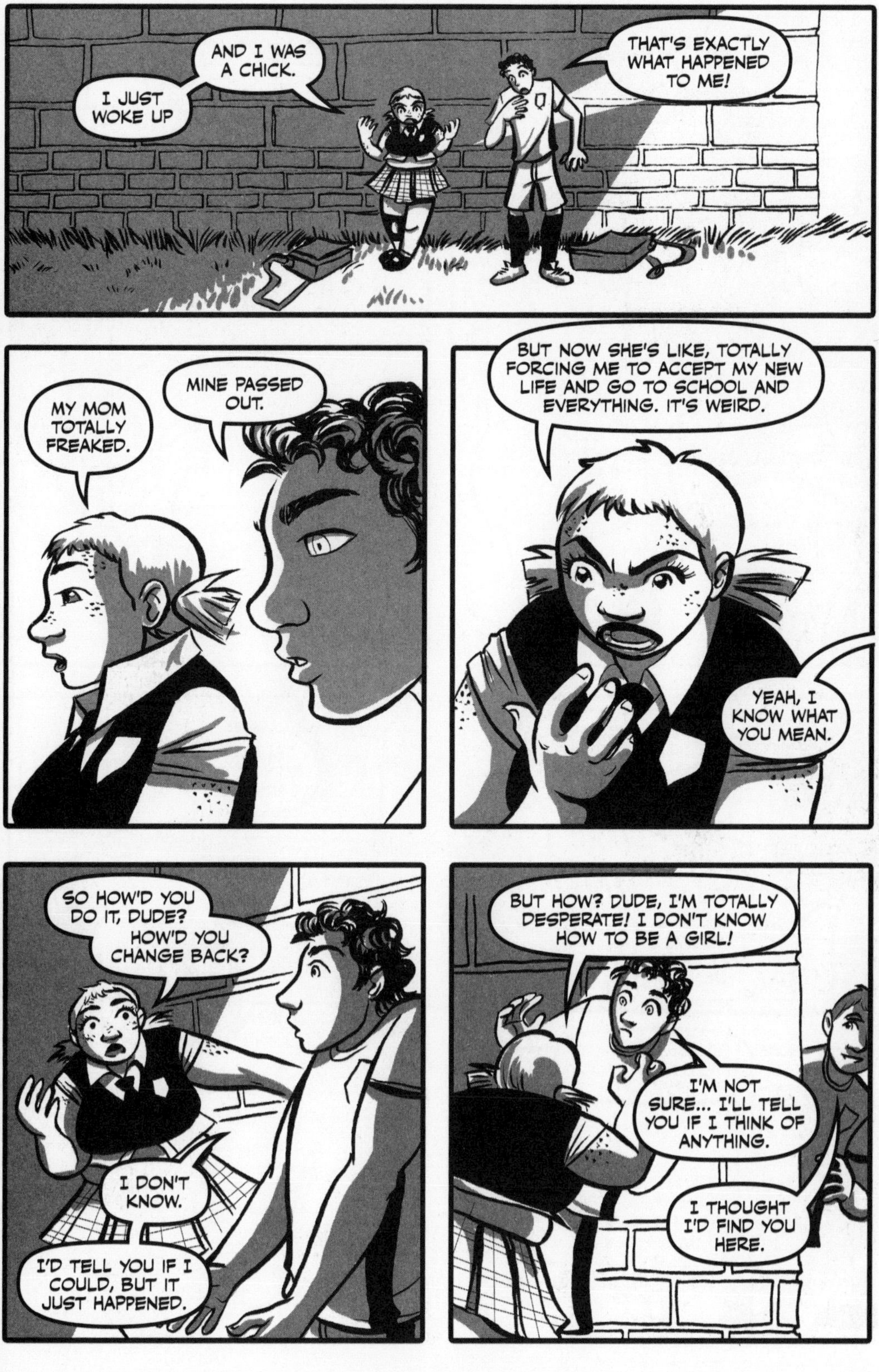
I JUST WOKE UP
AND I WAS A CHICK.
THAT'S EXACTLY WHAT HAPPENED TO ME!
MY MOM TOTALLY FREAKED.
MINE PASSED OUT.
BUT NOW SHE'S LIKE, TOTALLY FORCING ME TO ACCEPT MY NEW LIFE AND GO TO SCHOOL AND EVERYTHING. IT'S WEIRD.
YEAH, I KNOW WHAT YOU MEAN.
SO HOW'D YOU DO IT, DUDE?
HOW'D YOU CHANGE BACK?
I DON'T KNOW.
I'D TELL YOU IF I COULD, BUT IT JUST HAPPENED.
BUT HOW? DUDE, I'M TOTALLY DESPERATE! I DON'T KNOW HOW TO BE A GIRL!
I'M NOT SURE... I'LL TELL YOU IF I THINK OF ANYTHING.
I THOUGHT I'D FIND YOU HERE.

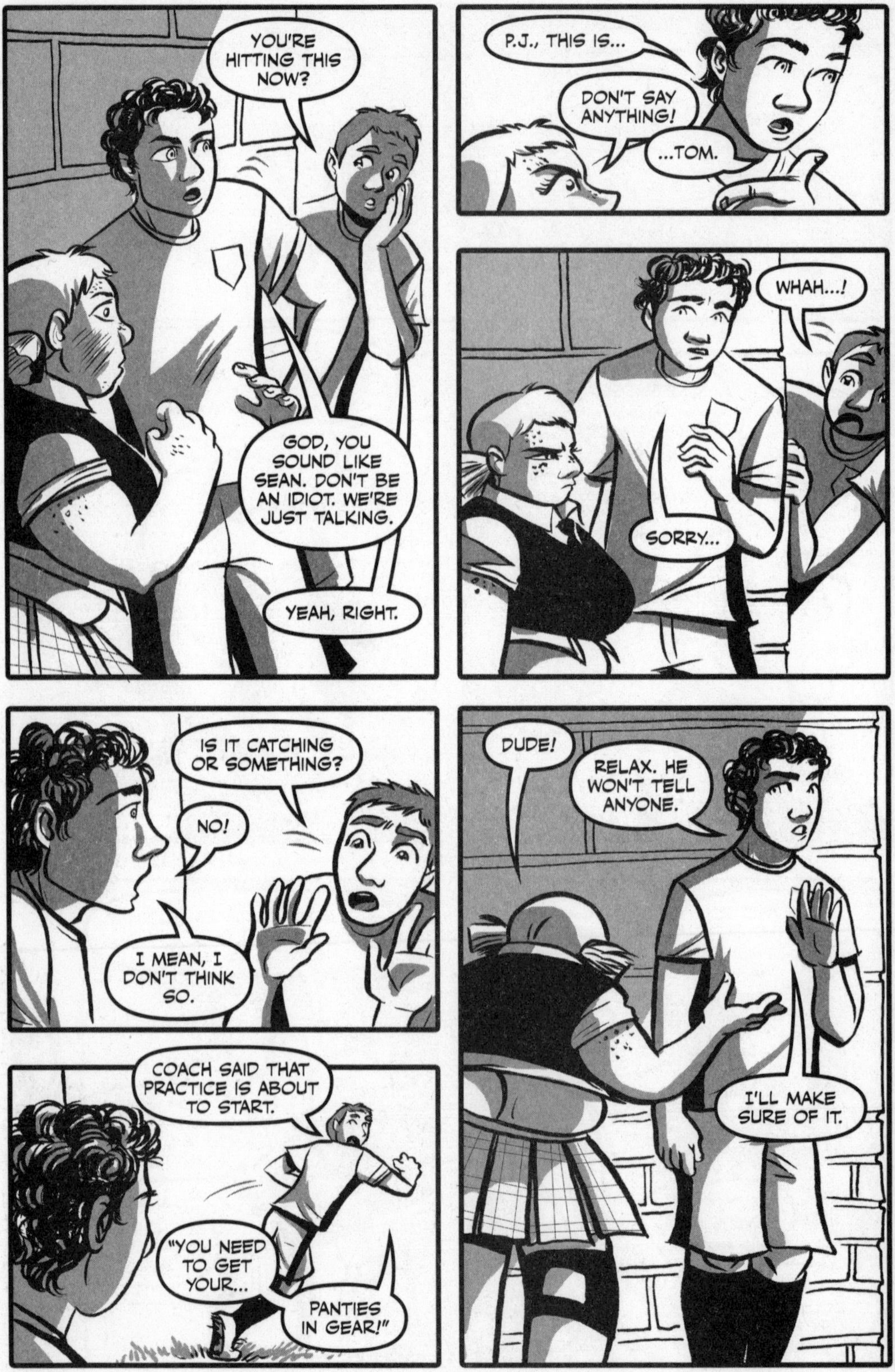
YOU'RE HITTING THIS NOW?
GOD, YOU SOUND LIKE SEAN. DON'T BE AN IDIOT. WE'RE JUST TALKING.
YEAH, RIGHT.
P.J., THIS IS...
DON'T SAY ANYTHING!
...TOM.
WHAH...!
SORRY...
IS IT CATCHING OR SOMETHING?
NO!
I MEAN, I DON'T THINK SO.
DUDE!
RELAX. HE WON'T TELL ANYONE.
I'LL MAKE SURE OF IT.
COACH SAID THAT PRACTICE IS ABOUT TO START.
"YOU NEED TO GET YOUR...
PANTIES IN GEAR!"

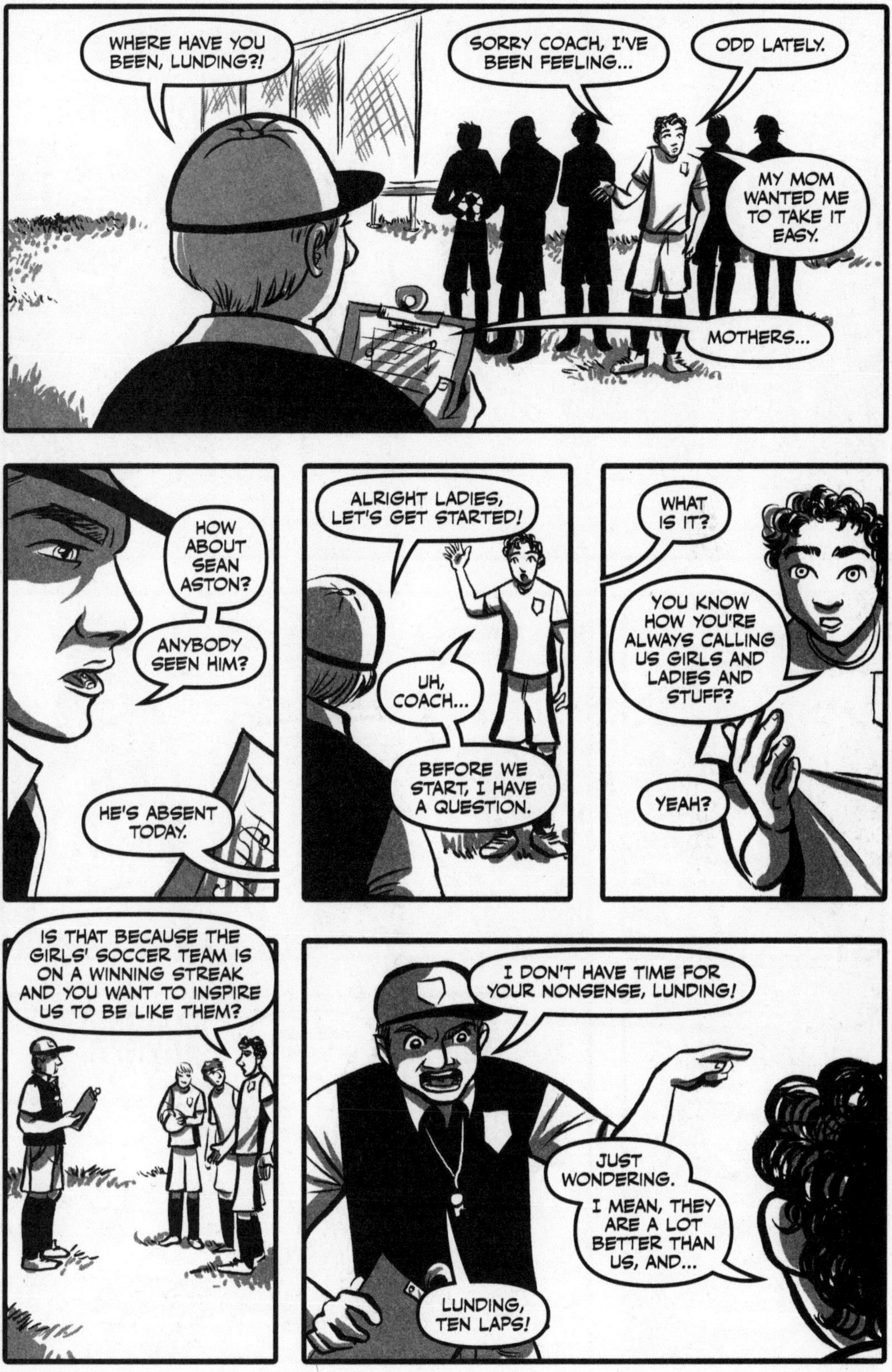
WHERE HAVE YOU BEEN, LUNDING?!
SORRY COACH, I'VE BEEN FEELING...
ODD LATELY.
MY MOM WANTED ME TO TAKE IT EASY.
MOTHERS...
HOW ABOUT SEAN ASTON?
ANYBODY SEEN HIM?
HE'S ABSENT TODAY.
ALRIGHT LADIES, LET'S GET STARTED!
UH, COACH...
BEFORE WE START, I HAVE A QUESTION.
WHAT IS IT?
YOU KNOW HOW YOU'RE ALWAYS CALLING US GIRLS AND LADIES AND STUFF?
YEAH?
IS THAT BECAUSE THE GIRLS' SOCCER TEAM IS ON A WINNING STREAK AND YOU WANT TO INSPIRE US TO BE LIKE THEM?
I DON'T HAVE TIME FOR YOUR NONSENSE, LUNDING!
JUST WONDERING.
I MEAN, THEY ARE A LOT BETTER THAN US, AND...
LUNDING, TEN LAPS!

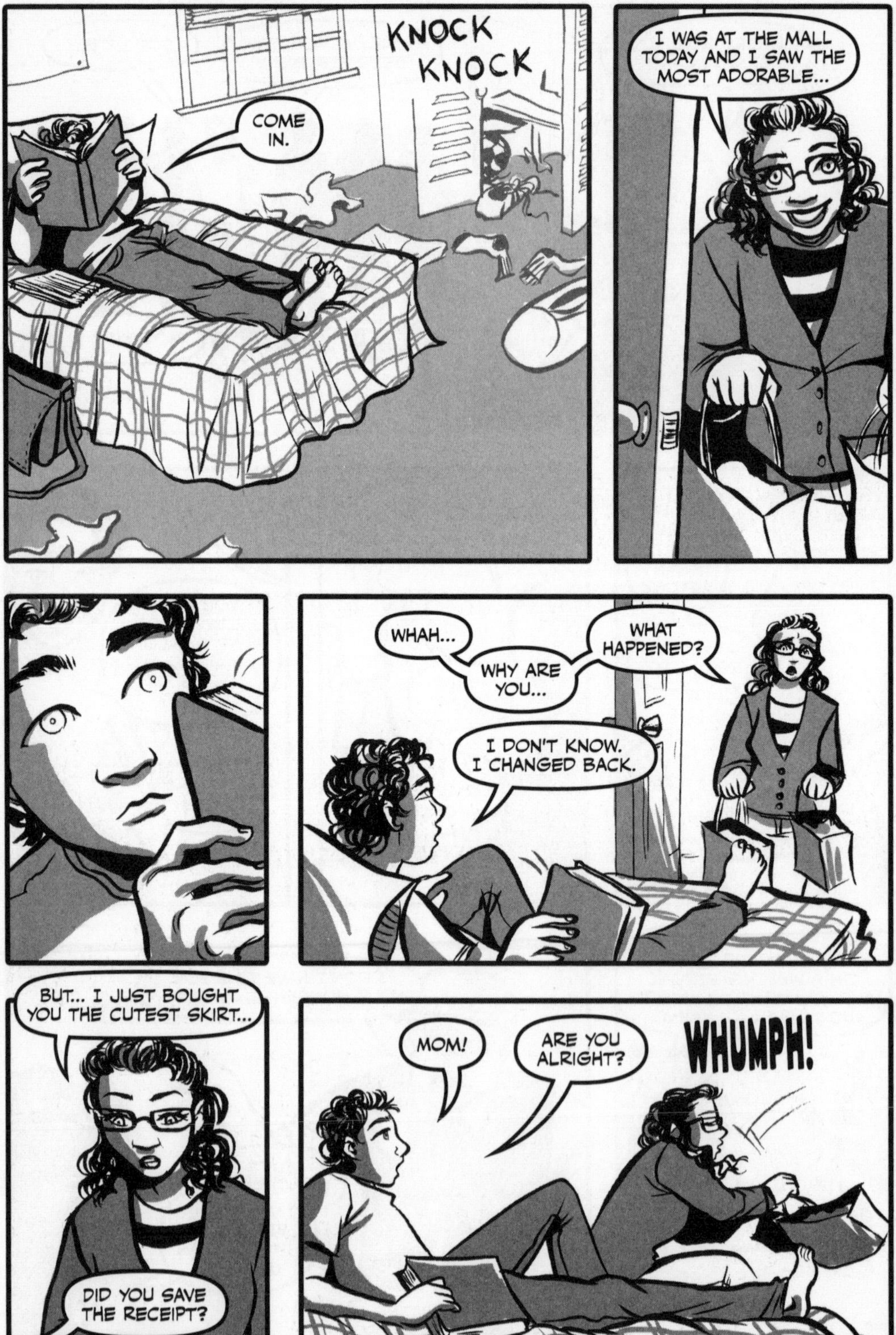
KNOCK KNOCK
COME IN.
I WAS AT THE MALL TODAY AND I SAW THE MOST ADORABLE...
WHAH...
WHY ARE YOU...
WHAT HAPPENED?
I DON'T KNOW. I CHANGED BACK.
BUT... I JUST BOUGHT YOU THE CUTEST SKIRT...
DID YOU SAVE THE RECEIPT?
MOM!
ARE YOU ALRIGHT?
WHUMPH!

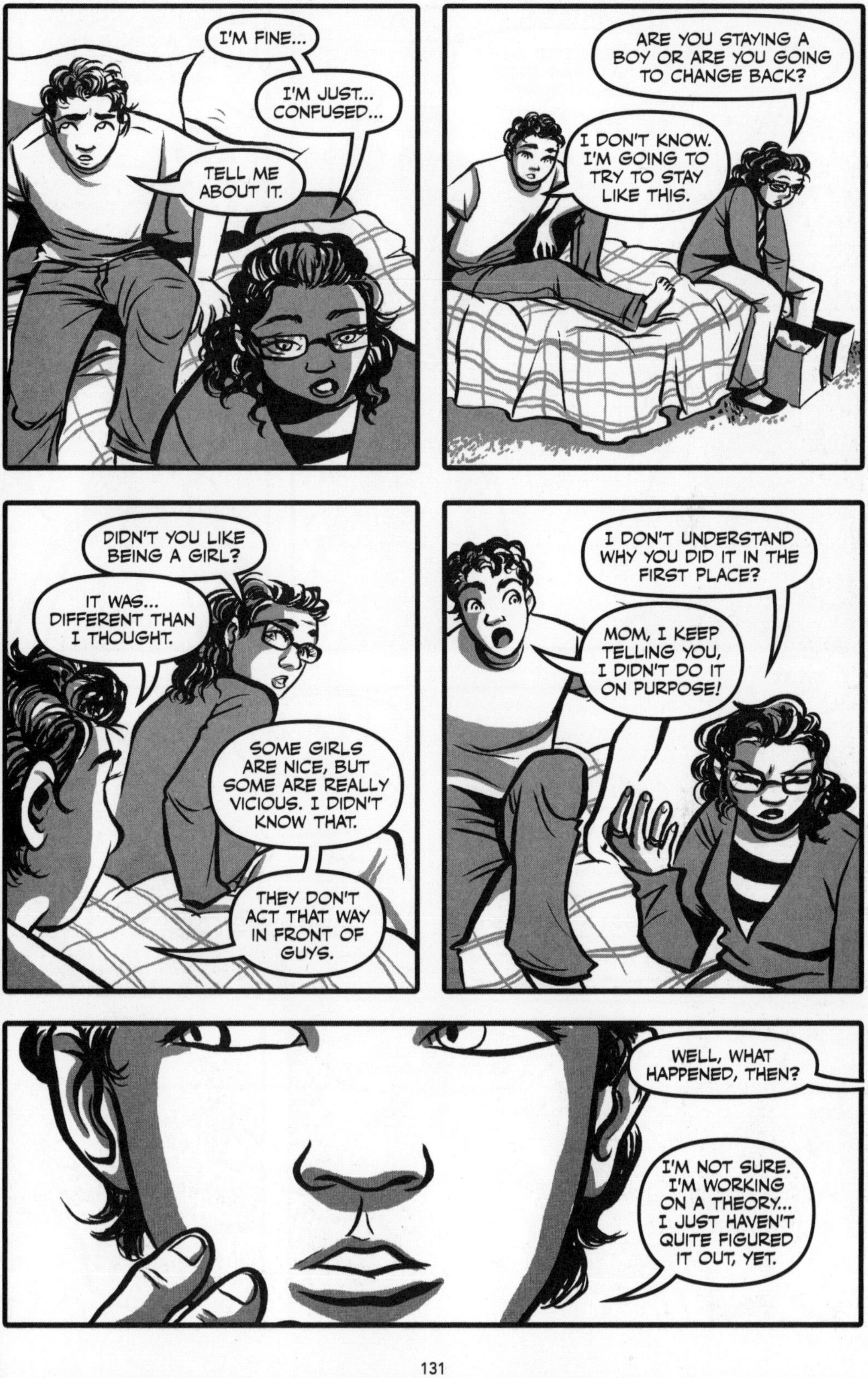
I'M FINE...
I'M JUST... CONFUSED...
TELL ME ABOUT IT.
ARE YOU STAYING A BOY OR ARE YOU GOING TO CHANGE BACK?
I DON'T KNOW. I'M GOING TO TRY TO STAY LIKE THIS.
DIDN'T YOU LIKE BEING A GIRL?
IT WAS... DIFFERENT THAN I THOUGHT.
SOME GIRLS ARE NICE, BUT SOME ARE REALLY VICIOUS. I DIDN'T KNOW THAT.
THEY DON'T ACT THAT WAY IN FRONT OF GUYS.
I DON'T UNDERSTAND WHY YOU DID IT IN THE FIRST PLACE?
MOM, I KEEP TELLING YOU, I DIDN'T DO IT ON PURPOSE!
WELL, WHAT HAPPENED, THEN?
I'M NOT SURE. I'M WORKING ON A THEORY... I JUST HAVEN'T QUITE FIGURED IT OUT, YET.

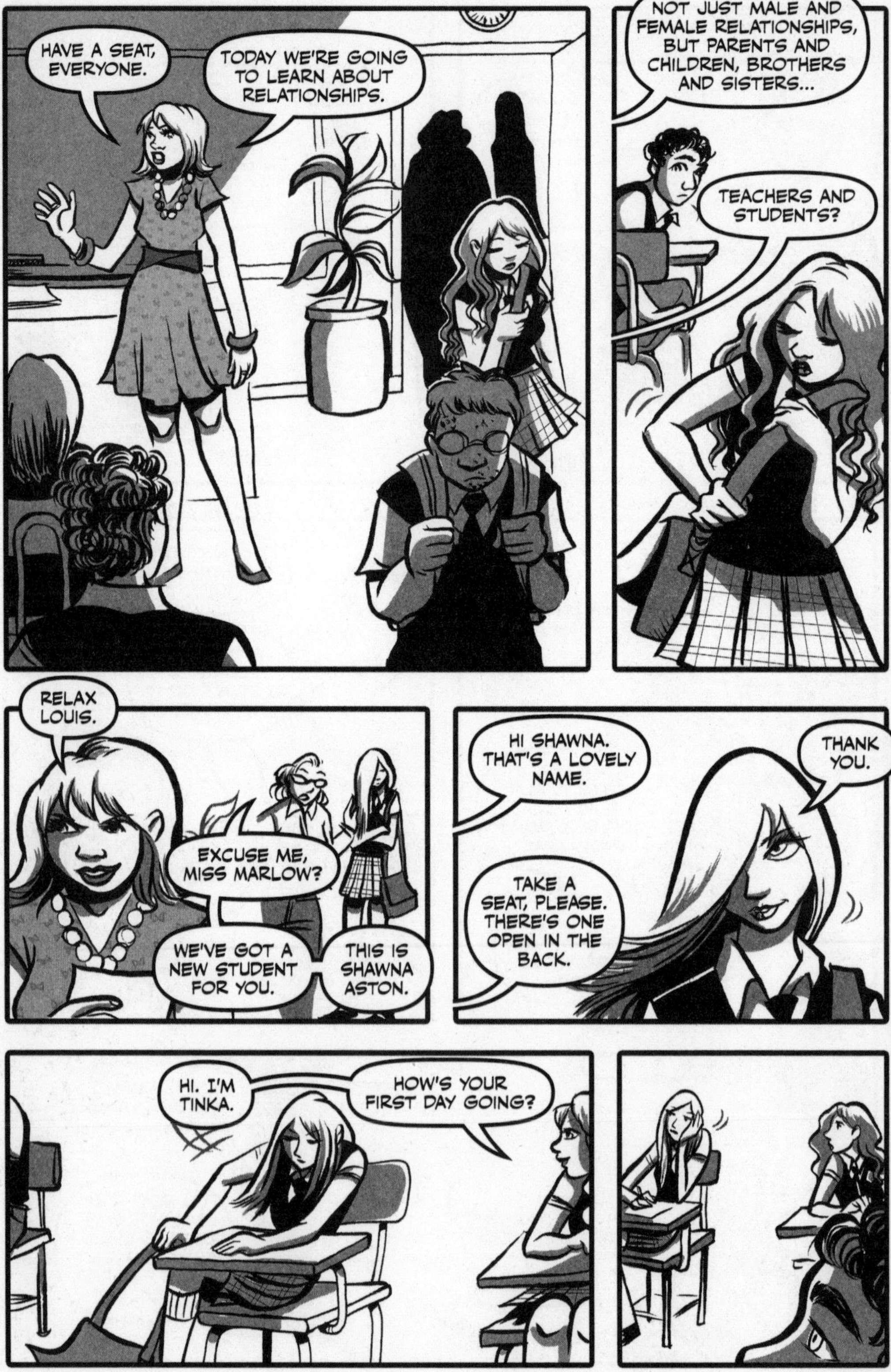
HAVE A SEAT, EVERYONE.
TODAY WE'RE GOING TO LEARN ABOUT RELATIONSHIPS.
NOT JUST MALE AND FEMALE RELATIONSHIPS, BUT PARENTS AND CHILDREN, BROTHERS AND SISTERS...
TEACHERS AND STUDENTS?
RELAX LOUIS.
EXCUSE ME, MISS MARLOW?
WE'VE GOT A NEW STUDENT FOR YOU.
THIS IS SHAWNA ASTON.
HI SHAWNA. THAT'S A LOVELY NAME.
THANK YOU.
TAKE A SEAT, PLEASE. THERE'S ONE OPEN IN THE BACK.
HI. I'M TINKA.
HOW'S YOUR FIRST DAY GOING?

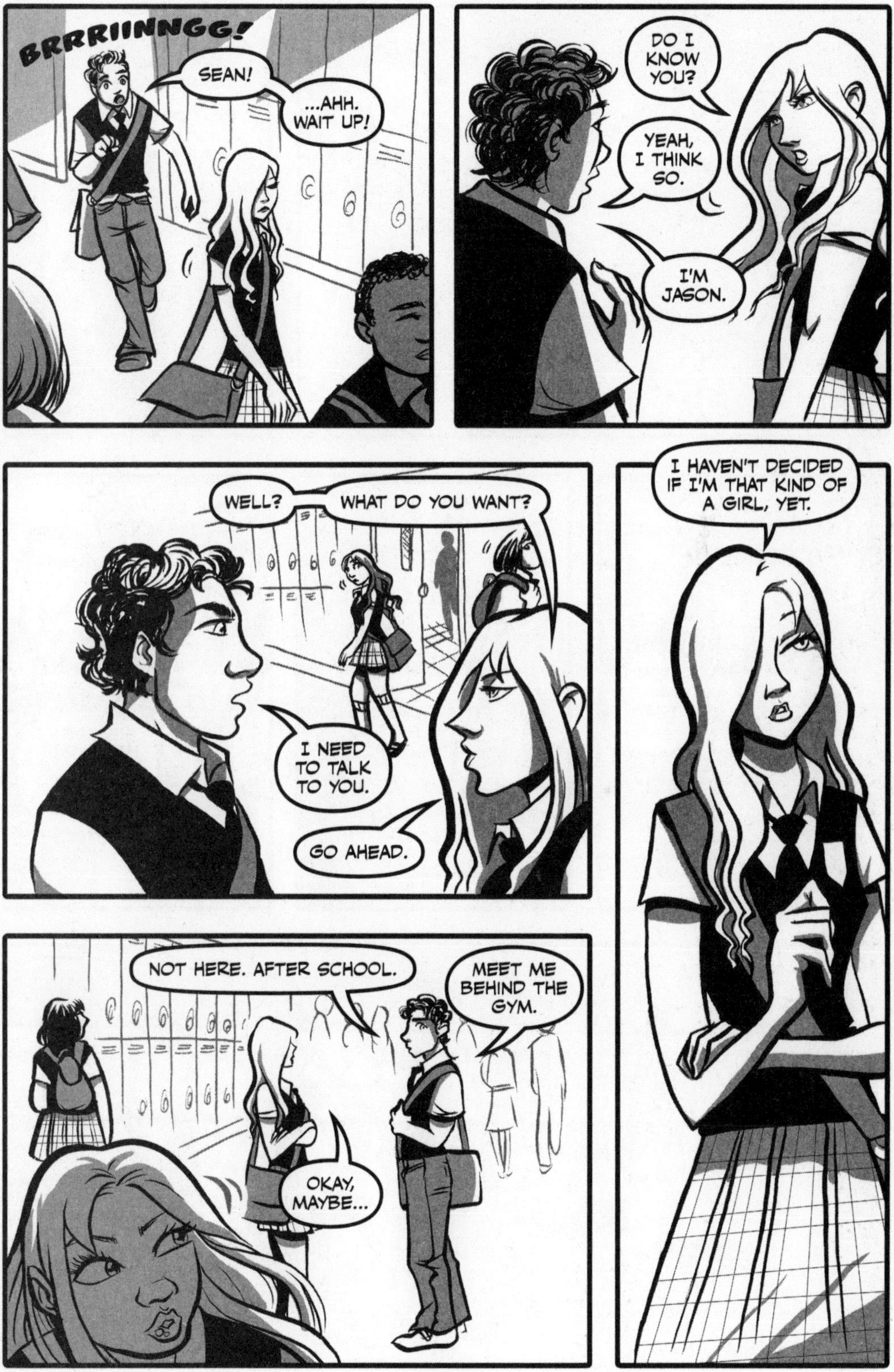
BRRRIINNGG!
SEAN!
...AHH. WAIT UP!
DO I KNOW YOU?
YEAH, I THINK SO.
I'M JASON.
WELL?
WHAT DO YOU WANT?
I NEED TO TALK TO YOU.
GO AHEAD.
I HAVEN'T DECIDED IF I'M THAT KIND OF A GIRL, YET.
NOT HERE. AFTER SCHOOL.
MEET ME BEHIND THE GYM.
OKAY, MAYBE...

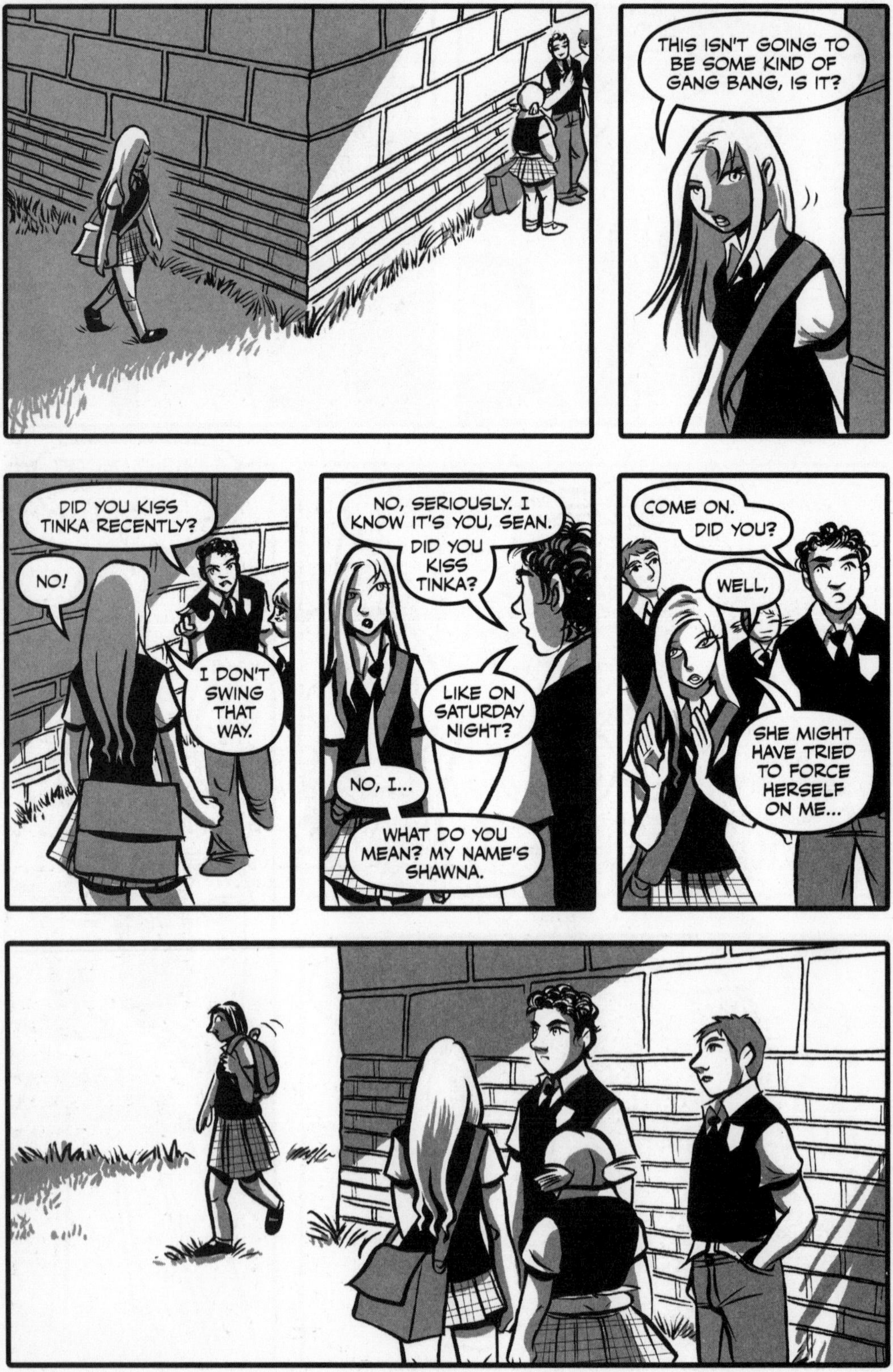
THIS ISN'T GOING TO BE SOME KIND OF GANG BANG, IS IT?
DID YOU KISS TINKA RECENTLY?
NO!
I DON'T SWING THAT WAY.
NO, SERIOUSLY. I KNOW IT'S YOU, SEAN.
DID YOU KISS TINKA?
LIKE ON SATURDAY NIGHT?
NO, I...
WHAT DO YOU MEAN? MY NAME'S SHAWNA.
COME ON. DID YOU?
WELL,
SHE MIGHT HAVE TRIED TO FORCE HERSELF ON ME...

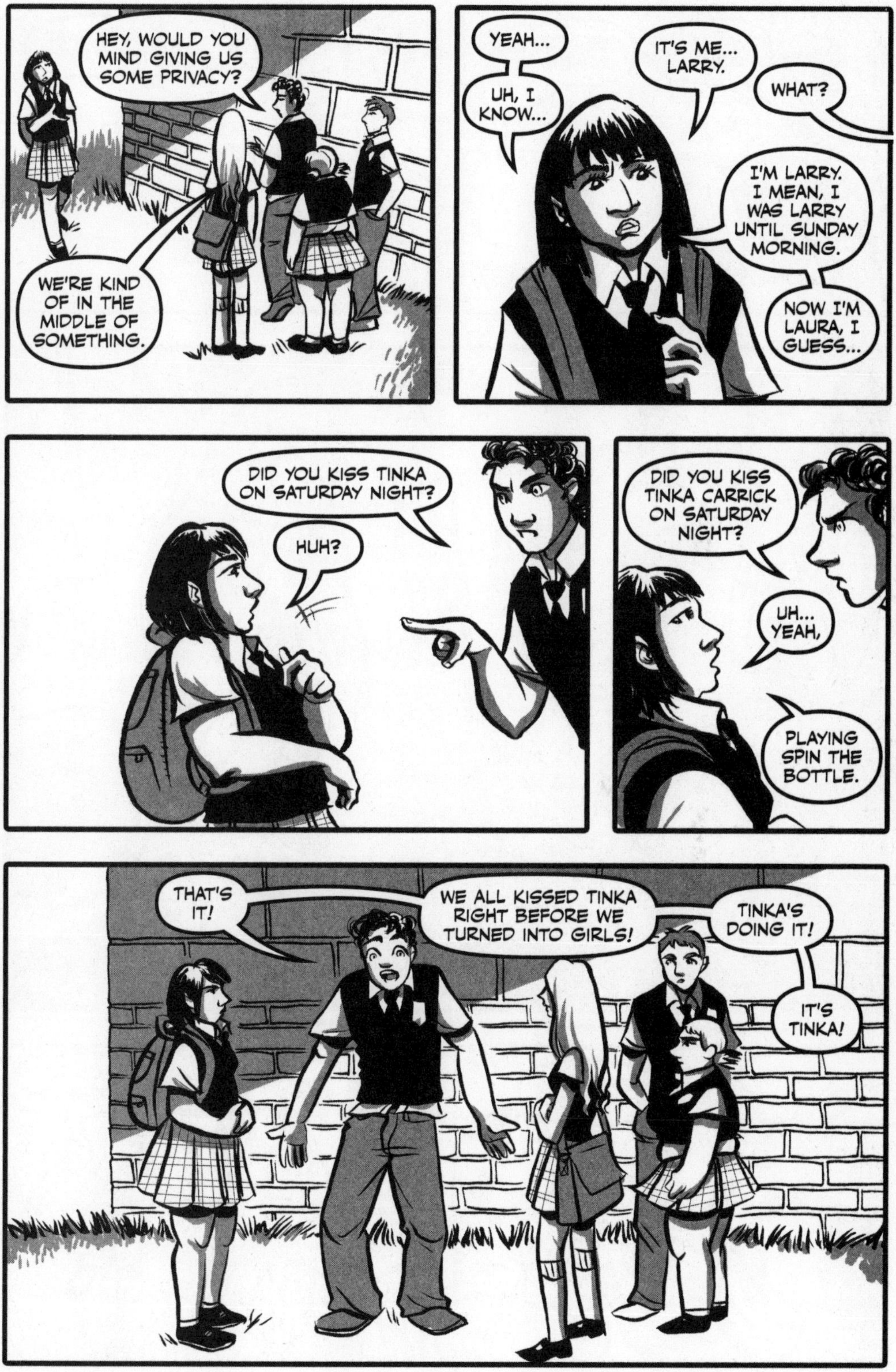
HEY, WOULD YOU MIND GIVING US SOME PRIVACY?
WE'RE KIND OF IN THE MIDDLE OF SOMETHING.
YEAH...
UH, I KNOW...
IT'S ME... LARRY.
WHAT?
I'M LARRY. I MEAN, I WAS LARRY UNTIL SUNDAY MORNING.
NOW I'M LAURA, I GUESS...
DID YOU KISS TINKA ON SATURDAY NIGHT?
HUH?
DID YOU KISS TINKA CARRICK ON SATURDAY NIGHT?
UH... YEAH,
PLAYING SPIN THE BOTTLE.
THAT'S IT!
WE ALL KISSED TINKA RIGHT BEFORE WE TURNED INTO GIRLS!
TINKA'S DOING IT!
IT'S TINKA!

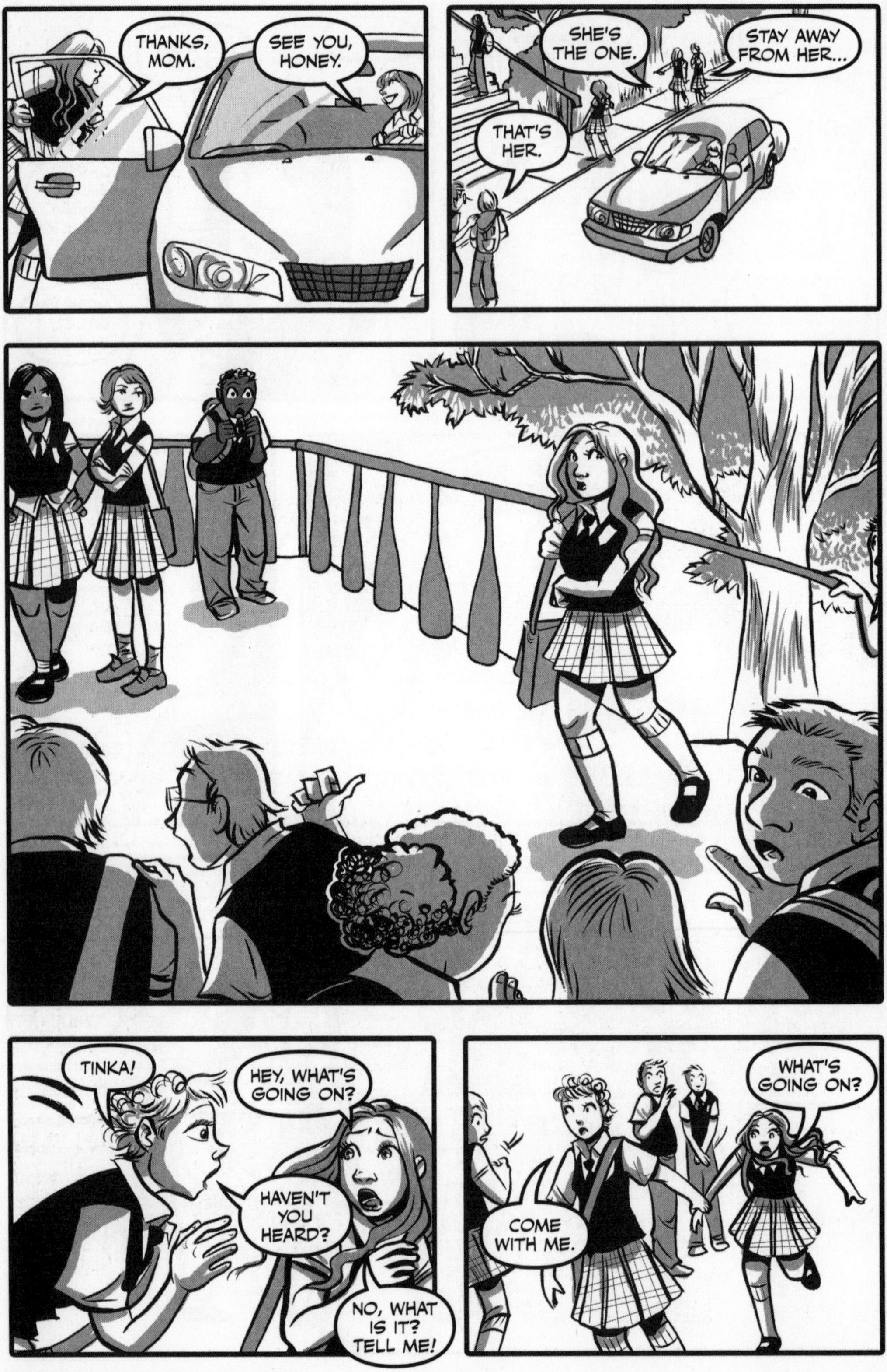
THANKS, MOM.
SEE YOU, HONEY.
SHE'S THE ONE.
STAY AWAY FROM HER...
THAT'S HER.
TINKA!
HEY, WHAT'S GOING ON?
HAVEN'T YOU HEARD?
NO, WHAT IS IT? TELL ME!
WHAT'S GOING ON?
COME WITH ME.

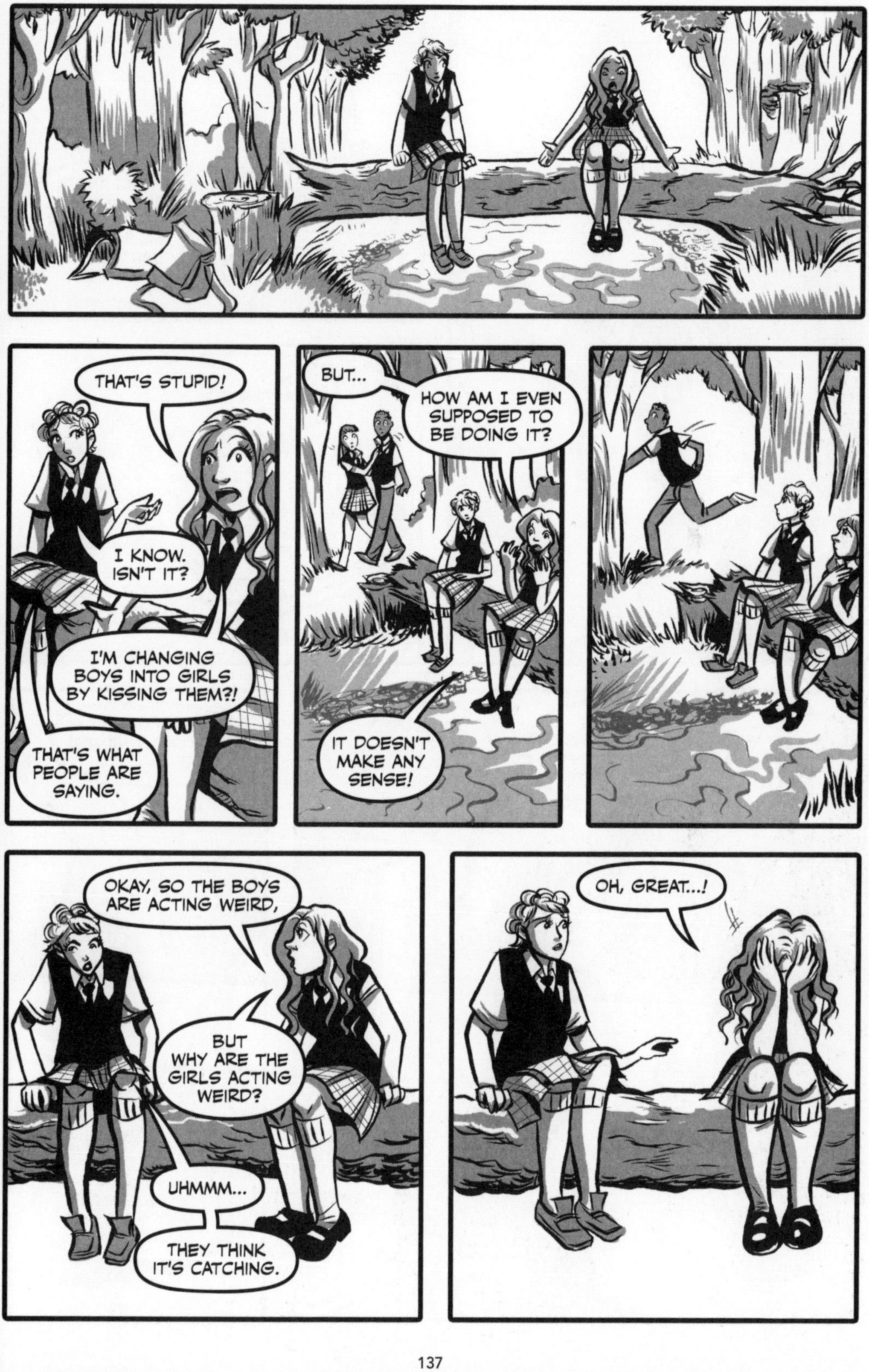
THAT'S STUPID!
I KNOW. ISN'T IT?
I'M CHANGING BOYS INTO GIRLS BY KISSING THEM?!
THAT'S WHAT PEOPLE ARE SAYING.
BUT...
HOW AM I EVEN SUPPOSED TO BE DOING IT?
IT DOESN'T MAKE ANY SENSE!
OKAY, SO THE BOYS ARE ACTING WEIRD,
BUT WHY ARE THE GIRLS ACTING WEIRD?
UHMMM...
THEY THINK IT'S CATCHING.
OH, GREAT...!

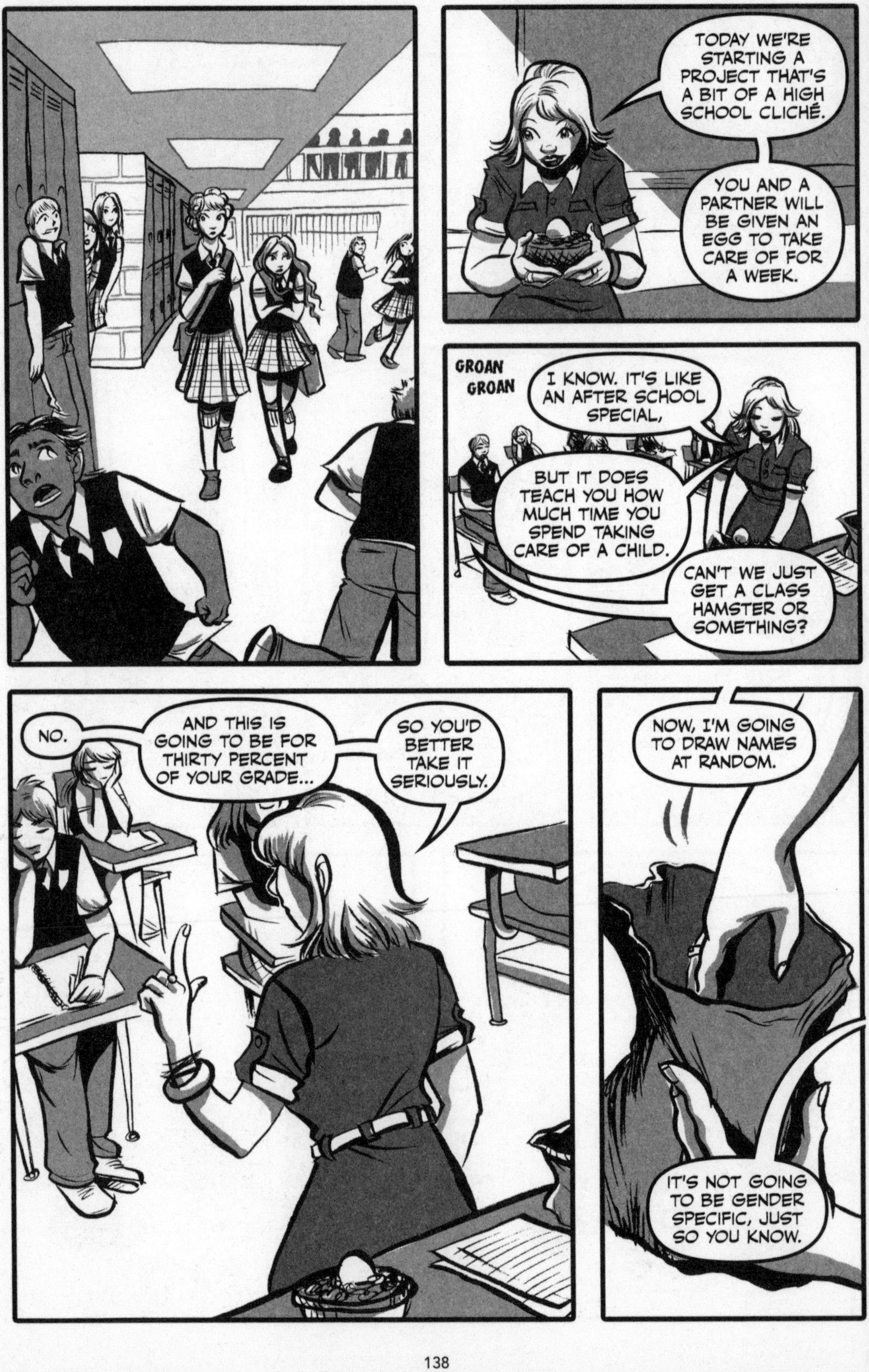
TODAY WE'RE STARTING A PROJECT THAT'S A BIT OF A HIGH SCHOOL CLICHÉ.
YOU AND A PARTNER WILL BE GIVEN AN EGG TO TAKE CARE OF FOR A WEEK.
GROAN GROAN
I KNOW. IT'S LIKE AN AFTER SCHOOL SPECIAL,
BUT IT DOES TEACH YOU HOW MUCH TIME YOU SPEND TAKING CARE OF A CHILD.
CAN'T WE JUST GET A CLASS HAMSTER OR SOMETHING?
NO.
AND THIS IS GOING TO BE FOR THIRTY PERCENT OF YOUR GRADE...
SO YOU'D BETTER TAKE IT SERIOUSLY.
NOW, I'M GOING TO DRAW NAMES AT RANDOM.
IT'S NOT GOING TO BE GENDER SPECIFIC, JUST SO YOU KNOW.

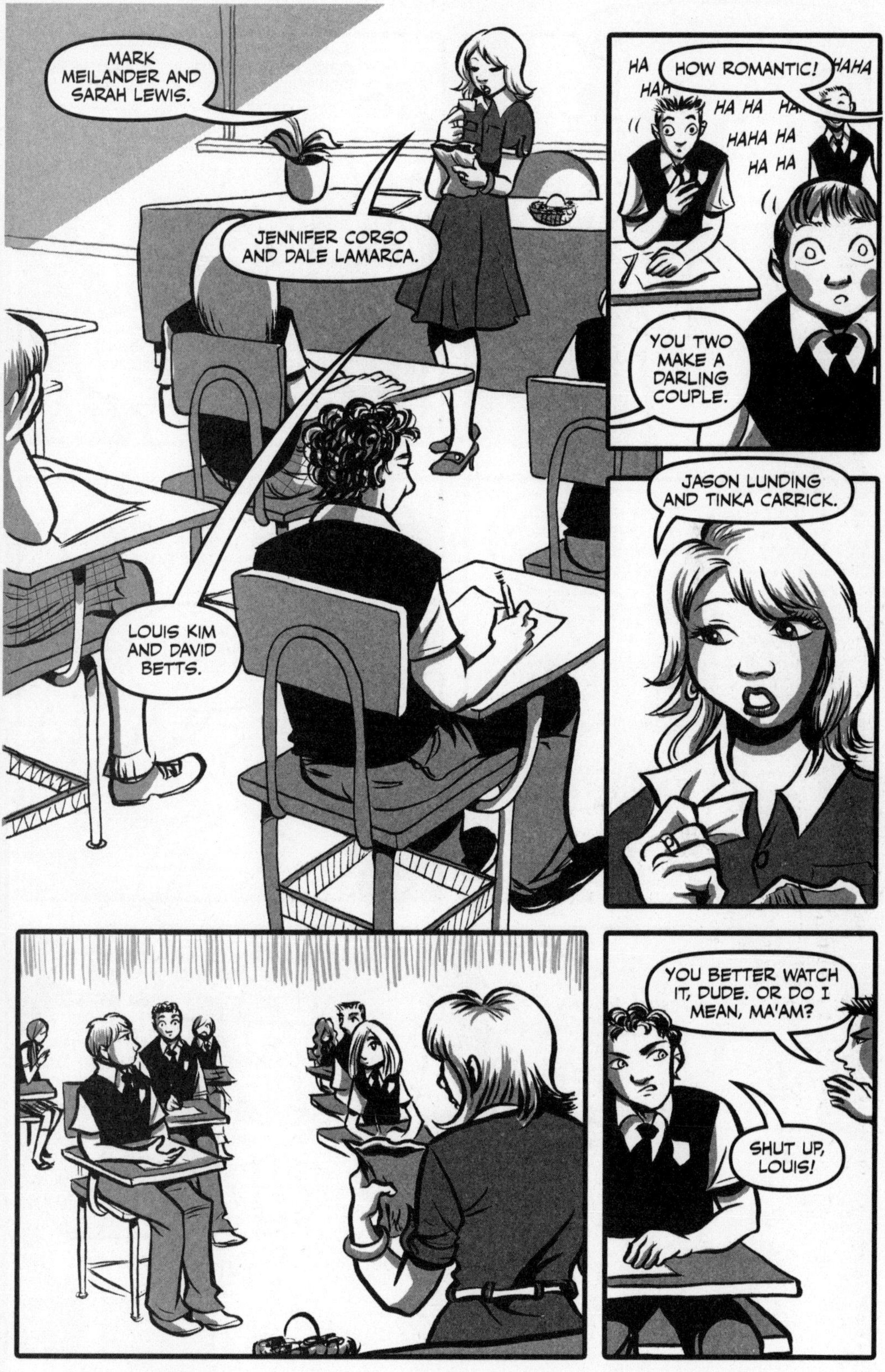
MARK MEILANDER AND SARAH LEWIS.
JENNIFER CORSO AND DALE LAMARCA.
LOUIS KIM AND DAVID BETTS.
HA HAH
HOW ROMANTIC!
HAHA
HA HA HA
HAHA HA
HA HA
YOU TWO MAKE A DARLING COUPLE.
JASON LUNDING AND TINKA CARRICK.
YOU BETTER WATCH IT, DUDE. OR DO I MEAN, MA'AM?
SHUT UP, LOUIS!

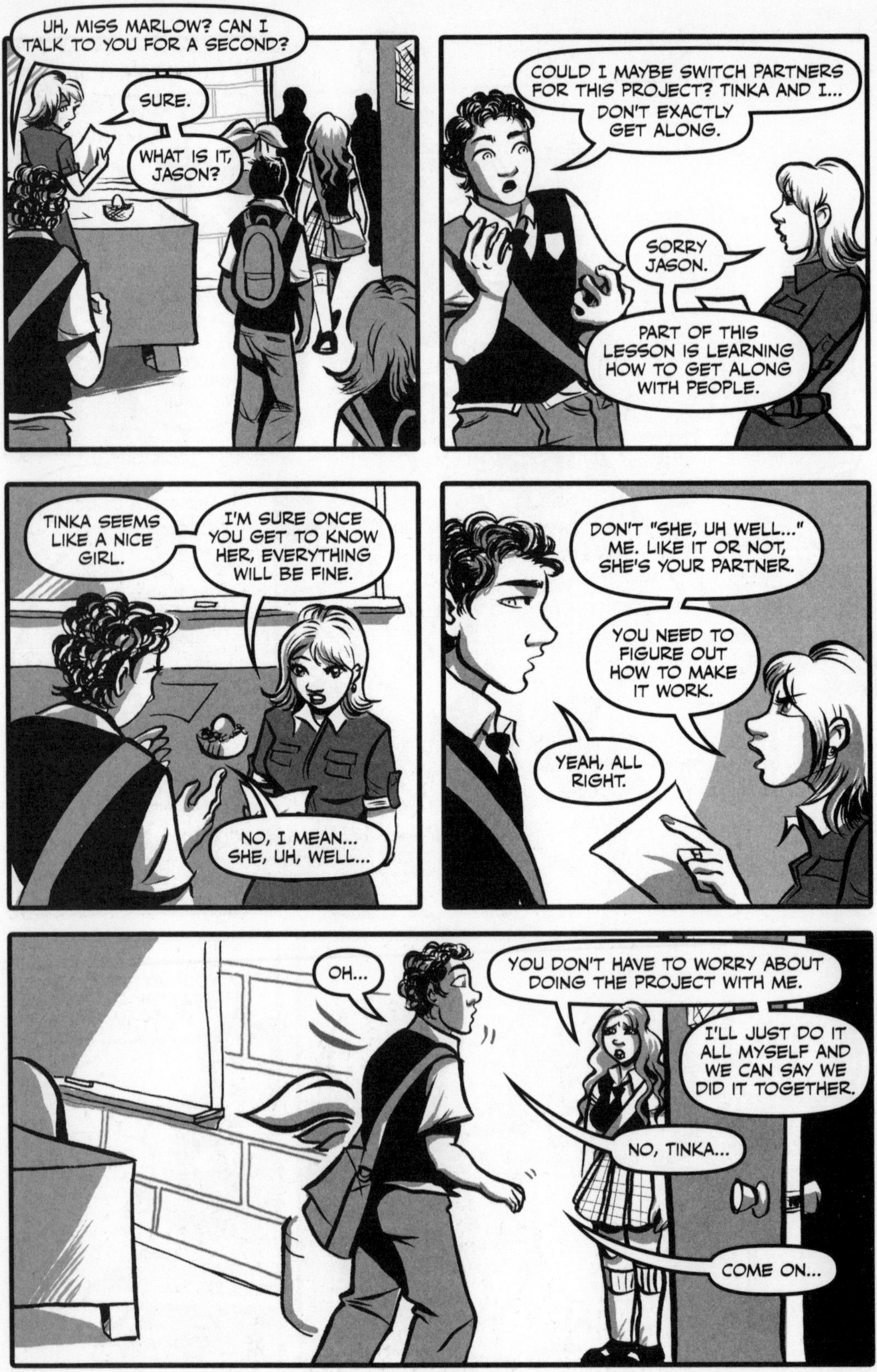
UH, MISS MARLOW? CAN I TALK TO YOU FOR A SECOND?
SURE.
WHAT IS IT, JASON?
COULD I MAYBE SWITCH PARTNERS FOR THIS PROJECT? TINKA AND I...
DON'T EXACTLY GET ALONG.
SORRY JASON.
PART OF THIS LESSON IS LEARNING HOW TO GET ALONG WITH PEOPLE.
TINKA SEEMS LIKE A NICE GIRL.
I'M SURE ONCE YOU GET TO KNOW HER, EVERYTHING WILL BE FINE.
NO, I MEAN... SHE, UH, WELL...
DON'T "SHE, UH WELL..." ME. LIKE IT OR NOT, SHE'S YOUR PARTNER.
YOU NEED TO FIGURE OUT HOW TO MAKE IT WORK.
YEAH, ALL RIGHT.
OH...
YOU DON'T HAVE TO WORRY ABOUT DOING THE PROJECT WITH ME.
I'LL JUST DO IT ALL MYSELF AND WE CAN SAY WE DID IT TOGETHER.
NO, TINKA...
COME ON...

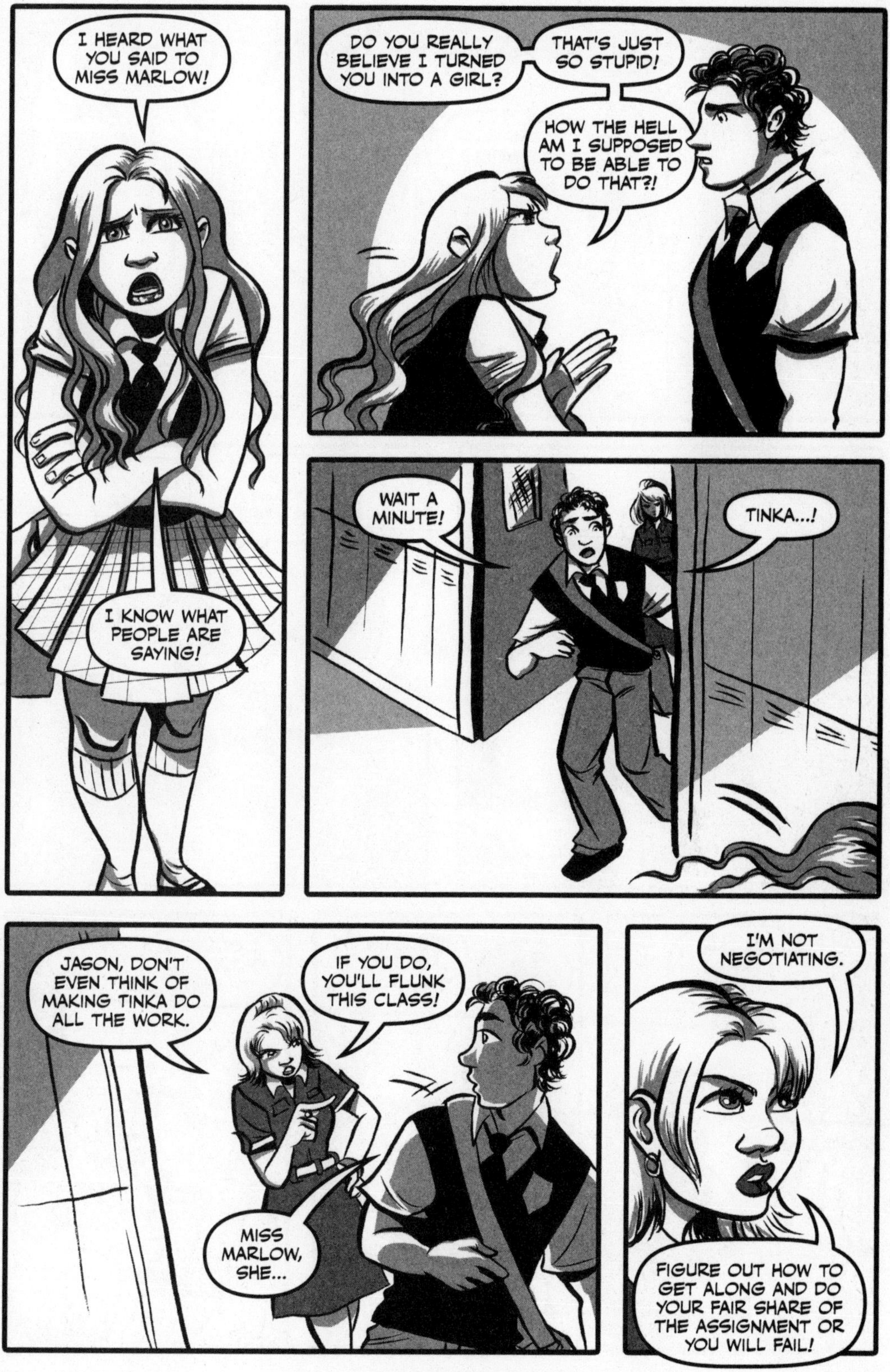

I HEARD WHAT YOU SAID TO MISS MARLOW!
I KNOW WHAT PEOPLE ARE SAYING!
DO YOU REALLY BELIEVE I TURNED YOU INTO A GIRL?
THAT'S JUST SO STUPID!
HOW THE HELL AM I SUPPOSED TO BE ABLE TO DO THAT?!
WAIT A MINUTE!
TINKA...!
JASON, DON'T EVEN THINK OF MAKING TINKA DO ALL THE WORK.
IF YOU DO, YOU'LL FLUNK THIS CLASS!
MISS MARLOW, SHE...
I'M NOT NEGOTIATING.
FIGURE OUT HOW TO GET ALONG AND DO YOUR FAIR SHARE OF THE ASSIGNMENT OR YOU WILL FAIL!

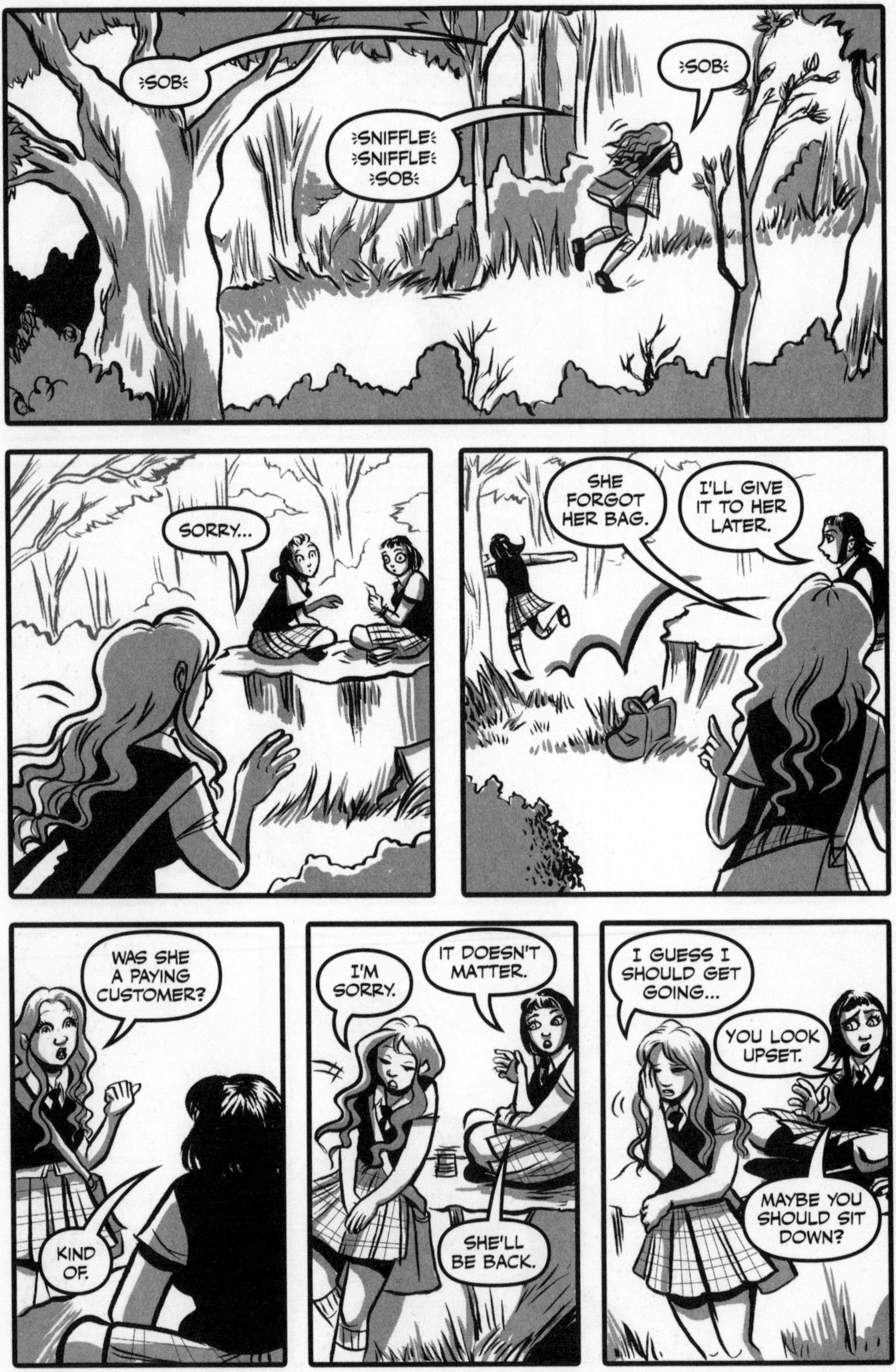

SOB
SNIFFLE SNIFFLE SOB
SOB
SORRY...
SHE FORGOT HER BAG.
I'LL GIVE IT TO HER LATER.
WAS SHE A PAYING CUSTOMER?
KIND OF.
I'M SORRY.
IT DOESN'T MATTER.
SHE'LL BE BACK.
I GUESS I SHOULD GET GOING...
YOU LOOK UPSET.
MAYBE YOU SHOULD SIT DOWN?

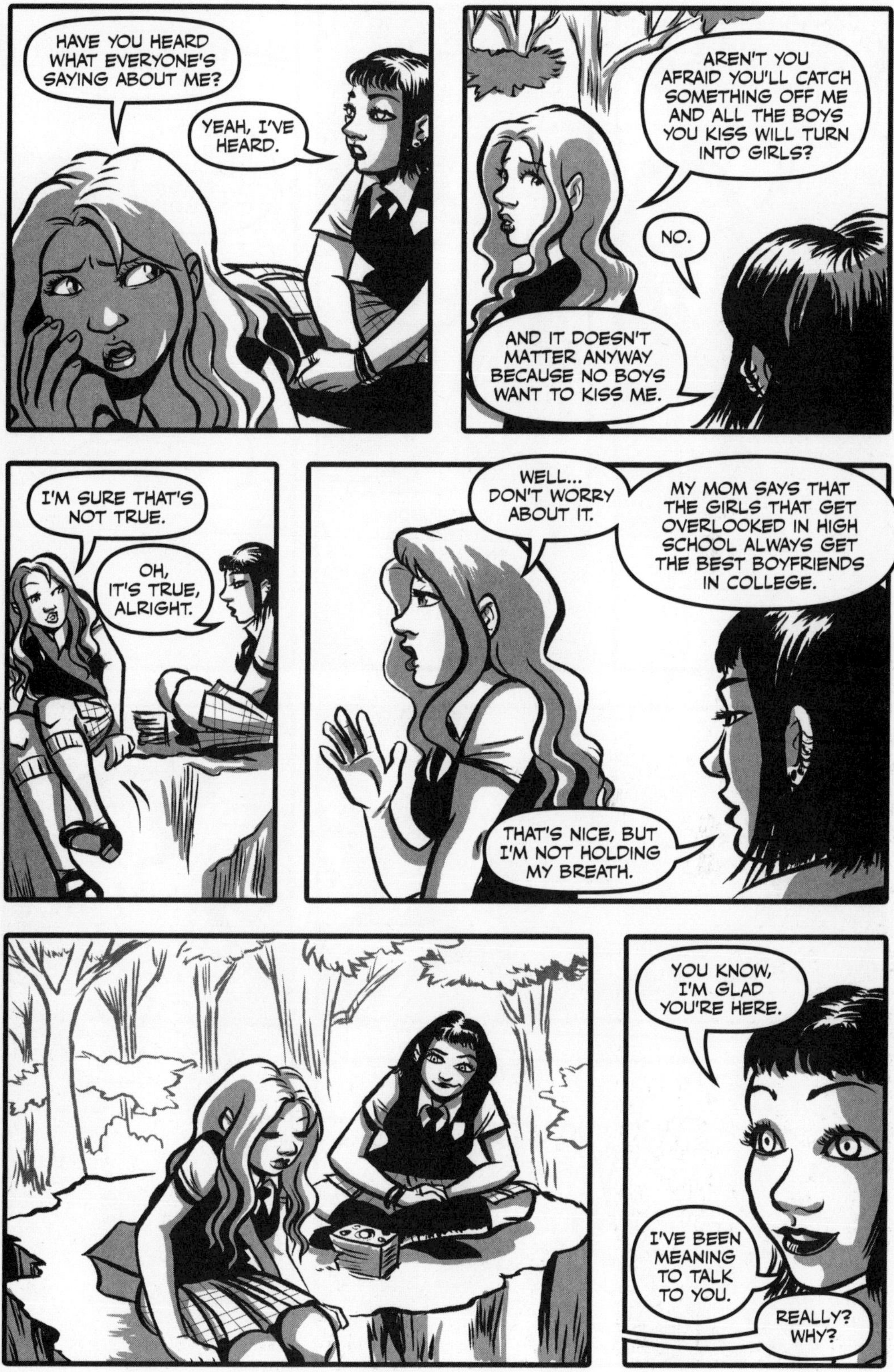
HAVE YOU HEARD WHAT EVERYONE'S SAYING ABOUT ME?
YEAH, I'VE HEARD.
AREN'T YOU AFRAID YOU'LL CATCH SOMETHING OFF ME AND ALL THE BOYS YOU KISS WILL TURN INTO GIRLS?
NO.
AND IT DOESN'T MATTER ANYWAY BECAUSE NO BOYS WANT TO KISS ME.
I'M SURE THAT'S NOT TRUE.
OH, IT'S TRUE, ALRIGHT.
WELL... DON'T WORRY ABOUT IT.
MY MOM SAYS THAT THE GIRLS THAT GET OVERLOOKED IN HIGH SCHOOL ALWAYS GET THE BEST BOYFRIENDS IN COLLEGE.
THAT'S NICE, BUT I'M NOT HOLDING MY BREATH.
YOU KNOW, I'M GLAD YOU'RE HERE.
I'VE BEEN MEANING TO TALK TO YOU.
REALLY? WHY?

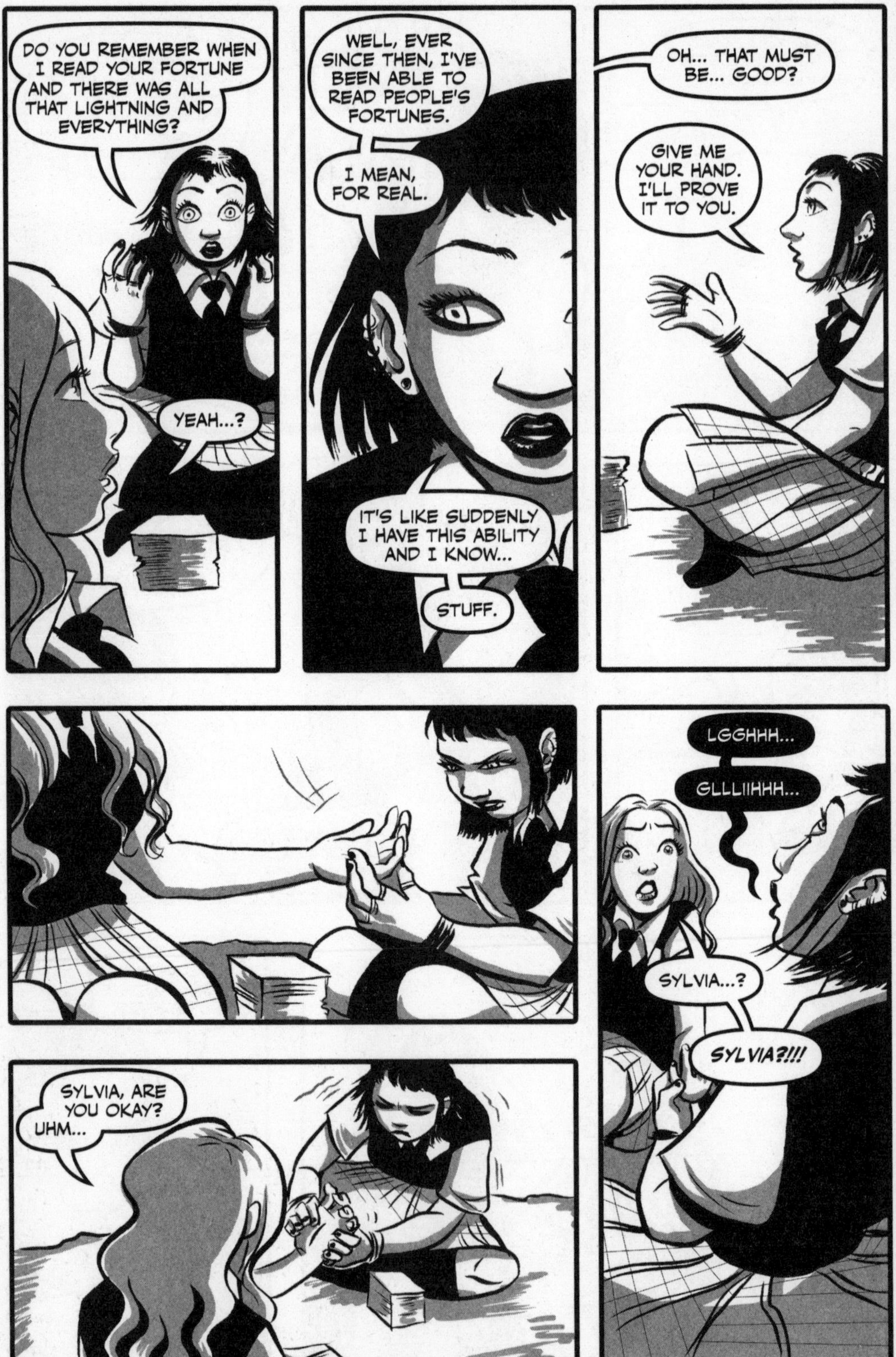
DO YOU REMEMBER WHEN I READ YOUR FORTUNE AND THERE WAS ALL THAT LIGHTNING AND EVERYTHING?
YEAH...?
WELL, EVER SINCE THEN, I'VE BEEN ABLE TO READ PEOPLE'S FORTUNES.
I MEAN, FOR REAL.
IT'S LIKE SUDDENLY I HAVE THIS ABILITY AND I KNOW...
STUFF.
OH... THAT MUST BE... GOOD?
GIVE ME YOUR HAND. I'LL PROVE IT TO YOU.
LGGHHH...
GLLLIIHHH...
SYLVIA...?
SYLVIA?!!!
SYLVIA, ARE YOU OKAY? UHM...

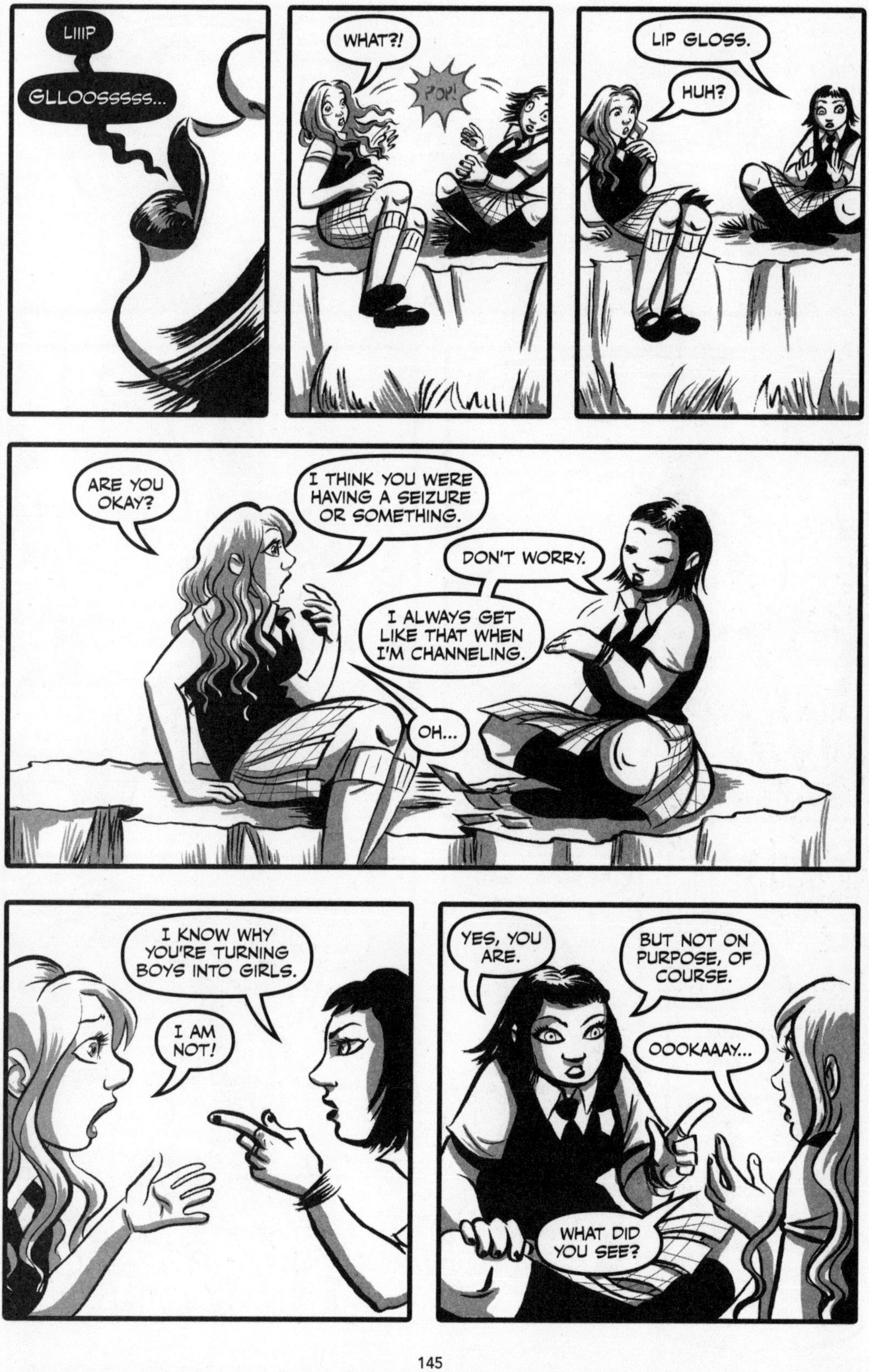
LIIIP
GLLOOSSSSS...
WHAT?!
POP!
LIP GLOSS.
HUH?
ARE YOU OKAY?
I THINK YOU WERE HAVING A SEIZURE OR SOMETHING.
DON'T WORRY.
I ALWAYS GET LIKE THAT WHEN I'M CHANNELING.
OH...
I KNOW WHY YOU'RE TURNING BOYS INTO GIRLS.
I AM NOT!
YES, YOU ARE.
BUT NOT ON PURPOSE, OF COURSE.
OOOKAAAY...
WHAT DID YOU SEE?

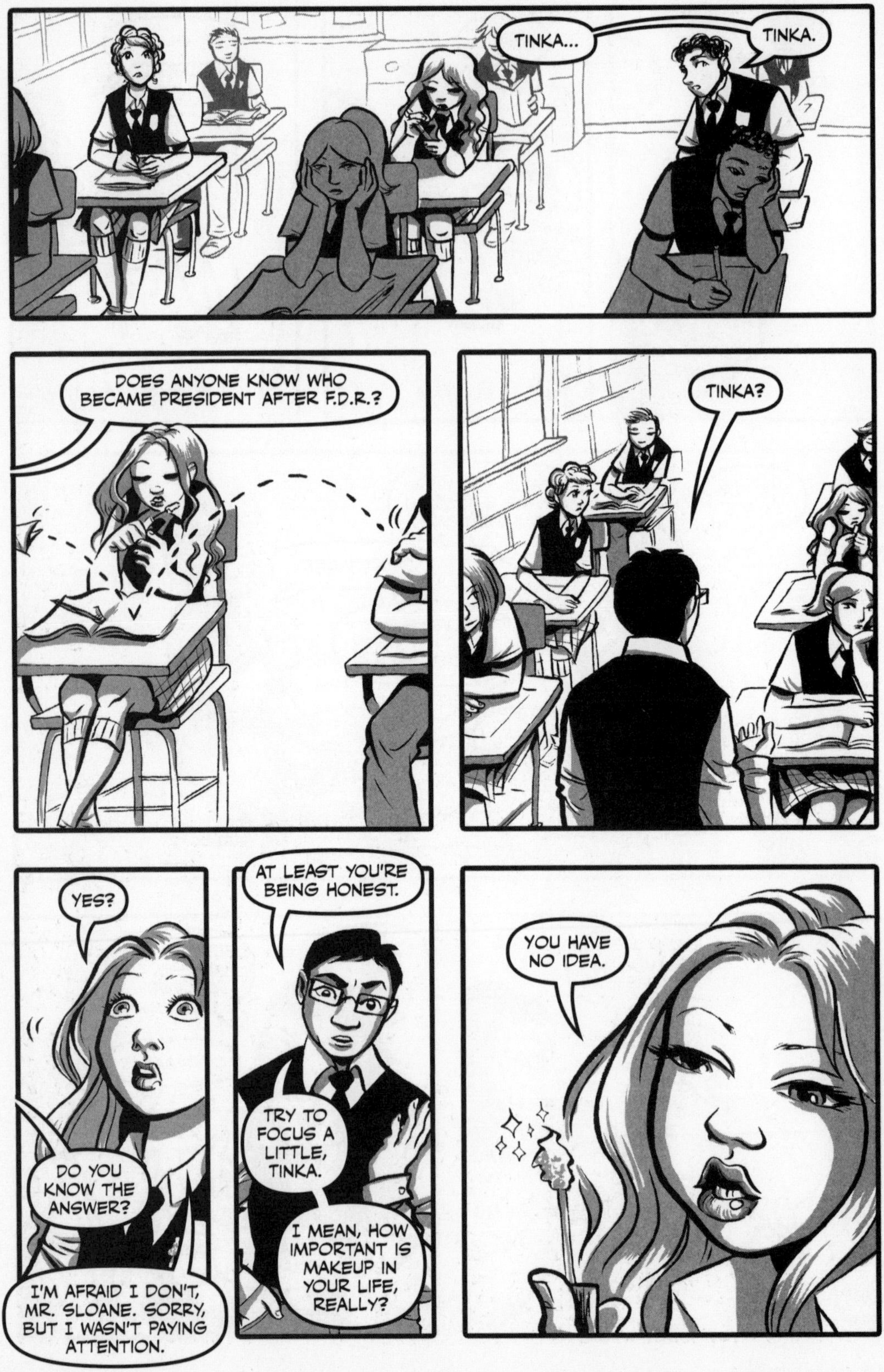
TINKA...
TINKA.
DOES ANYONE KNOW WHO BECAME PRESIDENT AFTER F.D.R.?
TINKA?
YES?
DO YOU KNOW THE ANSWER?
I'M AFRAID I DON'T, MR. SLOANE. SORRY, BUT I WASN'T PAYING ATTENTION.
AT LEAST YOU'RE BEING HONEST.
TRY TO FOCUS A LITTLE, TINKA.
I MEAN, HOW IMPORTANT IS MAKEUP IN YOUR LIFE, REALLY?
YOU HAVE NO IDEA.

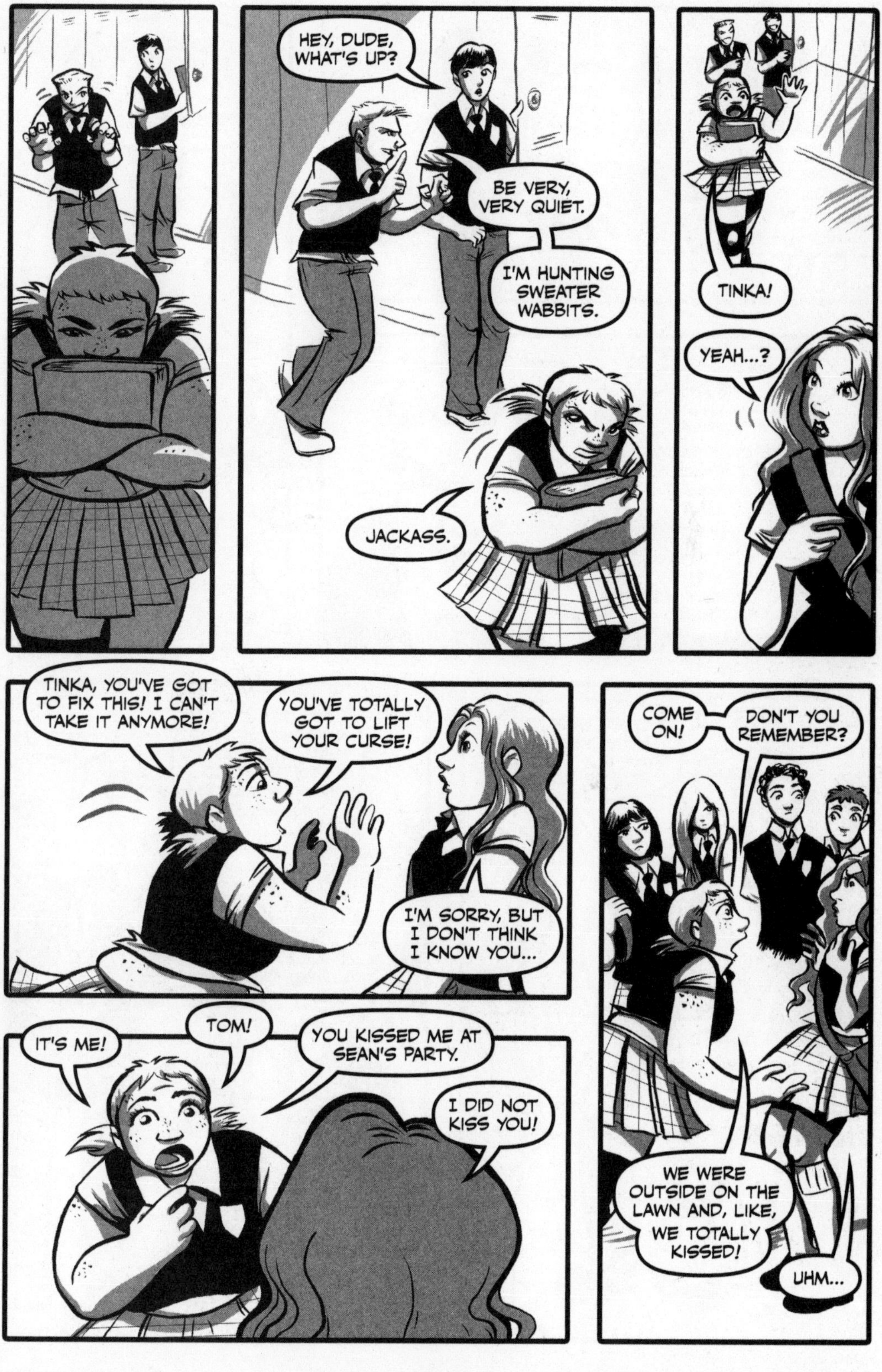
HEY, DUDE, WHAT'S UP?
BE VERY, VERY QUIET.
I'M HUNTING SWEATER WABBITS.
JACKASS.
TINKA!
YEAH...?
TINKA, YOU'VE GOT TO FIX THIS! I CAN'T TAKE IT ANYMORE!
YOU'VE TOTALLY GOT TO LIFT YOUR CURSE!
I'M SORRY, BUT I DON'T THINK I KNOW YOU...
IT'S ME!
TOM!
YOU KISSED ME AT SEAN'S PARTY.
I DID NOT KISS YOU!
COME ON!
DON'T YOU REMEMBER?
WE WERE OUTSIDE ON THE LAWN AND, LIKE, WE TOTALLY KISSED!
UHM...

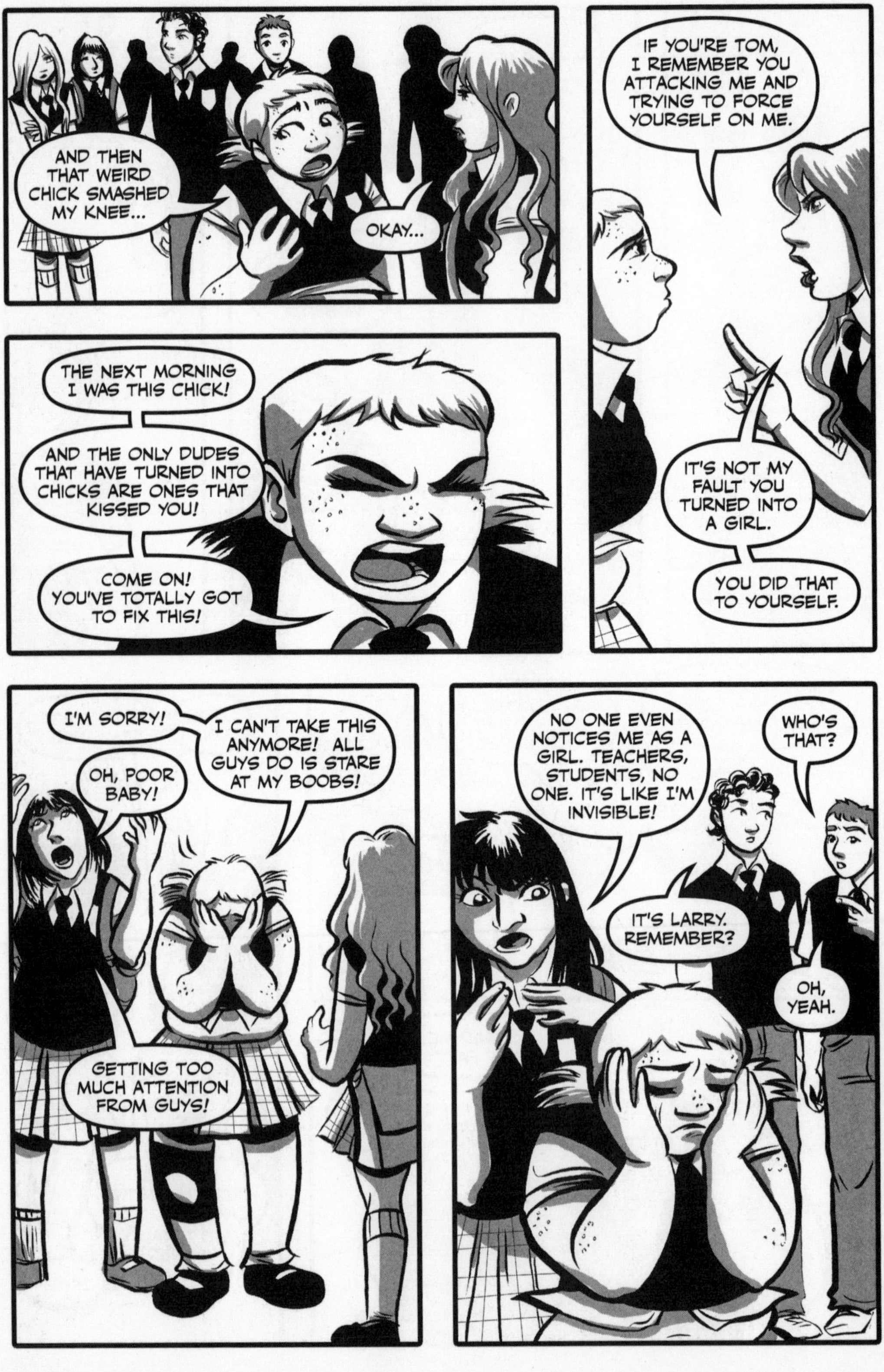
AND THEN THAT WEIRD CHICK SMASHED MY KNEE...
OKAY...
IF YOU'RE TOM, I REMEMBER YOU ATTACKING ME AND TRYING TO FORCE YOURSELF ON ME.
THE NEXT MORNING I WAS THIS CHICK!
AND THE ONLY DUDES THAT HAVE TURNED INTO CHICKS ARE ONES THAT KISSED YOU!
COME ON! YOU'VE TOTALLY GOT TO FIX THIS!
IT'S NOT MY FAULT YOU TURNED INTO A GIRL.
YOU DID THAT TO YOURSELF.
I'M SORRY!
I CAN'T TAKE THIS ANYMORE! ALL GUYS DO IS STARE AT MY BOOBS!
OH, POOR BABY!
GETTING TOO MUCH ATTENTION FROM GUYS!
NO ONE EVEN NOTICES ME AS A GIRL. TEACHERS, STUDENTS, NO ONE. IT'S LIKE I'M INVISIBLE!
WHO'S THAT?
IT'S LARRY. REMEMBER?
OH, YEAH.

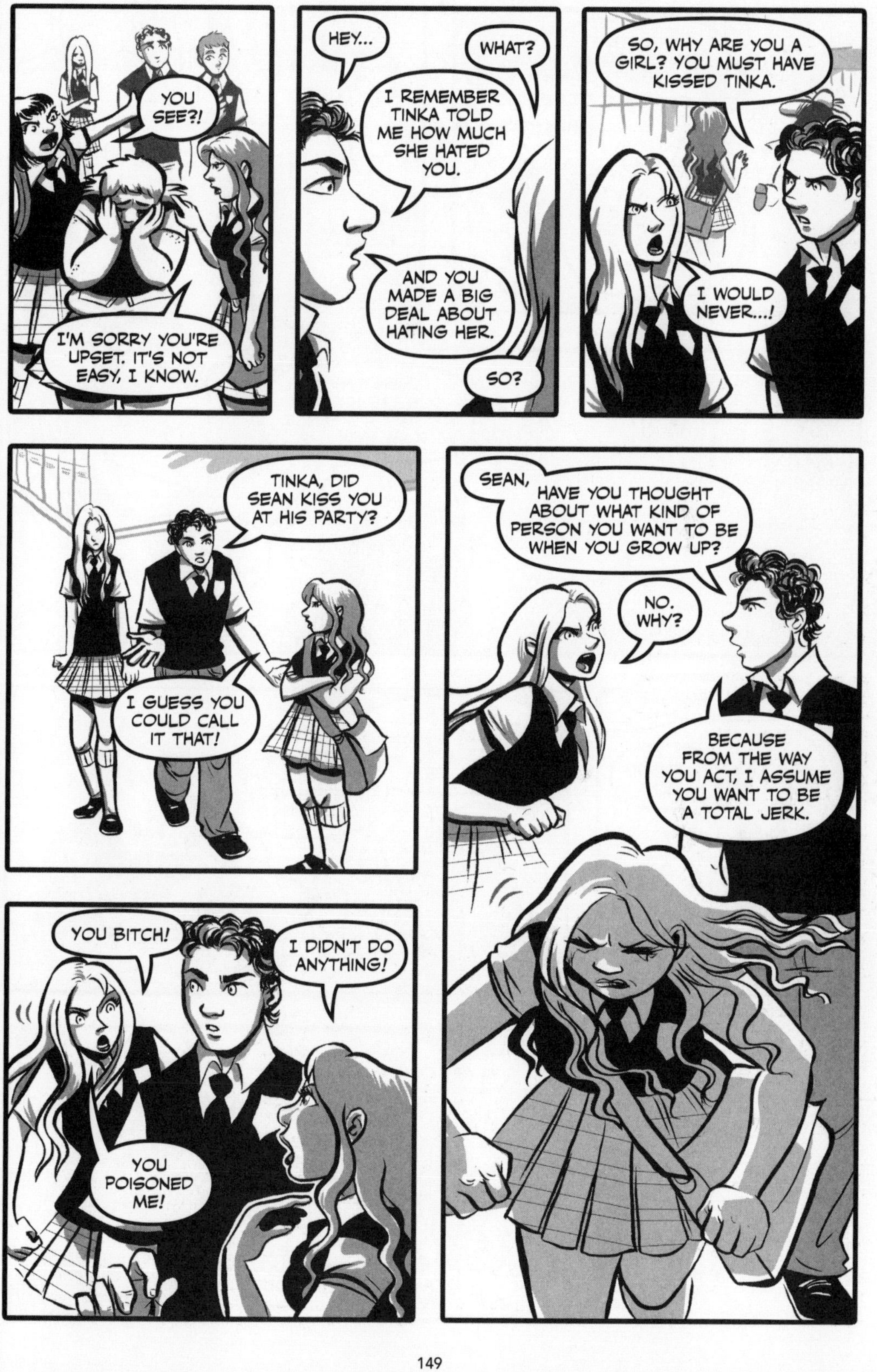
YOU SEE?!
I'M SORRY YOU'RE UPSET. IT'S NOT EASY, I KNOW.
HEY...
WHAT?
I REMEMBER TINKA TOLD ME HOW MUCH SHE HATED YOU.
AND YOU MADE A BIG DEAL ABOUT HATING HER.
SO?
SO, WHY ARE YOU A GIRL? YOU MUST HAVE KISSED TINKA.
I WOULD NEVER...!
TINKA, DID SEAN KISS YOU AT HIS PARTY?
I GUESS YOU COULD CALL IT THAT!
SEAN,
HAVE YOU THOUGHT ABOUT WHAT KIND OF PERSON YOU WANT TO BE WHEN YOU GROW UP?
NO. WHY?
BECAUSE FROM THE WAY YOU ACT, I ASSUME YOU WANT TO BE A TOTAL JERK.
YOU BITCH!
I DIDN'T DO ANYTHING!
YOU POISONED ME!

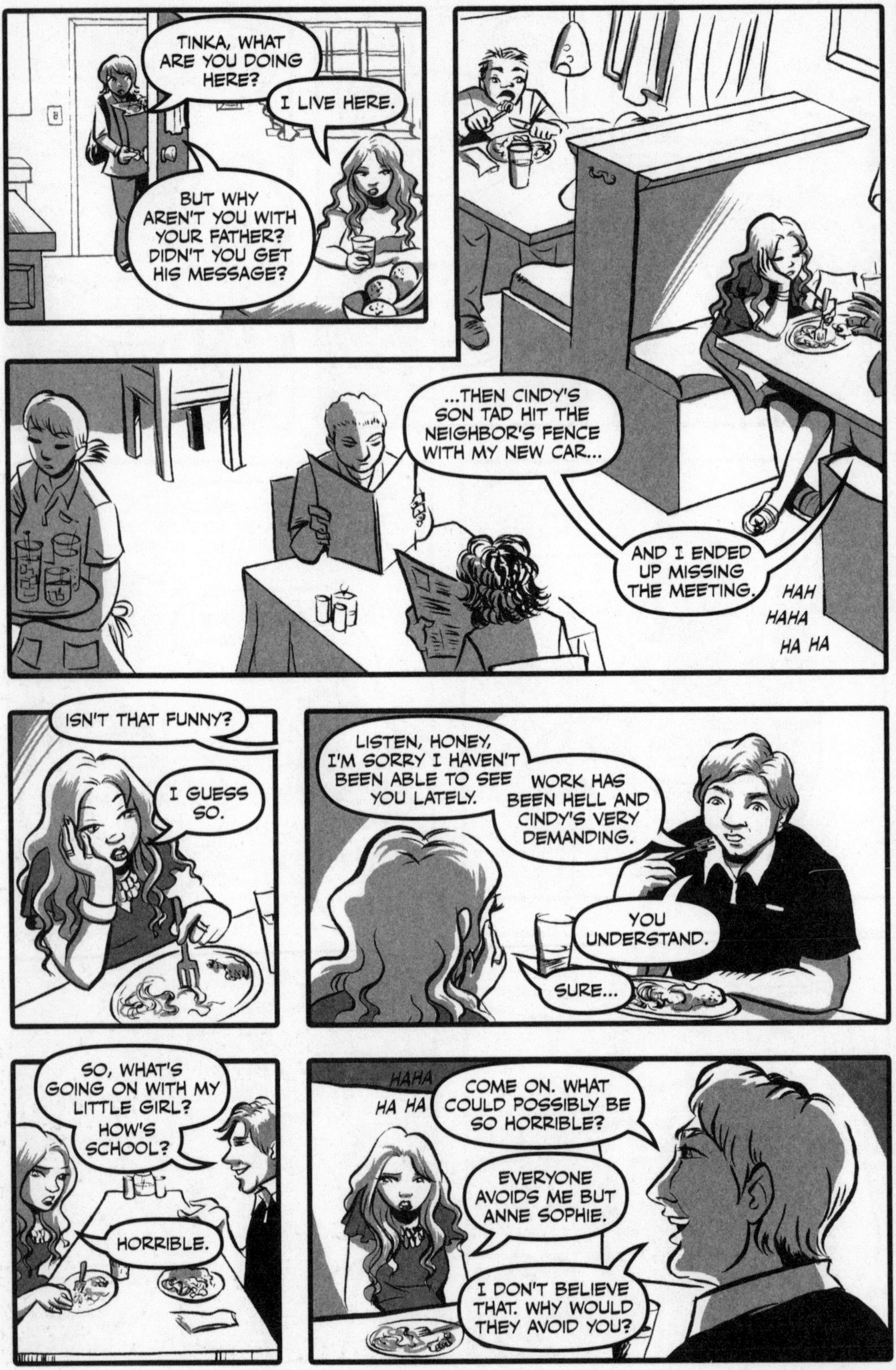
TINKA, WHAT ARE YOU DOING HERE?
I LIVE HERE.
BUT WHY AREN'T YOU WITH YOUR FATHER? DIDN'T YOU GET HIS MESSAGE?
...THEN CINDY'S SON TAD HIT THE NEIGHBOR'S FENCE WITH MY NEW CAR...
AND I ENDED UP MISSING THE MEETING.
HAH HAHA HA HA
ISN'T THAT FUNNY?
I GUESS SO.
LISTEN, HONEY, I'M SORRY I HAVEN'T BEEN ABLE TO SEE YOU LATELY.
WORK HAS BEEN HELL AND CINDY'S VERY DEMANDING.
YOU UNDERSTAND.
SURE...
SO, WHAT'S GOING ON WITH MY LITTLE GIRL? HOW'S SCHOOL?
HORRIBLE.
HAHA HA HA
COME ON. WHAT COULD POSSIBLY BE SO HORRIBLE?
EVERYONE AVOIDS ME BUT ANNE SOPHIE.
I DON'T BELIEVE THAT. WHY WOULD THEY AVOID YOU?

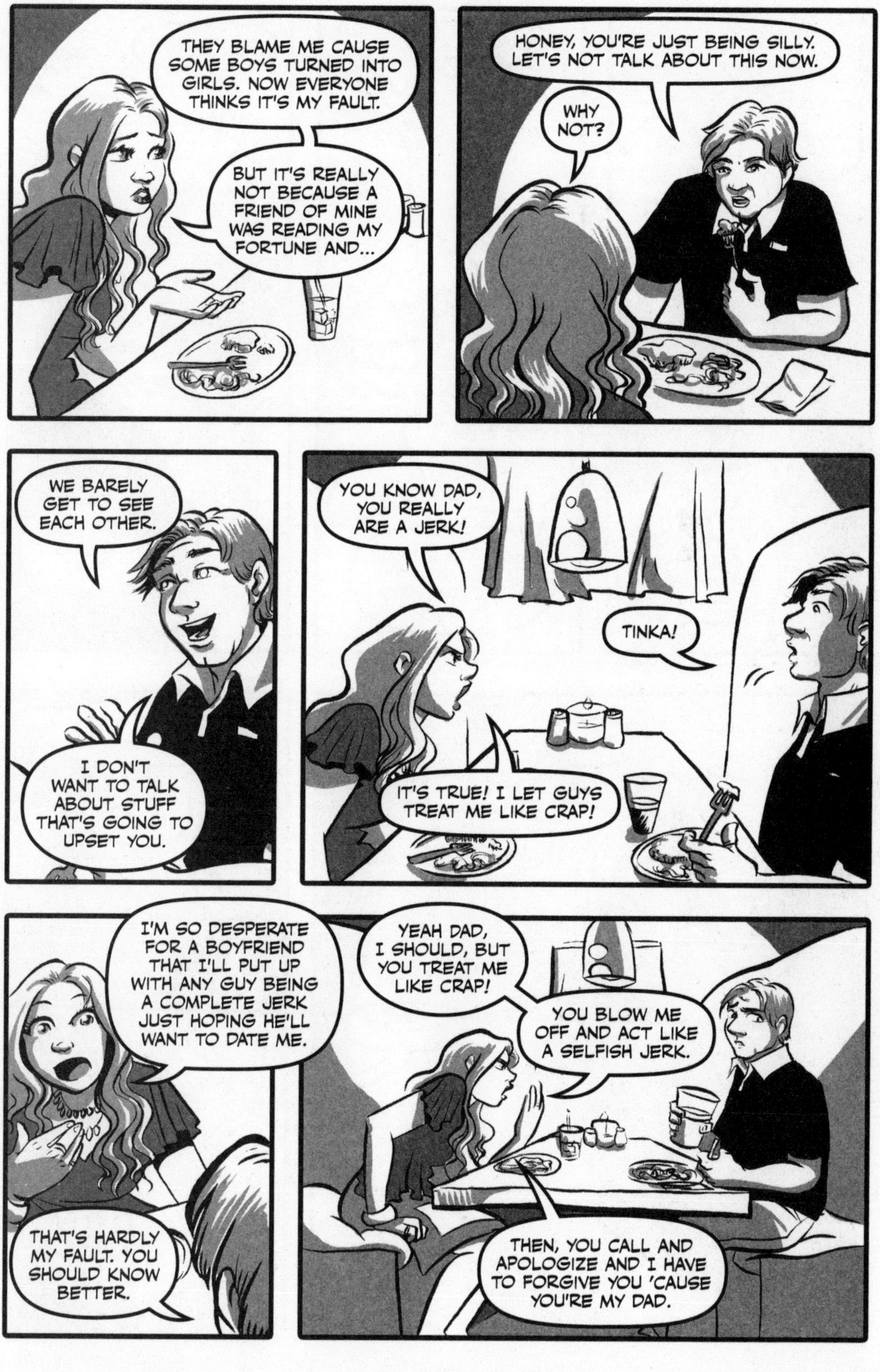
THEY BLAME ME CAUSE SOME BOYS TURNED INTO GIRLS. NOW EVERYONE THINKS IT'S MY FAULT.
BUT IT'S REALLY NOT BECAUSE A FRIEND OF MINE WAS READING MY FORTUNE AND...
HONEY, YOU'RE JUST BEING SILLY. LET'S NOT TALK ABOUT THIS NOW.
WHY NOT?
WE BARELY GET TO SEE EACH OTHER.
I DON'T WANT TO TALK ABOUT STUFF THAT'S GOING TO UPSET YOU.
YOU KNOW DAD, YOU REALLY ARE A JERK!
TINKA!
IT'S TRUE! I LET GUYS TREAT ME LIKE CRAP!
I'M SO DESPERATE FOR A BOYFRIEND THAT I'LL PUT UP WITH ANY GUY BEING A COMPLETE JERK JUST HOPING HE'LL WANT TO DATE ME.
THAT'S HARDLY MY FAULT. YOU SHOULD KNOW BETTER.
YEAH DAD, I SHOULD, BUT YOU TREAT ME LIKE CRAP!
YOU BLOW ME OFF AND ACT LIKE A SELFISH JERK.
THEN, YOU CALL AND APOLOGIZE AND I HAVE TO FORGIVE YOU 'CAUSE YOU'RE MY DAD.

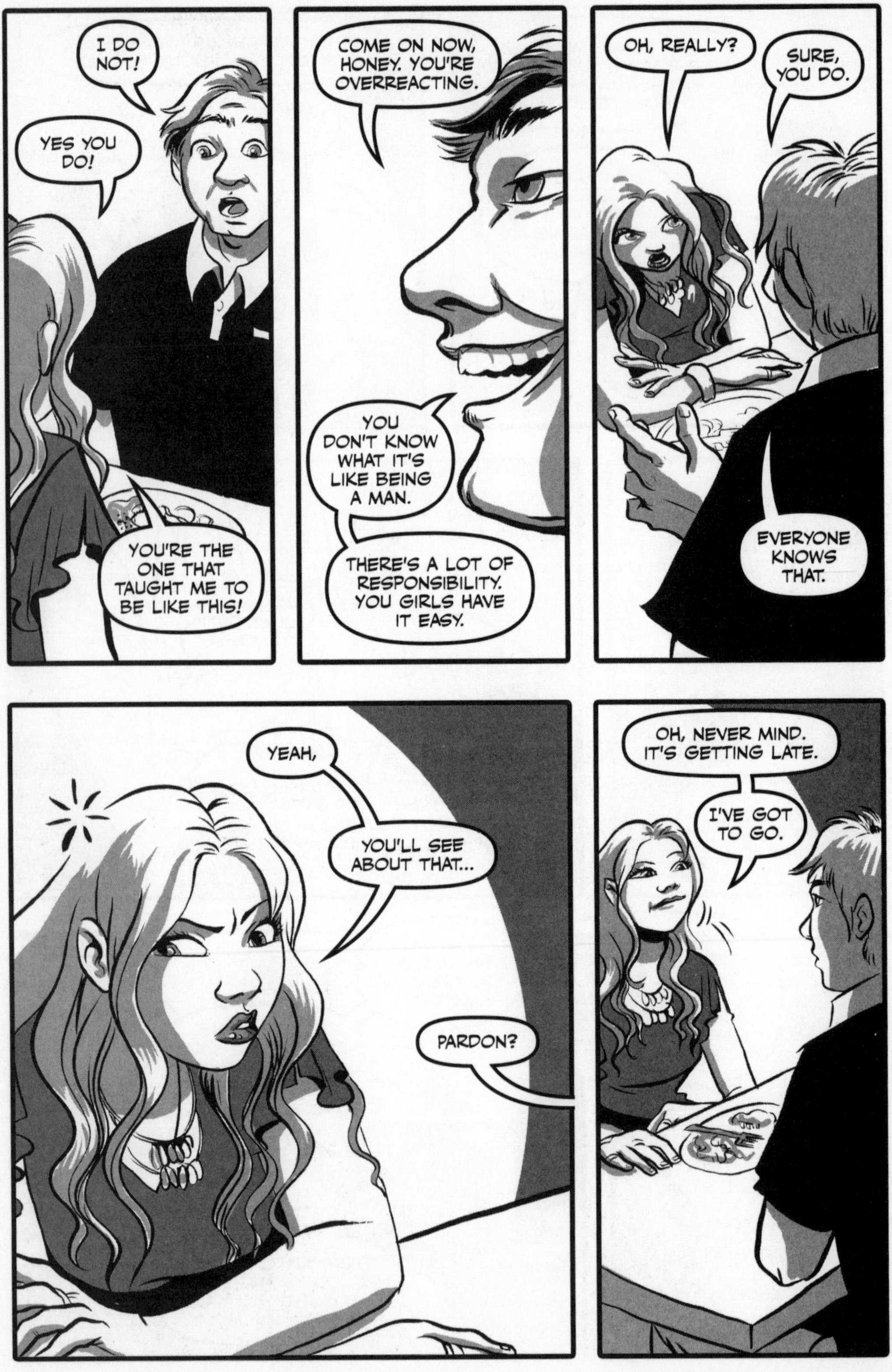
I DO NOT!
YES YOU DO!
YOU'RE THE ONE THAT TAUGHT ME TO BE LIKE THIS!
COME ON NOW, HONEY. YOU'RE OVERREACTING.
YOU DON'T KNOW WHAT IT'S LIKE BEING A MAN.
THERE'S A LOT OF RESPONSIBILITY. YOU GIRLS HAVE IT EASY.
OH, REALLY?
SURE, YOU DO.
EVERYONE KNOWS THAT.
YEAH,
YOU'LL SEE ABOUT THAT...
PARDON?
OH, NEVER MIND. IT'S GETTING LATE.
I'VE GOT TO GO.

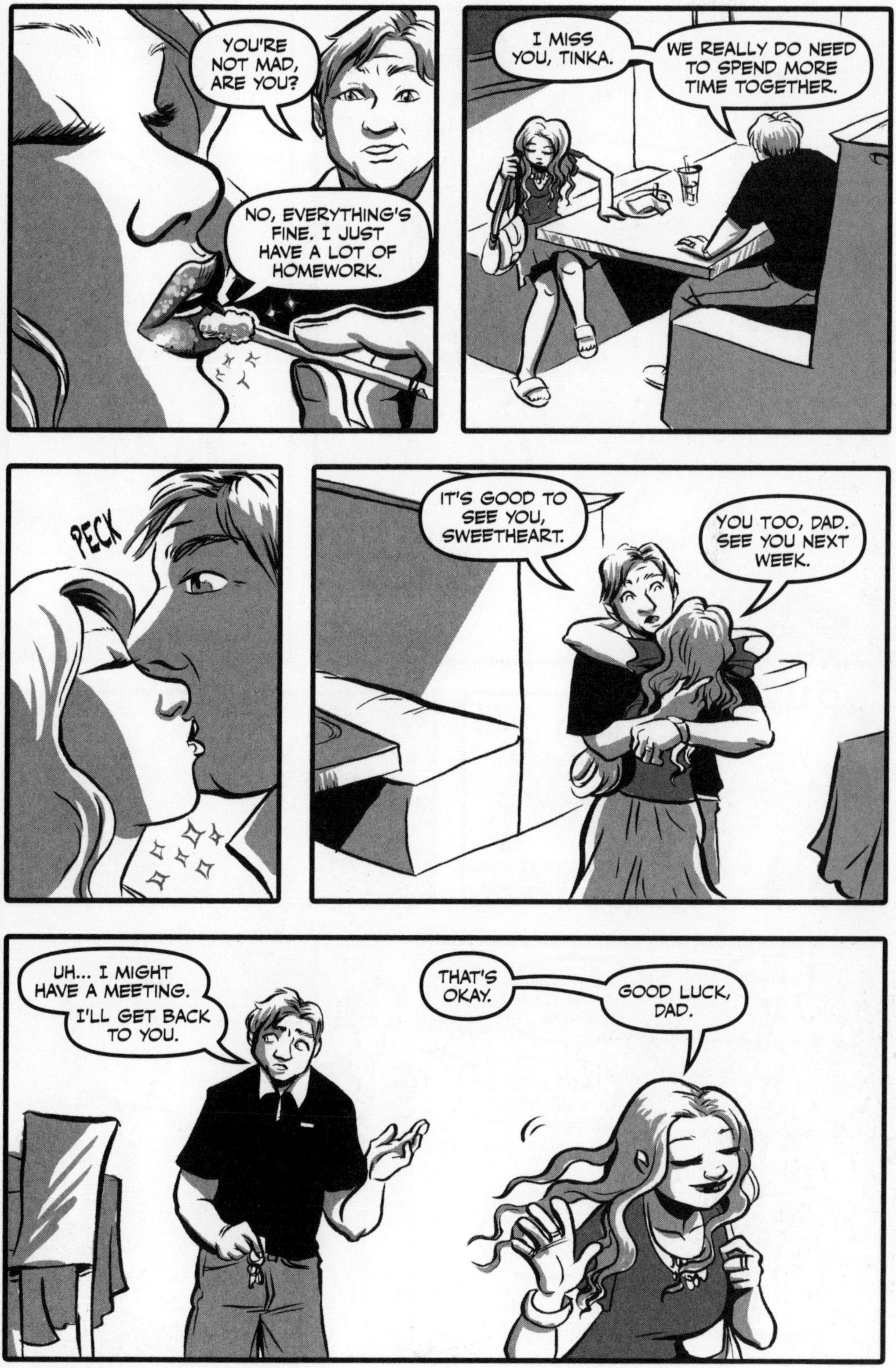
YOU'RE NOT MAD, ARE YOU?
NO, EVERYTHING'S FINE. I JUST HAVE A LOT OF HOMEWORK.
I MISS YOU, TINKA.
WE REALLY DO NEED TO SPEND MORE TIME TOGETHER.
PECK
IT'S GOOD TO SEE YOU, SWEETHEART.
YOU TOO, DAD. SEE YOU NEXT WEEK.
UH... I MIGHT HAVE A MEETING.
I'LL GET BACK TO YOU.
THAT'S OKAY.
GOOD LUCK, DAD.

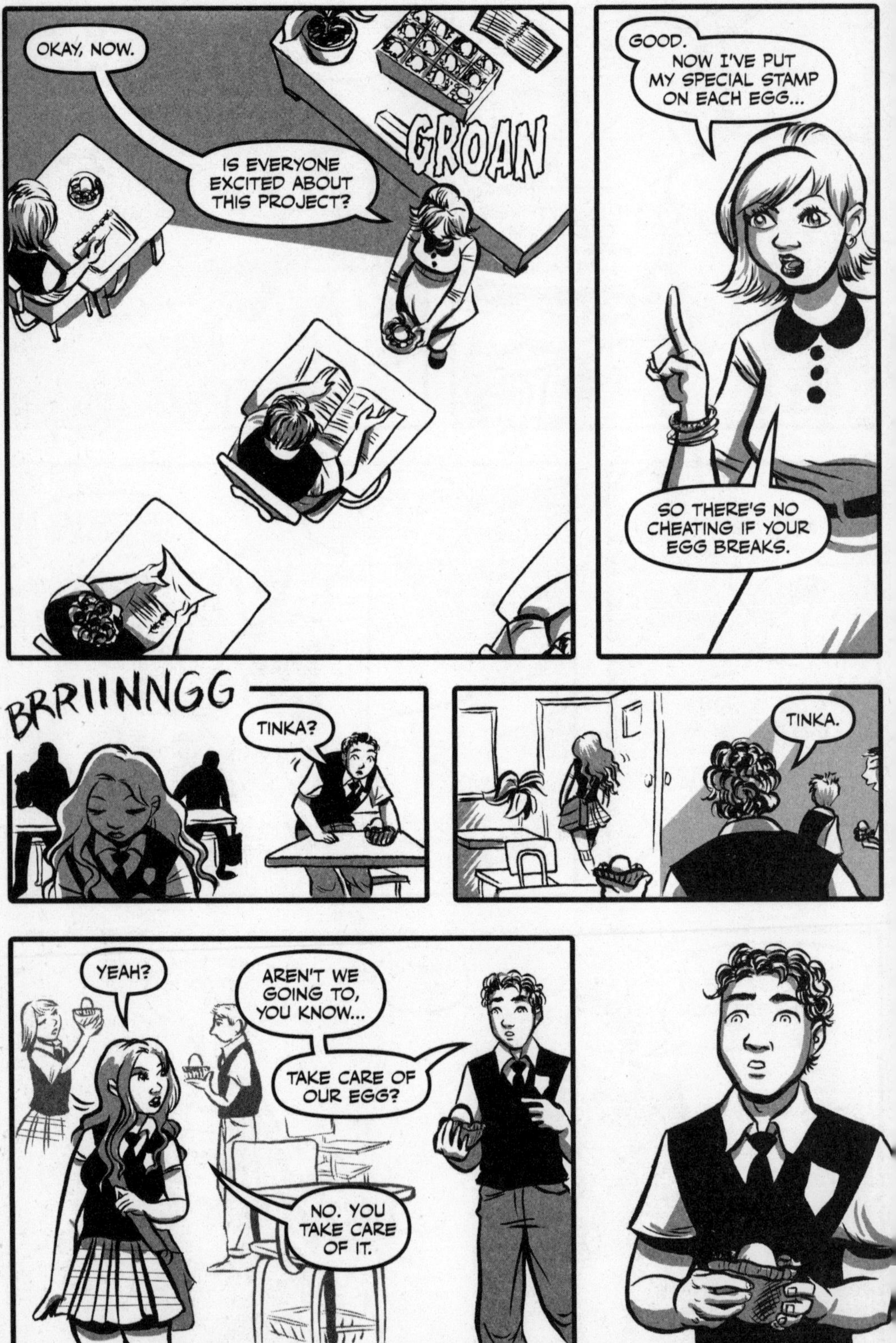

OKAY, NOW.
IS EVERYONE EXCITED ABOUT THIS PROJECT?
GROAN
GOOD.
NOW I'VE PUT MY SPECIAL STAMP ON EACH EGG...
SO THERE'S NO CHEATING IF YOUR EGG BREAKS.
BRRIINNGG
TINKA?
TINKA.
YEAH?
AREN'T WE GOING TO, YOU KNOW...
TAKE CARE OF OUR EGG?
NO. YOU TAKE CARE OF IT.

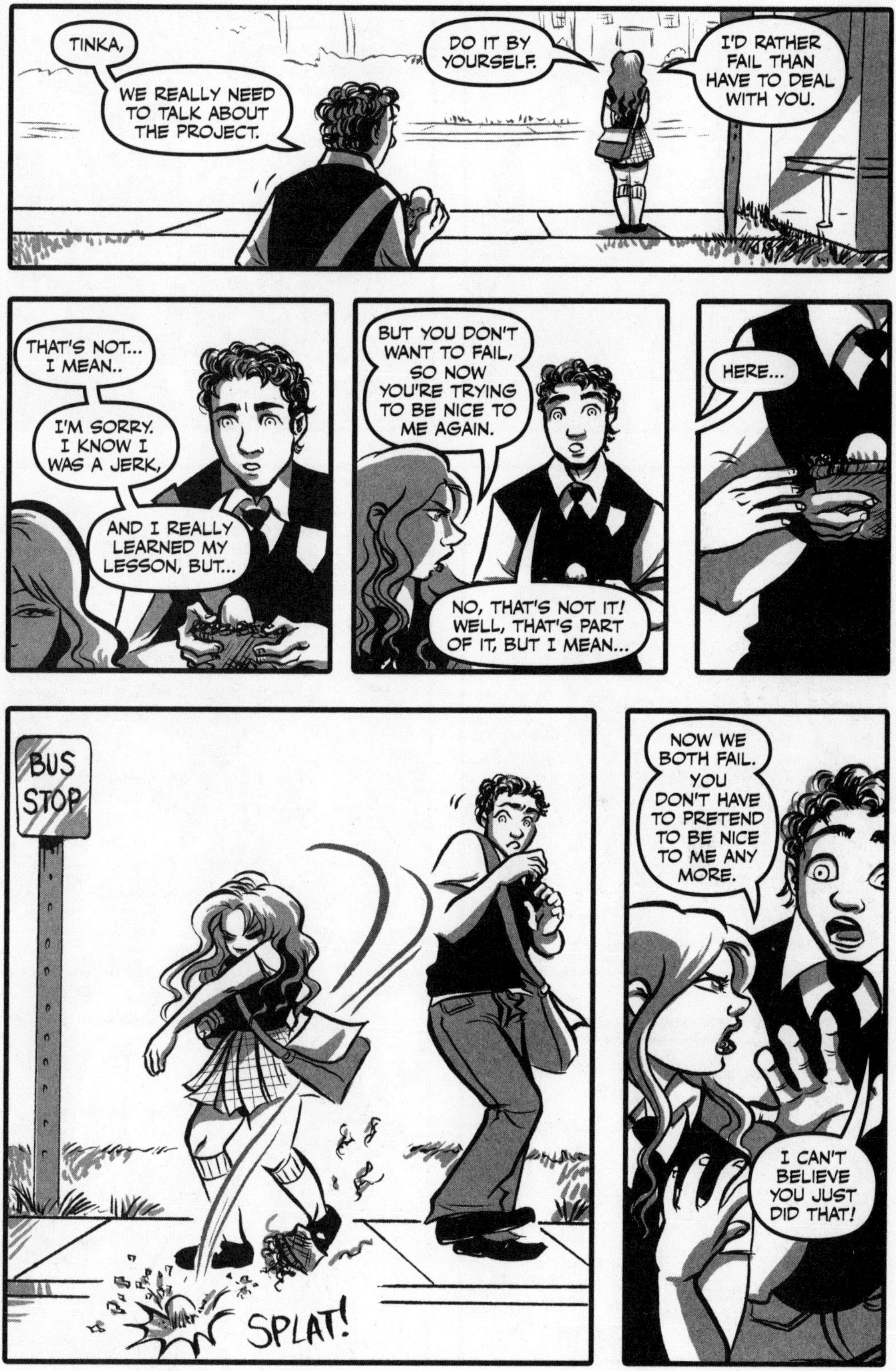
TINKA,
WE REALLY NEED TO TALK ABOUT THE PROJECT.
DO IT BY YOURSELF.
I'D RATHER FAIL THAN HAVE TO DEAL WITH YOU.
THAT'S NOT... I MEAN..
I'M SORRY. I KNOW I WAS A JERK,
AND I REALLY LEARNED MY LESSON, BUT...
BUT YOU DON'T WANT TO FAIL, SO NOW YOU'RE TRYING TO BE NICE TO ME AGAIN.
NO, THAT'S NOT IT! WELL, THAT'S PART OF IT, BUT I MEAN...
HERE...
BUS STOP
SPLAT!
NOW WE BOTH FAIL. YOU DON'T HAVE TO PRETEND TO BE NICE TO ME ANY MORE.
I CAN'T BELIEVE YOU JUST DID THAT!

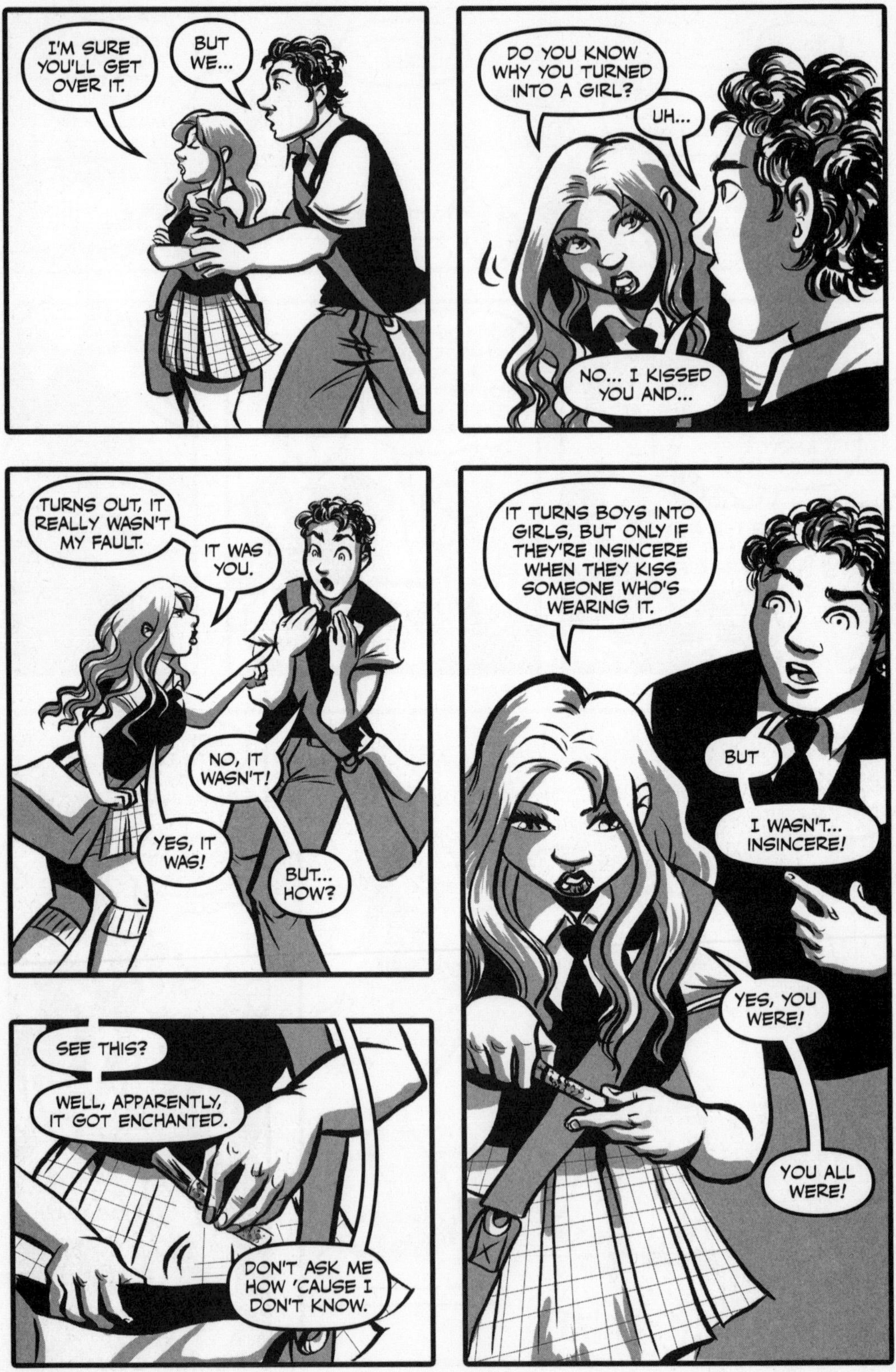
I'M SURE YOU'LL GET OVER IT.
BUT WE...
DO YOU KNOW WHY YOU TURNED INTO A GIRL?
UH...
NO... I KISSED YOU AND...
TURNS OUT, IT REALLY WASN'T MY FAULT.
IT WAS YOU.
NO, IT WASN'T!
YES, IT WAS!
BUT... HOW?
SEE THIS?
WELL, APPARENTLY, IT GOT ENCHANTED.
DON'T ASK ME HOW 'CAUSE I DON'T KNOW.
IT TURNS BOYS INTO GIRLS, BUT ONLY IF THEY'RE INSINCERE WHEN THEY KISS SOMEONE WHO'S WEARING IT.
BUT
I WASN'T... INSINCERE!
YES, YOU WERE!
YOU ALL WERE!

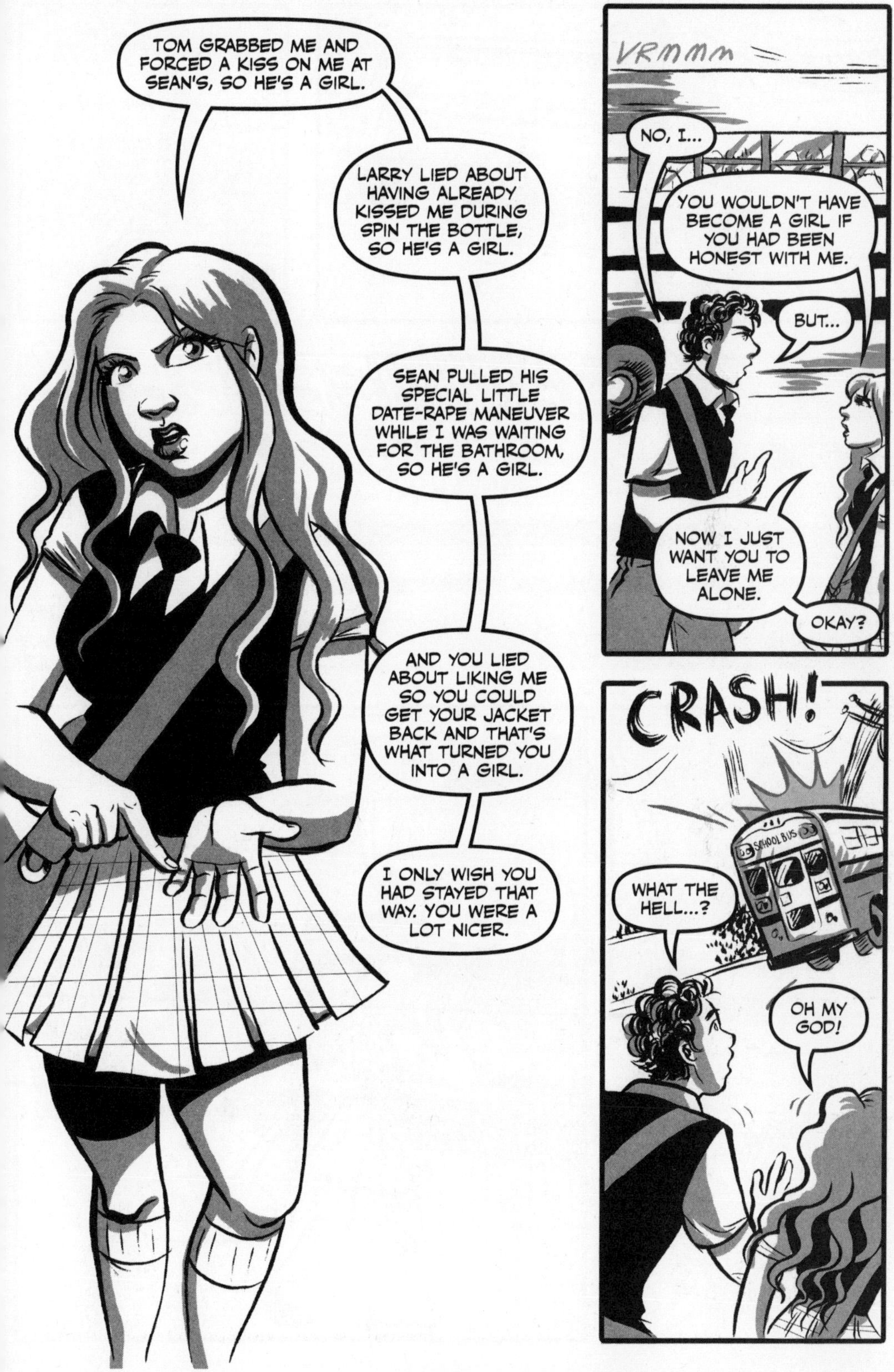
TOM GRABBED ME AND FORCED A KISS ON ME AT SEAN'S, SO HE'S A GIRL.
LARRY LIED ABOUT HAVING ALREADY KISSED ME DURING SPIN THE BOTTLE, SO HE'S A GIRL.
SEAN PULLED HIS SPECIAL LITTLE DATE-RAPE MANEUVER WHILE I WAS WAITING FOR THE BATHROOM, SO HE'S A GIRL.
AND YOU LIED ABOUT LIKING ME SO YOU COULD GET YOUR JACKET BACK AND THAT'S WHAT TURNED YOU INTO A GIRL.
I ONLY WISH YOU HAD STAYED THAT WAY. YOU WERE A LOT NICER.
VRMMM
NO, I...
YOU WOULDN'T HAVE BECOME A GIRL IF YOU HAD BEEN HONEST WITH ME.
BUT...
NOW I JUST WANT YOU TO LEAVE ME ALONE.
OKAY?
CRASH!
SCHOOL BUS
WHAT THE HELL...?
OH MY GOD!

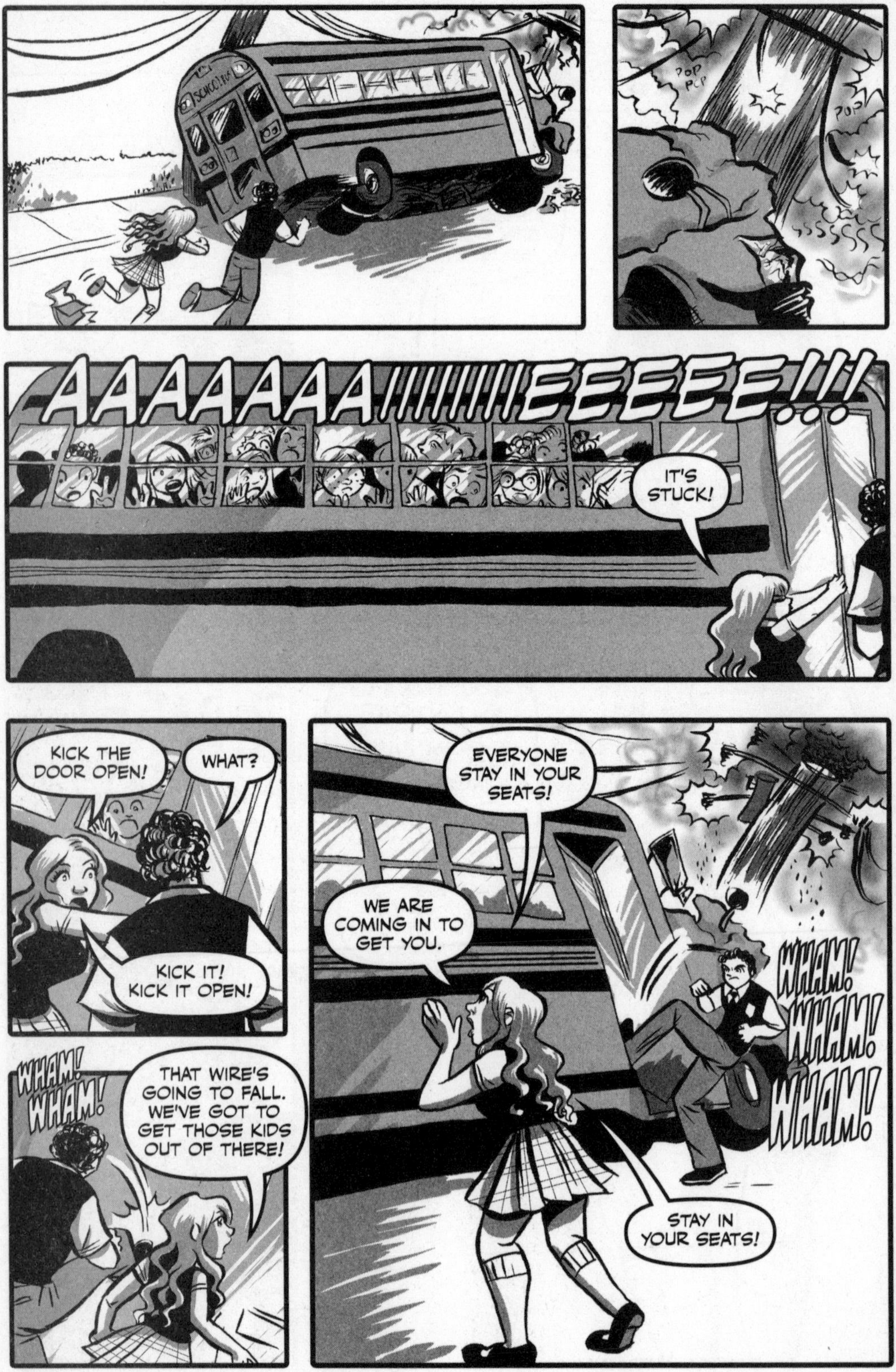
POP POP
POP
SSSSSSS
AAAAAAAIIIIIIIEEEEEE!!!
IT'S STUCK!
KICK THE DOOR OPEN!
WHAT?
KICK IT! KICK IT OPEN!
WHAM! WHAM!
THAT WIRE'S GOING TO FALL. WE'VE GOT TO GET THOSE KIDS OUT OF THERE!
EVERYONE STAY IN YOUR SEATS!
WE ARE COMING IN TO GET YOU.
WHAM! WHAM! WHAM!
STAY IN YOUR SEATS!

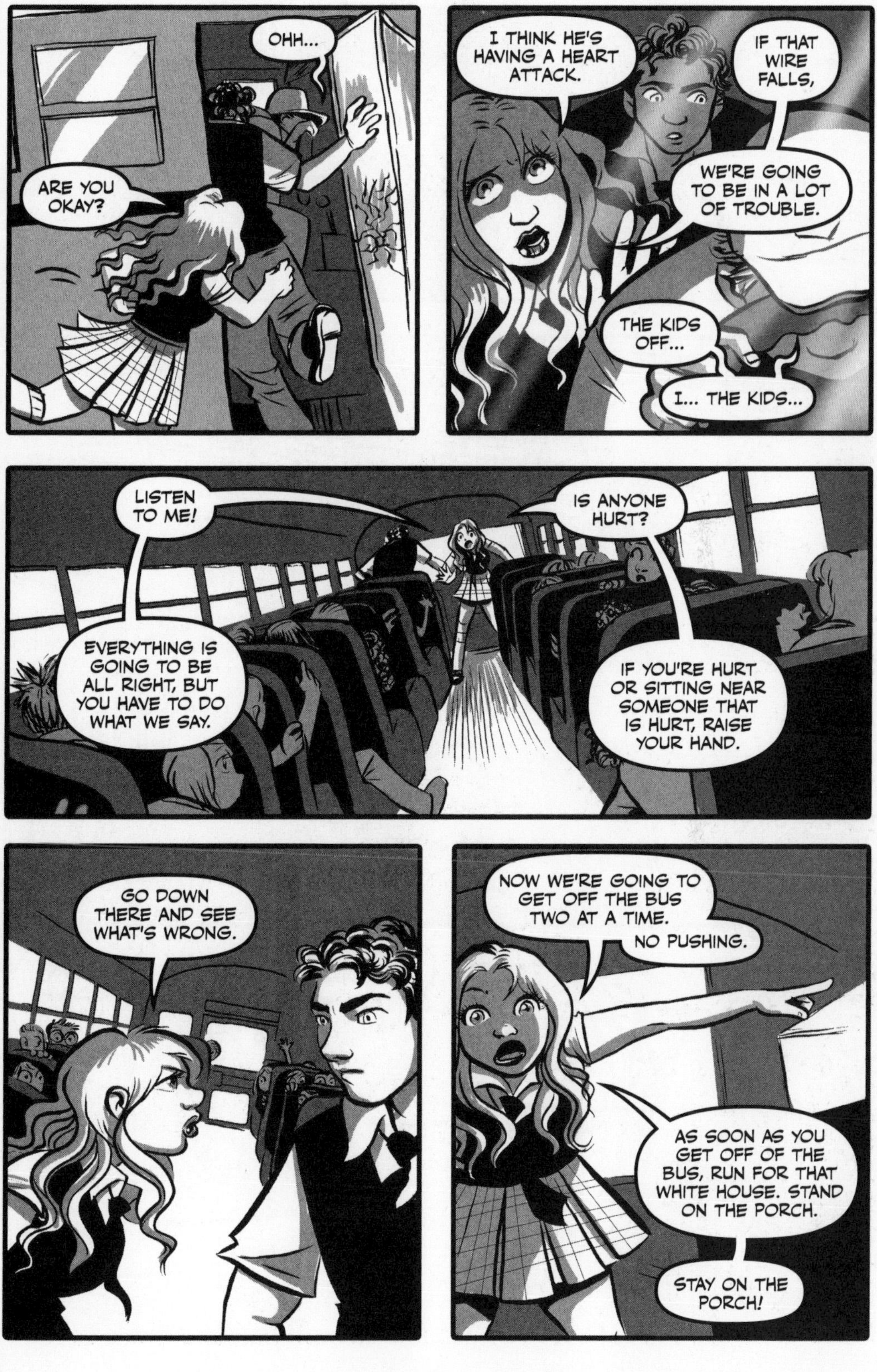
OHH...
ARE YOU OKAY?
I THINK HE'S HAVING A HEART ATTACK.
IF THAT WIRE FALLS,
WE'RE GOING TO BE IN A LOT OF TROUBLE.
THE KIDS OFF...
I... THE KIDS...
LISTEN TO ME!
EVERYTHING IS GOING TO BE ALL RIGHT, BUT YOU HAVE TO DO WHAT WE SAY.
IS ANYONE HURT?
IF YOU'RE HURT OR SITTING NEAR SOMEONE THAT IS HURT, RAISE YOUR HAND.
GO DOWN THERE AND SEE WHAT'S WRONG.
NOW WE'RE GOING TO GET OFF THE BUS TWO AT A TIME.
NO PUSHING.
AS SOON AS YOU GET OFF OF THE BUS, RUN FOR THAT WHITE HOUSE. STAND ON THE PORCH.
STAY ON THE PORCH!

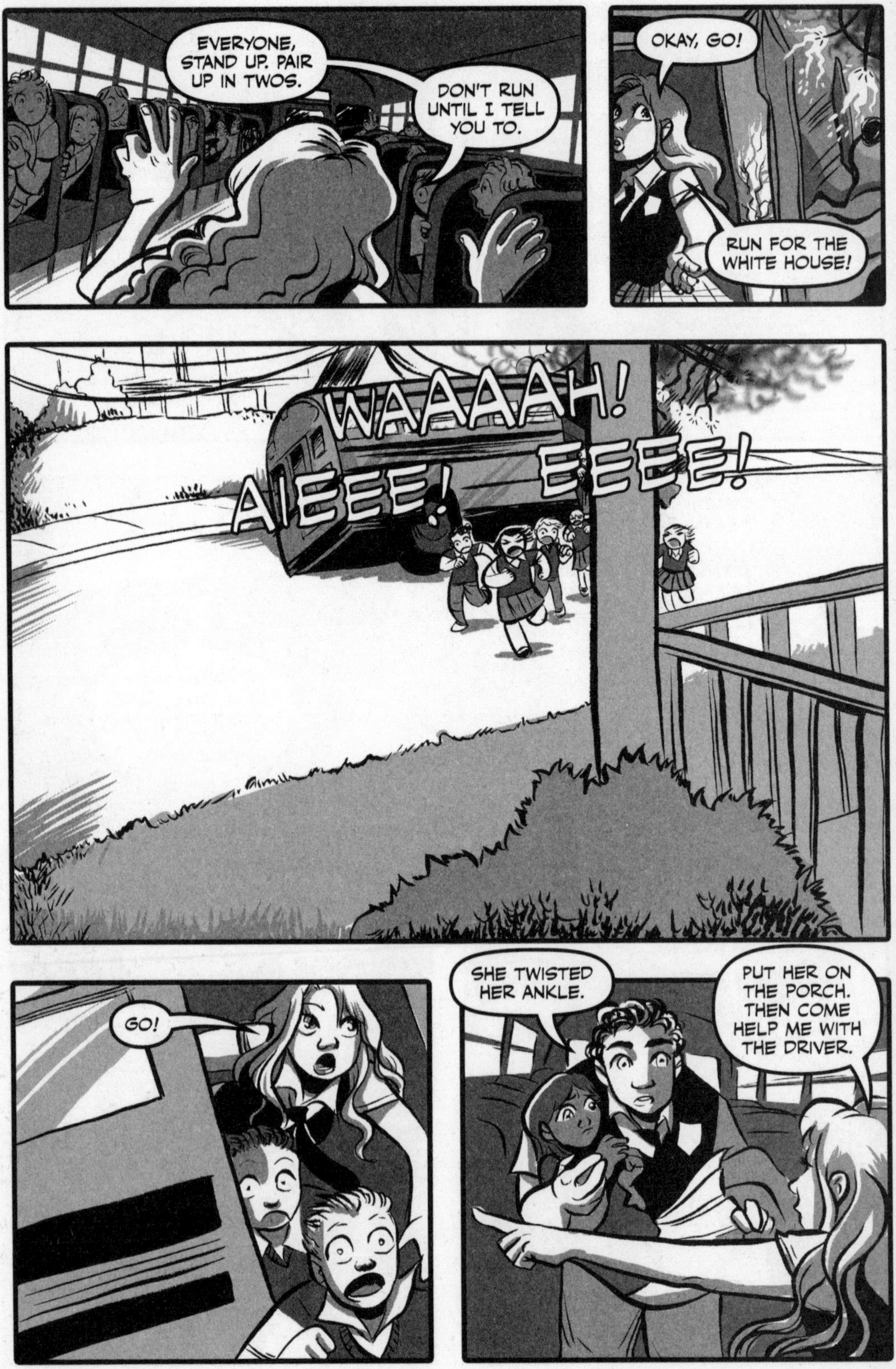
EVERYONE, STAND UP. PAIR UP IN TWOS.
DON'T RUN UNTIL I TELL YOU TO.
OKAY, GO!
RUN FOR THE WHITE HOUSE!
WAAAAAH!
AIEEEE!
EEEEE!
GO!
SHE TWISTED HER ANKLE.
PUT HER ON THE PORCH. THEN COME HELP ME WITH THE DRIVER.

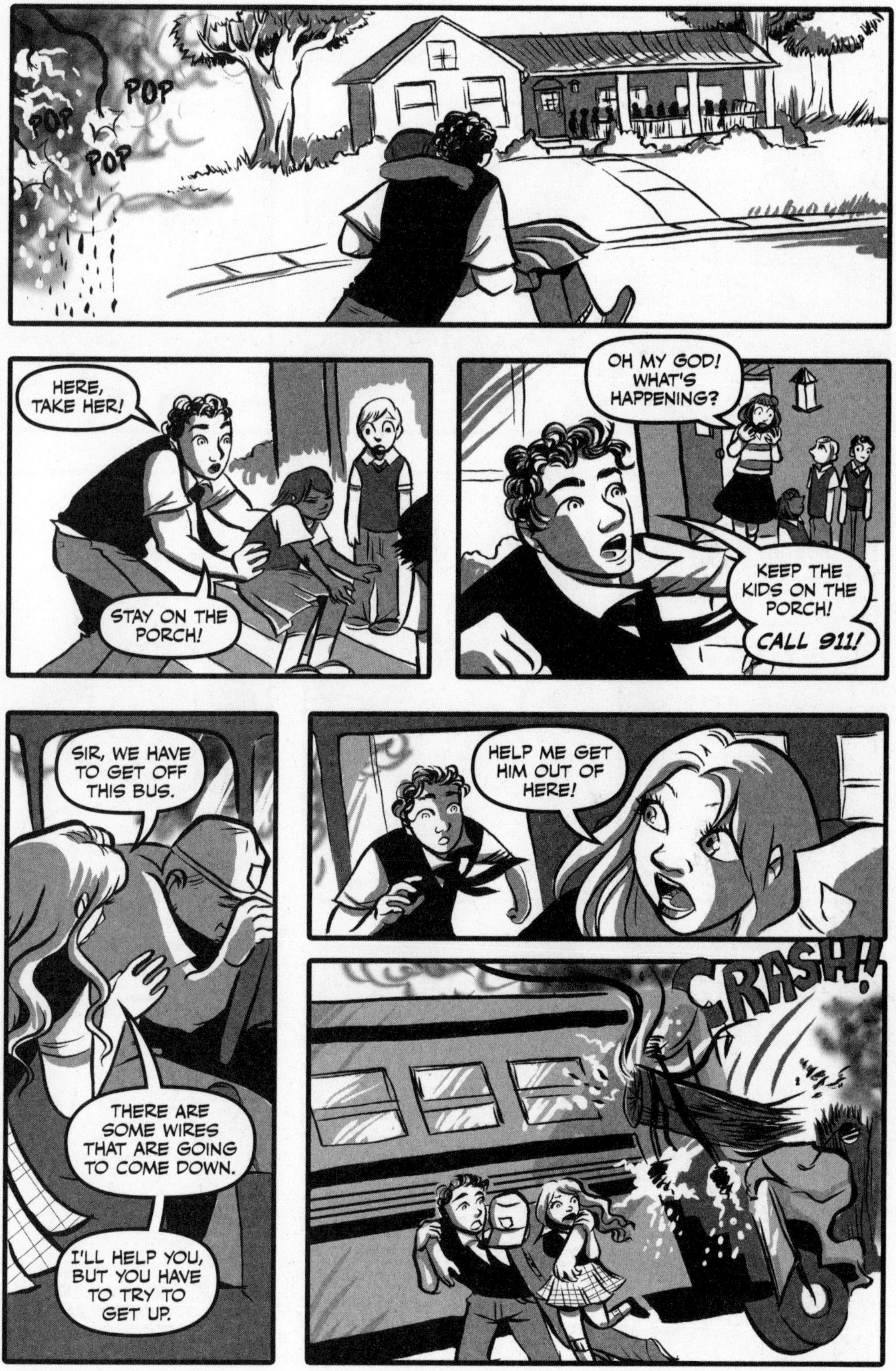
POP
POP
POP
HERE, TAKE HER!
STAY ON THE PORCH!
OH MY GOD! WHAT'S HAPPENING?
KEEP THE KIDS ON THE PORCH!
CALL 911!
SIR, WE HAVE TO GET OFF THIS BUS.
THERE ARE SOME WIRES THAT ARE GOING TO COME DOWN.
I'LL HELP YOU, BUT YOU HAVE TO TRY TO GET UP.
HELP ME GET HIM OUT OF HERE!
CRASH!

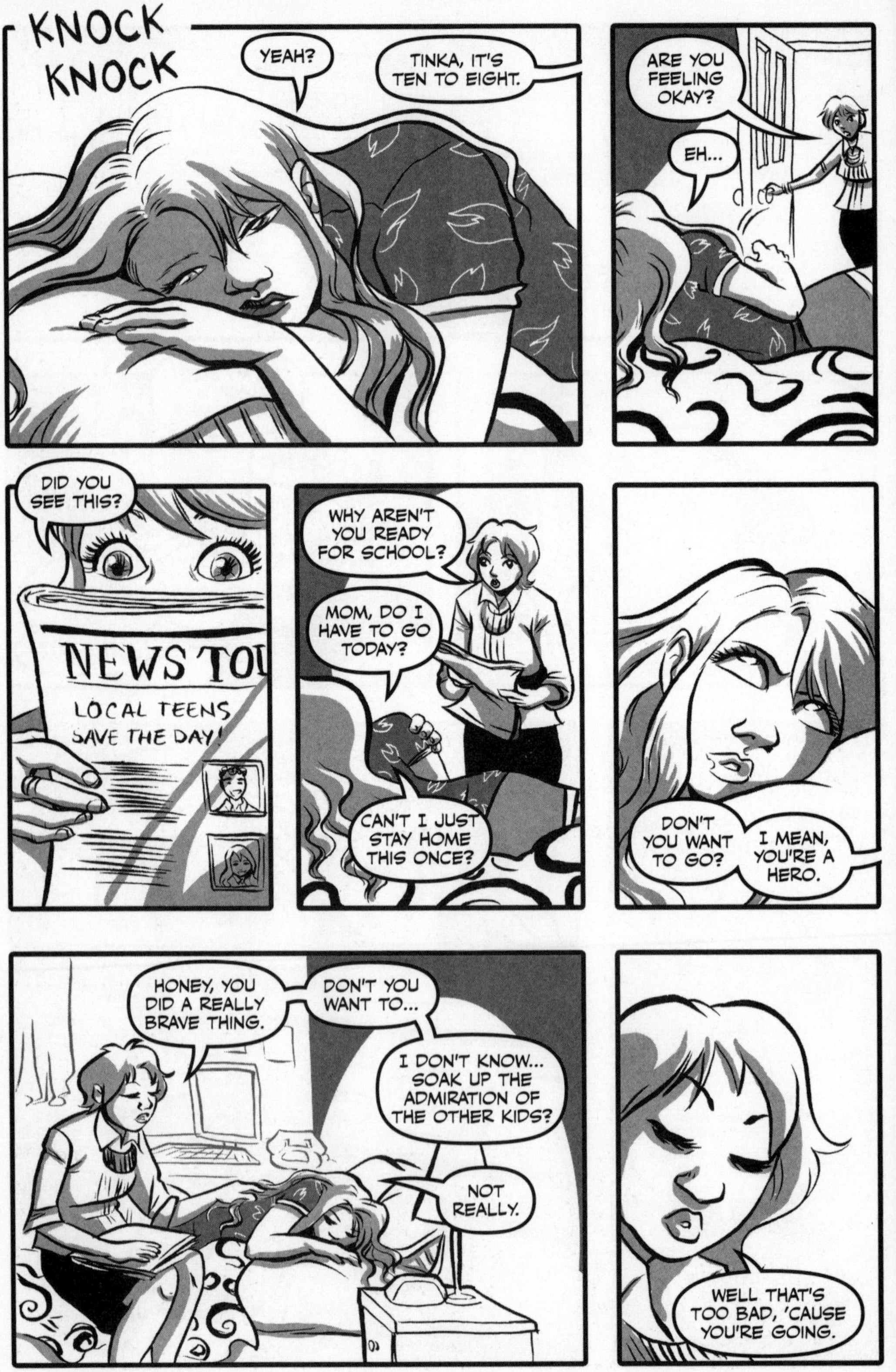
KNOCK KNOCK
YEAH?
TINKA, IT'S TEN TO EIGHT.
ARE YOU FEELING OKAY?
EH...
DID YOU SEE THIS?
NEWS TO
LOCAL TEENS SAVE THE DAY!
WHY AREN'T YOU READY FOR SCHOOL?
MOM, DO I HAVE TO GO TODAY?
CAN'T I JUST STAY HOME THIS ONCE?
DON'T YOU WANT TO GO?
I MEAN, YOU'RE A HERO.
HONEY, YOU DID A REALLY BRAVE THING.
DON'T YOU WANT TO...
I DON'T KNOW... SOAK UP THE ADMIRATION OF THE OTHER KIDS?
NOT REALLY.
WELL THAT'S TOO BAD, 'CAUSE YOU'RE GOING.

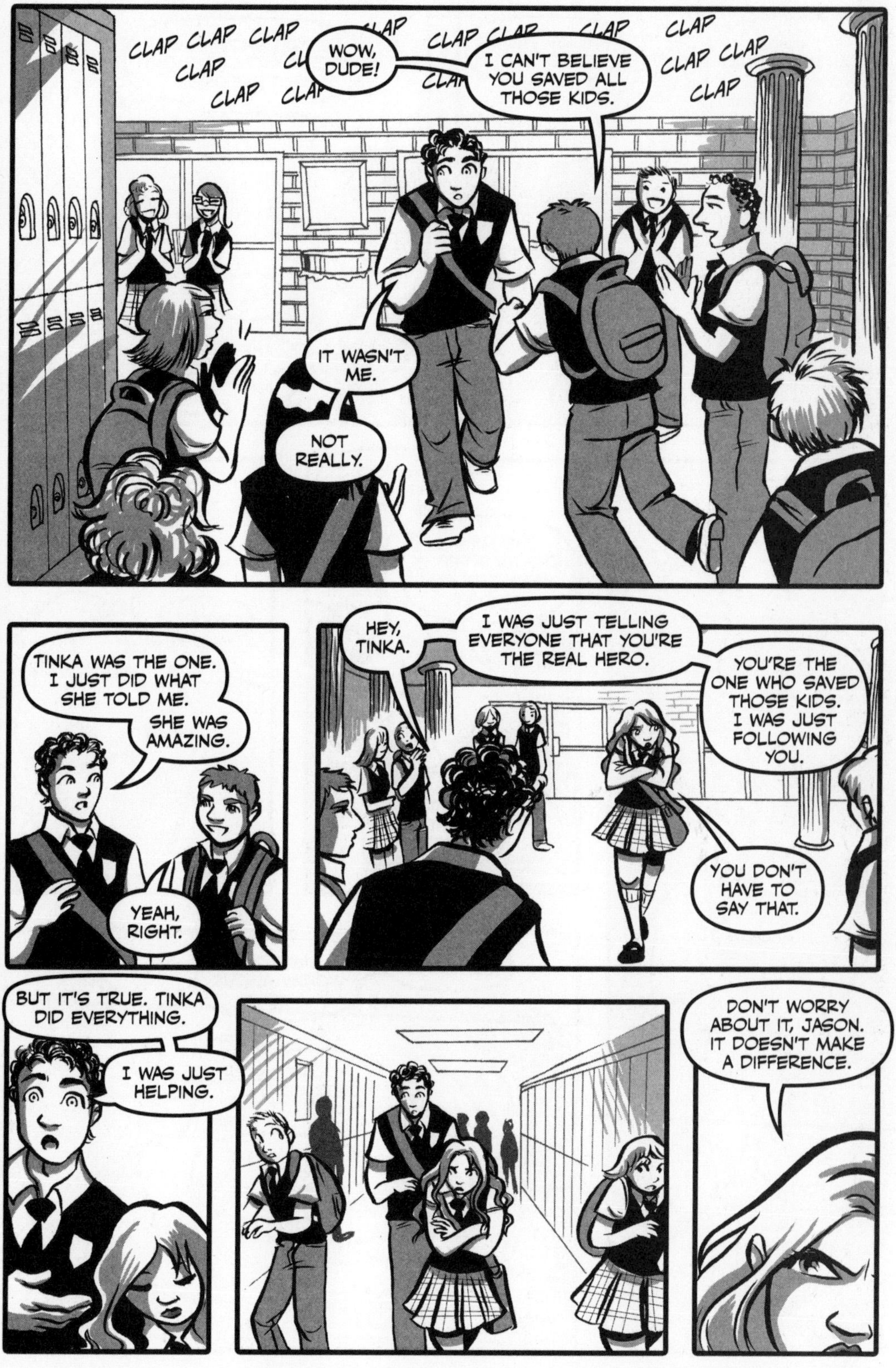
CLAP CLAP CLAP
CLAP
CLAP
WOW, DUDE!
CLAP CLAP
I CAN'T BELIEVE YOU SAVED ALL THOSE KIDS.
CLAP
CLAP CLAP
CLAP
IT WASN'T ME.
NOT REALLY.
TINKA WAS THE ONE. I JUST DID WHAT SHE TOLD ME.
SHE WAS AMAZING.
YEAH, RIGHT.
HEY, TINKA.
I WAS JUST TELLING EVERYONE THAT YOU'RE THE REAL HERO.
YOU'RE THE ONE WHO SAVED THOSE KIDS. I WAS JUST FOLLOWING YOU.
YOU DON'T HAVE TO SAY THAT.
BUT IT'S TRUE. TINKA DID EVERYTHING.
I WAS JUST HELPING.
DON'T WORRY ABOUT IT, JASON. IT DOESN'T MAKE A DIFFERENCE.

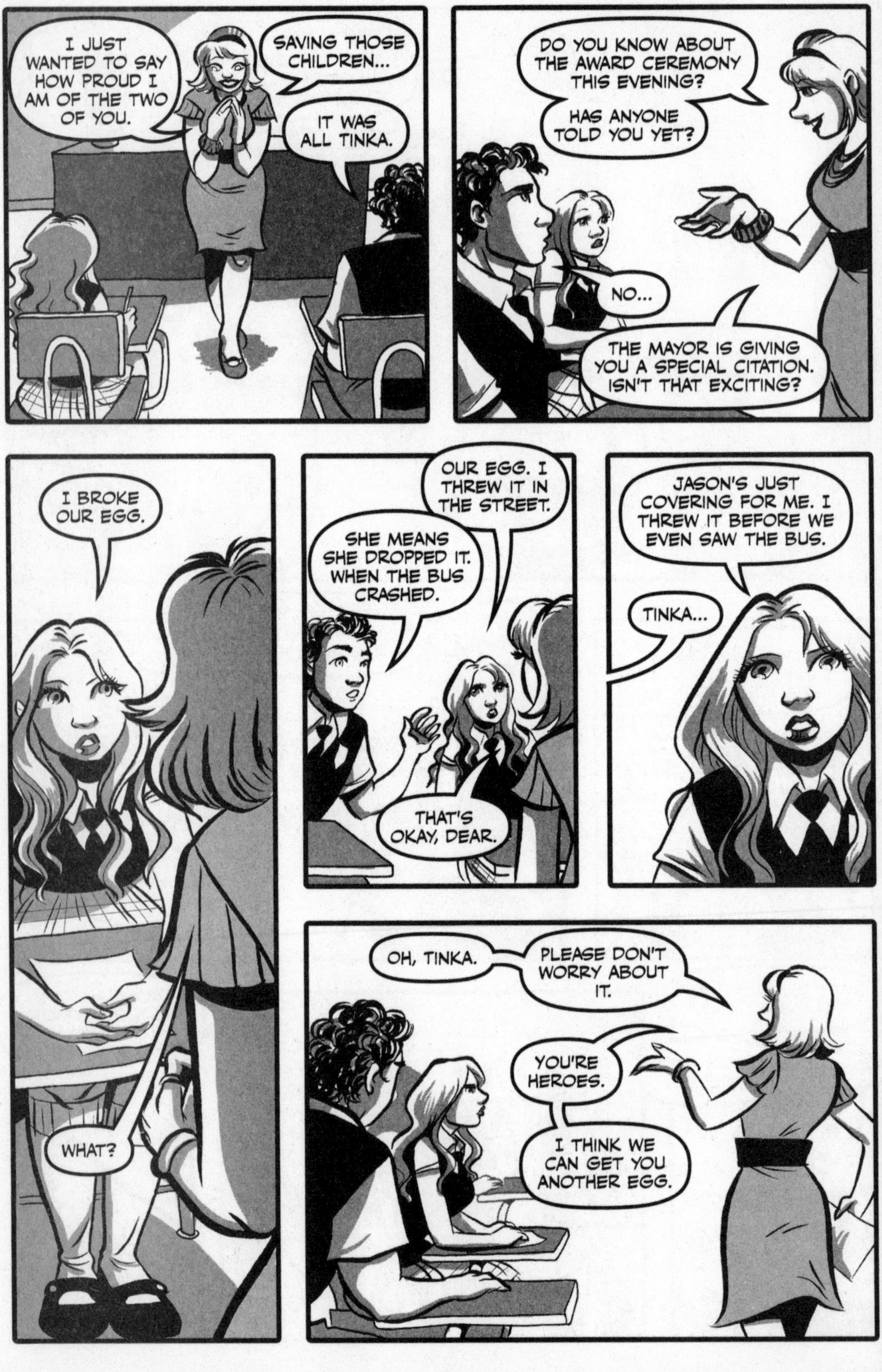
I JUST WANTED TO SAY HOW PROUD I AM OF THE TWO OF YOU.
SAVING THOSE CHILDREN...
IT WAS ALL TINKA.
DO YOU KNOW ABOUT THE AWARD CEREMONY THIS EVENING?
HAS ANYONE TOLD YOU YET?
NO...
THE MAYOR IS GIVING YOU A SPECIAL CITATION. ISN'T THAT EXCITING?
I BROKE OUR EGG.
WHAT?
OUR EGG. I THREW IT IN THE STREET.
SHE MEANS SHE DROPPED IT. WHEN THE BUS CRASHED.
THAT'S OKAY, DEAR.
JASON'S JUST COVERING FOR ME. I THREW IT BEFORE WE EVEN SAW THE BUS.
TINKA...
OH, TINKA.
PLEASE DON'T WORRY ABOUT IT.
YOU'RE HEROES.
I THINK WE CAN GET YOU ANOTHER EGG.

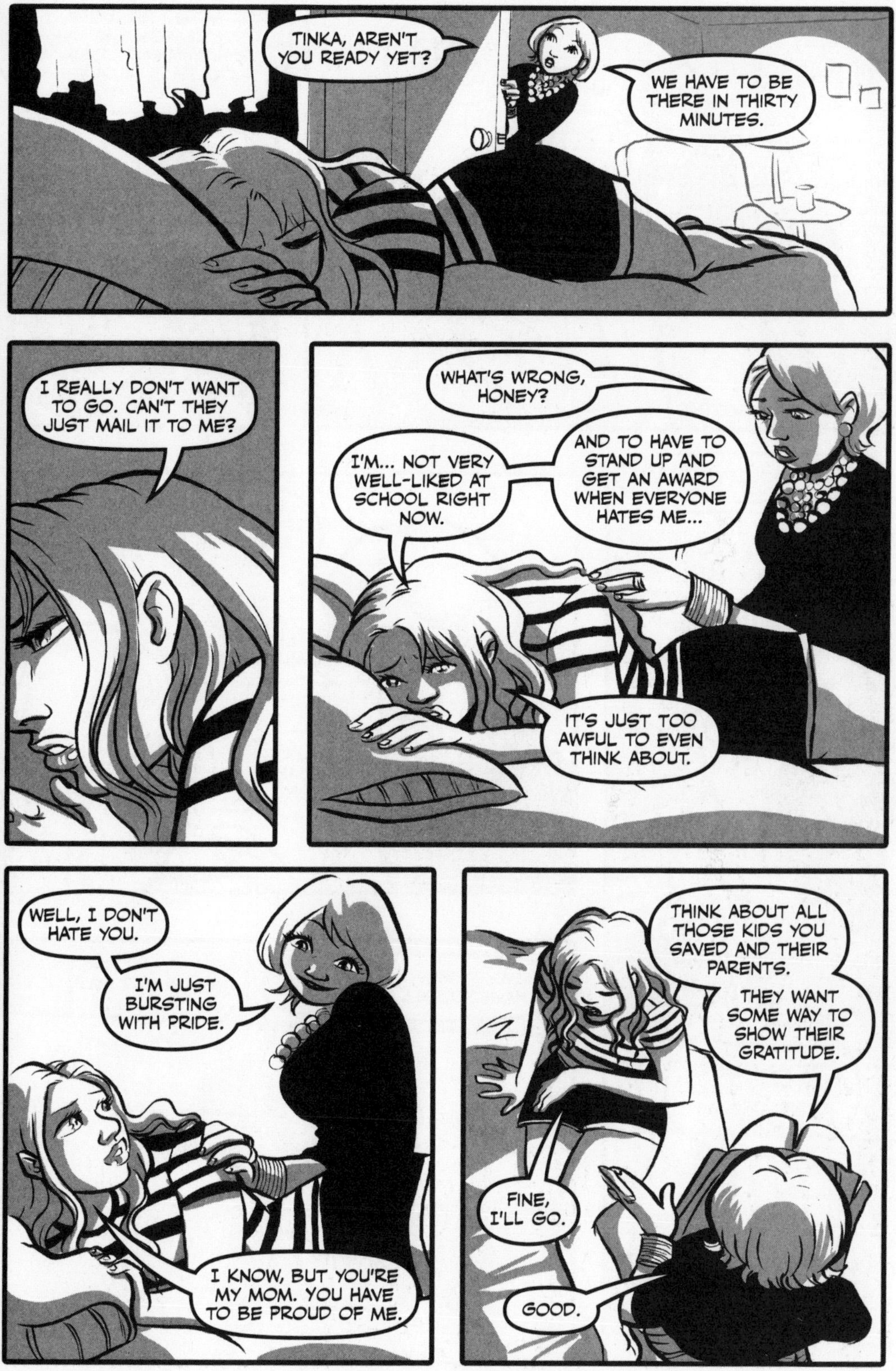
TINKA, AREN'T YOU READY YET?
WE HAVE TO BE THERE IN THIRTY MINUTES.
I REALLY DON'T WANT TO GO. CAN'T THEY JUST MAIL IT TO ME?
WHAT'S WRONG, HONEY?
I'M... NOT VERY WELL-LIKED AT SCHOOL RIGHT NOW.
AND TO HAVE TO STAND UP AND GET AN AWARD WHEN EVERYONE HATES ME...
IT'S JUST TOO AWFUL TO EVEN THINK ABOUT.
WELL, I DON'T HATE YOU.
I'M JUST BURSTING WITH PRIDE.
I KNOW, BUT YOU'RE MY MOM. YOU HAVE TO BE PROUD OF ME.
THINK ABOUT ALL THOSE KIDS YOU SAVED AND THEIR PARENTS.
THEY WANT SOME WAY TO SHOW THEIR GRATITUDE.
FINE, I'LL GO.
GOOD.

**Panel 1:**

WHAT?

YOU KNOW WHAT'S FUNNY?

**Panel 2:**

IN THAT SONG, RUDOLPH THE RED-NOSED REINDEER, THE ONLY REASON THE OTHER REINDEER END UP LIKING RUDOLPH IS BECAUSE HE SAVES CHRISTMAS.

I MEAN, THE OTHER REINDEER ARE JUST SO FAKE.

**Panel 3:**

I'M NOT FOLLOWING YOU.

AT LEAST THE JERKS AT MY SCHOOL ARE BEING HONEST.

THEY DIDN'T LIKE ME BEFORE AND THEY STILL DON'T LIKE ME NOW.

**Panel 4:**

TINKA, I DON'T THINK IT'S TOO HEALTHY TO BE ANALYZING CHRISTMAS CAROLS AS LIFE LESSONS. YOU'RE GIVING THE SONG A LITTLE TOO MUCH CREDIT.

YOU'RE PROBABLY RIGHT.

**Panel 5:**

UHM... THERE'S SOMETHING I HAVE TO TELL YOU, HONEY.

AND I'M REALLY SORRY.

WHAT?

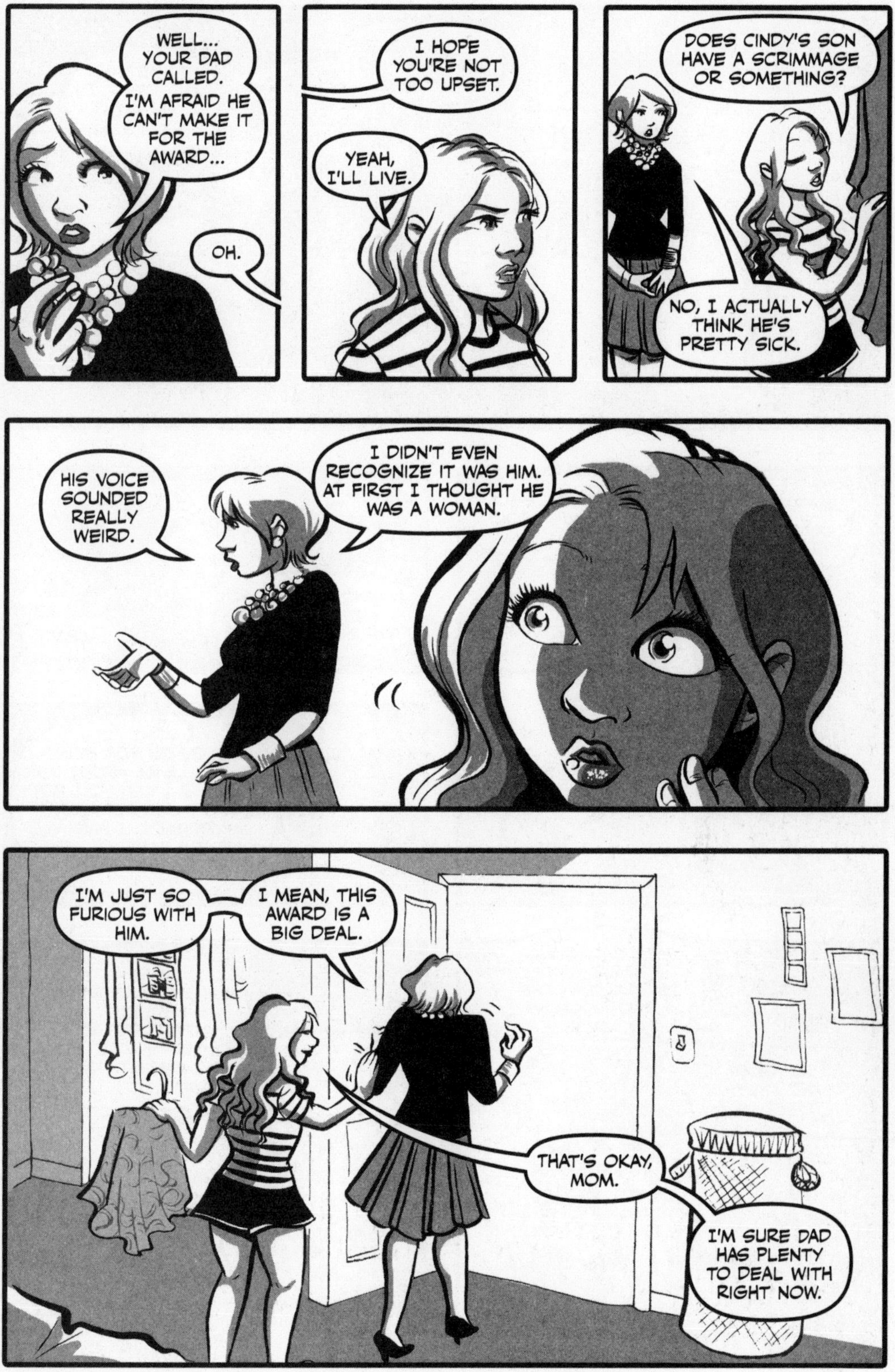
WELL... YOUR DAD CALLED.
I'M AFRAID HE CAN'T MAKE IT FOR THE AWARD...
OH.
I HOPE YOU'RE NOT TOO UPSET.
YEAH, I'LL LIVE.
DOES CINDY'S SON HAVE A SCRIMMAGE OR SOMETHING?
NO, I ACTUALLY THINK HE'S PRETTY SICK.
HIS VOICE SOUNDED REALLY WEIRD.
I DIDN'T EVEN RECOGNIZE IT WAS HIM. AT FIRST I THOUGHT HE WAS A WOMAN.
I'M JUST SO FURIOUS WITH HIM.
I MEAN, THIS AWARD IS A BIG DEAL.
THAT'S OKAY, MOM.
I'M SURE DAD HAS PLENTY TO DEAL WITH RIGHT NOW.

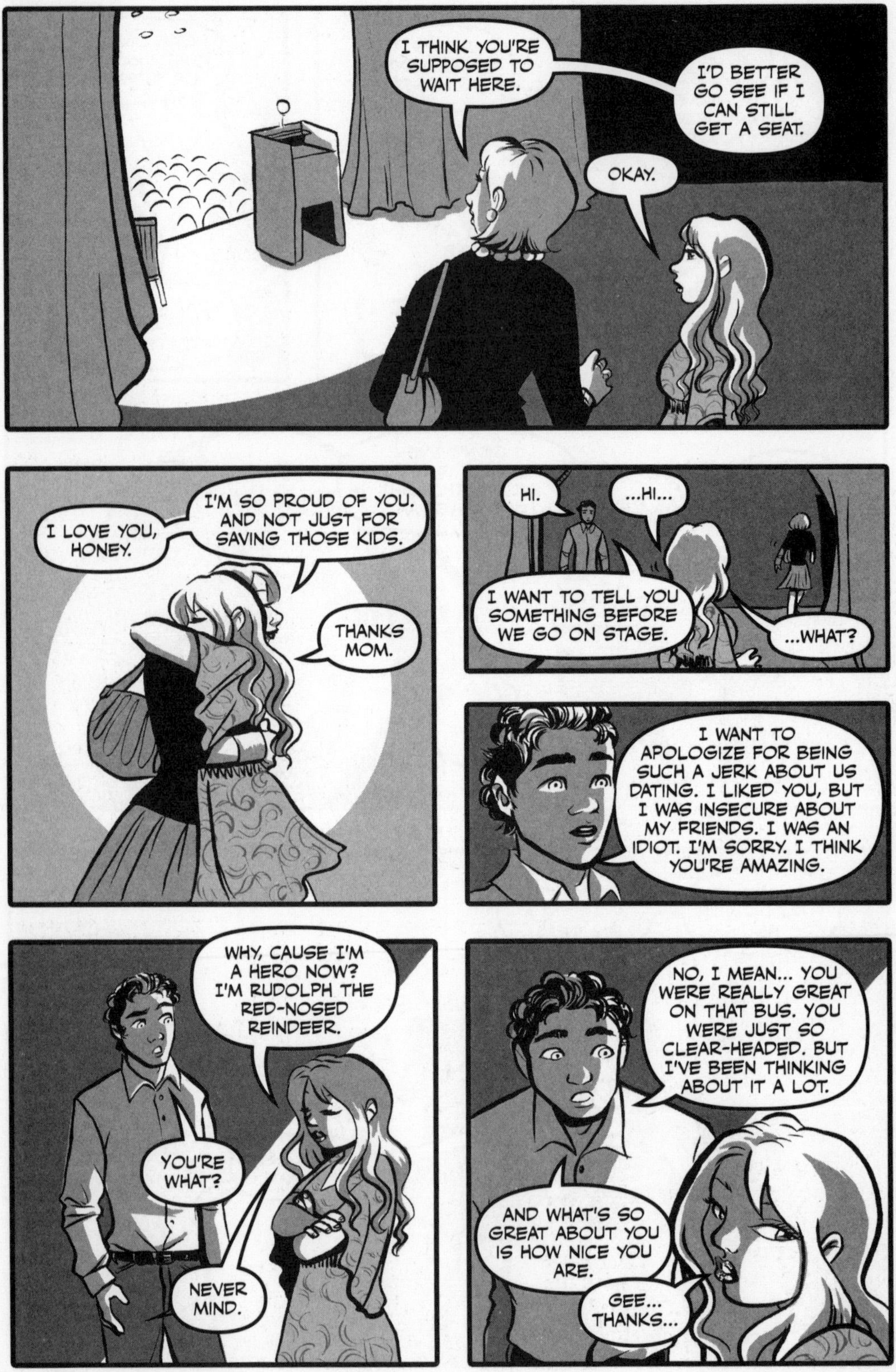
I THINK YOU'RE SUPPOSED TO WAIT HERE.
I'D BETTER GO SEE IF I CAN STILL GET A SEAT.
OKAY.
I LOVE YOU, HONEY.
I'M SO PROUD OF YOU. AND NOT JUST FOR SAVING THOSE KIDS.
THANKS MOM.
HI.
...HI...
I WANT TO TELL YOU SOMETHING BEFORE WE GO ON STAGE.
...WHAT?
I WANT TO APOLOGIZE FOR BEING SUCH A JERK ABOUT US DATING. I LIKED YOU, BUT I WAS INSECURE ABOUT MY FRIENDS. I WAS AN IDIOT. I'M SORRY. I THINK YOU'RE AMAZING.
WHY, CAUSE I'M A HERO NOW? I'M RUDOLPH THE RED-NOSED REINDEER.
YOU'RE WHAT?
NEVER MIND.
NO, I MEAN... YOU WERE REALLY GREAT ON THAT BUS. YOU WERE JUST SO CLEAR-HEADED. BUT I'VE BEEN THINKING ABOUT IT A LOT.
AND WHAT'S SO GREAT ABOUT YOU IS HOW NICE YOU ARE.
GEE... THANKS...

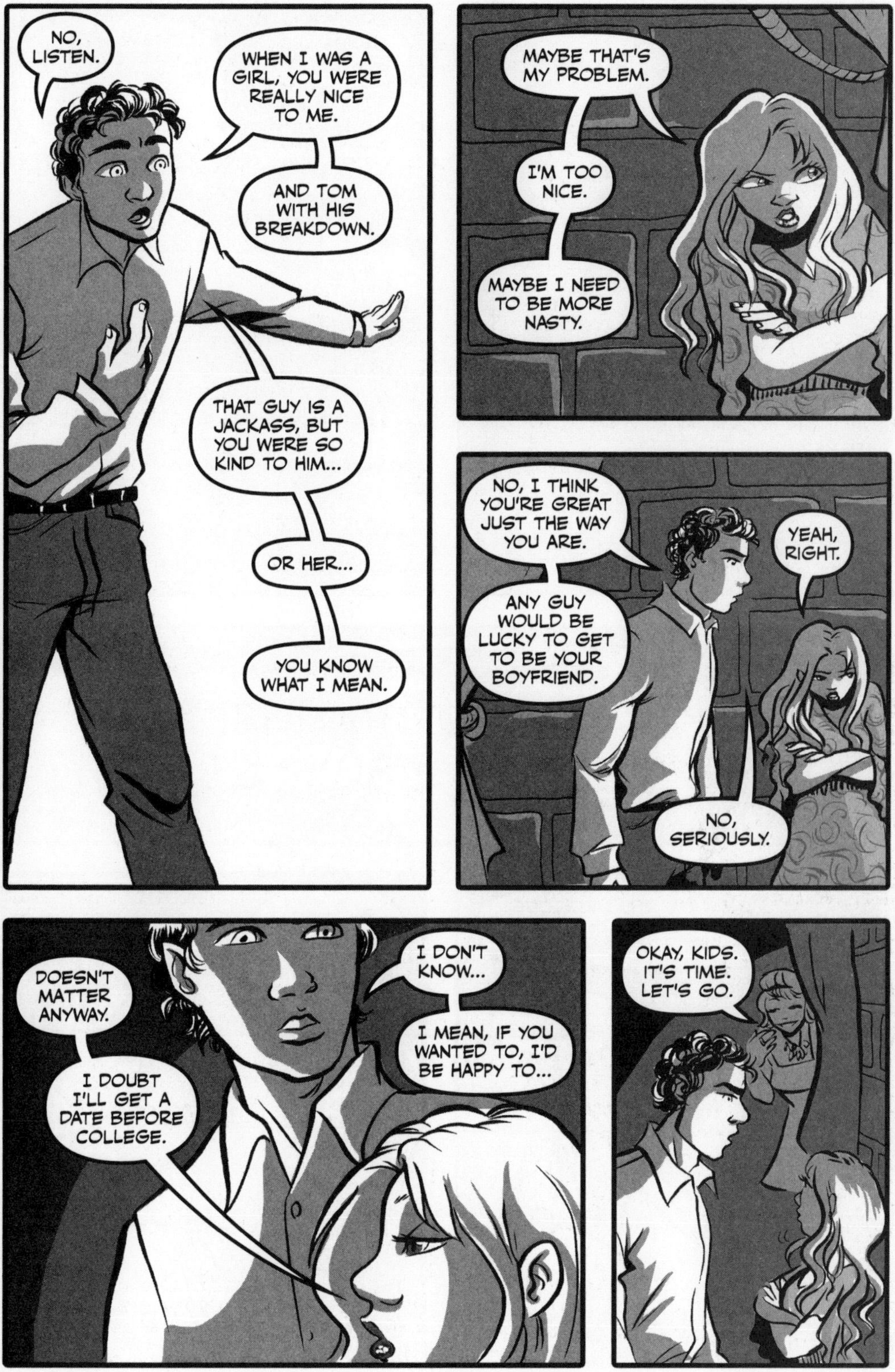
NO, LISTEN.
WHEN I WAS A GIRL, YOU WERE REALLY NICE TO ME.
AND TOM WITH HIS BREAKDOWN.
THAT GUY IS A JACKASS, BUT YOU WERE SO KIND TO HIM...
OR HER...
YOU KNOW WHAT I MEAN.
MAYBE THAT'S MY PROBLEM.
I'M TOO NICE.
MAYBE I NEED TO BE MORE NASTY.
NO, I THINK YOU'RE GREAT JUST THE WAY YOU ARE.
ANY GUY WOULD BE LUCKY TO GET TO BE YOUR BOYFRIEND.
YEAH, RIGHT.
NO, SERIOUSLY.
DOESN'T MATTER ANYWAY.
I DOUBT I'LL GET A DATE BEFORE COLLEGE.
I DON'T KNOW...
I MEAN, IF YOU WANTED TO, I'D BE HAPPY TO...
OKAY, KIDS. IT'S TIME. LET'S GO.

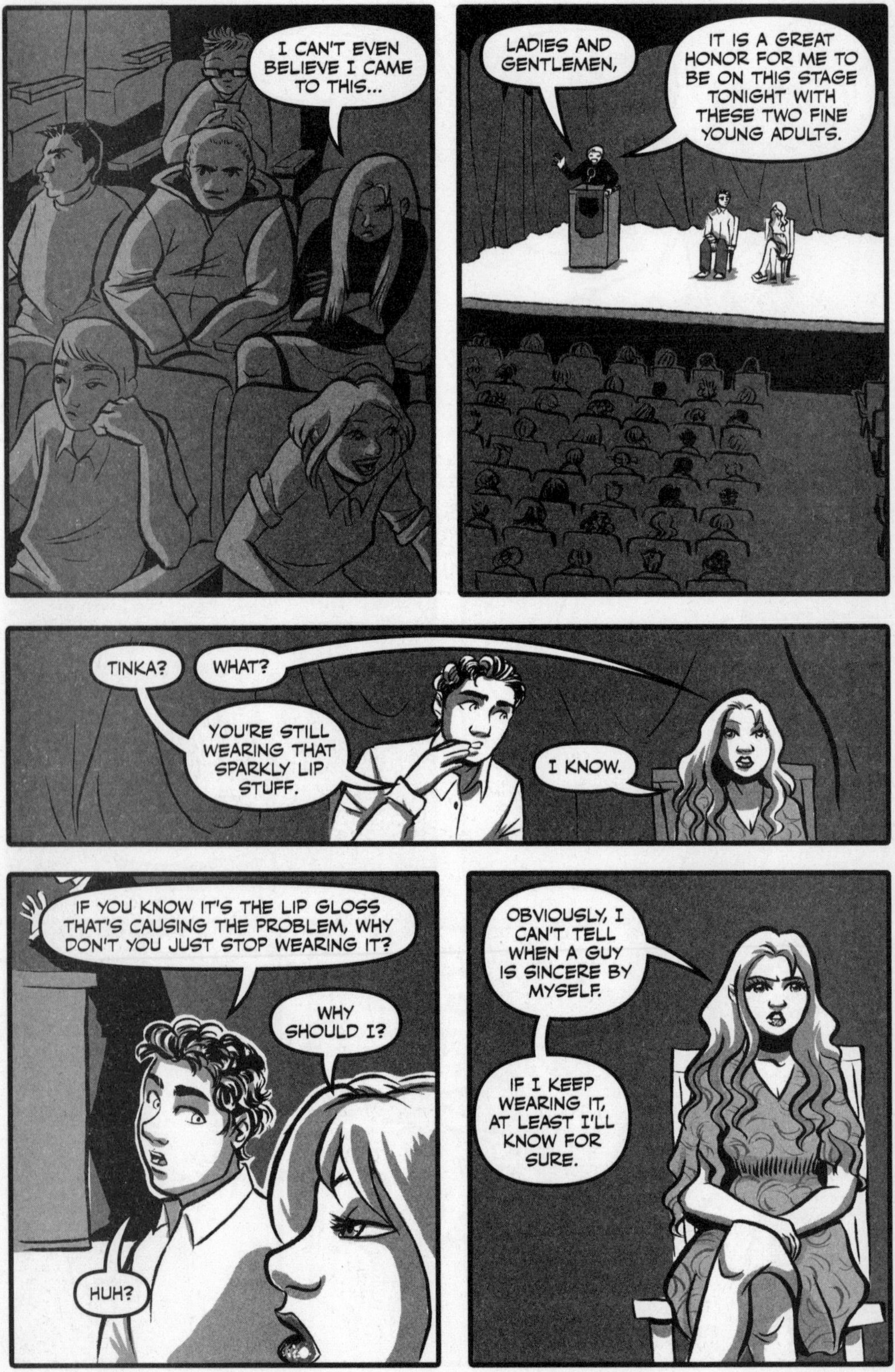
I CAN'T EVEN BELIEVE I CAME TO THIS...
LADIES AND GENTLEMEN,
IT IS A GREAT HONOR FOR ME TO BE ON THIS STAGE TONIGHT WITH THESE TWO FINE YOUNG ADULTS.
TINKA?
WHAT?
YOU'RE STILL WEARING THAT SPARKLY LIP STUFF.
I KNOW.
IF YOU KNOW IT'S THE LIP GLOSS THAT'S CAUSING THE PROBLEM, WHY DON'T YOU JUST STOP WEARING IT?
WHY SHOULD I?
HUH?
OBVIOUSLY, I CAN'T TELL WHEN A GUY IS SINCERE BY MYSELF.
IF I KEEP WEARING IT, AT LEAST I'LL KNOW FOR SURE.

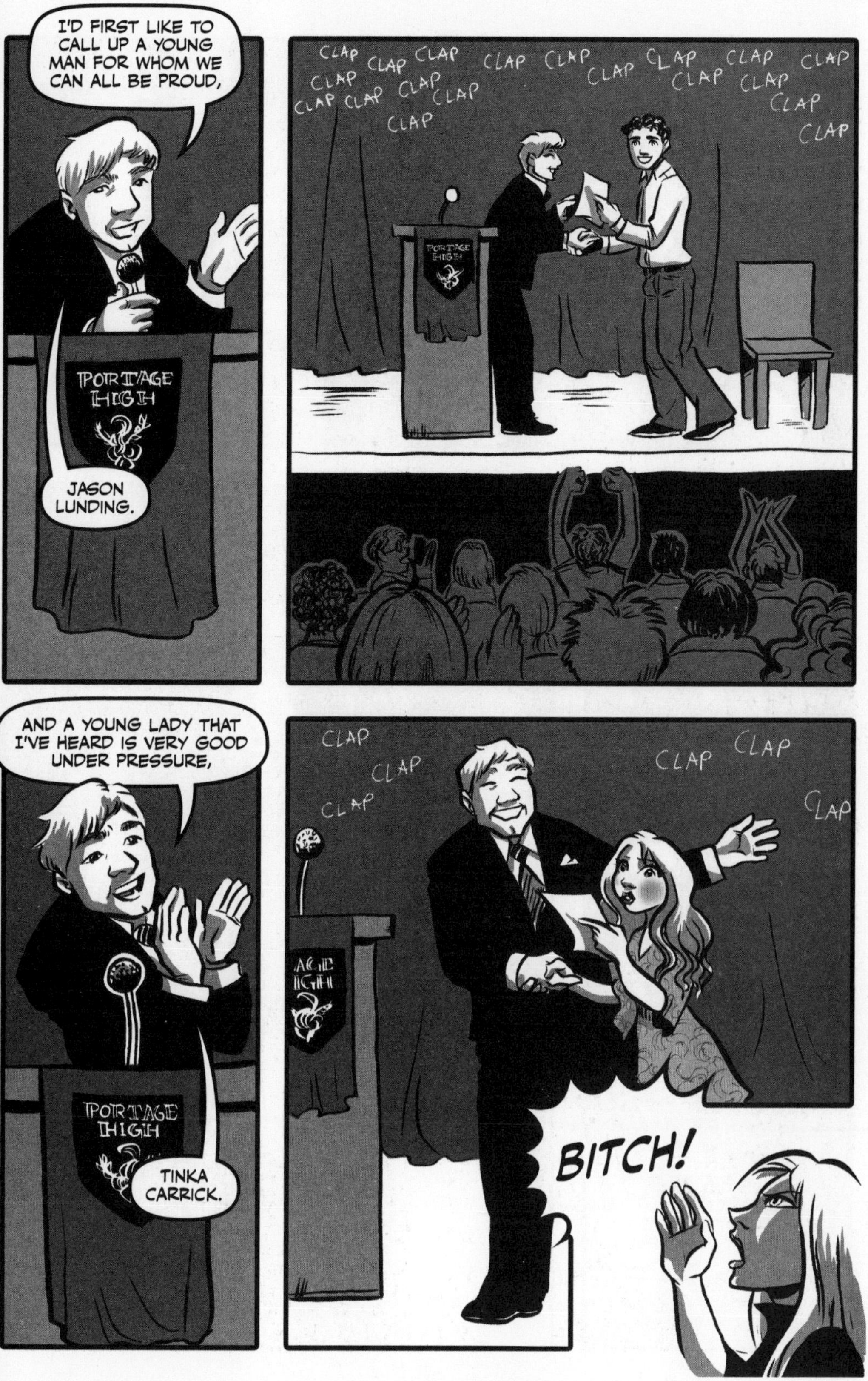
I'D FIRST LIKE TO CALL UP A YOUNG MAN FOR WHOM WE CAN ALL BE PROUD,
PORTAGE HIGH
JASON LUNDING.
CLAP CLAP CLAP CLAP CLAP CLAP CLAP CLAP CLAP CLAP CLAP CLAP CLAP CLAP CLAP CLAP CLAP CLAP
PORTAGE HIGH
AND A YOUNG LADY THAT I'VE HEARD IS VERY GOOD UNDER PRESSURE,
PORTAGE HIGH
TINKA CARRICK.
CLAP CLAP CLAP CLAP CLAP CLAP
BITCH!

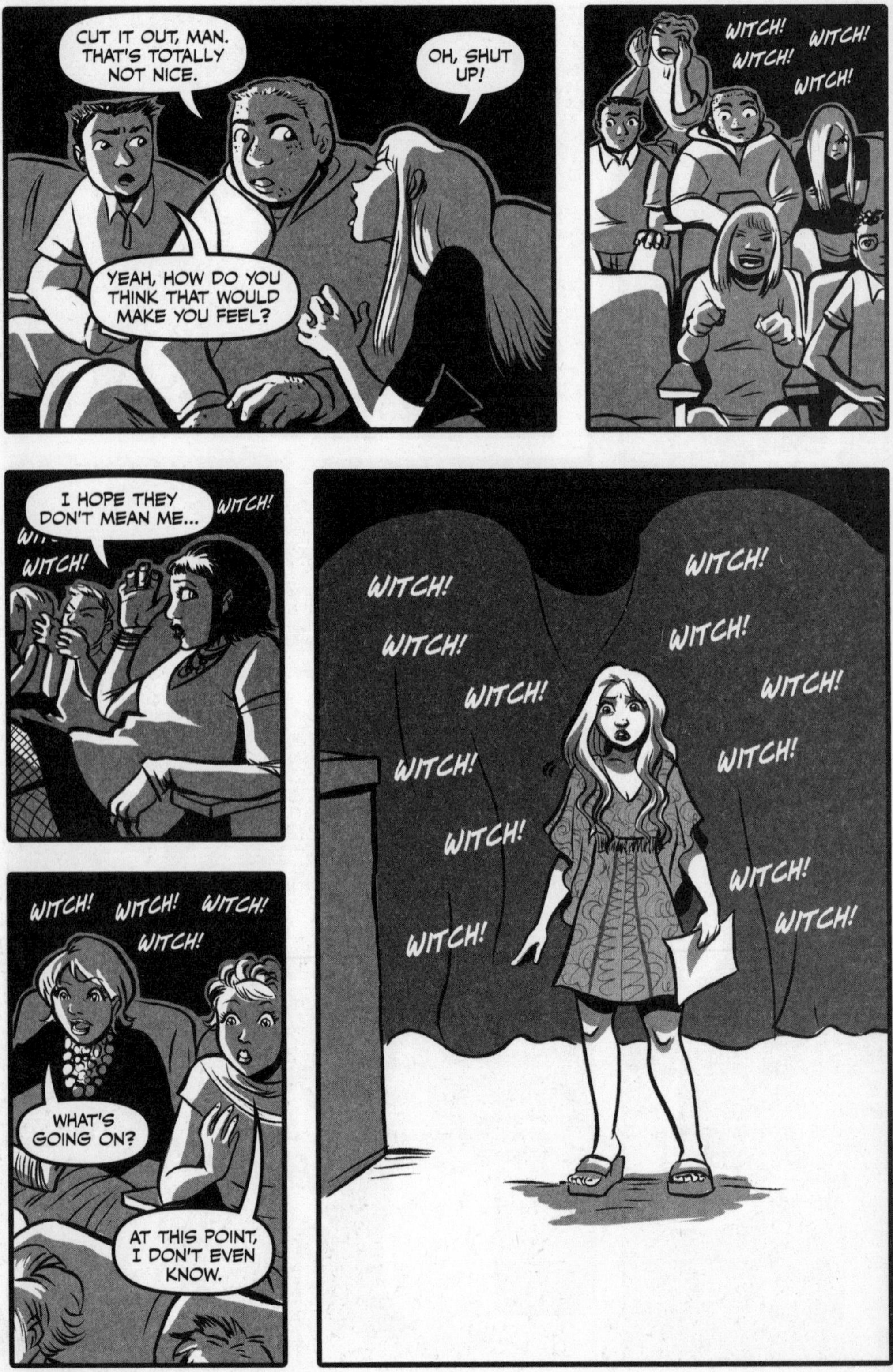
CUT IT OUT, MAN. THAT'S TOTALLY NOT NICE.
OH, SHUT UP!
YEAH, HOW DO YOU THINK THAT WOULD MAKE YOU FEEL?
WITCH! WITCH! WITCH! WITCH!
I HOPE THEY DON'T MEAN ME...
WITCH!
WITCH!
WITCH! WITCH! WITCH! WITCH!
WHAT'S GOING ON?
AT THIS POINT, I DON'T EVEN KNOW.
WITCH! WITCH! WITCH! WITCH! WITCH! WITCH! WITCH! WITCH! WITCH! WITCH! WITCH! WITCH!

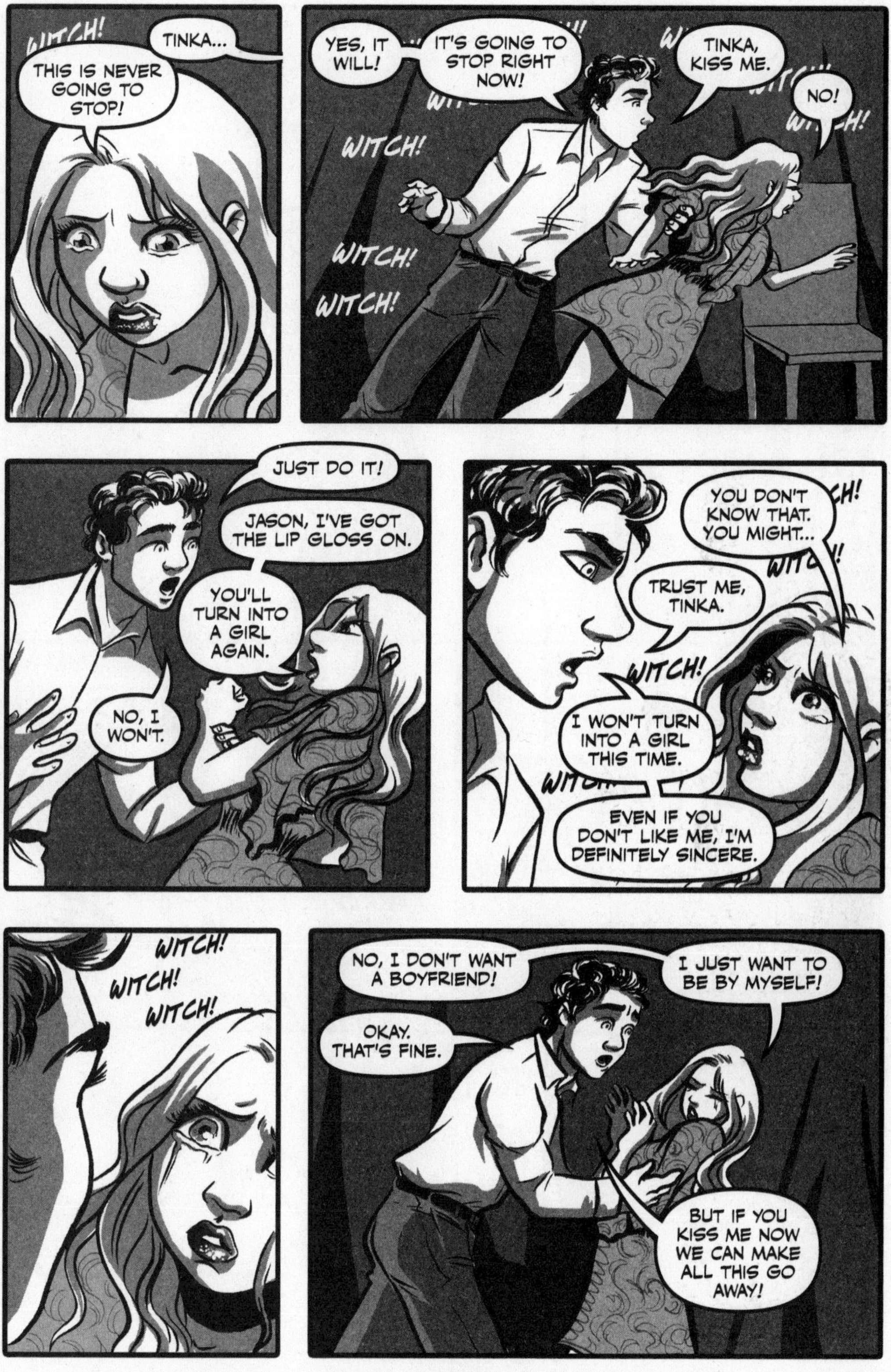
WITCH!
TINKA...
THIS IS NEVER GOING TO STOP!
YES, IT WILL!
IT'S GOING TO STOP RIGHT NOW!
TINKA, KISS ME.
NO!
WITCH!
WITCH!
WITCH!
JUST DO IT!
JASON, I'VE GOT THE LIP GLOSS ON.
YOU'LL TURN INTO A GIRL AGAIN.
NO, I WON'T.
YOU DON'T KNOW THAT. YOU MIGHT...
TRUST ME, TINKA.
WITCH!
I WON'T TURN INTO A GIRL THIS TIME.
EVEN IF YOU DON'T LIKE ME, I'M DEFINITELY SINCERE.
WITCH!
WITCH!
WITCH!
NO, I DON'T WANT A BOYFRIEND!
I JUST WANT TO BE BY MYSELF!
OKAY. THAT'S FINE.
BUT IF YOU KISS ME NOW WE CAN MAKE ALL THIS GO AWAY!

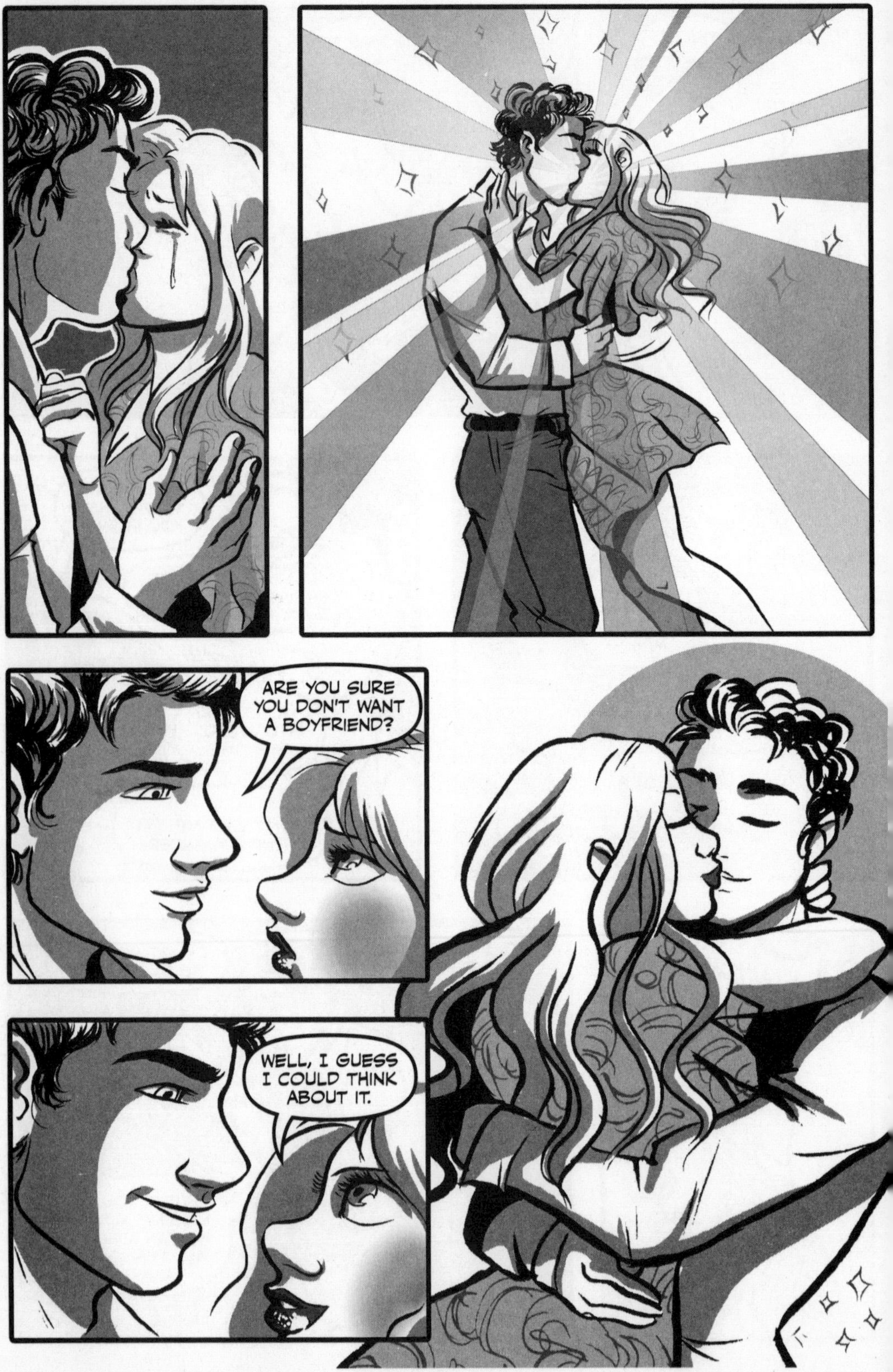
ARE YOU SURE YOU DON'T WANT A BOYFRIEND?
WELL, I GUESS I COULD THINK ABOUT IT.

## Adrianne Ambrose

is a native of Cleveland, OH. Two of her favorite words are "snack" and "nap". She also finds the word "carcass" unreasonably funny for no apparent reason. She is the author of *Confessions of a Virgin Sacrifice*, *What I Learned From Being a Cheerleader*, *Fangs for Nothing*, and *The Urchin*. She lives in the Bay Area with her husband, daughter, and a school of rabid land piranhas. Check out her blog at adrianneambrose.com and her twitter feed @adrianneambrose.

## Monica Gallagher

is an avid lipstick wearer and former rollergirl who currently lives in Baltimore with her boyfriend and their two dueling cats. Monica prefers to draw her comics while accompanied by rain, podcasts, and coffee. She finds the occasional (okay, regular) wine bar interruption to be perfectly acceptable. Her work has been previously published in Oni Press's *JAM! Tales From the World of Roller Derby*. To check out Monica's weekly webcomic *Bonnie N. Collide, Nine to Five* as well as her other work, visit www.eatyourlipstick.com.

# OTHER BOOKS FROM ONI PRESS...

**12 REASONS WHY
I LOVE HER**

By Jamie S. Rich & Joëlle Jones
144 pages, 6x9 Trade Paperback
Black and White
ISBN 978-1-932664-51-5

**THE AVALON CHRONICLES,
VOL. 1: ONCE IN A
BLUE MOON**

By Nunzio DeFilippis,
Christina Weir, & Emma Vieceli
162 pages, 6x9 Hardcover
Black and White
ISBN: 978-1-934964-75-0

**FESTERING ROMANCE**

By Renee Lott
184 pages, 6x9 Trade Paperback
Black and White
ISBN 978-1-934964-18-7

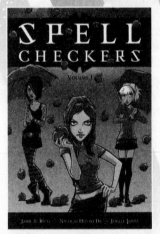

**SCOTT PILGRIM, VOL. 1:
SCOTT PILGRIM'S
PRECIOUS LITTLE LIFE**

By Bryan Lee O'Malley
194 pages, 6x9 Hardcover
Full Color
ISBN 978-1-62010-000-4

**SPELL CHECKERS, VOL. 1**

By Jamie S. Rich,
Nicolas Hitori De
& Joëlle Jones
152 pages, Digest
Black and White
ISBN 978-1-934964-32-3

**WET MOON, VOL. 1:
FEEBLE WANDERINGS**

By Ross Campbell
168 pages, 6x9 Trade Paperback
Black and White
ISBN 978-1-932664-07-2

*For more information on these and other fine Oni Press comic books and
graphic novels, visit www.onipress.com. To find a comic specialty store in your
area, call 1-888-COMICBOOK or visit www.comicshops.us.*